T0353645

# Lecture Notes in Computer Science    15358

Founding Editors

Gerhard Goos
Juris Hartmanis

Editorial Board Members

Elisa Bertino, *Purdue University, West Lafayette, IN, USA*
Wen Gao, *Peking University, Beijing, China*
Bernhard Steffen, *TU Dortmund University, Dortmund, Germany*
Moti Yung, *Columbia University, New York, NY, USA*

The series Lecture Notes in Computer Science (LNCS), including its subseries Lecture Notes in Artificial Intelligence (LNAI) and Lecture Notes in Bioinformatics (LNBI), has established itself as a medium for the publication of new developments in computer science and information technology research, teaching, and education.

LNCS enjoys close cooperation with the computer science R & D community, the series counts many renowned academics among its volume editors and paper authors, and collaborates with prestigious societies. Its mission is to serve this international community by providing an invaluable service, mainly focused on the publication of conference and workshop proceedings and postproceedings. LNCS commenced publication in 1973.

Maurizio Naldi · Karim Djemame ·
Jörn Altmann · José Ángel Bañares
Editors

# Economics of Grids, Clouds, Systems, and Services

20th International Conference, GECON 2024
Rome, Italy, September 26–27, 2024
Proceedings

 Springer

*Editors*
Maurizio Naldi 🆔
LUMSA University
Rome, Italy

Jörn Altmann 🆔
Seoul National University
Seoul, Korea (Republic of)

Karim Djemame 🆔
University of Leeds
Leeds, UK

José Ángel Bañares 🆔
University of Zaragoza
Zaragoza, Zaragoza, Spain

ISSN 0302-9743          ISSN 1611-3349 (electronic)
Lecture Notes in Computer Science
ISBN 978-3-031-81225-5          ISBN 978-3-031-81226-2 (eBook)
https://doi.org/10.1007/978-3-031-81226-2

© The Editor(s) (if applicable) and The Author(s), under exclusive license
to Springer Nature Switzerland AG 2025

This work is subject to copyright. All rights are solely and exclusively licensed by the Publisher, whether
the whole or part of the material is concerned, specifically the rights of translation, reprinting, reuse of
illustrations, recitation, broadcasting, reproduction on microfilms or in any other physical way, and transmission
or information storage and retrieval, electronic adaptation, computer software, or by similar or dissimilar
methodology now known or hereafter developed.
The use of general descriptive names, registered names, trademarks, service marks, etc. in this publication
does not imply, even in the absence of a specific statement, that such names are exempt from the relevant
protective laws and regulations and therefore free for general use.
The publisher, the authors and the editors are safe to assume that the advice and information in this book
are believed to be true and accurate at the date of publication. Neither the publisher nor the authors or the
editors give a warranty, expressed or implied, with respect to the material contained herein or for any errors
or omissions that may have been made. The publisher remains neutral with regard to jurisdictional claims in
published maps and institutional affiliations.

This Springer imprint is published by the registered company Springer Nature Switzerland AG
The registered company address is: Gewerbestrasse 11, 6330 Cham, Switzerland

If disposing of this product, please recycle the paper.

# Preface

We are glad to introduce the proceedings of the 20th International Conference on the Economics of Grids, Clouds, Systems, and Services (GECON 2024). The conference was held during September 26–27th, 2024, and hosted by Libera Università Maria SS. Assunta (Lumsa), Rome, Italy.

The conference series, which started in 2003, is now firmly established as a place of convergence among economics and computer science researchers, with the ultimate aim of building a strong multidisciplinary community in the increasingly important areas of future ICT systems and economics.

Economics underpins many critical aspects of Information and Communication Technology (ICT), from pricing and resource allocation to innovation, policy, and market structure. It plays a central role in shaping the development, deployment, and sustainability of ICT systems and services. For example, the ICT infrastructure, such as data centers, cloud services, and networks, requires significant investment and incurs ongoing operational costs. Economics helps in efficiently allocating resources of ICT systems and services, to maximize productivity, reduce costs, and ensure optimal utilization of ICT assets.

Moreover, the relationship between ICT and economics is a two-way street, since the development of technologies, such as Large Language Models (LLMs) and the economics behind such models also economically impacts the development, deployment, and usage of ICT systems. A conference such as GECON, therefore, plays a leading role due to its blending of skills and knowledge from both worlds.

We received 36 submissions in response to our call for papers. Each paper was peer-reviewed by at least three members of the international Program Committee (PC). Based on significance, novelty, and scientific quality, we selected 12 full papers, which are included in this book. Additionally, 10 shorter work-in-progress and two new-idea papers were integrated in the volume.

The full papers were organized around five themes:

- Function as a Service: Resource Management and QoS
- Cloud Business Models, Pricing, trading, network neutrality
- Edge Computing and Energy Awareness
- AI/Forecasting/Prediction Sales.
- Resource Management in Cloud Applications: Simulation, Streaming Processing and Workflows

## Industry Session

The industry session titled "Harnessing Large Language Models, Vector Search Engines, and the Synergy with Knowledge Graphs" brought as panellists Gert De Geyter and Somayeh Koohborfardhaghighi from Deloitte, Kacper Łukawski from Qdrant, and Prabhakar Thanikasalam from Flex. The session offered an immersive exploration into the transformative potential of Large Language Models (LLMs), vector search engines, and their seamless integration with knowledge graphs. By converging these cutting-edge technologies, unprecedented opportunities for innovation, efficiency, and insight across diverse industry sectors are unlocked. The insightful discussion explored how advanced AI technologies are reshaping the future of the supply chain industry.

## Keynotes

This year's GECON featured two keynotes, evenly distributed across the two days of the conference, addressing topics that span privacy, data sharing coordination, and aspects on the innovative process in artificial intelligence (AI). Short papers of those two keynotes are also included in this book.

The keynote speaker on the first day was Prof. Evangelos Pournaras, from the University of Leeds, UK. Prof. Pournaras' keynote, "Collective privacy recovery: Data-sharing coordination via decentralized artificial intelligence" dealt with collective privacy, which involves safeguarding the privacy of groups, communities, or populations in the age of big data, where personal data aggregation and advanced analytics can reveal sensitive information about collective behaviour, characteristics, and patterns. The keynote presented a mechanism, to automate and scale-up complex collective arrangements for privacy recovery using decentralized AI.

The keynote speaker on the second day was Prof. Arianna Martinelli, from the Institute of Economics of Scuola Superiore Sant'Anna, Pisa, Italy. Her keynote, "Patents and the technological evolution of AI "tackled the issue of patents. Patents are critical to the technological evolution of AI, providing a legal framework that encourages investment, innovation, and competition. The keynote examined some aspects of the innovative process in AI, delving into the role that government grants and government departments played in the development of AI.

September 2024

Maurizio Naldi
Jörn Altmann
José Ángel Bañares
Karim Djemame

# Acknowledgments

Any conference is the fruit of the work of many people, and GECON 2024 was no exception. In particular, we wish to thank the authors, whose papers made up the body of the conference, as well as the members of the Programme Committee and the reviewers, who devoted their time to review the papers on a tight time schedule. We wish to thank the keynote speakers, for bringing new viewpoints and inputs to the GECON community. Furthermore, we would like to thank Jorge Nakahara Junior, Elke Werner, Pooja Srinivasan, Ronan Nugent and the whole team at Springer, who continue an established tradition of publishing GECON proceedings in the renowned Lecture Notes in Computer Science (LNCS) series. Finally, we wish to thank the attendees, whose interest in the conference is the main driver for its organization.

# Organization

## Executive Committee

### Conference Chair

Maurizio Naldi      Libera Università Maria SS. Assunta (LUMSA), Italy

### Conference Vice-chairs

Karim Djemame      University of Leeds, UK
Jörn Altmann      Seoul National University, South Korea
José Ángel Bañares      Zaragoza University, Spain
Bruno Tuffin      Inria, France

### Local Conference Organization

Maurizio Naldi      Libera Università Maria SS. Assunta (LUMSA), Italy
Paolo Fantozzi      Libera Università Maria SS. Assunta (LUMSA), Italy
Valerio Rughetti      Libera Università Maria SS. Assunta (LUMSA), Italy

### Public Relations Chair

José Ángel Bañares      Zaragoza University, Spain

### Program Chairs

Vlado Stankovski      University of Ljubljana, Slovenia
Bruno Tuffin      Inria, France
Bernhard Egger      Seoul National University, South Korea

### Special Sessions and Tutorial Chair

Jörn Altmann      Seoul National University, South-Korea

# Program Committee

| | |
|---|---|
| Alvaro Arenas | IE University, Spain |
| Unai Arronategui | University of Zaragoza, Spain |
| Ashraf Bany Mohamed | University of Jordan, Jordan |
| Orna Agmon Ben-Yehuda | University of Haifa, Israel |
| Rajkumar Buyya | University of Melbourne, Australia |
| María Emilia Cambronero | University of Castilla-La Mancha, Spain |
| Emanuele Carlini | ISTI-CNR, Italy |
| Jeremy Cohen | Imperial College London, UK |
| Massimo Coppola | ISTI-CNR, Italy |
| Daniele D'Agostino | CNR-IMATI, Italy |
| Patrizio Dazzi | ISTI-CNR, Italy |
| Alex Delis | University of Athens, Greece |
| Luca Ferrucci | Università di Pisa, Italy |
| Sebastian Floerecke | University of Passau, Germany |
| Felix Freitag | Universitat Politècnica de Catalunya, Spain |
| Yodit Gebrealif | Addis Ababa Science and Technology University, Ethiopia |
| Daniel Grosu | Wayne State University, USA |
| Bahman Javadi | Western Sydney University, Australia |
| Songhee Kang | Software Policy and Research Institute, South Korea |
| Odej Kao | TU Berlin, Germany |
| Tobias Knoch | Erasmus MC, Netherlands |
| Somayeh Koohborfardhaghighi | University of Amsterdam, Netherlands |
| Dieter Kranzlmüller | Ludwig Maximilian University of Munich, Germany |
| Wool-Rim Lee | Seoul National University, South Korea |
| Patrick Maillé | IMT Atlantique, France |
| Marco Netto | IBM, Brazil |
| Mara Nikolaidoy | Harokopio University, Greece |
| Umara Noor | International Islamic University, Pakistan |
| Alberto Nuñez | Complutense University of Madrid, Spain |
| Frank Pallas | TU Berlin, Germany |
| Dana Petcu | West University of Timisoara, Romania |
| Ioan Petri | Cardiff University, UK |
| Congduc Pham | University of Pau and the Adour Region, France) |
| Zahid Rashid | Seoul National University, South Korea |
| Rizos Sakellariou | University of Manchester, UK |
| Dongnyok Shim | Konkuk University, South-Korea |
| Vlado Stankovski | University of Ljubljana, Slovenia |

| Burkhard Stiller | University of Zurich, Switzerland |
| Stefan Tai | TU Berlin, Germany |
| Luis Veiga | Universidade de Lisboa, Portugal |
| Ramin Yahyapour | GWDG - University of Göttingen, Germany |
| Muhammad Zakarya | Abdul Wali Khan University Mardan, Pakistan |

## Subreviewers

| Ivan Mercanti | Università degli study di Perugia, Italy |
| Carlo Taticchi | Università degli study di Perugia, Italy |
| Narges Mehran | University of Salzburg, Austria |

## Steering Committee

| Karim Djemame | University of Leeds, UK |
| Jörn Altmann | Seoul National University, South Korea |
| José Ángel Bañares | Zaragoza University, Spain |
| Orna Agmon Ben-Yehuda | Technion, Israel |
| Steven Miller | Singapore Management University, Singapore |
| Omer F. Rana | Cardiff University, UK |
| Gheorghe Cosmin Silaghi | Babeş-Bolyai University, Romania |
| Vlado Stankovski | University of Ljubljana, Slovenia |
| Konstantinos Tserpes | Harokopio University of Athens, Greece |
| Maurizio Naldi | Libera Università Maria SS. Assunta (LUMSA), Italy |

# Contents

**Edge Computing and Energy Awareness**

# Keynotes

# Privacy as a Collective Value and How to Protect in the Era of AI

Evangelos Pournaras[✉][iD]

School of Computer Science, University of Leeds, Leeds, UK
`e.pournaras@leeds.ac.uk`

**Abstract.** This extended keynote abstract outlines research on a new paradigm of data sharing designed to recover privacy for data providers, while reducing costs and risks of service providers, who collect personal sensitive data. This paradigm is based on the novel idea of coordinated data sharing within a community, the data collective, which makes automated and scalable collective arrangements of how to share data using decentralized artificial intelligence.

**Keywords:** privacy recovery · coordination · data collective · data sharing · artificial intelligence

## 1 Privacy Loss is a Coordination Deficit

The large-scale loss of privacy poses a significant threat to personal freedoms and democracy. However, are we prepared to handle personal data as a limited resource and share it collectively under the principle: *as little as possible, as much as necessary?*

Currently, data-sharing decisions cannot strike a balance between protecting privacy and maintaining the quality of online services that rely on shared data. See Fig. 1 as an example. Without a collective agreement on what data to share, with whom, and for what purpose, privacy is often compromised, while businesses face increased costs and risks.

It is proposed that significant privacy gains could be achieved if individuals, acting as a *data collective*, coordinate to share only the minimum data needed to run online services at the required quality level. This work demonstrates how decentralized artificial intelligence can automate and scale up such complex collective arrangements for privacy enhancement. For the first time, *attitudinal, intrinsic, rewarded*, and *coordinated* data-sharing approaches are compared in a highly realistic living-lab experiment, involving over 27,000 real data disclosures. See Fig. 2 as an outline of this study. Using causal inference and cluster analysis, we identify the key factors that predict privacy and examine five distinct data-sharing behaviors.

---

This is an extended abstract of a keynote talk based on earlier published work [1].

© The Author(s), under exclusive license to Springer Nature Switzerland AG 2025
M. Naldi et al. (Eds.): GECON 2024, LNCS 15358, pp. 3–6, 2025.
https://doi.org/10.1007/978-3-031-81226-2_1

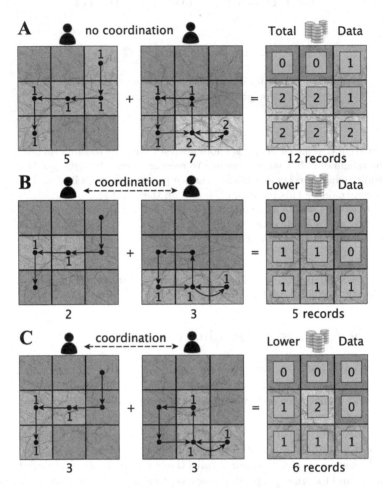

**Fig. 1.** A toy example on how collective arrangements of data sharing recover significant privacy. Individuals coordinate to collectively choose at which geographical areas to share and not share their location. (A) Default data-sharing. Two individuals (e.g. drivers) move within an area of 3×3= 9 possible locations (e.g. points of interest). When repeatedly sharing their Global Positioning System (GPS) location (default), they reveal sensitive information that can even disclose their identity. Yet, these shared data can be redundant in practice in several practical scenarios. (B) Finding the highest traffic density areas or (C) prioritizing accurate traffic density estimation in the city center over the outskirts can be both achieved with half (or even lower) the original data, while reducing privacy risks with fairer data sharing among individuals. Adopted from [1].

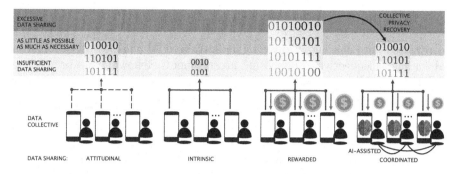

**Fig. 2.** Data-sharing commons exhibit coordination failures. Although individuals may rationally aim to share a sufficient amount of data, they often end up sharing too little on their own. When incentives are introduced, data sharing becomes excessive, leading to significant privacy loss. However, by introducing coordination via a decentralized AI-based decision-support system, privacy can be substantially recovered, while still maintaining the desired quality of service. These hypotheses are explored under four distinct data-sharing conditions: (i) *attitudinal*, (ii) *intrinsic*, (iii) *rewarded*, and (iv) *coordinated*. Adopted from [1].

## 2 Key Results and Findings

Three key findings are illustrated:

1. Coordinated data sharing proves to be more efficient, as it enhances privacy for individuals, while lowering costs for service providers. This approach relies on accessing less but higher-quality data, in contrast to rewarded data sharing, where people often disclose excessive or unnecessary information.
2. The most critical factors influencing individuals' data-sharing decisions are the data collector and the context. However, in situations where data is shared in exchange for rewards, leading to privacy loss, the type of data being shared becomes the primary consideration.
3. Individuals display five major behavioral shifts when moving from intrinsic to rewarded data sharing. These behaviors are consistent, yet mutually reinforcing. Notably, the findings demonstrate that coordinating data sharing comes as advantage for all key beneficiaries: individuals experience a significant recovery of privacy, while service providers achieve cost reductions. Additionally, the results highlight that substantial privacy recovery can be achieved within the framework of a data collective. This represents a transformative shift from the conventional view of privacy as a personal concern to understanding it as a collective value—a public good shared among a community of citizens sharing data responsibly.

# 3   Implications and Discussion

Coordinated data sharing, assisted by decentralized AI, enables the automation and scaling of collective data-sharing arrangements, following the principle of "*as little as possible, as much as necessary*". This coordination would otherwise be too complex and costly to implement manually.

The findings also reveal that data collectives provide clear advantages for online service providers that gather or access data in a coordinated manner: data collection costs are significantly reduced, and the data are used more effectively to maintain the required quality of service. This can lead to further notable cost savings, such as lower expenses for data storage, security, energy, carbon footprint, and legal disputes, which are more likely when handling excessive personal data.

This framework could serve as the foundation for alternative data-market designs, promoting business models rooted in social innovation without an over-dependence on vast amounts of free personal data. Additionally, data collectives may offer a solution to the current lack of transparency in generative AI models such as ChatGPT. Coordinated data sharing could be used to train open, more transparent AI models that are ethically aligned with community values, forming a new kind of "curriculum" for AI training, driven by data collectives.

This comprehensive understanding of the factors influencing data-sharing decisions is a basis towards a long-awaited revival of privacy in the digital age.

**Acknowledgments.** Evangelos Pournaras is supported by a UKRI Future Leaders Fellowship (MR/ W009560/1): "*Digitally Assisted Collective Governance of Smart City Commons–ARTIO*".

**Disclosure of Interests.** The author has no competing interests to declare that are relevant to the content of this article.

# References

1. Pournaras, E., Ballandies, M.C., Bennati, S. and Chen, C.F.: Collective privacy recovery: Data-sharing coordination via decentralized artificial intelligence. PNAS nexus **3**(2), 29 (2024)

# Patents and the Technological Evolution of AI

Arianna Martinelli$^{(\boxtimes)}$ (iD)

Scuola Superiore Sant'Anna, Pisa, Italy
a.martinelli@santannapisa.it
https://www.santannapisa.it/it/arianna-martinelli

**Keywords:** AI · patent data · Technology analysis

Artificial Intelligence (AI), defined as "a machine-based system that can, for a given set of human-defined objectives, make predictions, recommendations, or decisions influencing real or virtual environments" [30], encompasses devices capable of mimicking human-like cognitive functions, such as understanding, learning, reasoning, and interacting. AI is anticipated to have a broad transformative effect on economies and societies, as it has the potential to revolutionize production processes and people's behaviours. Historical parallels can be drawn with other pivotal technologies, such as the steam engine, electricity, and computers, which have been associated with profound transformations in socioeconomic systems. These technologies are often linked to the development and diffusion of general-purpose technologies (GPTs) characterized by high levels of pervasiveness, dynamism, and complementarity [8]. Concerning AI, Various studies have sought to conceptually [34] and empirically investigate the extent to which AI can already be considered a fully-fledged GPT and its relationship to other emerging technologies within the "Industry 4.0 paradigm" [27].

Given its transformative potential, economists are increasingly focused on studying the diffusion of AI and its effects [3]. A prominent area of investigation has been the impact of AI on productivity growth and employment. While it is likely that AI will enhance productivity in the long run [16], the implications for employment and the timing of these changes remain unclear [1]. Additional research has broadened the scope of analysis to consider specific measures that could mitigate the potential adverse effects of AI, such as ad-hoc taxation and reforms of intellectual property rights [25], as well as reforms in education and training [34]. Beyond its effects on firm performance and employment, AI can profoundly influence the innovation process [9] by facilitating the emergence of new ideas [2].

This talk aims to present a new approach to assess the effect of government funding on the development of AI. I will proceed in three steps. First, I'll explore the suitability of patents, the most common data source for innovative activities, in identifying AI developments. Second, I will highlight the empirical challenges associated with assessing the effect of government funding on innovative activity, in general, and on AI development in particular. Third, and finally, I'll discuss a

© The Author(s), under exclusive license to Springer Nature Switzerland AG 2025
M. Naldi et al. (Eds.): GECON 2024, LNCS 15358, pp. 7–12, 2025.
https://doi.org/10.1007/978-3-031-81226-2_2

new methodology based on patent citation networks, capable of addressing these challenges with an application to the AI domain.

Since Griliches' seminal paper [18], patents have increasingly been used to study various aspects of the innovation process. However, the conventional limitations associated with patent data (i.e., not all inventions are patented, and not all concepts can be patented) are further complicated by the broad scope of AI technology. AI technologies include an array of techniques and methods specific to different application domains (e.g., industrial robots, autonomous vehicles, medical technologies). More than in other technological fields, AI spans fundamental research and applied innovation, raising questions about the appropriateness of relying solely on patent data. Additionally, advancements in AI are often fueled by the increasing availability of complementary technologies developed in related domains. These complexities have triggered a growing body of literature discussing sampling strategies for analyzing AI through patent data. The foundation of this discourse often involves defining AI and establishing its boundaries. Taxonomies such as those proposed by Fujii and Managi [15] and the European Patent Office [13] appear somewhat conservative, concentrating primarily on computational models, while the OECD [31] provides a more expansive definition oriented towards AI applications, including image processing and digital devices, as emphasized by Cockburn et al. [9], particularly about robotics. The OECD [6] report noted that different definitions yield significantly varied patent samples. Moreover, the report highlights the shortcomings of focusing exclusively on patents without considering other potentially valuable data sources, such as scientific publications and software releases on platforms like GitHub.

In addition to issues regarding sampling strategies for identifying technological domains and defining AI, further empirical challenges arise when examining the role of government funding in facilitating technological progress. Numerous studies have explored the effects of government funding on returns from R&D investments [21] or evaluated the effectiveness of R&D subsidies [4,7,10] and government grants [22,33] on private innovation, yielding varied results contingent on the specific context analyzed. However, from an evolutionary standpoint, where technological progress is viewed as local, cumulative, and irreversible [11], government intervention may influence not only the rate of technological advancement but also its directional trajectory. Empirical evidence concerning the impact of government funding on the direction of technical change is limited, often concentrating on narrowly defined notions of directionality [5] or relying on specific historical case studies [20,29]. The empirical difficulty in linking government policy interventions to specific innovations or technological developments arises mainly from the fact that government funding typically occurs in the early stages of development, when market failure arguments are most pronounced, making it challenging to assess their impact in the long term, when technology finally reaches the market [19].

To address these issues, it is essential to identify a data source that captures government intervention and to employ a method for tracing long-term technological development. In this regard, patents can serve as a valuable data source. Depending on the legal framework, government involvement can be traced through various means [14]. For instance, in the United States, patents can be directly assigned[1] to federal agencies, national laboratories, and state departments, or they may include Government Interest Statements in the patent texts. Since the enactment of the Bayh-Dole Act in 1980, contractors have been able to retain patent ownership of federally funded research; however, they are required to disclose any government interest in their patents. In terms of methodology, network analysis —specifically "connectivity analysis" [23] – enables tracing long-term technological advancements. Initially developed to study knowledge flows within publication and citation networks, this methodology has increasingly been applied to patent data to identify emerging technological trajectories within specific domains. Following its seminal application to fuel cell technology, connectivity analysis has proven effective in examining technological evolution across various fields, including medical innovation [28], semiconductors [12], and local area networks (LANs) [32]. For instance, Martinelli [26] employed this method on a patent citation network related to telecommunication switching industry. The analysis documents the paradigmatic shift from circuit switching to packet switching, highlighting the changes in engineering heuristics, required competencies, and technological bottlenecks involved in this transition.

In Iori, Martinelli and Mina [24], we leverage connectivity analysis to assess how US government intervention steers the innovative process in AI. Through an econometric analysis, the paper identifies the effect of government funding on the "trajectory effect". The starting point of the analysis was identifying a suitable data source covering AI inventions. This study uses only patent data as the focus is unfolding the evolution of downstream inventions rather than AI-related scientific breakthroughs. The sample of AI-related patents has been constructed using both International Patent Classification (IPC) codes and keywords validated through expert interviews. The final sample includes 114,670 USPTO (United States Patent and Trademarks Office) patents granted from 1976 to 2019 retrieved in the EPO-PATSTAT database (Autumn 2019 version). As expected, the group of the most important assignees of these patents changes over time. While in the early phase, these are well-known ICT companies (e.g. IBM, AT&T, Texas Instrument), later on, new companies emerge (e.g. Microsoft). The connectivity analysis identifies the main technological trajectory, highlighting the evolution of speech-recognition techniques. Starting from early patents adapting technologies used for character recognition to a new application, we can trace a series of technological inventions cumulative leading to digital assistant technologies (and products). Concerning the government impact, we find that 4526 patents (about 4% of the sample) have some form of government involvement, with the Department of Defense and its Navy, Army and Air Force divisions supporting most of these inventions. This paper's findings indicate that these patents significantly impact the cumulative development of AI, with patents filed (and therefore owned) by federal and state agencies exerting the strongest influence. The effect of government funding is particularly pronounced during the

---

[1] The *assignee* is the entity that has the property right to the patent.

early stages of technology development. This diminishing impact on technology development is consistent with the complementarity between public and private funding. Private incentives for innovative activities are prominent when a trajectory is established and technological uncertainty decreases. Interestingly, the effect is negative when, following existing literature [17], we use forward citation to measure cumulative innovation. This difference hints that the network-based indicator captures a different aspect of technological development related to long-term technological evolution, accounting for a longer-lasting effect of some inventions on subsequent developments.

To conclude, combining patent data and network analysis techniques provides the ground for empirically grasping technology dynamics. Interestingly, this "toolbox", which mixes established data sources and new methods, has been proven to be suitable for studying a difficult-to-identify technology such as AI. Hopefully, the presented results can inspire more empirical work to understand drivers, incentives, and characteristics of AI innovative process, possibly extending the scope of the investigation to other complementary technologies.

# References

1. Acemoglu, D., Restrepo, P.: Artificial intelligence, automation and work. Working Paper 24196, National Bureau of Economic Research (2018). http://www.nber.org/papers/w24196
2. Aghion, P., Jones, B.F., Jones, C.I.: Artificial intelligence and economic growth. Working Paper 23928, National Bureau of Economic Research (2017). http://www.nber.org/papers/w23928
3. Agrawal, A., Gans, J., Goldfarb, A.: The Economics of Artificial Intelligence: An Agenda. University of Chicago Press (2019)
4. Akcigit, U., Grigsby, J., Nicholas, T., Stantcheva, S.: Taxation and innovation in the twentieth century. Q. J. Econ. **137**(1), 329–385 (2021)
5. Azoulay, P., Graff Zivin, J.S., Li, D., Sampat, B.N.: Public R&D investments and private-sector patenting: evidence from NIH funding rules. Rev. Econ. Stud. **86**(1), 117–152 (2018)
6. Baruffaldi, S., et al.: Identifying and measuring developments in artificial intelligence making the impossible possible. Working Paper 2020/05, OECD Science, Technology and Industry Working Papers (2020). https://doi.org/10.1787/5f65ff7e-en
7. Bloom, N., Griffith, R., Van Reenen, J.: Do r&d tax credits work? evidence from a panel of countries 1979–1997. J. Public Econ. **85**(1), 1–31 (2002)
8. Bresnahan, T.F., Trajtenberg, M.: General purpose technologies 'engines of growth'? J. Econom. **65**(1), 83–108 (1995)
9. Cockburn, I.M., Henderson, R., Stern, S.: The impact of artificial intelligence on innovation. Working Paper 24449, National Bureau of Economic Research (2018). http://www.nber.org/papers/w24449
10. Dechezleprêtre, A., Einiö, E., Martin, R., Nguyen, K.T., Van Reenen, J.: Do tax incentives increase firm innovation? an rd design for r&d, patents, and spillovers. Am. Econ. J. Econ. Pol. **15**(4), 486–521 (2023)
11. Dosi, G.: Technological paradigms and technological trajectories: a suggested interpretation of the determinants and directions of technical change. Res. Policy **11**(3), 147–162 (1982)

12. Epicoco, M.: Knowledge patterns and sources of leadership: mapping the semiconductor miniaturization trajectory. Res. Policy **42**(1), 180–195 (2013)
13. EPO: Patents and the fourth industrial revolution (2017)
14. Fleming, L., Greene, H., Li, G., Marx, M., Yao, D.: Government-funded research increasingly fuels innovation. Science **364**(6446), 1139–1141 (2019)
15. Fujii, H., Managi, S.: Trends and priority shifts in artificial intelligence technology invention: a global patent analysis. Econom. Anal. Policy **58**, 60–69 (2018)
16. Ai and the economy: Furman, J., Seamans, R. Innov. Policy Econ. **19**, 161–191 (2019)
17. Galasso, A., Schankerman, M.: Patents and cumulative innovation: causal evidence from the courts. Q. J. Econ. **130**(1), 317–369 (2014)
18. Griliches, Z.: Patent statistics as economic indicators: a survey. J. Econom. Lit. **28**(4), 1661–1707 (1990)
19. Griliches, Z.: The search for r&d spillovers. Scand. J. Econ. **94**, S29–S47 (1992)
20. Gross, D.P., Sampat, B.N.: America, jump-started: World war ii r&d and the takeoff of the us innovation system. Am. Econom. Rev. **113**(12), 3323–56 (2023)
21. Hall, B.H., Mairesse, J., Mohnen, P.: Chapter 24 - measuring the returns to r&d. In: Hall, B.H., Rosenberg, N. (eds.) Handbook of the Economics of Innovation, Volume 2, Handbook of the Economics of Innovation, vol. 2, pp. 1033–1082. North-Holland (2010)
22. Howell, S.T.: Financing innovation: evidence from r&d grants. Am. Econom. Rev. **107**(4), 1136–64 (2017)
23. Hummon, N.P., Dereian, P.: Connectivity in a citation network: The development of DNA theory. Social Netw. **11**(1), 39–63 (1989)
24. Iori, M., Martinelli, A., Mina, A.: The direction of technical change in ai and the trajectory effects of government funding. Working Paper 41, LEM Working Paper (2021). https://www.lem.sssup.it/WPLem/2021-41.html
25. Korinek, A., Stiglitz, J.E.: Artificial intelligence and its implications for income distribution and unemployment. Working Paper 24174, National Bureau of Economic Research (2017). http://www.nber.org/papers/w24174
26. Martinelli, A.: An emerging paradigm or just another trajectory? understanding the nature of technological changes using engineering heuristics in the telecommunications switching industry. Res. Policy **41**(2), 414–429 (2012)
27. Martinelli, A., Mina, A., Moggi, M.: The enabling technologies of industry 4.0: examining the seeds of the fourth industrial revolution. Indust. Corporate Change **30**(1), 161–188 (2021)
28. Mina, A., Ramlogan, R., Tampubolon, G., Metcalfe, J.: Mapping evolutionary trajectories: applications to the growth and transformation of medical knowledge. Res. Policy **36**(5), 789–806 (2007)
29. Mowery, D.C.: Military r&d and innovation. In: Hall, B.H., Rosenberg, N. (eds.) Handbook of the Economics of Innovation, Volume 2, Handbook of the Economics of Innovation, vol. 2, pp. 1219–1256. North-Holland (2010)
30. OECD: Recommendation of the council on artificial intelligence. adopted on 22 May 2019 after a proposal by the Expert Group on Artificial Intelligence at the OECD (AIGO). http://oe.cd/ai
31. OECD: OECD Science, Technology and Industry Scoreboard 2017 (2017). https://www.oecd-ilibrary.org/content/publication/9789264268821-en
32. Roberto Fontana, A.N., Verspagen, B.: Mapping technological trajectories as patent citation networks. an application to data communication standards. Econom. Innov. New Technol. **18**(4), 311–336 (2009)

33. Santoleri, P., Mina, A., Di Minin, A., Martelli, I.: The Causal Effects of R&D Grants: Evidence from a Regression Discontinuity. Rev. Econom. Stat. 1–42 (2022)
34. Trajtenberg, M.: Ai as the next gpt: a political-economy perspective. Working Paper 24245, National Bureau of Economic Research (2018). https://www.nber.org/system/files/chapters/c14025/c14025.pdf

# Function as a Service: Resource Management and QoS

# Marginal Cost of Computation as a Collaborative Strategy for Resource Management at the Edge

Emanuele Carlini[2], Patrizio Dazzi[1], Luca Ferrucci[1], Jacopo Massa[1], and Matteo Mordacchini[3(✉)]

[1] Department of Computer Science, University of Pisa, Pisa 56126, Italy
patrizio.dazzi@unipi.it, jacopo.massa@phd.unipi.it
[2] ISTI-CNR, National Research Council, Pisa 56124, Italy
emanuele.carlini@isti.cnr.it
[3] IIT-CNR, National Research Council, Pisa 56124, Italy
matteo.mordacchini@iit.cnr.it

**Abstract.** This paper explores an extended applications' cost function to model the willingness of Edge data centres to accommodate additional users in decentralized edge computing environments. By enhancing the Marginal Computing Cost per User (MCU) concept, we introduce a dynamic cost factor influenced by the number of users currently served. Through extensive simulations conducted on the PureEdgeSim platform, we evaluate the impact of this variable MCU on system performance across various configurations. The results reveal a critical trade-off between cost sensitivity (i.e., collaboration willingness) of Edge data centres and optimization potential. This work offers insights into user allocation strategies in heterogeneous edge systems and sets the stage for future research into non-linear MCU configurations and diverse application workloads.

**Keywords:** Self-Organization · Cloud-Edge Continuum · Marginal Cost

## 1 Introduction

Edge computing holds the promise of enhancing the performance of applications that require high interactivity and low latency by bringing computation and storage closer to end-users. This paradigm shift provides significant infrastructural support for applications that may struggle with the inherent delays of traditional cloud-based solutions. Edge computing spans a diverse range of infrastructure, from widespread small data centres to localized computational units, from general-purpose hardware to specialized GPUs and various accelerators, and from traditional virtual machines to lightweight WebAssembly (WASM, a complementary technology to Linux containers) containers. This heterogeneity necessitates sophisticated strategies for managing the interactions among

© The Author(s), under exclusive license to Springer Nature Switzerland AG 2025
M. Naldi et al. (Eds.): GECON 2024, LNCS 15358, pp. 15–27, 2025.
https://doi.org/10.1007/978-3-031-81226-2_3

all involved entities. The allocation of applications to resources within an edge computing environment involves complex decisions. These decisions require consensus among various stakeholders and often involve factors beyond straightforward resource matching, such as political, economic, or other considerations. To manage these allocations effectively and ensure scalability, many state-of-the-art solutions avoid relying on a centralized authority [3,12]. Instead, they employ distributed or decentralized approaches [1,2,4,7,11]. However, existing solutions often assume equal participation from all stakeholders, which can overlook different actors' unique needs and constraints. The decision to allocate resources is not solely based on matching resource availability with user requests; it also involves evaluating various factors that may not be directly related to monetary considerations. For instance, two parties with identical resources might have different criteria for hosting decisions based on non-technical factors such as political or economic interests. To address these complexities, we propose a new cost function that extends the Marginal Computational Cost of a User (MCU) concept introduced by Ferrucci, Mordacchini, and Dazzi [5]. This extended cost function incorporates the "willingness" of a party to accept additional users. This willingness is modelled as a function concerning the number of users served by a particular "instance" of a given application in a real-world scenario, as explained in Sect. 4. Employing extensive simulations, we show that the MCU is a good metric to express the "willingness" of an entity to serve additional users. The experimentation is performed by changing the parameters of the function representing such cost, studying the behaviour of a system under variation of such parameters. Specifically, we demonstrate that our approach effectively balances the need to minimize resource usage – such as memory, CPUs, storage, and bandwidth – to reduce the overall cost represented by the MCU function.

The remainder of this paper is subdivided as follows. Section 2 presents the formal definition and concept of the MCU and the associated propositions. Section 3 presents the formal definition of the problem and illustrates the approach we propose. Section 4 describes the experimental methodology, objectives and datasets adopted for assessing the proposed solution, the experimental results achieved, their description and analysis. Finally, Sect. 5 draws concluding remarks and highlights future work directions.

## 2    Marginal Computing Cost

In economics, *marginal cost* refers to the change in total cost resulting from the production of one additional unit of a product, essentially the cost of producing one more item [10]. Unlike the *average cost*, which is the total cost divided by the number of units produced, the marginal cost pertains specifically to the cost of the last (marginal) unit produced.

When the cost function $C$ is continuous and differentiable, the marginal cost $MC$ is given by the first derivative of the cost function concerning the quantity of output $Q$:

$$MC(Q) = \frac{\partial C}{\partial Q} \tag{1}$$

For non-differentiable cost functions, the marginal cost can be defined as:

$$\overline{MC}(Q) = \frac{\Delta C}{\Delta Q} \tag{2}$$

where $\Delta$ signifies a change of one unit.

**Marginal Computing Cost of a User.** In this paper, we apply the concept of marginal cost to define the *marginal computing cost per user* (MCU). In a previous study [5], we defined MCU simply as the additional computational resources required by a service to accommodate one more user. In this study, MCU is designed to represent the willingness of an Edge data centre to accept additional users rather than the actual computational cost incurred. This approach allows for a more flexible and realistic resource allocation modelling in edge computing environments.

**Definition 1.** *The marginal computing cost per user for an application $A$, currently serving $k$ users, measures the willingness to serve $x$ more users in the form of additional resources needed. It is denoted as $MCU_{A,k,x}$.*

This metric aids in analyzing the resource dynamics of applications. If $TC_{A,k}$ is the total cost for application $A$ serving $k$ users, the average cost per user is defined as:

$$AvgU_{A,k} = \frac{TC_{A,k}}{k} \tag{3}$$

Based on these definitions, we can assess whether serving additional users (and, thus, the willingness to do it) with the existing application instances or to create new instances is beneficial. This depends on the relationship between $AvgU_{A,k}$ and $MCU_{A,k,1}$. We define $\Delta_{cost(A,k,1)}$ as the difference between the average cost and the marginal computing cost when adding one user:

$$\Delta_{cost(A,k,1)} = AvgU_{A,k} - MCU_{A,k,1} \tag{4}$$

$\Delta_{cost(A,k,1)}$ indicates the advantage of serving one more user with an existing application instance. Therefore, it drives the decision-making process of an Edge data centre. In fact, if this value is positive, allocating additional users to the existing instance is beneficial. In case of a request to add $x$ additional users to $k$ already being served, the decision process can be described as a rule of thumb:

$$\Delta_{cost(A,k,x)} \implies \begin{cases} \text{Allocate additional users} & \text{if } > 0, \\ \text{Reject the users} & \text{if } <= 0, \end{cases} \tag{5}$$

## 3   Problem Definition and Proposed Solution

This paper explores the trade-offs that arise from different collaboration schemes in a decentralized Edge system. Specifically, we analyze the impact on system performance when Edge data centres exhibit varying degrees of collaboration. We assume that Edge data centres host a heterogeneous set of application instances. Users are initially assigned to their nearest Edge data centre to minimize latency, which is the primary factor influencing users' Quality of Experience (QoE). Each application has specific latency limits that constrain the eligible Edge data centres for serving its users.

---

**Algorithm 1.** Actions performed by a generic Edge $E_i$ at a time step $t$

---

1: **Input:** $\mathcal{N}$ = set of neighbors of $E_i$

2: Randomly choose a neighbor $E_j$ from $\mathcal{N}$
3: Let $\tilde{A}$ be the set of apps having instances in both $E_i$ and $E_j$
4: **if** $\tilde{A} \neq \emptyset$ **then**
5:    **if** $W_i \geq W_j$ **then**
6:       Let $\tilde{A}_l = \{A_k \in \tilde{A} \mid l(u_{i,k}, E_j) \leq l_k\}$
7:       Let $\mathcal{A} = \{A_k \in \tilde{A}_l \mid MCU_{A_k, u_{jk}, u_{ik}} + w_j \leq W_j\}$
8:       **if** $\mathcal{A} \neq \emptyset$ **then**
9:          $A_m = \max_{A_k \in \mathcal{A}} \Delta_{cost(A_k, u_{jk}, u_{ik})}$
10:         Direct the users of $u_{ik}$ to use the instance on $E_j$
11:         Turn off the instance on $E_i$
12:      **end if**
13:   **else**
14:      Let $\tilde{A}_l = \{A_k \in \tilde{A} \mid l(u_{j,k}, E_i) \leq l_k\}$
15:      Let $\mathcal{A} = \{A_k \in \tilde{A}_l \mid MCU_{A_k, u_{ik}, u_{jk}} + w_j \leq W_j\}$
16:      **if** $\mathcal{A} \neq \emptyset$ **then**
17:         $A_m = \max_{A_k \in \mathcal{A}} \Delta_{cost(A_k, u_{ik}, u_{jk})}$
18:         Direct the users of $u_{jk}$ to use the instance on $E_i$
19:         Turn off the instance on $E_j$
20:      **end if**
21:   **end if**
22: **end if**

---

Neighboring Edge data centres collaborate by exchanging groups of users of their running applications, reducing the number of active instances. This approach reduces overall energy consumption and frees resources to host new users and applications. Our proposed algorithm dynamically adjusts user allocation based on real-time resource consumption evaluations at each Edge data centre. However, each Edge data centre can limit its level of collaboration by setting constraints on its willingness to accept new users, measured by the MCU function. An Edge data centre will accept additional users from a neighbour only if the resulting MCU does not exceed its resource limits. In doing this, we do not use the MCU as a direct measure of the computational cost but rather as an indicator of the Edge data centre's willingness to accommodate additional users. This perspective enables dynamic adjustments based on resource availability and collaboration policies among Edge data centres.

This self-organizing behaviour is implemented using the steps described in Algorithm 1. We define a function $l(u_{hk}, E_a)$ that checks if the latency limits $l_k$ of an application $A_k$ are met for all the members of its subset $h$ of users $u_{hk}$ when assigned to Edge data centre $E_a$; $w_a$ represents the current resource occupancy of $E_a$, while $W_a$ is its maximum capacity. In Algorithm 1, an Edge $E_i$ randomly selects a neighbor $E_j$ (line 2 of Algorithm1). They exchange information to identify the set $\tilde{A}$ of applications with active instances on both. They compare their occupancies, $w_i$ and $w_j$. The Edge with lower occupancy checks if it can host additional users. If $E_j$ has lower occupancy, it calculates the MCU for all applications on $E_i$ whose users can be moved to $E_j$ without violating latency limits (lines 6-7). If any application in $\tilde{A}$ satisfies $MCU_{A_k, u_{jk}, u_{ik}} + w_j \leq W_j$, the users on $E_i$ of $A_k \in \tilde{A}$ that maximises the $\Delta_{cost}$ function are redirected to $E_j$ (lines 9-10), and the instance on $E_i$ is turned off (line 11). The roles are reversed if $E_i$ has lower occupancy.

## 4    Experimental Setup and Evaluation

In this section, we present the results of our study with different MCUs using PureEdgeSim [9], a simulator based on CloudSimPlus [6] that supports various Edge-Cloud scenarios. PureEdgeSim allows the simulation of Edge devices, their characteristics, and the modelling of user-generated requests submitted to these devices.

For the geographic placement of Edge data centres, we used the EUA Dataset[1] from Lai et al. [8]. This dataset includes location information for Edge resources from the Australian Communications and Media Authority (ACMA), precisely the positions of cellular base stations in Melbourne. The dataset fixes the number of Edge data centres at 125, each covering a range of 450 to 750 m in a simulation area of about $1.71\,\text{km}^2$.

To ensure users are initially served by an application instance meeting their QoE requirements, we distributed applications and users uniformly. Each Edge data centre has the same resources, allowing us to study various scenarios by changing application types and MCU functions, extending the study by Ferrucci, Mordacchini, and Dazzi [5].

For application footprints, we used the Alibaba cluster-trace-microservices-v2021 dataset[2], containing runtime metrics of microservices. We applied the k-means algorithm to cluster these microservices into eight reference applications. This process ensures the selected applications represent different resource footprints in a modern IDC. The following assumptions apply to our model:

---

[1] https://github.com/swinedge/eua-dataset.
[2] https://github.com/alibaba/clusterdata.

1. Any application type can run on any Edge data centre.
2. There is at most one instance of each application type per Edge data centre.
3. All Edge data centres can communicate and be reached by any user.

The resources simulated include *VCPUs* and *RAM*, representing the number of Virtual CPUs and memory required by an application type. Each Edge data centre has a fixed capacity of 36 VCPUs and 48 Gbytes of RAM, based on a ratio of the capacity used in Alibaba's cluster traces. In our experiments, we extracted eight application types from the Alibaba dataset. Each application type $A_i$ is characterised by a fixed cost $C_{A_i}^{fix}$ (resources needed to start an instance for a single user) and a variable cost $C^{var}$ (for each additional user), which corresponds to the $MCU_{A_i,k,1}$. We used a uniform distribution of applications and users to ensure that each user is initially served by an application instance that meets their QoE requirements. This approach randomly places the same number of users within the range of each Edge data centre, which then serves them. These users are further uniformly distributed across different application types. Each Edge data centre has the same amount of resources, allowing us to study the behaviour of different application types and MCU functions in various scenarios, building on the study in [5].

Starting from the work in [5], in this paper we have defined a new different variable Marginal Computing cost function, in addition to the constant functions evaluated in the previous work, giving the function $MCU_{A_i,1,1} = 1/8 * C_{A_i}^{fix}(R)$, 12.5% of application startup cost, where $R$ is the resource type ( VCPU or RAM ). Such function is a **polynomial** Marginal computing cost function concerning the number of yet served users on a specific Edge data centre and is defined by the following formula:

$$MCU_{A_i,k,1} = MCU_{A_i,1,1} + MCU_{A_i,1,1} * c * k^{Exp} \tag{6}$$

where $c$ is a predefined coefficient, which represents the growth rate of the Marginal cost function. In our experiments, $c$ is in $\{0, 0.05, 0.1\}$, where $c = 0$ represents a constant MCU function. $Exp$ represents a predefined constant exponent that allows the study of non-linear Marginal cost functions in future works.

Table 1 shows the different application types and the corresponding fixed costs. Our experiments simulated a scenario with three users generating tasks of a given application type on each Edge data centre. Given eight application types, we have $8 * 125 * 3 = 3000$ users. Given the different MCU functions studied and defined for the tests, we considered a total of 3 different scenarios: a scenario with a constant MCU function and two scenarios with linear MCU functions, with respectively $c = 0.05$ and $c = 0.1$.

Another parameter considered in our simulations is the function used to simulate and measure the real-time latency, that is, the simulated time, in milliseconds, to send a message over the communication channel, either between a user (its mobile device, actually) and an Edge data centre or between two Edge data centres. Such function is the following:

$$f_{latency}(d, Edgedatacenter) = ChanLat_{fix} + dist(d, Edgedatacenter) * C_{Lat}$$

**Table 1.** $C_{A_i}^{fix}(R)$ for each application type, for 8 apps tests

| Type | VCPU | Ram (Mbyte) |
|------|------|-------------|
| $A_1$ | 0.318 | 898 |
| $A_2$ | 0.08 | 763 |
| $A_3$ | 0.174 | 833 |
| $A_4$ | 0.057 | 466 |
| $A_5$ | 0.153 | 1023 |
| $A_6$ | 0.195 | 646 |
| $A_7$ | 0.077 | 609 |
| $A_8$ | 0.082 | 909 |

The function is composed of two parts:

- a fixed part, $ChanLat_{fix}$, which is dependent on the communication channel type; in our experiments, it is fixed at $ChanLat_{fix} = 0.02$ seconds and also includes the component of the latency that depends on the bandwidth of the channel and the dimension of the packet sent;
- a linear part, proportional to the Euclidean distance $dist(d, Edgedatacentre)$ between the Edge data centre hosting the instance of the serving application and the user's device or Edge data centre $d$. The $C_{Lat}$ predefined constant represents the latency cost for each unit of distance and is fixed in our tests at $C_{Lat} = 0.00006$ seconds.

Given the predefined values for $ChanLat_{fix}$ and $C_{Lat}$ and the minimum and maximum distance of a user from the closest base station, we can obtain a range for the latency belonging to the interval $Lat = [20, 42.5]$ milliseconds inside a 5G cell, which is typical for a cell of such cellular network generation. For each type of application, we also specified a maximum latency of the network link that has been chosen *a priori* randomly, in the range $MaxLinkLat = [0.07, 0.1]$ seconds.

Our simulation is divided into iterations that occur at discrete time intervals. Each Edge data centre behaves like an agent that initiates the algorithm once per iteration. In our scenario, an iteration is started every 30 seconds, and every experiment has a simulated duration time of 15 minutes, so the number of iterations is fixed to 29. All the various experiment parameters (number of users, applications, datasets, latency calculation, users and Edge data center distributions, duration of the experiment, etc.) are chosen to allow a direct comparison with similar experiments in our previous paper [5].

### 4.1   Experimental Evaluation: Results

In this section, we present the experimental evaluation results of our proposed approach, which focuses on the variable MCU presented in 6. This approach introduces variability in the cost associated with exchanging users, which impacts the overall resource management and latency within the system. Unlike the fixed MCU used in previous works, this dynamic approach provides a more realistic simulation of the varying costs in real-world scenarios: such *costs* transcend the simple monetary value or occupancy of resources and represent the willingness of the party to add new users to a computation on a certain Edge data centre, exchanging them from another Edge data centre as explained in Sect. 3. If the *costs* of hosting such users on a unique Edge data centre are more significant than the *costs* to maintain such users on the other Edge data centre ( expressed by the MCU of the exchanged users ), the exchange is avoided, leading to a reduction in the total costs of the system and, consequently, also a better load balancing in the workload of the Edge data centres.

This section comprises three parts: the dynamics of active instances, resource footprint, and latency. For the baseline comparison, we refer to the previous work [5] when $c = 0$ and $Exp = 1$. Our experiments will consider 3000 users, 8 applications, and varying values of $c$, while $Exp$ is fixed to 1, leading to different linear Marginal computing cost functions. In future work, further tests with a value of $Exp > 1$ will be performed. We limited the number of users to 3000 due to the computational complexity of the simulator.

**Dynamics of the Active Instances.** The dynamics of the active instances of the applications hosted by the edge infrastructure are depicted in subfigures (c) of Figs. 1, 2, and 3. When $c = 0$ and $Exp = 1$ (linear MCU), the graph demonstrates a gradual reduction in the number of active instances from an initial value of 1.0 to approximately 0.5 by iteration 25, consistent with the findings of the baseline. This indicates that the system efficiently consolidates users into fewer instances, optimising resource usage. In contrast, for $c = 0.05$ and $Exp = 1$, the number of active instances starts at 1.0 and decreases to around 0.95 by iteration 25. The higher $c$ value results in a less significant reduction as the cost of moving users increases. When $c = 0.1$ and $Exp = 1$, the active instances remain almost stable around 0.98, showing minimal consolidation due to the increased cost sensitivity. These results suggest that while our approach effectively reduces the number of active instances, the impact of the cost factor $c$ plays a significant role in determining the extent of optimising the total costs, in accordance to the willingness expressed by the operator in the MCU function.

**Resource Footprint.** The impact of varying MCU on the overall resource footprint of the system is shown in subfigures (a) and (b) of Figs. 1, 2, and 3. For $c = 0$ and $Exp = 1$, memory usage decreases significantly from 0.16 to 0.12 by iteration 25, consistent with the baseline. This reduction reflects efficient memory consolidation with a linear MCU and no additional cost factor. However, for $c = 0.05$ and $Exp = 1$, memory usage starts at 0.13 and reduces slightly to around 0.125. The presence of a cost factor limits the level of consolidation, as some memory usage remains necessary to avoid excessive costs from exchanging users. When $c = 0.1$ and $Exp = 1$, memory usage remains stable at around 0.126

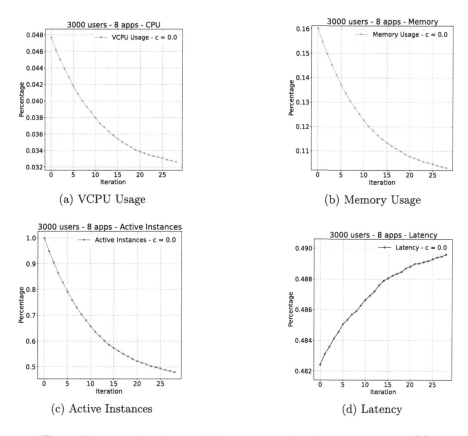

**Fig. 1.** Dynamics for $c = 0$ and $Exp = 1$ - Baseline from previous work [5]

with minimal reduction, indicating that higher costs associated with exchanging users significantly restrict memory optimisation but lead to an increase in load balancing and, as expressed by the MCU function itself, a reduction in total costs for the party. Notably, the CPU usage trends closely mirror memory usage across the different configurations. As the cost factor increases, the extent of optimisation diminishes similarly for both CPU and memory, highlighting the consistent impact of the dynamic MCU function on resource consolidation. As for the dynamics of the active instances, the presence of a cost factor $c$ crucially determines the given optimisation, helping parties to express concisely the trade-off between merely resource optimisation and the actual costs represented by the MCU function.

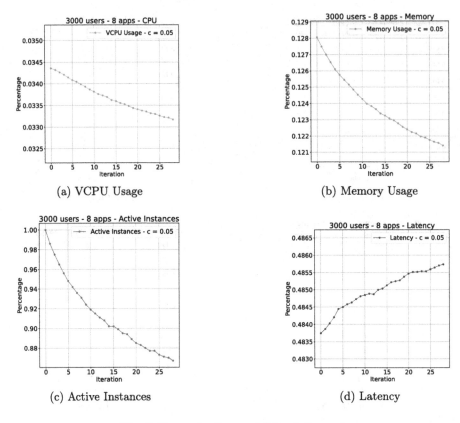

**Fig. 2.** Dynamics for $c = 0.05$ and $Exp = 1$

**Latency.** The latency dynamics are depicted in subfigures (d) of Figs. 1, 2, and 3, highlighting how latency is affected by the different MCU configurations. For $c = 0$ and $Exp = 1$, latency slightly decreases from 0.49 to around 0.48, showing that latency constraints are well-maintained despite user consolidation, consistent with the baseline. For $c = 0.05$ and $Exp = 1$, latency remains relatively stable, starting at 0.485 and ending at around 0.483. The system effectively manages latency while moderately consolidating users. When $c = 0.1$ and $Exp = 1$, latency shows minimal variation, staying around 0.484. The high cost of exchanging users ensures latency remains stable but limits optimisation benefits. These results demonstrate that our approach effectively maintains latency constraints even when higher costs limit resource consolidation.

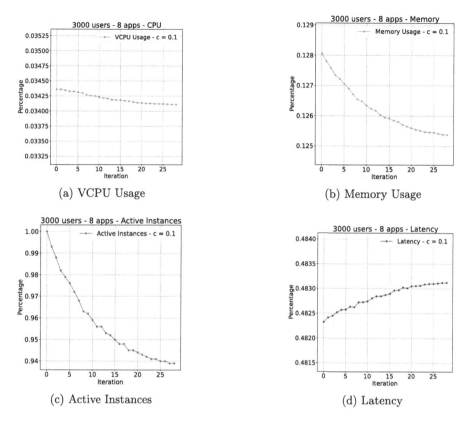

**Fig. 3.** Dynamics for $c = 0.1$ and $Exp = 1$

## 5   Conclusions

This paper presented extended cost functions to model the willingness of edge data centres to accept additional users in a decentralized edge computing environment. The marginal computing cost per user (MCU) concept was expanded to incorporate a dynamic cost factor based on the number of users served. Extensive simulations were conducted using the PureEdgeSim platform to evaluate the impact of this variable MCU on system performance under different parameter configurations. The results demonstrate that our approach effectively balances the dual objectives of optimizing resource usage through user consolidation, while also reducing the overall cost as represented by the MCU function. When the MCU exhibited linear growth, systems with higher growth coefficients showed less significant reductions in active instances and resource footprint over time. This indicates that a higher cost sensitivity inhibits the extent of optimization. Notably, latency constraints were well-maintained even for scenarios with limited consolidation due to higher costs. This work provides insights into how modelling the flexible willingness of edge data centres via a variable MCU can influence the collaborative user allocation process in decentralized edge systems. It also highlights the trade-off between resource optimization on one hand, and costs expressed by the MCU on the other. Future work will explore non-linear MCU configurations and different types of real-world application workloads and infrastructure topologies to continue assessing this approach under varied conditions. Overall, the proposed solution presents a viable strategy for managing heterogeneous edge systems with self-interested participants.

**Acknowledgments.** This project has received funding from the European Union's Horizon Europe research and innovation programme under Grant Agreement No 101092950 (EDGELESS project).

# References

1. Carlini, E., et al.: Smartorc: smart orchestration of resources in the compute continuum. Front. High Perform. Comput. **1**, 1164915 (2023)
2. Carlini, E., Coppola, M., Dazzi, P., Mordacchini, M., Passarella, A.: Self-optimising decentralised service placement in heterogeneous cloud federation. In: 2016 IEEE 10th International Conference on Self-adaptive and Self-organizing Systems (SASO), pp. 110–119. IEEE (2016)
3. Ferrer, A.J., Becker, S., Schmidt, F., Thamsen, L., Kao, O.: Towards a cognitive compute continuum: an architecture for ad-hoc self-managed swarms. In: 2021 IEEE/ACM 21st International Symposium on Cluster, Cloud and Internet Computing (CCGrid), pp. 634–641. IEEE (2021)
4. Ferrucci, L., Mordacchini, M., Coppola, M., Carlini, E., Kavalionak, H., Dazzi, P.: Latency preserving self-optimizing placement at the edge. In: Proceedings of the 1st Workshop on Flexible Resource and Application Management on the Edge, pp. 3–8. FRAME '21, ACM, New York, NY, USA (2021)
5. Ferrucci, L., Mordacchini, M., Dazzi, P.: Decentralized replica management in latency-bound edge environments for resource usage minimization. IEEE Access **12**, 19229–19249 (2024). https://doi.org/10.1109/ACCESS.2024.3359749
6. Filho, M.C.S., Oliveira, R.L., Monteiro, C.C., Inácio, P.R.M., Freire, M.M.: Cloudsim plus: A cloud computing simulation framework pursuing software engineering principles for improved modularity, extensibility and correctness. In: 2017 IFIP/IEEE Symposium on Integrated Network and Service Management (IM), pp. 400–406 (2017)
7. Korontanis, I., et al.: Inter-operability and orchestration in heterogeneous cloud/edge resources: The accordion vision. In: Proceedings of the 1st Workshop on Flexible Resource and Application Management on the Edge, pp. 9–14 (2020)
8. Lai, P., et al.: Optimal edge user allocation in edge computing with variable sized vector bin packing. In: ICSOC (2018)
9. Mechalikh, C., Takta, H., Moussa, F.: Pureedgesim: A simulation toolkit for performance evaluation of cloud, fog, and pure edge computing environments. In: 2019 International Conference on High Performance Computing Simulation (HPCS), pp. 700–707 (2019)
10. O'Sullivan, A., Sheffrin, S.M.: Economics: Principles in Action. Pearson Prentice Hall, Upper Saddle River, NJ (2003)

11. Russo, G.R., Mannucci, T., Cardellini, V., Presti, F.L.: Serverledge: Decentralized function-as-a-service for the edge-cloud continuum. In: 2023 IEEE International Conference on Pervasive Computing and Communications (PerCom), pp. 131–140. IEEE (2023)
12. Surya, K., Rajam, V.M.A.: Novel approaches for resource management across edge servers. Int. J. Netw. Distrib. Comput. **11**(1), 20–30 (2023). https://doi.org/10.1007/s44227-022-00007-0

# FaaS@Edge: Bringing Function-as-a-Service to Voluntary Computing at the Edge

Catarina Gonçalves[1], José Simão[1,2] , and Luís Veiga[1(✉)]

[1] INESC-ID, Instituto Superior Técnico, Universidade de Lisboa, Lisboa, Portugal
catarinagoncalves@gsd.inesc-id.pt, luis.veiga@tecnico.ulisboa.pt
[2] Instituto Superior de Engenharia de Lisboa (ISEL/FIT), Lisboa, Portugal
jose.simao@isel.pt

**Abstract.** Function-as-a-Service (FaaS) is an emerging cloud computing model ideal for processing vast amounts of data generated by the
Internet of Things. However, existing FaaS approaches struggle to leverage resources efficiently on distributed edge devices. Our work presents
FaaS@Edge, a solution that employs volunteered resources from edge
nodes, discovered through the IPFS network, to deploy functions using
the Apache OpenWhisk framework and enhancing the system's scalability and efficiency. This approach supports various language runtimes,
ensuring near-universal deployability on edge devices. Our evaluation
demonstrates that FaaS@Edge introduces a latency overhead for function submission but achieves similar invocation times compared to a
local OpenWhisk deployment. FaaS@Edge maintains high request success rates, with overall request success rates around 98% for both submission and invocation. These results confirm that FaaS@Edge provides
a viable and efficient model for FaaS deployment in edge computing environments, facilitating low latency and efficient resource utilization.

**Keywords:** Function-as-a-Service · Edge Computing · Cloud
Computing · Volunteer Computing · Peer-to-Peer Data Networks

## 1 Introduction

Function-as-a-Service (FaaS) is an emerging paradigm aimed to simplify Cloud
Computing and overcome its drawbacks by providing a simple interface to deploy
event-driven applications that execute the function code, without the responsibility of provisioning, scaling, or managing the underlying infrastructure [12,18].
In the FaaS model, the management effort is detached from the responsibilities
of the consumer, since the cloud provider transparently handles the lifecycle,
execution, and scaling of the application. This model was originally proposed

---

Work partially developed while as a Visiting Researcher with the Hybrid Cloud Computing Group at IBM Research Europe – Zurich.

© The Author(s), under exclusive license to Springer Nature Switzerland AG 2025
M. Naldi et al. (Eds.): GECON 2024, LNCS 15358, pp. 28–42, 2025.
https://doi.org/10.1007/978-3-031-81226-2_4

for the cloud but has since been explored for deployments in geographically distributed systems [6]. With the expansion of the Internet of Things, the cloud has become an insufficient solution to respond to the growing amounts of data transmitted and the variety of Internet of Things applications that require low latency and location-aware deployments, as stated by CISCO [20]. This led to the introduction of the Edge Computing paradigm, designed to reduce the overload of information sent to the cloud through the Internet, by bringing the resources and computing power closer to the end user and processing the data at the edge of the network, e.g., recently for AI workloads [10,13].

The intersection between Function-as-a-Service and Edge Computing presents a captivating area of research and innovation since the growing demand for low latency, real-time applications urges the need to explore the integration of FaaS in Edge Computing devices. At the same time, this integration also needs to address its inherent challenges, such as managing distributed architectures, optimizing resource allocation, and ensuring compatibility with the heterogeneous characteristics of edge devices.

Most cloud service platforms still rely on centralized architectures and services that are neither designed to operate on resource-constrained environments, nor on the heterogeneous devices that characterize edge systems. Solutions to bring Function-as-a-Service deployments to the edge of the network have been explored [8,16] but few have managed to realize efficient resource provisioning and allocation [5], by leveraging volunteered resources in a completely distributed and decentralized manner [3].

Our contribution consists of a FaaS@Edge system that uses volunteer resources from multiple users, that are announced and discovered through the IPFS network, to submit and invoke user functions on their volunteered edge devices using the Apache OpenWhisk framework.

The rest of the paper is structured as follows: Sect. 2 describes FaaS@Edge's architecture and algorithms, alongside the implementation details of our solution. Section 3 presents the evaluation of our prototype. Section 4 presents an analysis of the related work in Cloud Computing including Function-as-a-Service, Edge Computing, and Peer-to-Peer Content, Storage and Distribution. Finally, Sect. 5 wraps up the paper with our closing remarks.

## 2 Architecture

FaaS@Edge represents a distributed and decentralized middleware framework designed to facilitate Function-as-a-Service (FaaS) deployments across a network of volunteer edge computing devices. This framework aims to minimize execution latency, optimize resource utilization, and enhance the distribution and availability of content within edge environments. The architecture of FaaS@Edge necessitates that participating nodes be equipped with specific components, as illustrated in Fig. 1:

- FaaS@Edge's middleware running as daemon;

- An initialized IPFS Kubo node;
- The IPFS daemon;
- An OpenWhisk stack running as a Java process (if the node is supplying its resources to execute function requests).

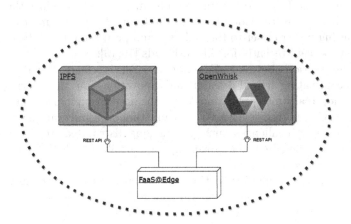

**Fig. 1.** FaaS@Edge participant node's complete components.

**Distributed Architecture.** The architecture of FaaS@Edge is built upon the IPFS peer-to-peer framework, leveraging a Kademlia-based Distributed Hash Table (DHT) for its operations. This DHT is instrumental in associating content identifiers with the node identifiers and IP addresses that host the content, enabling efficient lookup, routing, and retrieval mechanisms that are crucial for large-scale content distribution, aided by built-in caching features. With every FaaS@Edge node accessible via IPFS and uniquely identified by a PeerID - a SHA-256 multihash of the node's public key - the system facilitates a distributed and decentralized approach to resource discovery. Nodes can broadcast resource availability, namely memory, on IPFS, encapsulating the memory offered in files tagged with specific strings and content identifiers (CIDs), which other nodes can then discover to deploy their functions effectively.

The system has two roles, suppliers that offer resources and clients that look for the best place to run their functions. Each node can have either one or both roles. The nodes that are running the OpenWhisk component are described as the suppliers and are the ones volunteering their resources to the system, indicating the maximum memory amount they are willing to offer in the start command. However, all nodes can send function deployment requests. During the initialization of a node, the CIDs of all the possible offer values (ranging from 128 MB to 512 MB, in power of 2 sizes) are calculated with IPFS' only-hash option in the add command and stored to be used by the supply and discovery algorithms.

---

**Algorithm 1:** Supplier's resource supplying algorithm.

---

**Data:** $suppActiveOffersMap, suppOfferPlan$
**Function** SupplyResources($freeRes, maxRes$):
    $usedRes \leftarrow ResourcesInUse(freeRes, maxRes)$
    $removeSupplierOffers()$
    $offerCount, offerSize \leftarrow suppOfferPlan.CalculateOffers()$
    **foreach** $offerCount, offerSize$ **do**
        $newOffer \leftarrow CreateOffer(offerSize)$
        $suppActiveOffersMap.Add(newOffer)$

---

The following data structures are used in the resource scheduling algorithms:

- **Offer** contains the *resources* a supplier node is offering and is published in IPFS as a text file with the string faas-edge-MEM, where MEM is the memory being offered (only one offer file is published per memory amount, the rest is incremented/decremented in the map presented next);
- **Supplier's Active Offers Map** keeps a record of the *number of offers* made of each *resource value*;
- **Available Offer** contains the *resources* and *supplier IP address* of an offer discovered in IPFS.

Algorithm 1 is executed by a supplier node upon its initial integration into the system or whenever its resource availability fluctuates, either due to the allocation of a function or by freeing resources following a deployment failure. The node starts by calculating the amount of resources currently in use, given the maximum value of resources it is willing to provide and the current value of free resources it has. Then, all active offers are removed in order to calculate the offers that match the current resource availability. This is achieved by making the IPFS client to remove the offer file's *pin* per each size of active offer, the remaining offers are simply decremented in the supplier's active offers map. Given the distributed nature of IPFS and its caching capabilities, there is no direct way to delete a file, only to *unpin* it from storage and let the garbage collector reclaim it. Meanwhile, requests routed to now unavailable resources are replayed; randomness in clients sorting offers promotes selecting others available (Algorithm 3).

After this, the algorithm will calculate the number and size of offers to be made, according to the respective offering plan. For each of these, it will then use Algorithm 2 to publish the file in IPFS and create a new offer object that is added to the supplier's active offers map. Adding the offer files to IPFS during each resource availability update can serve as an offer refresh and help to ensure liveness. Algorithm 2 starts by checking if the node already has active offers of that value in its offers map, or if it needs to make the offer available in IPFS. To do so, the node retrieves the string representative of that offer value and calls the IPFS client to add a file with the string to its distributed file system. If the publishing operation was successful or there was no need to publish, because at least one offer of that memory value was already being made in IPFS, the

---

**Algorithm 2:** Supplier's create offer algorithm.

---

**Data:** $suppActiveOffersMap, IPFSClient$
**Result:** $newOffer$
**Function** CreateOffer($offerRes$):
    **if** $suppActiveOffersMap[offerRes.Value] < 1$ **then**
        $offerStr \leftarrow GetResourcesString(offerRes)$
        $ok \leftarrow IPFSClient.Add(offerStr)$
        **if** $ok = false$ **then**
            **return** $Error($"Unable to create offer"$)$

    /* Only add to IPFS if there are no active offers of that memory value,
      otherwise, just create the new offer to add to the map.         */
    $newOffer \leftarrow NewOffer(offerRes)$
    **return** $newOffer$

---

**Algorithm 3:** Algorithm to schedule function in supplier node.

---

**Function** Schedule($fnConfig$):
    $resNeeded \leftarrow fnConfig.Resources$
    $availOffers \leftarrow DiscoverResources(resNeeded)$
    $availOffers \leftarrow RandomOrder(availOffers)$
    **foreach** $offer$ $in$ $availOffers$ **do**
        $fnStatus \leftarrow SubmitFunction(fnConfig, offer, self.IP)$
        **if** $fnStatus = ok$ **then**
            $deployedFn \leftarrow DeployedFn(fnConfig, offer.SuppIP)$
            $functionsMap.Add(deployedFn)$
            **return** $fnStatus$

    **return** $Error($"Unable to schedule function"$)$

---

function can finally create a new offer object containing the resources being offered.

When the supplier node has available resources to supply, it can follow several options on how to arrange different combinations of resource offers. These offering plans will achieve different results when it comes to effective resource utilization, fragmentation, and resource allocation. The different offering plan options are the following:

- **Balanced** - Provides the same number of offers for each size, without exceeding its maximum resource capacity.
- **Overbook** - Generates all the possible resource combinations that it can offer, thus overbooking its available resources. This approach favors resource utilization and avoids fragmentation since there are offers of all sizes. Free resources will be a result of the different supply and demand in the system.
- **Balanced Ranges** - Equivalent to the Balanced option except the offer sizes are limited within one of the following ranges: Small (128 MB), Medium (256 MB), or Large (512 MB).
- **Overbook Ranges** - Equivalent to the Overbook option except the offer sizes are limited within one of the ranges Small, Medium, and Large presented above.
- **Random Balanced** - Each supplier node randomly chooses the offering plan between the Balanced and the three Balanced Ranges plans.

– **Random Overbook** - Each supplier node randomly chooses the offering plan between the Overbook and the three Overbook Ranges plans.

The resource discovery method occurs when a client node receives a function submission request with specified resource limits. In this process the node determines the minimum necessary memory size and obtains the relevant CID. It then uses IPFS's to find providers and identify up to 20 potential suppliers by their IPFS addresses, creating Available Offer objects for each, detailing the resources and supplier node's IP address.

Algorithm 3 is called when a user's submission request is received through the CLI application that interacts with FaaS@Edge's daemon, containing the function's configuration (source code's CID, function's name, function's runtime type, and resources needed). It takes the resources needed for the deployment and uses the previously described action to find a set of available offers. Then, this set of offers is sorted in random order, to contribute to spread the load and thus avoid overloading any supplier nodes. Finally, it will iterate over the sorted offers, and send a SubmitFunction message, through the node's remote client, containing the function's configuration, the offer to be used, and the node's own IP address.

When the supplier node's receives a function submission message from a client node it starts by signaling the use of the resources provided in that offer, triggering the update of the supplied offers to adjust to the decrease in the node's available resources. Then it calls the OpenWhisk component, passing the function's configuration so that it can retrieve the source code file from IPFS using its CID, and insert/create the function in OpenWhisk. If the creation is successful, the node stores a new local function object in a map, where it keeps the functions of each client node, to be able to invoke them when requested, and informs the client node of the successful deployment. In case of failure, the supplier's resources are released, and an error message is returned to the client node that requested the deployment.

**Implementation Details.** Figure 2 provides an overview of FaaS@Edge's node software components, interfaces, and their relationships. Note that only the supplier nodes need to include the OpenWhisk Client Wrapper and Function Manager components. The main components are:

**Node** - Super component that drives the initialization of all other components, receiving the configuration parameters from the user through the CLI tool, and passing them to its internal components. The node makes its scheduling services available to the other nodes and to the user through interfaces exposed via REST API;

**Scheduler** - Responsible for the function deployments and subsequent invocations, exposes interfaces to the user, to inject requests, and to remote nodes, allowing them to send message requests to deploy/invoke functions in this node. Interacts with the Discovery component to find available resources for a deployment;

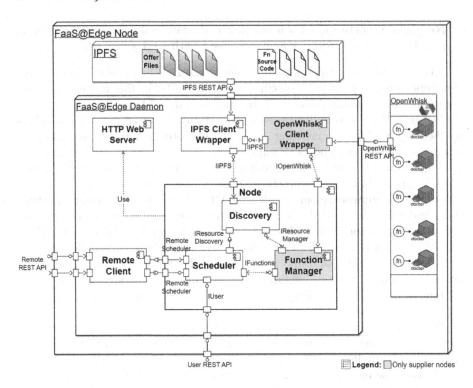

**Fig. 2.** FaaS@Edge's components and interfaces.

**Discovery** - Implements the resource discovery algorithms to find resources offered by other provider nodes and to oversee the supplier node's resources and offers, according to the offering plan. Interacts with the IPFS Client Wrapper to add offer files to IPFS, query the DHT to find providers, and get the CID of each offer value;

**Function Manager** - Manages function deployments in the local node's OpenWhisk platform via OpenWhisk Client Wrapper. Provides an interface used by the Scheduler to submit and invoke functions requested by other nodes and interacts with the Discovery component to validate the use of the node's resources for deployments and release them in case an error is received from OpenWhisk;

**IPFS Client Wrapper** - Wraps the Go client library for the HTTP RPC API exposed by IPFS' daemon in order to provide a simplified interface that isolates the use of IPFS at our middleware's level from IPFS' core API that provides direct access to the core commands;

**OpenWhisk Client Wrapper** - Wraps the Go client library for the Open-Whisk API to access the running OpenWhisk services, isolating our middleware's function management from OpenWhisk's API details. Exposes an interface to be used by the Function Manager component to insert, invoke, and delete functions and enforces the system limit for how much memory a function can allocate, defined during the function's insertion in OpenWhisk;

**HTTP Web Server** - Serves REST API endpoints and redirects requests to the respective FaaS@Edge components. The server is started by the Node component once the user issues a *start* command.

We selected OpenWhisk and IPFS due to their widespread usage. Our architecture could be adapted to other: open-source FaaS frameworks (e.g. OpenFaaS, Knative); P2P structured overlays, e.g., Chord, CAN; P2P storage, e.g., Freenet.

Finally, FaaS@Edge provides a CLI tool to consume the REST API, similar to OpenWhisk's CLI tool, that allows users to perform the following operations: `Start` - Start running a new FaaS@Edge node; `Exit` - Shut down the instance node; `Submit` - Submit a user function in FaaS@Edge.; `Invoke` - Invoke a function previously submitted in FaaS@Edge.

## 3   Evaluation

To evaluate the FaaS@Edge prototype, we used a configuration consisting of a cluster deployment setup, illustrative of an edge deployment, of 1 to 15 virtual machines with 2 vCPUs and 2048MB of RAM and a remote client node on a geographically distant machine with 2 vCPUs and 4096MB of RAM. In order to test our system accordingly, we used FaaS workload functions that we developed, using the Go language, to be supported by our prototype and use some typical FaaS scenarios [18, 21]:

- **Content Hashing** - Receives data contents as a function parameter and generates the SHA256 hash of that content. The resulting hash is returned to the user if requested.
- **Database Query** - The user can request the initialization of an in-memory database that stores information regarding a library's books in JSON format. Then, the user can query the database for any specific book by passing its International Standard Book Number (ISBN) as a parameter.
- **Image Transformation** - Receives a public image URL which is used to get the image data using HTTP. Then, performs a transformation to flip the image vertically and returns the image data in base64 format.

Our study compared FaaS@Edge's overhead and performance with local OpenWhisk on edge devices, analyzing function latency, bandwidth, CPU, memory usage, and success rates. We examined how different offering plans, particularly the Balanced plan, affected these metrics across six deployment setups.

- Local deployment of OpenWhisk on a single node instance;
- One client node and one supplier node on the same machine;
- One client node and one supplier node on remotely distant machines;
- Five nodes with two supplier nodes and three client nodes on the same machine;
- Ten nodes with five supplier nodes and four client nodes on the same machine, and a client node on a remote machine;

– Fifteen nodes with eight supplier nodes and six client nodes on the same machine, and a client node on a remote machine.

The remainder of this section presents the results of our evaluation.

**Function Latency.** Fig. 3 presents the distribution of the submission latency times for each of the deployments mentioned previously, measured since the client nodes sent the submission requests until an answer was received, excluding the time it took the supplier node available to create the function in OpenWhisk. The values observed are situated between the interval of 0.02 s and 0.1 s, and the lower latency values belong to the 2 nodes and 5 nodes deployments, and higher values correspond to the 15 nodes deployment.

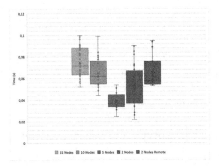
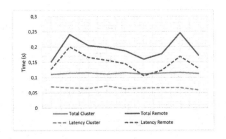

**Fig. 3.** Submission latency times per nodes (Box plot).

**Fig. 4.** Submission times comparison between client node in cluster machine and remote machine.

The function memory values specified in a submission request have an important role in our algorithms to select the available provider, contrary to the function types that have no influence, but the results returned relatively close values of overhead time, which indicates a leveled distribution of the different sizes of resources as a result of our offering strategy.

Figure 4 provides a comparison between the submission times obtained by client nodes located in a cluster machine, where the supplier nodes are also running, and the client node in a remote machine. A remote client node spends ≈70% more time during resource discovery and/or exchanging of messages to fulfill the submission request.

Figure 5 presents the distribution of the latency times obtained for each of the deployments, again, excluding the time it takes for the function to execute in OpenWhisk. The results fitted all within an interval of 0.04 s, as predicted since the invocation request has no additional overhead from resource discovery or scheduling algorithms, already handled during the function's submission.

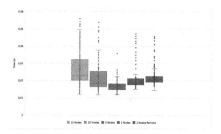

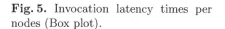

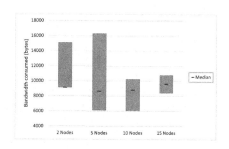

**Fig. 5.** Invocation latency times per nodes (Box plot).

**Fig. 6.** Bandwidth consumed per nodes.

These results only consider *warm start* invocations, where there is already a running container, as a way to normalize their averages. The image transformation function (that is more CPU demanding) revealed a significantly higher total invocation time than the rest, which was spent in OpenWhisk. The function memory allocation values do not cause significant implications on the total and latency invocation times.

Contrary to what we witnessed with the submission times, the remote client took only 2.9% more invocation total time, indicating that the physical distance between nodes can have an impact on IPFS' lookup protocol during the resource discovery but does not impose a lot of added time on the execution of invocation requests (maintaining an acceptable network throughput).The results show that using FaaS@Edge is slower than local deployment but still offers practical benefits. Submissions through FaaS@Edge take about 90.9% longer than local deployment, while invocations are 25.5% slower. Despite this, the slight delay in FaaS@Edge can be deemed acceptable, particularly as it allows less powerful edge nodes to leverage the FaaS model without relying on cloud providers. The minimal performance loss is especially favorable considering users are likely to make more invocation than submission requests in FaaS@Edge.

**Bandwidth Consumed per Node.** Fig. 6 presents the overall bandwidth consumed by the supplier node instances in the different deployments during test executions with each fulfilling an arbitrary number of requests. Notice that the amplitude of bandwidth values decreases with the increase of nodes in the deployment and the median values are all situated between 8659B and 9604B (showing that increased scale improves load balancing to a significant extent). Bandwidth consumption over time typically suffered 2–3 increases of transmitted bandwidth by intervals of ≈3000B, with the exception of the image transformation function which also revealed an increase in the received data due to an HTTP request performed to retrieve the image data. The Bandwidth consumed per node did not show any direct relation to the number of requests a supplier node executed, thus we can simply conclude that the average consumption during the program's execution in an edge device is admissible and does not hinder the node's performance.

**CPU and Memory Usage per Node.** The CPU and Memory used per node metrics were retrieved periodically over time on both supplier and client nodes, during each test execution. The average CPU usage observed in supplier nodes and client nodes for each deployment gradually decreased from 5.61% to 2.31% as the number of nodes in the deployments increased, indicating an efficient utilization of the extra resources and good load balancing between the supplier nodes. The usage in client nodes is also significantly lower (averaging between 0.30%-0.80% CPU) than in supplier nodes seeing as the latter are the ones satisfying the requests and running the OpenWhisk platform thus using more processing power.

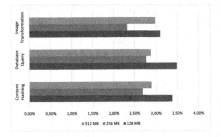

**Fig. 7.** CPU usage per node and memory value for each function type.

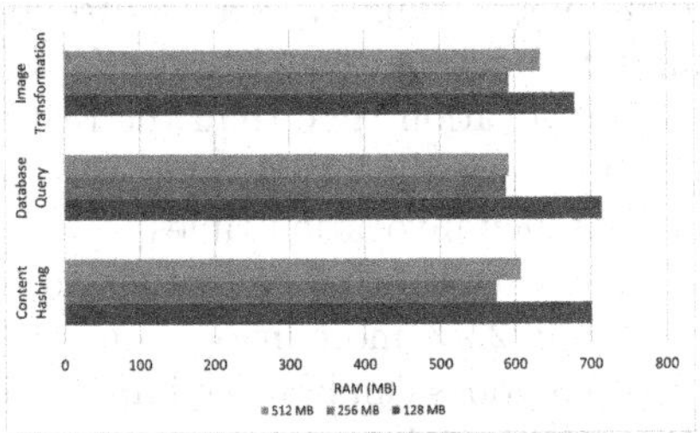

**Fig. 8.** Memory used per node and memory value for each function type.

Figure 7 and Fig. 8 show that functions with 128MB of memory consumed the most CPU and memory resources, which we attribute to increased memory-disk swapping, which degraded performance. Despite this, the overall resource consumption for all memory allocations was deemed reasonable, ensuring that edge devices remain efficient for other functionalities while partaking in the FaaS@Edge network.

**Request Success Rate.** The request success rate measures how many user requests to submit and invoke a function the FaaS@Edge system was able to successfully fulfill, which directly translates into the resource discovery and scheduling algorithms' effectiveness and, in turn, the user's satisfaction.

Table 1 shows varying success rates for different FaaS functions and memory sizes during tests. Image transformation had the highest success rate, while database queries saw more failures, often due to supplier node crashes, not resource issues. The offering plan had minimal effect on bandwidth, CPU, or memory, suggesting stable resource availability and demand-supply balance, without network scaling or churn impacting resource allocation.

**Table 1.** Request Success Rate by Function Type and Memory

|  | Request Success Rate | |
|---|---|---|
| Function Type | Submission | Invocation |
| Content Hashing | 99.49% | 100.00% |
| Database Query | 95.16% | 94.98% |
| Image Transformation | 100.00% | 100.00% |
| Function Memory | | |
| 128 MB | 95.24% | 97.28% |
| 256 MB | 99.49% | 98.73% |
| 512 MB | 100.00% | 100.00% |
| *Total Requests* | 98.76% | 98.69% |

## 4   Related Work

Function-as-a-Service, first presented by Amazon, in the form of Lambda functions, allows the consumer to run their function code automatically, at a more fine-grained level, when a request occurs, i.e., an event is triggered, without having to provision virtual machine instances or monitor and upgrade the system. A widely used open source example of this technology is Apache OpenWhisk.

WOW [11] is a prototype for a WebAssembly runtime environment, as a lightweight alternative to traditional container runtimes, designed mainly for serverless computing at the edge. It introduces the components to support the WebAssembly runtime, similar to Docker's container runtime support, using the Apache OpenWhisk framework.

Our work is also related to volunteer computing approaches, where users offer their unused resources to build a large computational infrastructure. A well-known example is SETI@home [2], a volunteer computing project that uses Internet-connected computers to analyze radio signals in search of extraterrestrial intelligence. It uses the BOINC [1] software platform for volunteer computing, but the system is only designed for this specific set of applications, although there are other extensions of BOINC for cycle-sharing applications, such as the nuBOINC system [19]. Caravela [17] is a completely decentralized Edge Cloud system that utilizes volunteered user resources where users can deploy their applications using Docker containers. Peers in Caravela can act as suppliers, publishing offers to supply their resources, buyers, searching for resource offers in order to deploy a container, or traders, registering and mediating the offers made within their resource region.

As computational progress evolves rapidly on a global scale with the emergence of increasingly more powerful processors, cloud storages have been more sought after to handle these data management functions. However, the typical characteristics of centralized management and single-entity infrastructure providers which are linked to cloud storages may pose several privacy and security concerns and threaten data accessibility and availability [9]. Peer-to-Peer

Data Networks aim to overcome these issues by creating overlay networks where peers can autonomously share their resources with each other. While other data-sharing and content distribution approaches like Content Delivery Networks [14], that addressed the lack of dynamic management of Web content, focus on fulfilling the customer's (often a company) requirements for performance and Quality-of-Service, Peer-to-Peer Data Networks' main goal is to efficiently locate and transfer files across peers (often final users) [15].

IPFS [7] is a decentralized file system merging DHTs, block exchanges, and version control to create a peer-to-peer network. It uses a Kademlia-based DHT for peer discovery and content location, with data stored in content-addressed chunks forming a Merkle DAG for retrieval. The BitSwap protocol manages data distribution, where peers exchange lists of content identifiers for the chunks they want or offer. Support for publish-subscribe notifications was also added [4].

The previous systems address some of the aspects that we tackle in our work, but none achieves the implementation of all aspects. Apache OpenWhisk is a framework for FaaS deployments, but it was not intentionally designed to maintain performance in an edge environment and does not feature content distribution. WOW targets wasm that could run at browsers at the edge, but it focuses mostly on reducing cold starts and does not address decentralization at the edge specifically. Caravela uses a peer-to-peer network with similar capabilities as IPFS and introduces the execution of long-running container applications, however, it is not designed for FaaS deployments. SETI@home uses large-scale volunteer computing, but still relies on a centralized server. IPFS focuses on content storage and distribution, which is highly important in peer-to-peer edge environments but involves no computation execution by itself.

## 5 Conclusion

In this study, we introduced FaaS@Edge, a novel decentralized framework designed to implement Function-as-a-Service (FaaS) within edge computing environments by utilizing the resources of edge nodes to deploy user functions via Apache OpenWhisk. Our observations revealed that while the middleware introduces a significant bootstrapping overhead (nearly doubling the latency time for function submission compared to a local OpenWhisk deployment), the invocation times remained comparably low, which is advantageous considering the typically higher frequency of invocations relative to submissions. Moreover, the system's bandwidth consumption, CPU, and memory usage were found to be within acceptable ranges for edge devices, and FaaS@Edge demonstrated a high success rate in function deployment and execution.

Regarding future work, our objectives include enhancing FaaS@Edge's functionality by developing a mechanism that allows users to deploy functions using methods beyond source code files and custom runtimes, such as Docker containers or binary-compatible executables.

**Acknowledgements.** This work was supported by national funds through FCT, Fundação para a Ciência e a Tecnologia, under project UIDB/50021/2020 (DOI:10.54499/

UIDB/50021/2020). This work was supported by: "DL 60/2018, de 3-08 - Aquisição necessária para a atividade de I&D do INESC-ID, no âmbito do projeto SmartRetail (C6632206063-00466847)". This work was supported by the CloudStars project, funded by the European Union's Horizon research and innovation program under grant agreement number 101086248.

# References

1. Anderson, D.P.: BOINC: a platform for volunteer computing. J. Grid Comput. **18**(1), 99–122 (2020)
2. Anderson, D.P., Cobb, J., Korpela, E., Lebofsky, M., Werthimer, D.: Seti@ home: an experiment in public-resource computing. Commun. ACM **45**(11), 56–61 (2002)
3. Antelmi, A., D'Ambrosio, G., Petta, A., Serra, L., Spagnuolo, C.: A volunteer computing architecture for computational workflows on decentralized web. IEEE Access **10**, 98993–99010 (2022)
4. Antunes, J., Dias, D., Veiga, L.: Pulsarcast: scalable, reliable pub-sub over P2P nets. In: Yan, Z., Tyson, G., Koutsonikolas, D. (eds.) IFIP Networking Conference, IFIP Networking 2021, Espoo and Helsinki, Finland, June 21–24, 2021, pp. 1–6. IEEE (2021)
5. Ascigil, O., Tasiopoulos, A.G., Phan, T.K., Sourlas, V., Psaras, I., Pavlou, G.: Resource provisioning and allocation in function-as-a-service edge-clouds. IEEE Trans. Serv. Comput. **15**(4), 2410–2424 (2021)
6. Baldini, I., et al.: Serverless computing: current trends and open problems. In: Research advances in cloud computing, pp. 1–20. Springer (2017)
7. Balduf, L., et al.: The cloud strikes back: Investigating the decentralization of IPFS. In: Proceedings of the 2023 ACM on Internet Measurement Conference, IMC '23, New York, NY, USA, pp. 391–405. Association for Computing Machinery (2023)
8. Baresi, L., Mendonça, D.F.: Towards a serverless platform for edge computing. In: 2019 IEEE International Conference on Fog Computing (ICFC), pp. 1–10. IEEE (2019)
9. Daniel, E., Tschorsch, F.: IPFS and friends: a qualitative comparison of next generation peer-to-peer data networks. IEEE Commun. Surv. Tutor. **24**(1), 31–52 (2022)
10. Freitag, F., Wei, L., Liu, C.-H., Selimi, M., Veiga, L.: Server-side adaptive federated learning over wireless mesh network. In: International Conference on Information Technology & Systems, pp. 289–298. Springer (2023)
11. Gackstatter, P., Frangoudis, P.A., Dustdar, S.: Pushing serverless to the edge with webassembly runtimes. In: 2022 22nd IEEE International Symposium on Cluster, Cloud and Internet Computing (CCGrid), pages 140–149. IEEE (2022)
12. Jonas, E., et al.: Cloud programming simplified: a Berkeley view on serverless computing. arXiv preprint arXiv:1902.03383 (2019)
13. Mathur, A., et al.: On-device federated learning with flower. arXiv preprint arXiv:2104.03042 (2021)
14. Pallis, G., Vakali, A.: Insight and perspectives for content delivery networks. Commun. ACM **49**(1), 101–106 (2006)
15. Pathan, A.-M.K., Buyya, R., et al.: A taxonomy and survey of content delivery networks. Grid computing and distributed systems laboratory, University of Melbourne, Technical report 4(2007):70 (2007)

16. Pfandzelter, T., Bermbach, D.: tinyfaas: a lightweight FAAS platform for edge environments. In: 2020 IEEE International Conference on Fog Computing (ICFC), pp. 17–24. IEEE (2020)
17. Pires, A., Simão, J., Veiga, L.: Distributed and decentralized orchestration of containers on edge clouds. J. Grid Comput. **19**(3), 36 (2021)
18. Raith, P., Nastic, S., Dustdar, S.: Serverless edge computing–where we are and what lies ahead. IEEE Internet Comput. **27**(3), 50–64 (2023)
19. Silva, J.N., Veiga, L., Ferreira, P.: nuBOINC: BOINC extensions for community cycle sharing. In: 2008 Second IEEE International Conference on Self-Adaptive and Self-Organizing Systems Workshops, pp. 248–253. IEEE (2008)
20. C. Systems. Fog computing and the internet of things: extend the cloud to where the things are. White paper (2016)
21. Yussupov, V., Breitenbücher, U., Leymann, F., Müller, C.: Facing the unplanned migration of serverless applications: a study on portability problems, solutions, and dead ends. In: Proceedings of the 12th IEEE/ACM International Conference on Utility and Cloud Computing, UCC'19, New York, NY, USA, pp. 273–283. Association for Computing Machinery (2019)

# FaaS-Utility: Tackling FaaS Cold Starts with User-Preference and QoS-Driven Pricing

Henrique Santos[1], José Simão[1,2] (ID), and Luís Veiga[1(✉)] (ID)

[1] INESC-ID, Instituto Superior Técnico, Universidade de Lisboa, Lisboa, Portugal
`henriquesantos@gsd.inesc-id.pt, luis.veiga@tecnico.ulisboa.pt`
[2] Instituto Superior de Engenharia de Lisboa (ISEL/FIT), Lisboa, Portugal
`jose.simao@isel.pt`

**Abstract.** This study introduces FaaS-Utility, a novel approach aimed at optimizing Function-as-a-Service (FaaS) systems by addressing the critical issue of cold starts, which significantly impede system performance. By introducing a utility function informed by customer preferences and pricing goals, our methodology prioritizes resource allocation to enhance service quality effectively. We implement this strategy within Apache OpenWhisk, demonstrating its integration into a real-world FaaS platform. Our evaluation reveals that the proposed approach notably improves system performance, particularly in over-provisioned states, by reducing latency up to 2.37 times with a maximum additional cost of only 30%. While our method performs best in cold environments, it also maintains performance when applied in warm settings, offering a balanced solution between client and provider through adaptive pricing.

**Keywords:** Serverless Computing · Resource Allocation · Performance Optimization · Cold Start Mitigation

## 1 Introduction

Presently, more sophisticated, dynamic and elastic applications, with reduced latency and better resource use, are made possible by serverless computing and the Function-as-a-Service model (also know as FaaS) [15]. Current implementations of the Function-as-a-Service architecture such as Amazon AWS Lambda and Microsoft Azure Functions focus deeply on the optimization of systems resources and performance while paying little attention to the individual preferences of each customer.

Current scheduling mechanisms [8,12,24,25,31] attempt to maximize available resources for the least cost, be that cost resource consumption or execution time. Customers tend to wish for execution times to be as low as possible, however, this is in general terms, as not all customers are the same when it comes to urgency. One customer might just be requesting a project to be done by the end

---

Work partially developed while as a Visiting Researcher with the Hybrid Cloud Computing Group at IBM Research Europe – Zurich.

© The Author(s), under exclusive license to Springer Nature Switzerland AG 2025
M. Naldi et al. (Eds.): GECON 2024, LNCS 15358, pp. 43–57, 2025.
https://doi.org/10.1007/978-3-031-81226-2_5

of the day and has little interest in when it is done in a few minutes or an hour, while another customer might need a request to be done as soon as possible; this information can be leveraged by providers, by employing fewer resources when they are scarce, while reducing the price charged to users [23].

We propose an extension to the scheduling mechanism in FaaS that takes into account these customer differences in priority, as well as provide monetary profits for the provider using our proposal by adjusting the price of the service depending on the priority desired by the customer. This is embodied in a scheduling optimization in the Function-as-a-Service model that receives input from the customer to assist its execution for a more intelligent and focused quality of service. This entails that a customer using our system will be provided a few additional options, depending on the server's state, when attempting to issue requests, such as monetary discounts for slower execution times or extra monetary costs for her request to be completed promptly. The latter is presented in case the system is saturated and unable to confidently complete customer requests in the initially expected time frame.

The rest of the paper is structured as follows: Sect. 2 discuss some research on serverless computing, specifically focusing on FaaS, its scalability issues, and the cold start problem. Section 3 elaborates on the architecture of the FaaS-Utility system, highlighting how it incorporates user preferences into resource allocation, alongside the details of the implementation of FaaS-Utility within the Apache OpenWhisk platform. Section 4 discusses the methodology and results of the system evaluation, assessing the effectiveness of our approach in mitigating cold starts and improving performance. Finally, Sect. 5 concludes the paper with a summary of our findings and potential avenues for future research.

## 2   Related Work

Cloud computing is structured into various service layers, including traditional models like Infrastructure-as-a-Service (IaaS), Platform-as-a-Service (PaaS), and Software-as-a-Service (SaaS), as well as the more recent Backend-as-a-Service (BaaS), and Function-as-a-Service (FaaS), with this work focusing on the latter. BaaS and FaaS are both considered serverless, and are frequently used in conjunction because they share operational characteristics (such as no resource management) [7,9,17].

FaaS allows developers to deploy code in the cloud without managing hardware, offering greater abstraction compared to PaaS, where the provider manages data and server state. FaaS provides transparent scalability, unlike PaaS, where users must plan how to scale, focusing solely on deploying specific application functions [2]. Low latency is crucial for real-time applications like emergency vital sign monitoring, where quick paramedic response is essential. User-wearable sensors play a key role in health monitoring. Edge computing, driven by the need for low latency, leverages serverless frameworks to manage server operations, network, load balancing, and scaling tasks [13,14]. The cold start delay, which is seen as a delay in setting up the environment in which functions are executed, is one of the most significant FaaS performance issues [28,29]. Popular systems most frequently use a pool of warm containers, reuse the containers, and regularly call routines to reduce cold start delay. However, these techniques squander resources like memory, raise costs, and lack knowledge of function invocation trends over time. In other words, while these solutions reduce cold start delay through fixed processes, they are not appropriate for environments with dynamic cloud architecture [27].

In the work in [27], the authors proposed an intelligent method that chooses the optimum strategy for maintaining the containers running in accordance with the function invocations over time in order to lessen cold start delay and to consider resource usage. While in the work [3], the authors assume that the FaaS platform is a "black box" and use process knowledge to reduce the number of cold starts from a developer perspective. They proposed three strategies to reduce cold starts: the naive approach, the extended approach, and the global approach. Additionally, they introduced a lightweight middleware designed to work in tandem with the functions, aiding in the effective mitigation of cold start occurrences.

While numerous studies focus on cloud computing optimization [11,12,18], the potential revenue benefits from these optimizations are often overlooked [4]. We discuss both sides of the aspects. When it comes to scheduling, the provider can use optimization techniques to improve the customer experience with little to no thought to the financial implications. Pricing is one the most relevant issues in cloud computing cost methodologies that aim to maximize revenue. Providers use optimization techniques in scheduling to boost customer experience, sometimes neglecting financial outcomes, while recent advancements in cloud computing pricing strategies aim to optimize revenue.

In distributed systems, scheduling is frequently studied to establish a connection between requests and available resources. For clusters [19], clouds [10], and cloud-edge (Fog) systems [16,20,22], numerous solutions have been put forth.

In the work presented in [18], the authors offer a cutting-edge scheduling system for FaaS that is QoS-Aware and implemented in Apache OpenWhisk. By adding a Scheduler component, which takes over from the Controller's load balancing function and allows more scheduling policies, they extended Apache OpenWhisk. In this new design, incoming requests are routed through the Scheduler rather than the Controller in order to be immediately scheduled to the Invokers.

Cloud ecosystems' viability is based on effective service pricing [4] and an energy-aware architecture with sensible resource pricing, although many studies focus more on reducing energy consumption than on pricing and billing strategies [4,21]. Pricing strategy is pivotal in attracting clients who aim for the highest service quality at minimal costs, while cloud service providers focus on boosting income and cutting costs through advanced technologies [1]. The dynamic nature of service demands and quality necessitates a flexible pricing approach beyond fixed pricing, allowing consumers to pay for actual usage and enabling providers to offer fair, competitive rates [4]. Our system offers improvements over existing models by adopting flexible pricing and user-focused optimization, aiming to better balance quality and cost in cloud computing services.

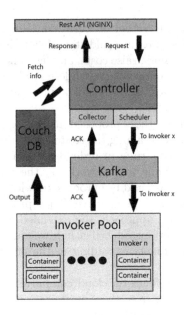

**Fig. 1.** General architecture with newly added scheduler and Collector component. (Color figure online)

## 3    Architecture

In this section, we first present an overview of Apache OpenWhisk's systems, more specifically its scheduling methodology, followed by our proposed scheduling extension which is subdivided into two components: i) during an under-provisioned server state, and ii) an over-provisioned server state. Apache Open-Whisk facilitates the creation, invocation, and outcome querying of functions through a REST interface, using a Controller to assign tasks to a pool of Invokers based on a hashing method and Invoker status [31]. After receiving the request, the Invoker uses a Docker container to carry out the function. Functions are commonly referred to as actions within Apache OpenWhisk. The Invoker sends the outcomes to a CouchDB-based Database after the function execution is complete and notifies the Controller of its completion. The Controller then returns to clients the outcomes of the function executions [31].

**Scheduler Extension.** In our extended version of the Apache OpenWhisk architecture, we add a newly updated scheduler with all of our requirements for the pricing utility function, as well as an updated Collector to allow us to extend the capabilities of warm container creation with no additional overhead. Both of these extra components are shown in Fig. 1 as the green and blue containers. Clients initiate requests via a REST interface, which are processed by the Controller using information from CouchDB and a utility function to determine the appropriate Invoker. The Invoker executes the request, and upon completion, updates CouchDB and sends an acknowledgment back to the Controller for future optimization. To accommodate varying system states, a number of pricing options are offered, allowing clients to select from two initial choices in over-provisioned states and three additional ones in under-provisioned states, enabling a tailored service experience.

---

**Algorithm 1:** Over-provisioned scheduling algorithm

---

$Action \leftarrow A$
$ActionContainer \leftarrow Action$
**for all** $Invokers$ **do**
  **if** $BusyPoolSize = MaxPoolSize$ **then**
    continue
  **else if** $ActionContainer \in FreePool$ **then**
    $FreePool \leftarrow FreePool \setminus ActionContainer$
    $BusyPool \leftarrow BusyPool \cup ActionContainer$
    **return**
  **else if** $PreWarmPoolSize > 0$ **and** $Invoker = HomeInvoker$ **then**
    $PreWarmPool \leftarrow PreWarmPool \setminus PreeWarmContainer$
    $ActionContainer \leftarrow PreWarmContainer$
    $BusyPool \leftarrow BusyPool \cup ActionContainer$
  **else if** $FreePoolSize + BusyPoolSize = MaxPoolSize$ **then**
    $FreePool \leftarrow FreePool \setminus LeastRecentContainer$
  **else**
    $ActionContainer \leftarrow ColdContainer$
    $BusyPool \leftarrow BusyPool \cup ActionContainer$
  **end if**
**end for**
$Queue \leftarrow Queue \cup Action$

---

**Pricing Options for the Client.** Two initial pricing options are provided: *Basic* Version which merely finishes the request with no additional benefits; or *Premium* that completes the request with additional Invokers, but the additional resources used for a faster execution of the request will come at a discounted price. This second option is to use the request to create warm containers for this particular client's repeated uses, resulting in future quicker execution times.

When servers are under-provisioned, leading to potential request queues, three additional pricing tiers are introduced: *Standard priority* maintains normal costs without altering request scheduling priority; *Urgent priority* increases scheduling precedence at a higher cost for time-sensitive tasks; and *Reduced priority* lowers both cost and scheduling priority for users with flexible timelines.

These pricing options cater to different user needs, allowing them to choose based on urgency and cost considerations, like a user needing immediate database error correction versus a student with no immediate project deadlines.

**Scheduling During an Over-Provisioned State.** If no special pricing mechanism is applied, scheduling functions normally, but with an added premium: the scheduler will distribute actions across all Invokers to enhance efficiency. This approach benefits clients by ensuring faster execution for repeated requests and optimal Invoker selection for speed, regardless of the Invoker's identity. Clients can also customize their use of the pricing models, applying the *Premium* selectively to specific actions or triggers to optimize cost and performance.

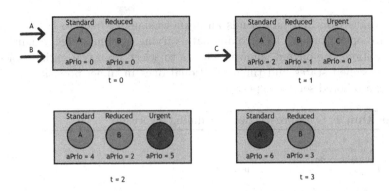

**Fig. 2.** Four seconds of execution of the priority queue scheme. (Color figure online)

The enhanced scheduler algorithm, detailed in Algorithm 1, introduces a nuanced queuing strategy, triggering action queuing when Invokers are semi-saturated, a more flexible approach compared to the original algorithm's condition of full saturation. This adjustment is particularly effective in over-provisioned states, ensuring that the scheduler optimally utilizes available resources.

Key modifications, marked in the pseudo-code in blue and red, include bypassing pre-warm containers for new container creation on alternative Invokers, and a more exhaustive search for available Invokers rather than settling for the first one found. These enhancements aim to improve resource allocation and system responsiveness by dynamically adapting to the current load on Invokers.

All of the results of the multiple executions of the action are received by the controller. The cost of the requested deployment by the client is calculated as a ratio between the cost without the extra Invokers and the total cost of all resources used. Consequently, the cost the client will be charged is given by:

$$final\ cost = \alpha \times c + (1 - \alpha) \times C \qquad (1)$$

where $\alpha$ is the ratio of the cost that remains static, $c$ is the cost of the deployment under default conditions, and $C$ is the total cost of all resources used. This creates a situation where if no additional actions were deployed on other Invokers, the final costs are equal to the normal pricing model.

**Scheduling During an Under-Provisioned State.** The existing First-In-First-Out (FIFO) priority method, used when server saturation leads to action queuing, offers a low urgency solution for clients. We defend the need for a more advanced priority-aware system that accelerates resolution for time-sensitive requests at an additional cost, also providing options for clients seeking discounts in less urgent situations. A possible scheme (left as future work) can utilize a unique priority value, "aPrio" (absolute priority), which can be adjusted based on the request's urgency level, allowing distinction between requests with identical aPrio values using FIFO. This scheme is visualized in Fig. 2, illustrating how different priority levels ($p_1$, $p_2$, $p_3$) could influence the queue management over time. Yellow requests are in the queue while red requests are the selected actions for when resources are freed. The pricing model utilized is similar to what is offered during the over-provisioned state. The final cost is given by:

$$final\,cost = \alpha \times c + (1 - \alpha) \times \frac{cp}{p_1} \tag{2}$$

where $\alpha$ is the percentage of cost that remains static, $c$ is the cost of the specific action, $p$ represents the value of the priority system used for the action, and $p_1$ is the value of the reduced priority system.

## 3.1  Implementation Details

The solution proposed for over-provisioned state has two main goals: (1) set up containers for future workloads, and if possible (2) combine the work of all Invokers for an even faster possible execution. Thus, we tackled both problems separately, starting with the more architecturally demanding problem (1).

Invokers in Apache OpenWhisk operate independently without knowledge of each other's conditions, limiting the ability to dynamically create containers based on system-wide states and preventing the generation of empty warm containers. The controller, with some awareness of the Invoker pool's state, becomes a focal point for managing container allocation, particularly in over-provisioned scenarios where additional action invocations don't strain existing resources due to container isolation. Increased workload on the controller and Kafka during over-provisioned states introduces minimal overhead, as Kafka is designed for high throughput and low latency, capable of handling significant data volumes. This system design ensures that resource augmentation in an over-provisioned state does not compromise Invoker performance, though it warrants attention during performance evaluation.

To enhance the algorithm in 'ShardingContainerPoolBalancer.scala' within Apache OpenWhisk, the proposed modification involves extending the search for available Invokers beyond the first one found, aiming to engage multiple Invokers to prepare or execute the action. This approach is designed to ensure the action is spread across all potential Invokers, whether to prepare warm containers or create cache data, addressing a key objective. By executing the action on all available Invokers, the system capitalizes on the quickest response, as the fastest Invoker will deliver the result back to the controller, optimizing performance. To achieve this, the scheduling function must be adjusted so its completion criteria are met only after all Invokers have been considered, ensuring comprehensive action distribution. Additionally, the modification seeks to preserve the stability of the home Invoker metric, allowing users to opt-out of this enhanced functionality if desired.

## 4  Evaluation

In this section, we will address the system performance and the assessed metrics. We deploy the system with Apache OpenWhisk on a development environment based on Docker. The base open source code of Apache OpenWhisk is extended to the requirements presented by the architecture in Sect. 3. Data is assumed to be stored locally, or on some cloud storage in the same location.

**FaaS Benchmarks.** Four FaaS workloads (F1-F4) are used in the evaluation of our system those being: Sleep functions, File hashing, Video transformation, and Image classification, taken from FaaS benchmarking found in the literature [6]:

- F1 - Sleep functions: a simple, low-overhead operation that can be used to measure infrastructural overheads, in our case the scheduling infrastructure, of a FaaS platform.
- F2 - File hashing: a relatively simple operation that can be used to test the ability of the system to handle file inputs and outputs.
- F3 - Video Transformation: it exercises many of the key features of a FaaS system, such as scalability, concurrency, and performance. Video transformation tasks, such as transcoding, are typically compute-intensive and require parallel processing. This makes them well-suited to assess system ability to handle high levels of concurrency and scale horizontally.
- F4 - Image classification: a complex operation that requires significant computational resources and can be used to test the ability of the system to handle more demanding workloads. Additionally, Image classification is a common use case of real-world usage in FaaS [18], especially in machine learning applications [26,30].

**Metrics.** The performance of our system is evaluated using three key metrics: Latency (time for request processing and response), Scheduling delay (time from request readiness to execution, reflecting the scheduler's efficiency), and Resource usage (assessing how well the system utilizes memory and CPU). To understand memory consumption and system overload, we analyze logs from OpenWhisk components, specified in the docker-compose.yml file, which helps in identifying performance bottlenecks and resource management. These metrics are measured and compared with the Apache OpenWhisk default scheduler.

**Evaluation Environment.** The evaluation environment for the updated Apache OpenWhisk scheduler involved a minimal cluster setup with one container per OpenWhisk component and three invokers managed by a single *Controller*, designed to stress-test the system. Testing variables included the types of actions, the volume of requests, and the concurrency of users, with each test conducted in either a 'cold' or 'warm' server state to simulate varying user demands and assess the system's responsiveness without needing repeated authentication. JMeter, an open-source tool, was employed to assess the performance of web applications, APIs, and other services by simulating numerous user interactions to identify potential bottlenecks under various load conditions.

The system's evaluation involved actions F1, F2, F3, and F4 to examine various operational aspects, from quick tasks and delay measurements to CPU-intensive processes. Each action was tested in Default, Base, and Spread versions to compare, respectively: i) the original OpenWhisk system, ii) the modified version without enhancements, and iii) the version with new functionalities, enabling a thorough analysis of the system's adaptability and performance in diverse computing environments. During testing, all actions are established in the test setup phase, and the time spent on this initial creation is not included in the test metrics since it does not impact the modified components of the updated system. To evaluate the enhanced scheduler, two distinct sub-environments were crafted, reflecting the system's initial state before each specific test is conducted.

**1. Cold Sub-environment _"C"_:** we sought to evaluate our system as the worst case possible where all currently existing warm containers within the invokers mismatch the invoked action. This allow us to evaluate our system when handling cold invocations, and how well it successfully warms up the system to generate the best user experience. This was achieved through the mass invocation of a "hello world" action which simply returns "hello user" to the user. The mass invocation comprises 100 parallel invocation calls using JMeter, by setting up a thread group with 100 users and 1 call each. The execution of the tests ignores this environment setup and is done after all containers within the invokers enter the paused state.

**2. Warm Sub-environment _"W"_:** a fully cold environment is not entirely realistic, as prewarm and warm containers contribute heavily towards faster request execution times, and are the backbone of FaaS systems. As such for the same set of tests as the sub-environment 1, we evaluated our system under a warm environment where only prewarm and warm containers of the action to be invoked were present. In the same way as achieved in sub-environment 1, the warm environment was made with 100 concurrent calls for the specific action related to the test. Once again this execution time was not taken into consideration during the test. JMeter was set up with 100 users with one HTTP request each.

Two different pieces of hardware were used for testing to accurately determine potential system degradation caused by our scheduler.

- **Hardware _"A"_:** a machine representative of a typical low-mid cloud server instance with an Intel® Core™i7 CPU @ 2.60 GHz processor with 4 physical cores and 8 threads on UbuntuLTS 64-bit.
- **Hardware _"B"_:** a machine representative of a more capable cloud server instance, but where resource usage optimization is still challenging, to assess the extent of potential gains to be achieved at scale. This hardware B uses a Intel(R) Core(TM) i7 CPU @ 3.20 GHz, 6 Physical Core(s), 12 Logical Processor(s).

## 4.1   Performance Evaluation

A total of 6 tests were made to evaluate our newly augmented scheduler. These tests vary in both sub-environment and hardware. Each test is referred to by the test number, which sub-environment it uses followed by which hardware it utilizes, for example, "Test 1 (W-A)" is test number 1 and uses both a Warm sub-environment and hardware A. The full analysis is described in [5], with detailed results for each action (F1-F4) used; we leave here the main findings.

Test 1 (W-A), focused just on preliminary determining if our Base scheduler performed similarly to Default, employing solely F1 only for simplicity. Results show our enhanced scheduler performed slightly better under the same circumstances, so we could use it for previous versions of workloads on OpenWhisk.

Test 2 (C-A) and Test 6 (C-B) both seek to evaluate the use case for our functionality. This situation was a cold environment at first, followed by the use of our new functionality to set up the warm container, and finalising with a heavy amount of requests for the specific action. We were able to confirm that our functionality was able to benefit the system in terms of reduced latency, variance, and total execution time for faster execution actions, where the cold start delay is previously more noticeable. We were able to conclude that hardware can indeed affect the value provided by our functionality, as we were only able to see significant improvements for F4 function in more powerful hardware B.

Test 3 (W-A), 4 (W-A), and Test 5 (W-B) check the performance of the scheduler during less ideal circumstances, those being in the case where a warm environment already exists for the requested action. We were able to conclude the lack of parallelism potential from the hardware itself was the main bottleneck, as the new scheduler would overload the Invokers leading to performance degradation. Test 4 (W-A) specifically focused on confirming this parallelism roadblock by independently doing the same amount of requests as the Action-Spread functionality would do but using the original version of the scheduler. Thus, our proposed functionality needs not be used for already ideally warm environments, as it may lead to unnecessary additional overloading of the system.

## 4.2   Utility Function Evaluation

The enhanced scheduler's performance analysis includes evaluating its impact on client costs and provider resource consumption, focusing on critical metrics like latency reduction, execution time, and the utility function's alpha parameter. Table 1 offers a comparative overview, detailing the trade-offs between performance improvements and resource usage, aiding stakeholders in assessing the scheduler's efficiency and cost-effectiveness in a concise manner.

The effectiveness of the enhanced scheduler varies with different scenarios, particularly showing limited benefits in already warm environments like in Test 3, where additional invocations did not mitigate the risk of cold starts and led to performance degradation. However, the introduction of a variable pricing factor, $\alpha$, influenced by the seller, can adjust the final cost, offering a mechanism to counteract the performance drop or unnecessary resource usage, enabling a negotiation space between the client and the seller for better interaction and agreement on the service value.

**Table 1.** Utility evaluation

| Test | Latency decrease | Total time decrease | Extra resources | $\alpha$ | Cost |
|---|---|---|---|---|---|
| $2 - F1$ | 2.37x | 1.44x | 1.32x | 0.8 | 1.06x |
| | | | | 0.6 | 1.13x |
| | | | | 0.4 | 1.19x |
| $2 - F2$ | 0.73x | 1.03x | 1.36x | 0.8 | 1.07x |
| | | | | 0.6 | 1.14x |
| | | | | 0.4 | 1.21x |
| $2 - F4$ | 0.76x | 0.92x | 1.36x | 0.8 | 1.07x |
| | | | | 0.6 | 1.14x |
| | | | | 0.4 | 1.21x |
| $3 - F1$ | 0.78x | 0.80x | 3x | 0.8 | 1.4x |
| | | | | 0.6 | 1.8x |
| | | | | 0.4 | 2.2x |
| $3 - F2$ | 0.98x | 0.98x | 3x | 0.8 | 1.4x |
| | | | | 0.6 | 1.8x |
| | | | | 0.4 | 2.2x |
| $6 - F1$ | 1.67x | 1.12x | 1.36x | 0.8 | 1.06x |
| | | | | 0.6 | 1.14x |
| | | | | 0.4 | 1.19x |
| $6 - F2$ | 0.71x | 1.05x | 1.4x | 0.8 | 1.08x |
| | | | | 0.6 | 1.16x |
| | | | | 0.4 | 1.24x |
| $6 - F4$ | 1.13x | 1.03x | 1.4x | 0.8 | 1.08x |
| | | | | 0.6 | 1.16x |
| | | | | 0.4 | 1.24x |

Hardware variations also impact the scheduler's performance benefits, as observed in tests 2 and 6, with different hardware setups. The scheduler's performance varied significantly between hardware types, with certain tests showing better latency improvements on weaker hardware. The adjustment of the $\alpha$ value by the seller can make the resource use more cost-effective for the client, especially if enhanced performance justifies additional resource consumption, highlighting a nuanced trade-off between resource use, performance gain, and cost.

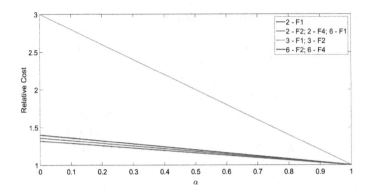

**Fig. 3.** Cost's behaviour depending on $\alpha$ values

Finally, Fig. 3 studies how the system's environmental awareness affects the seller's pricing leverage and the overall cost-effectiveness of the scheduler. The functionality's deployment in its intended cold environment versus an unnecessary warm environment demonstrates the adaptive cost strategy's role in ensuring that the scheduler's use aligns with its designed benefits, thereby optimizing the balance between performance enhancement and resource expenditure.

## 5    Conclusion

We created a scheduler extension architecture that considers user preferences when adjusting scheduling to provide a higher quality of service to the user. Apache OpenWhisk was used to implement our solution. For over-provisioned system conditions a new functionality that we named "Action-Spreading" was implemented to allow warm containers to be set up for a reduced cost in preparation for an influx of requests. We evaluated our enhanced scheduler through a series of tests.

We concluded that under over-provisioned system conditions, it provided a substantial benefit for the client with a latency decrease of up to 2.37 times for only a maximum of 30% additional cost. We also were able to conclude that should the scheduler be used under unforeseen system conditions it allows for a positive client-seller solution through the use of the proposed utility function management.

As future work, we consider that the development of priority-based queueing extensions for Kafka and other similar components (that do not have priority-aware mechanics in mind), specifically for FaaS systems, would be a great avenue for future research in this field. This would enable enforcing our proposed scheduling approach during an under-provisioned state, by being able to speed up requests from higher priority users or functions, while without hurting the scalability of the controller.

**Acknowledgements.** This work was supported by national funds through FCT, Fundação para a Ciência e a Tecnologia, under project UIDB/50021/2020 (DOI:10.54499/UIDB/50021/2020). This work was supported by: "DL 60/2018, de 3-08 - Aquisição necessária para a atividade de I&D do INESC-ID, no âmbito do projeto SmartRetail (C6632206063-00466847)". This work was supported by the CloudStars project, funded by the European Union's Horizon research and innovation program under grant agreement number 101086248.

# References

1. Al-Roomi, M., Al-Ebrahim, S., Buqrais, S., Ahmad, I.: Cloud computing pricing models: a survey. Int. J. Grid Distrib. Comput. **6**(5), 93–106 (2013)
2. Astrova, I., Koschel, A., Schaaf, M., Klassen, S., Jdiya, K.: Serverless, FaaS and why organizations need them. Intell. Dec. Technol. **15**(4), 825–838 (2021)
3. Bermbach, D., Karakaya, A.-S., Buchholz, S.: Using application knowledge to reduce cold starts in FaaS services. In: Proceedings of the ACM Symposium on Applied Computing, pp. 134–143, New York, NY, United States. ACM (2020)
4. Dibaj, S.R., Sharifi, L., Miri, A., Zhou, J., Aram, A.: Cloud computing energy efficiency and fair pricing mechanisms for smart cities. In: IEEE Electrical Power and Energy Conference (EPEC), pp. 1–6, New York, NY, United States. IEEE (2018)
5. dos Santos, H.d.C.R.: FaaS-utility. Master's thesis, Instituto Superior Técnico, U. Lisboa (2023)
6. Dukic, V., Bruno, R., Singla, A., Alonso, G.: Photons: lambdas on a diet. In: Proceedings of the 11th ACM Symposium on Cloud Computing, pp. 45–59, New York, NY, United States. ACM (2020)
7. Janakiraman, B.: Serverless (2016)
8. Kim, Y.K., HoseinyFarahabady, M.R., Lee, Y.C., Zomaya, A.Y.: Automated fine-grained CPU cap control in serverless computing platform. IEEE Trans. Parallel Distrib. Syst. **31**(10), 2289–2301 (2020)
9. Kounev, S., et al.: Serverless computing: what it is, and what it is not? Commun. ACM **66**(9), 80–92 (2023)
10. Lee, G., Chun, B., Katz, H.: Heterogeneity-aware resource allocation and scheduling in the cloud. In: Proceedings of the USENIX Workshop on Hot Topics in Cloud Computing (HotCloud), pp. 1–5, Portland, OR. USENIX Association (2011)
11. Lin, L., Li, P., Xiong, J., Lin, M.: Distributed and application-aware task scheduling in edge-clouds. In: Proceedings of the International Conference on Mobile Ad-Hoc and Sensor Networks (MSN), pp. 165–170, New York, NY, United States. IEEE (2018)
12. Madej, A., Wang, N., Athanasopoulos, N., Ranjan, R., Varghese, B.: Priority-based fair scheduling in edge computing. In: Proceedings of the IEEE International Conference on Fog and Edge Computing (ICFEC), pp. 39–48, New York, NY, United States. IEEE (2020)
13. Nastic, S., et al.: A serverless real-time data analytics platform for edge computing. IEEE Internet Comput. **21**(4), 64–71 (2017)
14. Palade, A., Kazmi, A., Clarke, S.: An evaluation of open source serverless computing frameworks support at the edge. In: Proceedings of the IEEE World Congress on Services (SERVICES), vol. 2642, pp. 206–211, New York, NY, United States. IEEE (2019)

15. Pfandzelter, T., Bermbach, D.: tinyfaas: a lightweight FaaS platform for edge environments. In: Proceedings of the IEEE International Conference on Fog Computing (ICFC), pp. 17–24, New York, NY, United States. IEEE (2020)
16. Pires, A., Simão, J., Veiga, L.: Distributed and decentralized orchestration of containers on edge clouds. J. Grid Comput. **19**(3), 36 (2021)
17. Roberts, M.: Serverless architectures (2018)
18. Russo, G.R., Milani, A., Iannucci, S., Cardellini, V.: Towards QoS-aware function composition scheduling in apache openwhisk. In: Proceedings of the IEEE International Conference on Pervasive Computing and Communications Workshops and other Affiliated Events (PerCom Workshops), pp. 693–698. IEEEAD. IEEE (2022)
19. Schwarzkopf, M., Konwinski, A., Abd-El-Malek, M., Wilkes, J.: Omega: flexible, scalable schedulers for large compute clusters. In: Proceedings of the ACM European Conference on Computer Systems, New York, NY, United States, pp. 351–364. ACM (2013)
20. Scoca, V., Aral, A., Brandic, I., De Nicola, R., Uriarte, R.B.: Scheduling latency-sensitive applications in edge computing. In: Proceedings of the International Conference on Cloud Computing and Services Science (CLOSER), pp. 158–168, New York, NY, United States. Springer (2018)
21. Sharifi, L., Cerdà-Alabern, L., Freitag, F., Veiga, L.: Energy efficient cloud service provisioning: keeping data center granularity in perspective. J. Grid Comput. **14**(2), 299–325 (2016)
22. Silva, J.N., Ferreira, P., Veiga, L.: Service and resource discovery in cycle-sharing environments with a utility algebra. In: 2010 IEEE International Symposium on Parallel & Distributed Processing (IPDPS), pp. 1–11 (2010)
23. Simão, J., Veiga, L.: Partial utility-driven scheduling for flexible SLA and pricing arbitration in clouds. IEEE Trans. Cloud Comput. **4**(4), 467–480 (2016)
24. Suresh, A., Somashekar, G., Varadarajan, A., Kakarla, V.R., Upadhyay, H., Gandhi, A.: Ensure: efficient scheduling and autonomous resource management in serverless environments. In: Proceedings of the IEEE International Conference on Autonomic Computing and Self-Organizing Systems (ACSOS), pp. 1–10, New York, NY, United States. IEEE (2020)
25. Suresh, A., Somashekar, G., Varadarajan, A., Kakarla, V.R., Upadhyay, H., Gandhi, A.: Ensure: efficient scheduling and autonomous resource management in serverless environments. In: Proceedings of the IEEE International Conference on Autonomic Computing and Self-Organizing Systems (ACSOS), pp. 1–10 (2020)
26. Tu, Z., Li, M., Lin, J.: Pay-per-request deployment of neural network models using serverless architectures. In: Proceedings of the Conference of the North American Chapter of the Association for Computational Linguistics: Demonstrations, PA, USA, pp. 6–10. Association for Computational Linguistics (2018)
27. Vahidinia, P., Farahani, B., Aliee, F.S.: Mitigating cold start problem in serverless computing: a reinforcement learning approach. IEEE Internet Things J. **10**(5), 3917–3927 (2023)
28. van Eyk, E., Iosup, A., Abad, C.L., Grohmann, J., Eismann, S.: A spec RG cloud group's vision on the performance challenges of FaaS cloud architectures. In: Companion of the 2018 ACM/SPEC International Conference on Performance Engineering, ICPE '18, New York, NY, USA, pp. 21–24. Association for Computing Machinery (2018)
29. Van Eyk, E., Iosup, A., Abad, C.L., Grohmann, J., Eismann, S.: A spec RG cloud group's vision on the performance challenges of FaaS cloud architectures. In: Proceedings of the Companion of the ACM/SPEC International Conference on Performance Engineering, New York, NY, United States, pp. 21–24. ACM (2018)

30. Xu, F., Qin, Y., Chen, L., Zhou, Z., Liu, F.: λDNN: achieving predictable distributed DNN training with serverless architectures. IEEE Trans. Comput. **71**(2), 450–463 (2021)
31. Yu, H., Irissappane, A.A., Wang, H., Lloyd, W.J.: Faasrank: learning to schedule functions in serverless platforms. In: Proceedings of the IEEE International Conference on Autonomic Computing and Self-Organizing Systems (ACSOS), New York, NY, United States, pp. 31–40. IEEE (2021)

# Icarus: A Testing-as-a-Service Utility for Serverless Functions

Thomas Tomtsis$^{(\boxtimes)}$ (iD) and Kyriakos Kritikos (iD)

University of the Aegean, Samos, Greece
ttomtsis@protonmail.com, kkritikos@aegean.gr

**Abstract.** Testing serverless functions differs significantly from that of conventional software products. Their distributed nature and event-driven architecture make test development inherently complex. Further, the development of functions and their tests often relies on using tools and software development kits managed by cloud providers, resulting in minimal control over the test execution environment and a lack of debugging tools. As such, we have developed the Icarus RESTful, open-source Testing-as-a-Service tool with a transparent and predictable operation, supplying the user with full control over test creation and execution. Icarus does not burden the user with details of a function's deployment across different providers, does not require the user to write any line of testing code and relies solely on using familiar open-source and well-known tools to automatically compose and execute functional and non-functional tests. Its experimental evaluation shows that it scales well with the user and workload increase, rapidly delivering test results to the user.

**Keywords:** Serverless · AWS Lambda · Google Cloud Functions · Functional Testing · Performance Testing

## 1 Introduction

Vendor lock-in is one of the biggest issues in Cloud Computing. The functional cost and the overall quality of an offered service is directly correlated with the business strategy of the Cloud Provider, thus aligning the Cloud Strategy of an organization with that of the Cloud Provider. While this offers an easy transition towards the Cloud, eventually this approach incurs sizable costs in the event of migration from one provider to another or in the event of investing in a private infrastructure. The complexity and cost of data migration and the cost of service and product transfer amongst providers are critical factors that usually impede Cloud adoption [1].

Serverless Computing is one of the latest developments in cloud computing, where the development and deployment of software foregoes the need of owning and managing IT infrastructure. It is based in the Function-as-a-Service (FaaS) model, where the foundational building block of applications are small, event-driven, single-responsibility pieces of code, named functions. In the FaaS model, function development must utilize the provider's Software Development Kits (SDKs) and conform to architectural

© The Author(s), under exclusive license to Springer Nature Switzerland AG 2025
M. Naldi et al. (Eds.): GECON 2024, LNCS 15358, pp. 58–67, 2025.
https://doi.org/10.1007/978-3-031-81226-2_6

requirements specified by the provider. At the same time, operating costs and scalability vary between providers due to different closed-source implementations of the FaaS paradigm. To make matters even more complicated, functions commonly utilize several other vendor specific implementations of supporting services, such as Message Queues or Serverless Databases, and may rely on proprietary optimization technologies (e.g. AWS Lambda Snap Start) or supporting solutions (e.g. Azure Durable Functions).

As such, it is evident that choosing a suitable Cloud Provider is paramount for a user or organization. This process is often complex and requires manually implementing tests to judge a provider's adequacy. These tests must be executed in the provider's infrastructure, thus incurring extra costs, or be executed in an environment that closely simulates it. The tests must be developed using the relevant vendor specific SDK's or tools. Simulating a vendor's infrastructure is challenging, since realistic scenarios are hard to recreate. At the same time, function development and deployment across different vendors requires working knowledge of each vendor's toolchain and services.

This paper addresses these shortcomings by developing a simple and easy to use RESTful service. This service, which is aptly named Icarus, simplifies the process of developing and executing automated tests across vendors and simultaneously abstracts the complexity of the function's lifecycle management. Users solely provide the location of the function's source code and the test configuration, while Icarus manages the entire lifecycle of the functions, creates and executes the tests, and produces a test report document. Our service utilizes the black box testing technique and supports the automated execution of both functional and performance tests across different cloud providers and respective function implementations. It has been developed as a Software-as-a-Service, thus realizing the vision of Testing-as-a-Service (TaaS) [2], and is available as an open-source software project on GitHub[1]. By utilizing our service, functional and non-functional issues may be detected early in the software development lifecycle without requiring specialized knowledge of vendor specific tools and services.

Compared to the related work, Icarus not only supports both testing kinds but also does not require the user to write any single line of testing code. Further, it parallelizes the execution for both functional and non-functional tests. In addition, the testing report supplies significant new knowledge, especially in the context of performance testing, as it incorporates a statistical performance model for the tested function, one per each cloud provider. This model incorporates all factors influencing function performance, including workload, resources (e.g., main memory size) and location. As such, it is more complete than other similarly constructed models within the literature. This new knowledge is of paramount importance not only for better understanding a function's performance features across different providers and configurations, but also for facilitating the user in the selection of the most suitable provider according to his/her needs.

The remainder of this paper is structured as follows. Section 2 reviews related work. Section 3 analyses the design and implementation of Icarus TaaS. Section 4 describes the way Icarus was experimentally evaluated and showcases the respective results. Finally, the last section concludes the paper and draws directions for further research.

---

[1] https://github.com/ttomtsis/icarus

## 2  Related Work

Testing serverless applications has been the subject of research during the last few years, mainly in the context of function performance testing and benchmarking. A stellar example of this has been the benchmarking suite developed by Copik et al. [3] which introduces a provider-agnostic FaaS platform model and a set of metrics for analyzing both function cost and performance. Please note that the work of Copik et al. [3] is among the few to use a characteristic set of serverless applications to evaluate their suite and does not simply rely on microbenchmarks, which are quite common throughout the literature but are not so useful and practical as they rely on very small functions.

Similarly, Maissen et al. [4] offer a benchmarking suite for four well-known FaaS platforms (e.g., AWS Lambda and Google Cloud Functions) that supports specific runtimes and relies extensively on Docker containers to manage the functions lifecycle. Apart from producing performance models, the suite includes a billing costs calculator.

Somu et al. [5]support function chaining (apart from single functions) and multiple function triggers for python3 functions and rely on JMeter to conduct load tests.

Malawski et al. [6] developed a benchmarking tool, able to execute well known benchmarks like Linmark, that relies on the Serverless Framework to manage the function lifecycle.

To the best of our knowledge, Icarus is a complete testing utility for serverless applications, enabling automated functional testing of serverless functions, a feature not exhibited so far amongst the already developed tools. Further, Icarus can perform a wide variety of non-functional testing, not being limited to load tests, supports all available function runtimes in AWS Lambda and Google Cloud Functions, and utilizes the novel Terraform CDK for Java to automate the process of deployment, thus not relying on complex container techniques or cloud provider CLI's. In addition, Icarus minimizes the user effort in configuring the function testing as there is a single configuration to supply for testing the function across multiple providers and regions in contrast to the other tools. Finally, Icarus can produce more precise statistical functional performance models by considering all factors that influence function performance, including function location, memory layout and in the case of Google Cloud Functions vCPU cores.

## 3  System Development

Icarus was developed using the waterfall model as the project's requirements were well-defined and improbable to change, at least during its development. As such, the project's lifecycle included four distinct phases: Requirements engineering, design, implementation, and validation/testing.

The project requirements were carefully produced and devised by considering the current gaps in the literature, the actual needs of function developers, especially in terms of testing, and the current best practices in SaaS development.

## 3.1 Functional Requirements

The functional requirements are summarized as follows:

- Provide automated support for both functional and non-functional testing guided by user-supplied testing configuration
- The user functional testing configuration must supply a suitable test case description to automatically produce and execute the right tests and as well as generate the functional testing report.

  - Simply speaking, each test case must include the function input to supply as well as the desired output and HTTP status code.
  - As such, each test case is executed by sending requests over the function based on the designated output and checking whether the produced output and received HTTP status code are the expected ones. This checking is incorporated in the respective functional testing report.

- As part of the test execution process, the target function's lifecycle would be managed by the application, abstracting the complexity away from the user.
- The user non-functional testing configuration includes the test parameters, the function's resource configurations and the metrics to be collected per each provider.

  - Test parameters must be specified by summing all user-created load profiles. Every load profile includes the number of concurrent users, the users think time, the ramp up, initial start delay of the profile and total load time. By chaining load profiles, we enable the execution of a wide range of performance tests.
  - A resource configuration includes the function's memory configuration, the deployed region and in case of Google Cloud Functions the number of vCPU cores.

- During non-functional testing for a specific provider, the system should deploy the function according to its resource configuration and then execute all its load profiles

  - Each load profile is executed multiple times and then the measurements being produced must be averaged.
  - All average measurements across all resource configurations must then be fed into a statistical tool to produce via linear regression the function's performance model for the current cloud provider. This model should be stored in the non-functional report along with all these average measurements associated to their load profile and resource configuration.

- User (profile) management functions, including user registration and authentication, must be implemented to enable the system to be used only by registered users.

  - Each user profile should be associated with a set of accounts that the user has on cloud providers he/she intends to exploit. These accounts are to be used by the system to conduct function deployments on behalf of the user.

## 3.2   Non-functional Requirements

The non-functional requirements set are summarized as follows:

- The system must support multiple concurrent users (at least 50) and respective requests
- The system should be performant (response time must be less than 5ms per request) and scalable
- The system should offer a high security level

  - It must support HTTPS
  - It must support basic user authentication with salting-based password hashing
  - It must support OAuth2 user authentication (with Auth0 as the default authentication provider) for those users that require using external authentication services
  - Access to services should be restricted to authenticated users
  - Each authenticated user should be able to solely see his/her own data

- The system must be developed in form of a RESTful API with high REST maturity

  - Testing must be performed asynchronously as it can take a long time to execute depending on the testing configuration length and the function execution time

- The system should operate across platforms by exploiting container technology
- The system should use an IaC (Infrastructure-as-Code) tool such that it can support function deployment across multiple serverless platforms
- The system must support at least the AWS Lambda and Google Cloud Function platforms. By supporting these two platforms we aim to compare the already intensely studied and industrially significant AWS Lambda with the less studied and gaining in popularity Google Cloud Functions

  - Icarus must support the novel Google Cloud Functions V2, which allows the manual configuration of vCPU cores. This can lead to the production of more complete statistical function performance models as we take into consideration another resource factor apart from the main memory size.

## 3.3   Application Design

During the design stage, we followed a top-down approach to the system design, by modelling suitable UML diagrams.

**Context Diagram.** Initially, we designed a context diagram (see Fig. 1) to set the boundaries of our application and define the external systems with which it will interoperate. Icarus would support two user types, visitors and authenticated users. Auth0 would be used as the default OAuth2 authentication provider. GitHub would be used when a user specifies a public GitHub repository as the source of the function's source code. This is a convenience feature, aiming to ease integrating Icarus into a project's development lifecycle. Google Cloud Platform and Amazon Web Services would be used to deploy the functions and their supporting infrastructure and destroy it upon completion of the test.

**Component Diagram.** Next, we designed our RESTful API's component diagram, shown in Fig. 2, to designate the API's internal architecture. Then, other diagrams followed like use-case diagrams and process diagrams. Due to the imposed size restrictions, we do not have the space to show all these diagrams. Thus, we stick to the component diagram to explain which are the API's main components, what is their intended functionality and how they interact with each other in which cases. Finally, we provide some implementation details, including the URL of the Icarus public repository on GitHub.

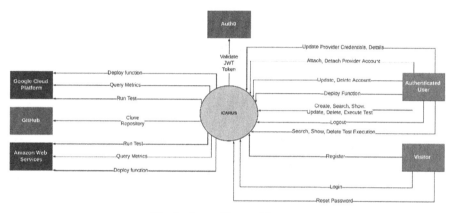

**Fig. 1.** Icarus Context Diagram

Icarus has been structured in several components to meet the project's requirements.

**Backbone Super-Component.** Encapsulates basic components required for test creation and execution. Prior to a test's creation and execution, Icarus requires a linked AWS or GCP account (which will be used to execute the tests and deploy the function), a description of the function to be tested (containing details like runtime, source code location etc.), and a resource configuration that contains details about the function's deployment. Each of these requirements is handled by a respective sub-component. *Function Service* manages the Function entities, *Provider Account Service* manages the user's cloud provider accounts, *Resource Configuration Service* manages the function configurations (memory layouts, regions, vCPU cores) on the cloud providers, *User Service* manages the application's users, *Test Service* manages test functionality common for both functional and performance tests (such as checking for the existence of the target function's source code prior to deploying), and *Test Execution Service* offers basic support functionality during test execution, such as report production and deletion of infrastructure after the tests have been completed.

**PostgreSQL Database.** Icarus uses a (PostgreSQL) database to store the required entities and user data.

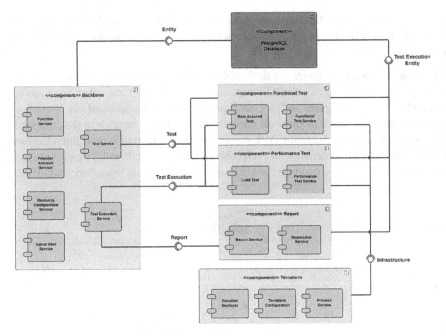

**Fig. 2.** Icarus Component Diagram

**Functional Test Super-Component.** The *Functional Test* super-component executes the functional tests. It mainly encompasses the *Functional Test Service* that handles the smooth creation and execution of each Rest Assured functional test as prescribed by the user configuration by using the *RestAssured Test* sub-component. Functional tests contain test cases and each test case contains test case members. Icarus creates a RestAssured test per each test case member associated with the functional test. RestAssured tests' creation and execution is done concurrently to improve performance.

**Performance Test Super-Component.** The *Performance Test* super-component is responsible for performance test execution. Similarly to the *Functional Test Service* super-component, the *Performance Test Service* sub-component handles the creation and execution of each performance test as prescribed by the user configuration by using the *Load Test* sub-component, which is responsible for the creation and configuration of a JMeter load test. When executing a performance test, Icarus refers to the resource configurations that have been associated with the test and deploys a number of different configurations for the function accordingly. The deployment of the different configurations is being handled by Terraform and as such Icarus has little effect on the performance of the deployment process. After deployment, Icarus creates a load test for every resource version of the deployed function and JMeter handles its execution.

**Report Super-Component.** The *Report* super-component manages the successful creation of a report document, containing the respective test execution's results. This is accomplished via subcomponents *Report Service* and *Regression Service*. In case of a performance test, *Regression Service* performs a linear regression analysis on the test results and adds the constructed performance model to the report. *Report Service* manages the creation and storage of a pdf report document by using Eclipse BiRT.

**Terraform Super-Component.** The Terraform super-component is used to manage the lifecycle of the functions, from creation to deletion. This is accomplished through its subcomponents, Function Deployer, Terraform Configuration and Process Service. The Function Deployer's purpose is twofold, it manages the creation of Terraform configuration files through the Terraform CDK for Java and interfaces with the local Terraform binary to deploy and delete the serverless functions and supporting infrastructure. The Process Service is a supporting component used by Function Deployer to execute Terraform commands in the local system using the host's Terraform binary. As its name suggests, Terraform Configuration is used to configure Terraform.

### 3.4 Icarus Implementation

The implementation of the Icarus service as an open-source Maven project relied on the Java 21 programming language and Spring Boot v3.1.5. Framework. As such Icarus functions as a RESTful web service utilizing Tomcat and listening for requests in port 8080. PostgreSQL v15.5 was used as the underlying database. To manage the lifecycle of the functions, Terraform v1.6.5 and the Terraform CDK for Java v0.19.0 were used. For automated performance testing, we chose the well-known JMeter v5.6.2 tool whereas for automated functional testing we relied on RestAssured v5.3.2. We utilized Eclipse's BiRT v4.8.0 for report generation.

## 4   Experimental Evaluation

The evaluation process focused on checking the system response time and its behavior when executing functional tests with varying workload. The function tested took the form of a pre-deployed 'hello world' type function deployed in AWS Lambda. The target function was warmed up before executing the test plan, enabling to exclude cold start delays incurred by AWS Lambda from our test results. In addition, the AWS region where the function was deployed had a sufficient instance number (1000 instances) to not incur throttling. Icarus and its PostgreSQL database were deployed in the local system. Further, user requests were authenticated by Icarus using Basic Authentication. Following this setup ensured that we were studying the internal performance characteristics of Icarus more closely and excluded any other moving parts and external systems.

Icarus was evaluated in a laptop (local system) with 8GB RAM and an Intel Core i5-1135G7 processor running Windows 11. We used the JMeter load testing tool with the Measure-Command PowerShell utility. JMeter executed a test plan in headless mode and the Measure-Command utility measured the execution time of the command.

We focused on two distinct scenarios as part of the evaluation process. The first scenario studied the application's performance under a varying number of concurrent users. Every user executes a functional test containing a single test case that checks if the function's response matches the string 'Hello World'. For every configuration of the first scenario (exact number of concurrent users), we executed the test thirty times and removed the two biggest and smallest execution times. Afterwards we divided the result by 26 and successfully calculated the average response time experienced across all users for that configuration of the scenario. We studied this scenario starting with ten concurrent users and scaling upwards to fifty concurrent users, in steps of ten.

The second scenario studied the application's performance under a steady number of thirty concurrent users with varying workload configurations. Each workload configuration consists of a steady number of test cases. Same as before, for every workload configuration the scenario was executed thirty times. We removed the two biggest and smallest execution times and divided the result by 26 to calculate the average response time per user experienced across all users for that workload configuration of the scenario. We studied this scenario starting with ten identical test cases and scaling upwards to forty test cases per user, in steps of ten.

To account for JMeter's initialization times, we conducted further experiments to measure the average initialization time of JMeter and thus redact it from the calculated average execution times. We created an empty test plan containing a thread group with zero loops and used Measure-Command to study JMeter's behavior. After conducting this experiment thirty times and calculating the average initialization time, we redacted it from the measurements we had obtained from both scenarios.

Below, we showcase the two experiment results in two graphs. Scenario A represents the first scenario, where we study the effects of the increasing concurrent user number, whereas scenario B represents the second scenario where we study the effects of thirty concurrent users with varying workloads. By studying the graphs, we can clearly see the linear increase in response time in both scenarios. This indicates that Icarus scales well with the increase of its workload (Fig. 3).

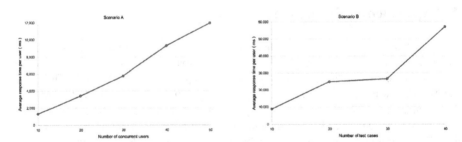

**Fig. 3.** Performance Test results for Scenarios A (left) and B (right)

## 5 Conclusions

In this paper, we presented the Icarus TaaS, a complete testing service that touches on a subject often ignored in related FaaS tools, the functional testing of serverless functions. Further, Icarus covers the non-functional function testing by also having the ability to produce more complete function performance models than those of the existing FaaS tools, for both the intensely studied AWS Lambda and the under-researched Google Cloud Functions, through incorporating resource features, such as vCPU cores and main memory size, as well as the function (deployment) location.

We aim to further expand the base functionality of Icarus by supporting multiple trigger types, complex function chains and serverless applications, thus covering a wider spectrum of serverless applications and use cases. In addition, we plan to support automated test case data generation as currently such data are given by the user in the test configuration. All these new features will provide more test automation and thus greatly reduce the test effort of the end users who will then be able to focus mainly on the core development task of function/serverless application implementation.

# References

1. Opara-Martins, J., Sahandi, R., Tian, F.: Critical review of vendor lock-in and its impact on adoption of cloud computing. In: International Conference on Information Society (i-Society 2014), pp. 92–97. IEEE, London, United Kingdom (2014)
2. Gao, J., Xiaoying Bai, Wei-Tek Tsai, Uehara, T.: Testing as a Service (TaaS) on Clouds. In: 2013 IEEE Seventh International Symposium on Service-Oriented System Engineering, pp. 212–223. IEEE, San Francisco, CA, USA (2013)
3. Copik, M., Kwasniewski, G., Besta, M., Podstawski, M., Hoefler, T.: SeBS: a serverless benchmark suite for function-as-a-service computing. In: Proceedings of the 22nd International Middleware Conference, pp. 64–78. ACM, Quebec City, Canada (2021)
4. Maissen, P., Felber, P., Kropf, P., Schiavoni, V.: FaaSdom: a benchmark suite for serverless computing. In: Proceedings of the 14th ACM international conference on distributed and event-based systems, pp. 73–84. ACM, Montreal, Quebec, Canada (2020)
5. Somu, N., Daw, N., Bellur, U., Kulkarni, P.: PanOpticon: a comprehensive benchmarking tool for serverless applications. In: 2020 International Conference on COMmunication Systems & NETworkS (COMSNETS), pp. 144–151. IEEE, Bengaluru, India (2020)
6. Malawski, M., Figiela, K., Gajek, A., Zima, A.: Benchmarking heterogeneous cloud functions. In: Heras, D.B., et al. (eds.) Euro-Par 2017: Parallel Processing Workshops, vol. 10659, pp. 415–426. Springer International Publishing, Cham (2018)

# Cloud Business Models, Pricing, Trading, Network Neutrality

# A Cloud Resources Portfolio Optimization Business Model - From Theory to Practice

Valentin Haag, Maximilian Kiessler, Benedikt Pittl, and  Erich Schikuta$^{(\boxtimes)}$ ⓘ

Faculty of Computer Science, University of Vienna, Vienna, Austria
{benedikt.pittl,erich.schikuta}@univie.ac.at

**Abstract.** Cloud resources have become increasingly important, with many businesses using cloud solutions to supplement or outright replace their existing IT infrastructure. However, as there is a plethora of providers with varying products, services, and markets, it has become increasingly more challenging to keep track of the best solutions for each application. Cloud service intermediaries aim to alleviate this problem by offering services that help users meet their requirements. The business model of such intermediaries is missing in current works and introduced in this paper. This paper aims to lay the groundwork for developing a cloud portfolio management platform and its business model, defined via a business model canvas. Furthermore, a prototype of a platform is developed offering a cloud portfolio optimization service, using two algorithms developed in previous research to create suitable and well-utilized allocations for a customer's applications. The developed business model forms the baseline for realizing cloud intermediaries on cloud markets.

**Keywords:** Cloud Economics · Portfolio Optimization · Business Model

## 1  Introduction

Over the past years, the cloud resource market has been one of the fastest-growing IT segments. The biggest providers, Amazon Web Services (AWS), Microsoft Azure, and Google Cloud, have seen annual sales increases of over 20% for several years. Just AWS itself reported a revenue of 90 Billion US dollars for the year 2023, and the entire cloud market achieved revenue of 545.8 Billion dollars worldwide with 19% growth compared to 2022 [1]. This large and expanding market has resulted not only in a growing cloud service provider (from here on, often referred to as CSPs) market but also in several methods of delivery of cloud resources to the customer.

One big challenge facing both industry and academia is finding a cost-effective solution when buying cloud capacities. Pittls' study [16] concludes that almost all observed resource requests were oversized and offered significant cost reduction potential, which lies not only in reducing the amount of resources bought but also in their composition. Depending on the planning period of the operations

ⓒ The Author(s), under exclusive license to Springer Nature Switzerland AG 2025
M. Naldi et al. (Eds.): GECON 2024, LNCS 15358, pp. 71–83, 2025.
https://doi.org/10.1007/978-3-031-81226-2_7

to be performed, a different mix of procurement from different market spaces is optimal. The author suggests tackling this problem via a cloud resource trading intermediary.

Offering a service that aids businesses in managing their cloud portfolio and proposing efficient allocations to run their applications, even across various providers, is of great interest in the market. While most larger CSPs offer some functionalities and services that claim to help prevent over-provisioning, like AWS Lambda and Fargate, it is ultimately not in the provider's best interest to reduce the costs for the customer. For the same reason, offering cross-platform support should not be expected of them either.

One way to better leverage the opportunities of the cloud market and make the market more accessible is the use of cloud intermediaries between the CSPs and the customer. Given that, this paper introduces a business model for a intermediary termed *Cloud Portfolio Manager*. The presented work has a twofold focus, on SaaS (business model) and IaaS (mangement of infrastructure resources), and addresses the following research questions:

– *Under what kind of business model could such an intermediary operate?* To answer this question, a detailed proposal and description of a viable business model for a cloud resource intermediary will be presented. Intermediaries in a similar fashion have been put forward, but as far as the authors' best knowledge, no conclusive business model exists on how these intermediaries could operate.
– *How could such a platform be implemented?* The other goal of this work is the design and implementation of a cloud resource intermediary.

Thus, the paper is structured as follows: The next Sect. 2 gives the reader a literature survey on the target research area. Section 3 focuses on cloud portfolio optimization theory, and two respective algorithms, a genetic and a greedy one, are described and their performance evaluated - this chapter is mainly based on previous work. In Sect. 4, we propose our proposal of a business model for a cloud portfolio management platform, consisting of the nine building blocks defined by the business model canvas framework of Osterwalder [13]. Based on the business model description, we present the implementation of our respective prototype in Sect. 5. Finally, Sect. 6 summarises the paper's findings, including what future work to expand upon the topic.

While we followed the basic Research Design principals [5], a solid evaluation of our artefact is outside of the scope of the paper, but can be found here [8].

## 2   State of the Art

The cloud market currently consists of many cloud service providers, each featuring various ways and markets for customers to access their products. There is no single space from which all suppliers can be accessed which slows down the development of multi-cloud environments [14]. The market is an oligopoly, dominated by the most prominent three players, Amazon Cloud Services (AWS), Microsoft Azure, and Google Cloud [12]. In the course of this work, we focus on AWS, the largest cloud service provider today, which offers three different resource markets with varying pricing models: *On-demand marketplace*, *Saving plans marketplace* and *Spot marketplace*.

The definition of a business model has not only been one of the earliest focuses of research, but also one of the most hotly debated. Almost every paper concerning this topic has defined its own take on this task, and to this day, there is no general agreement on a universally accepted definition. We follow the definition of [13], where a business model describes the rationale of how an organization creates, delivers, and captures value. Similar to the definition of the term, there is also a wide array of frameworks describing the elements a business model comprises. The paper will focus on the Business Model Canvas from Osterwalder and Pigneur [13], one of the most established and widely used frameworks today. This framework proposes to describe any business model with nine building blocks: (i) The *Customer Segment* block describes the groups a company tries to offer its products to. (ii) The *Value Proposition* describes the reason why a customer chooses to work with one business over others (iii) *Channels* describe the way a company reaches its customer segment to make its proposition of value. (iv) The different kinds of relationships companies can have with their customers are described in the block *Customer Relationships*. (v) The block *Revenue Streams* deals with the income a company receives from its customers. (vi) The *Key Resources* block describes the resources that allow the company to operate its business and earn revenues. (vii)The block *Key Activities* defines the activities a company must perform to be successful. They are necessary to create value and earn revenue, and they can differ widely depending on the company. (viii) *Key partnerships* are the suppliers and partners a business model includes to make it work. (ix) The last block *Cost Structure* of the Canvas deals with all operating costs of the business model.

Actual cloud broker implementations on the market are still sparse, while the high number of cloud service offerings makes it hard to find the right service as a customer [6]. For example, spot.io[1] offers a range of tools for customers to analyze, manage and optimize their cloud portfolios. While they offer services like Eco and Elasticgroup, with a similar value proposition of cost reduction for a customers cloud portfolio, their underlying optimization algorithms differs from ours. Additionally, Eco also relies on trading and reselling resources among their customers and does not factor in spot instances for its calculations. Densify[2] offers a cloud management and optimization service with a similar value proposition to our platform but differences regarding revenue stream and pricing model. Seeing as their pricing model is based on the number of instances

---

[1] https://spot.io/.
[2] https://www.densify.com/.

managed, Densify does not seem incentivized to reduce the number of instances used in a portfolio.

While a plethora of research has been conducted in the field of cloud intermediaries, the number of implementations on the market is limited. This situation, in conjunction with the fact that the services provided can vary wildly, has resulted in a lack of research concerning the business models of cloud brokers so far. Nevertheless, the work of Filiopoulou at al. [7] gives an overview of benefits, common pricing models, and an evaluation of cloud brokers. It is concluded that brokers assist companies in developing themselves and creating a more competitive environment for providers while earning revenues themselves. Other works such as [15] focus on the introduction of a cloud ecosystem as a generic framework where intermediates are foreseen, but no business model is described.

## 3    Portfolio Optimization Model

In the paper at hand we refer cloud portfolio optimization alogrithms which were introduced by Kiessler et al. [11]. This section summarizes the most important findings of our previous work.

The main goal of cloud portfolio management is usually achieving the lowest costs for running a specific set of applications over time. Some research like Jangjaimon and Tzeng [10] and Sharma et al. [19] tried to deal with this problem by creating a checkpointing mechanism or by focusing on preemptible servers in combination with concepts taken from financial modeling, to meet the requirements of applications when using spot instances. Meanwhile, Pittl et al. [16] took a more comprehensive approach to cloud portfolio management, which resulted in the findings that a more heterogeneous portfolio tends to be more cost-efficient. Cloud portfolio is defined as a set of *cloud instances*, which are used to run a set of *applications* on them. The main goal of our optimization problem, hereby, is finding a cost-efficient allocation of these applications and instances [11]. The problem is essentially a multi-dimensional packing problem, it is NP-hard, very complex to solve, and finding an optimal solution is usually not computationally feasible [4]. Therefore, we developed two optimization heuristics to find good approximations of an optimal solution. First, we developed a greedy algorithm called *Efficient Resource Inference for Cloud Hosting* (ERICH). It integrates the approach of the widely known bin packing algorithm first fit decreasing (FFD), combining it with the proposed portfolio management strategy by Hwang and Pedram [9]. Our second algorithm is a genetic algorithm named *Genetic Optimization of Resource Groupings* (GEORG) which outperformed ERICH in almost all evaluated secenarios [11].

# 4  Cloud Portfolio Manager Business Model

Based on Osterwalders Canvas [13] the proposed Cloud Portfolio Managers building blocks are shown in Fig. 1.

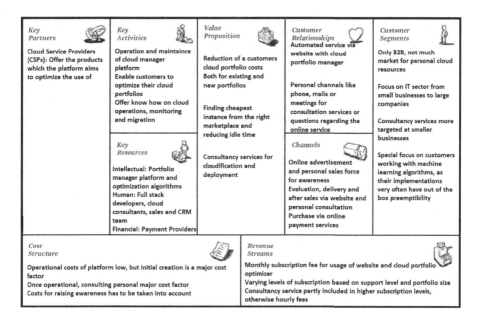

**Fig. 1.** Business Model Canvas [13] of Cloud Portfolio Manager

*Customer Segments.* For our customer segment, the sole focus will be on the B2B area, as consumers, so far, have little to no reason to purchase cloud resources for personal use. Within the B2B sector, a big emphasis will be put on the IT sector, ranging from small businesses to large companies, seeing as large parts of this sector move more and more of their IT infrastructure into the cloud such as Netflix, which moved its entire IT infrastructure to AWS [2]. Surprisingly, when it comes to smaller businesses start-up companies looking for cloud solutions prefer the reputation of a cloud provider over other aspects such as price, security, and reliability [17]. Hence, establishing a reputation should be a primary business goal. Besides this, the envisioned Portfolio Manager can increase its attractiveness to small businesses and start-ups by offering cloud consulting and optimization services.

One customer segment our business will specifically focus on within the IT sector are those companies, businesses, and possibly research facilities working with machine learning algorithms. These are uniquely well-suited to be run on cloud resources, as their implementations often offer out-of-the-box preemptibility like the previously mentioned PyTorch and Google TensorFlow [3,20].

*Value Proposition.* The primary value proposition, a cost reduction for their cloud portfolio, is unlike many other business models, targeting all customer segments. It can be applied to both existing portfolios and first-time cloud deployments. A portfolio can be set up in two ways: Either, directly via interacting with the Portfolio Manager via its website or via API. The API allows customers to integrate the Portfolio Manager with their own systems and automate the process of creating portfolios and creating allocations.

The previously mentioned cost reduction is achieved by a combination of choosing the cheapest instances from the right marketplace and reducing their idle time through continuous monitoring of the needs of the applications. The resulting benefit for the customer entails the direct cost reduction itself and offers easier access to the complex world of cloud computing, which could be especially useful for small and medium-sized businesses.

*Channels.* Listed here, we will address the channels used throughout the five phases of customer interaction through which we aim to reach our customers:

(i) *Awareness:* For the first phase, raising the customer's awareness of our service, a mixture of online advertisement and direct contact with potential customers through an in-house sales force seems applicable. Furthermore, targeted online advertisement, for example, via Google ads[3], word-of-mouth between different businesses as well as reach potential customers is trade fairs could be considered an option. (ii) *Evaluation:* Our website is the primary channel used for evaluation and the center of the operation. It provides example calculations, which showcase the potential cost reductions offered by the service and gives an overview of the pricing structure. (iii) *Purchase:* Regarding purchasing our products, many online payment services such as PayPal, Amazon Payments, and Credit cards are available and can be provided with relative ease. (iv) *Delivery:* The delivery of the optimization service to the customer can also be achieved through the platform's direct channel, either by direct customer interaction on the website or via API call. (v) *After sales:* On the website the user can overview his portfolios, optimizations, subscriptions, and general account information. A FAQ page as well as personal customer support can help to clear issues.

*Customer Relationships.* The website will be used for the majority of interactions, such as setting up an account, creating and managing a portfolio as well as for communicating with consumers. Another important aspect of this building block is the interaction between the consultancy force and the customers. Here, direct interaction with the customer is preferable, as service experience is valued even higher than the actual service quality in B2B services [18].

*Revenue Streams.* Regarding revenue streams, a plethora of options are available at first glance. However, most of them are not readily applicable to our platform for one reason or another, leaving us with one very widely used revenue stream as our primary source of revenue.

---

[3] https://ads.google.com/intl/de_at/home/.

The first option we want to discuss is advertisement. While it is the main revenue stream of many large online platforms such as YouTube and Facebook, the Cloud Portfolio Manager focuses on a too small audience.

Next, we have considered the option of transaction fees. This could be implemented on a usage-based model, where the customer would pay a certain amount for each optimization based on the portfolio size. The usage-based model does not lend itself well to a product that is meant for continuous optimization. This would either lead to a need to frequently pay for a new allocation or prevent customers from getting the full benefit of an approach that is meant to adapt to changing demands in their portfolio.

Another alternative would be a system based on a brokerage fee. In this case, a part of the cost reduction achieved by the Cloud Portfolio Manager would be taken as our revenue. The significant flaw with this idea, though, is that our system does not aim to directly access and manage the customer's cloud instances. This would result in customers needing to accurately and honestly report their current cloud expenses and their achieved cost reductions, which lends itself to be abused way too easily.

Finally, we propose that subscription fees are the revenue stream best suited to our business model. They tackle several disadvantages mentioned in the previously discussed systems, such as fitting well with a continuously running service, unlike pay-per-use transaction fees and a low entry barrier compared to a one-time charge. The subscription fee, due in a monthly interval, could either be based upon a system with different levels of subscriptions, offering support to differing sizes of cloud portfolios and varying levels of customer support, or directly scaling with the size of the optimized cloud portfolios.

As for revenue streams concerning the consultancy side of the business model, a classic hourly fee would most suit customers needing only a more minor assistance contingent. Another variant would be offering package deals with a fixed price, such as offering to help set up the first cloud portfolio for a customer. Finally, higher-level subscription models for the cloud portfolio optimizer platform could include a certain amount of consultancy services for free.

*Key Resources.* As for the differing categories of key resources, the following can be said: When it comes to physical key resources, there is little to be mentioned here. Financial key resources may also not play a huge role in starting off. Of course, financial resources such as cash or credit will be needed to set up the business, but due to its nature, these will be of a small volume.

Finally, when it comes to human key resources, the following groups can be expected to be part of those: Especially for development and improvements to the platform, further full-stack developers could be needed. Furthermore, a small team of cloud consultants would be responsible for providing customers. Besides that, a group of employees helping with sales and CRM-related topics should be employed as well.

*Key Activities.* The most important key activity of the business is the operation and maintenance of the Cloud Portfolio Manager platform. In this capacity, the platform offers the customer an automated service. Besides a simple interface to directly manipulate a portfolio, the main feature for management is the possibility to upload load profiles based upon which an optimized portfolio of instances is calculated and displayed to the customer.

In addition to the service provided by the platform, the other main activity is problem-solving for the customer by offering our consultancy service.

*Key Partnerships.* Within this building block, the most prevalent partnerships are the various CSPs for which the platform offers portfolio optimization. While actively managing the customer's portfolio is not part of the business plan so far, it is crucial to the platform's functionality to access the instances and their respective pricing offered by the various providers. If the business grows beyond a small scale, it would be possible for certain activities, such as customer support or cloud consulting, to be outsourced to external partners, which would turn these into key partnerships as well.

*Cost Structure.* The cost structure of the business model is intended to lean towards being value-driven, focusing on creating value for the customer. As the business operates online with a web platform at its center, scaling should be achievable relatively easily.

## 5   Portfolio Manager Prototype

This section will present the prototype of our Cloud Portfolio Manager. It will present an overview of important pages and showcase the various functionalities of the application. The main motivation is to gather product and pricing information automatically from cloud providers so that matching providers can used for pending cloud workloads.

After authentication, the *instance page* becomes accessible as shown in Fig. 2 contains information about available instances from the various providers. For our prototype, we chose a range of instances from the four biggest CSPs: AWS, Google Cloud, Microsoft Azure, and Alibaba. The list on this page gives an overview of each instance's main attributes: provider, name, market space, capacity, and price.

The *Apps and portfolios* page is depicted in Fig. 3. The left side lists the user's applications and details like mean resource demand, demand variance, preemptibility, and starting and finishing time. On the right side of the page is a list of the user's portfolio, including details like which providers should be considered for any possible allocation, a minimum quality of service, the number of apps in the portfolio, and a list of which applications exactly the portfolio consists of.

To create a new application or portfolio, two green buttons depict a plus sign on each side of the page. These open the respective application and portfolio forms, as seen in Fig. 4a and Fig. 4b. To create an application, the user has to fill out the application form, including a unique name, mean resource demand, demand variance, a checkbox for preemtibility, and finally, the starting and finishing time chosen via a date-time picker. Should the user wish to create a portfolio, the portfolio form requires a unique name and a minimum quality of service, which gives a percentage of time the apps in the portfolio are required to run. e portfolio form also requires the user to choose at least one CSP to be considered for allocations and which apps should make up the portfolio. To ensure suitable inputs for both forms, they also feature various checks, giving instant feedback to invalid inputs, such as an application's finishing time before its starting time. The user can update each application and portfolio by clicking the yellow button, which displays a pen icon for every application and portfolio.

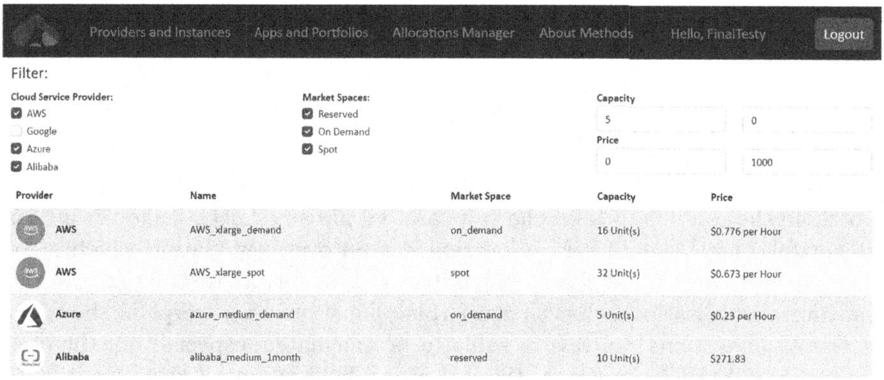

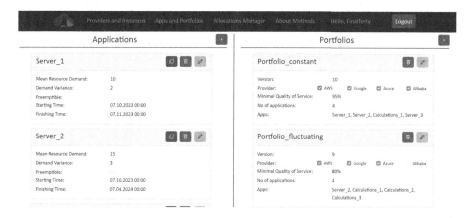

**Fig. 2.** Instances page

**Fig. 3.** Apps and portfolios page overview

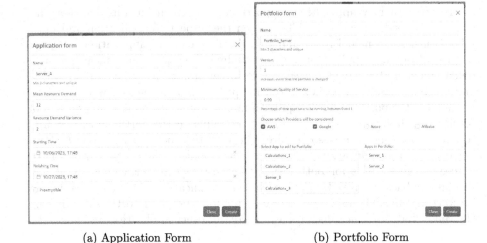

(a) Application Form          (b) Portfolio Form

**Fig. 4.** Screenshots of application and portfolio forms

The *Allocations Page* as shown in Fig. 5 is the primary feature of the Cloud Portfolio Manager: creating allocations for cloud portfolios. The user has a drop-down menu at the top of the page, which lists their created portfolios. Choosing a portfolio shows its details on the side, and all already existing allocations for this portfolio are below. Every allocation has an overview stating which algorithm was used, which portfolio version it was made for, its total costs, and the mean overall utilization achieved with this allocation: an excerpt is shown in Fig. 6b. As allocations can take a while to be calculated, especially in the case of using the GEORG algorithm, there is also a field stating if the allocation is already completed. Below the general stats are two fields, which can be extended by clicking on them. The first contains a complete list of all instances used for this allocation and some statistics like capacity, price, and the beginning and end of the instance's run time. The second field contains more detailed statistics about the allocation, such as separate statistics for reserved, on-demand, and spot instances. To create a new allocation, the"New Allocation" button opens a form where the user can choose which algorithm should be used such as shown in Fig. 6a.

**Fig. 5.** Allocations page overview

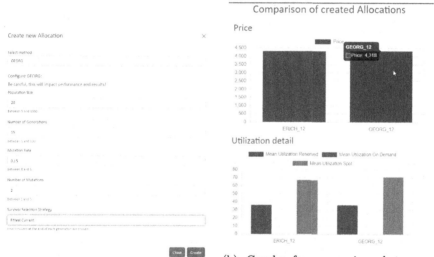

(a) Form for creating a new GEORG allocation (excerpt of paramters)

(b) Graphs for comparison between a GEORG and ERICH allocation for an example portfolio

**Fig. 6.** Details on allocation page

# 6   Conclusion and Future Work

The main contribution of the paper is the development of a business model for a Cloud Portfolio Manager which was implemented including two optimization algorithms. The work is seen as a corner-stone towards adopting Cloud interme-diaries in industry. As the cloud computing market has been on a meteoric rise over the past years and is still expanding, the topic of cloud portfolio manage-ment will likely keep or expand its relevance in the coming years. Future work will see the prototype developed into a fully functional public platform operat-ing with our business model or a modification of it. Therefore, feedback from practitioners is required and the business model itself needs to be tightly evalu-ated along the Research Design framework. Furthermore, the platform's offered services can be extended by various monitoring functionalities and direct control of portfolios via the platform. .

# References

1. Statista Online Services: Annual revenue of amazon web services (AWS) from 2013 to 2022. https://www.statista.com/statistics/233725/development-of-amazon-web-services-revenue/. Accessed 7 Aug 2024
2. Amazon Web Services: Netflix in AWS (2017). https://aws.amazon.com/solutions/case-studies/netflix-kinesis-data-streams/
3. Pytorch Foundation: Pytorch Checkpoints (2023). https://pytorch.org/tutorials/recipes/recipes/saving_and_loading_a_general_checkpoint.html
4. Chekuri, C., Khanna, S.: On multidimensional packing problems. SIAM J. Comput. **33**(4), 837–851 (2004)
5. Creswell, J.: Research design (2012)
6. Elhabbash, A., Samreen, F., Hadley, J., Elkhatib, Y.: Cloud brokerage: a systematic survey. ACM Comput. Surv. **51**(6) (2019)
7. Filiopoulou, E., Mitropoulou, P., Michalakelis, C., Nikolaidou, M.: The rise of cloud brokerage: business model, profit making and cost savings. In: Bañares, J.Á., Tserpes, K., Altmann, J. (eds.) Economics of Grids, Clouds, Systems, and Services, pp. 19–32. Springer, Cham (2017)
8. Haag, V.: A cloud portfolio manager - a novel business model, Master's thesis, University of Vienna (2024)
9. Hwang, I., Pedram, M.: Portfolio theory-based resource assignment in a cloud com-puting system. In: 2012 IEEE Fifth International Conference on Cloud Computing, pp. 582–589. IEEE (2012)
10. Jangjaimon, I., Tzeng, N.F.: Effective cost reduction for elastic clouds under spot instance pricing through adaptive checkpointing. IEEE Trans. Comput. **64**(2), 396–409 (2013)
11. Kiessler, M., Haag, V., Pittl, B., Schikuta, E.: Optimization heuristics for cost-efficient long-term cloud portfolio allocations. In: International Conference on Information Integration and Web, pp. 309–323. Springer (2022)
12. Law, M.: Technology biggest cloud providers 2023 (2023). https://technologymagazine.com/top10/top-10-biggest-cloud-providers-in-the-world-in-2023
13. Osterwalder, A., Pigneur, Y.: Business Model Generation: A Handbook for Vision-aries, Game Changers, and Challengers, vol. 1. Wiley (2010)
14. Petcu, D.: Multi-cloud: expectations and current approaches. In: Proceedings of the 2013 International Workshop on Multi-Cloud Applications and Federated Clouds, pp. 1–6 (2013)

15. Pittl, B., Mach, W., Schikuta, E.: A classification of autonomous bilateral cloud SLA negotiation strategies. In: Proceedings of the 18th International Conference on Information Integration and Web-based Applications and Services, pp. 379–388 (2016)

16. Pittl, B., Mach, W., Schikuta, E.: Cost-evaluation of cloud portfolios: an empirical case study. In: Proceedings of the 9th International Conference on Cloud Computing and Services Science (CLOSER), pp. 132–143. SciTePress (2019)

17. Repschlaeger, J., Erek, K., Zarnekow, R.: Cloud computing adoption: an empirical study of customer preferences among start-up companies. Electron. Mark. **23**(2), 115–148 (2013)

18. Roy, S., Sreejesh, S., Bhatia, S.: Service quality versus service experience: an empirical examination of the consequential effects in B2B services. Ind. Market. Manag. **82**, 52–69 (2019)

19. Sharma, P., Irwin, D., Shenoy, P.: Portfolio-driven resource management for transient cloud servers. Proc. ACM Measur. Anal. Comput. Syst. **1**(1), 1–23 (2017)

20. TensorFlow: Tensorflow Checkpoints. https://www.tensorflow.org/guide/checkpoint (2023)

# ISP Pricing and Platform Pricing Interaction Under Net Neutrality

Luis Guijarro[✉][iD], Vicent Pla[iD], and José Ramón Vidal[iD]

Universitat Politècnica de València Camino de Vera, s/n. 46022 València, Spain
{lguijar,jrvidal}@dcom.upv.es, vpla@upv.es

**Abstract.** We analyze the effects of enforcing vs. exempting access ISP from net neutrality regulations when platforms are present and operate two-sided pricing in their business models. This study is conducted in a scenario where users and Content Providers (CPs) have access to the internet by means of their serving ISPs and to a platform that intermediates and matches users and CPs, among other service offerings. Our hypothesis is that platform two-sided pricing interacts in a relevant manner with the access ISP, which may be allowed (a hypothetical non-neutrality scenario) or not (the current neutrality regulation status) to apply two-sided pricing on its service business model. We conclude that the platforms are extracting surplus from the CPs under the current net neutrality regime for the ISP, and that the platforms would not be able to do so under the counter-factual situation where the ISPs could apply two-sided prices.

**Keywords:** Platform · Internet Service Providers · Net neutrality · Two-sided pricing

## 1 Introduction

Net neutrality has been debated intensively since it first was advocated two decades ago. And it has been regulated worldwide, prominently in the US and in the EU. There are multiple approaches to the net neutrality concept. We focus on the one which prevents a two-sided pricing scheme to be applied by an access Internet Service Provider (ISP) in order for Content Providers (CPs) reaching the access ISP's subscribers from a different ISP [2].

It has been claimed by access ISPs that charging a side payment to the CPs, which is forbidden by net neutrality regulations, would contribute to the upgrade of the infrastructure needed to support the huge amount of traffic that flows from the CPs to the users. This rationale has recently been proposed under the concept of "direct compensation" or "fair share".

We do not aim to contribute to the general debate on net neutrality under the current facade [4]. Instead, we will focus on the fact that CPs (e.g., newspapers) not only need access ISP in order to reach users that subscribe to their services, but also need platforms (e.g., Google News) that intermediate and match

© The Author(s), under exclusive license to Springer Nature Switzerland AG 2025
M. Naldi et al. (Eds.): GECON 2024, LNCS 15358, pp. 84–93, 2025.
https://doi.org/10.1007/978-3-031-81226-2_8

CPs against users. These platforms do not abide to an equivalent net neutrality regulation, and therefore have been applying two-sided pricing mechanisms, which allows them to actively manage the cross-network effects operating in such business models.

Our focus is then to analyze the effects of enforcing vs. exempting access ISP from net neutrality regulations when platforms are present and operate two-sided pricing in their business models. Our hypothesis is that platform two-sided pricing interacts in a relevant manner with the access ISP, which may be allowed (an hypothetical non-neutrality scenario) or not (the current neutrality regulation status) to apply two-sided pricing on their service business model.

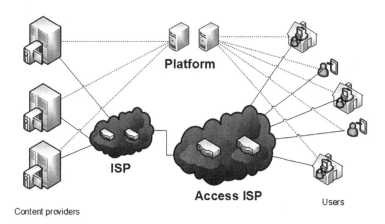

**Fig. 1.** Scenario

## 2 Economic Model

We model a scenario as depicted in Fig. 1, where users and CPs have access to the internet by means of their serving ISPs and to a platform that intermediates and matches users and CPs, among other service offering. Therefore, both ISPs and platform are necessary for the users to subscribe and use the services provided by the CPs. And both ISPs and platform create their respective stand alone value with additional (although typically more basic) services.

### 2.1 Users' Subscription

We model a mass of $N_u$ non-atomic users that are potential subscribers of both the access ISP and the platform, so that if they do subscribe to both of them, they will be able to enjoy the service provided by the CPs. The users are homogeneous in all their characteristics except in the value of the outside option, which we assume is drawn independently from a uniform distribution over the unity interval $[0, 1]$.

The users are charged a fee $\beta$ by the platform and a price $b'$ by the access ISP, per traffic unit that is downloaded from the CPs. If an average traffic $\omega$ is assumed for the traffic downloaded by one user from one CP, then we can set $b = b'\omega$ as the price per CP that the access ISP charges to a user.

The users derive a stand-alone value $r_u$ from the combined platform-access-ISP service. And they derive an additional value that is increasing in the number of CPs offering their contents through the platform and the access ISP. If the number of joined CPs is $n_c$, this additional value, assuming a linear dependence, is $\delta n_c$, so that $\delta$ models the intensity of the cross-group network effect that the CP side exerts on the users.

Putting all the above modeling decisions together, the expression for the utility that a user derives if he/she subscribes to the combined service is:

$$u = r_u + \delta n_c - \beta - b n_c = r_u - \beta + (\delta - b)n_c \tag{1}$$

Note that the above expression has similarities with the common modeling of the utility derived by the users of a platform when they are charged both a participation fee $\beta$ and a transaction fee $b$ [3]. Nevertheless, in this work, as it will be detailed below, these fees are charged by different agents.

Finally, since the outside option $u_0$ of each user is uniformly distributed in the unity interval, the number of users that will subscribe to the combined service $n_u$ can be computed as:

$$\frac{n_u}{N_u} = \text{Prob}\{u_0 \leq u\} =$$

$$= \text{Prob}\{u_0 \leq r_u - \beta + (\delta - b)n_c\}$$

$$= \begin{cases} 0 & \text{if } r_u - \beta + (\delta - b)n_c < 0 \\ r_u - \beta + (\delta - b)n_c & \text{if } 0 \leq r_u - \beta + (\delta - b)n_c \leq 1 \\ 1 & \text{if } 1 < r_u - \beta + (\delta - b)n_c \end{cases} \tag{2}$$

## 2.2  CPs' Decisions

We model a mass of $N_c$ non-atomic CPs that are willing to offer their contents to the users, which are reachable by means of the combined platform-ISPs service. The CP's business model is based on advertisement. The CPs are homogeneous in all their characteristics except in the benefit of the outside option, which we assume it is drawn independently from a uniform distribution over the unity interval $[0, 1]$.

A CP is charged a fee $\alpha$ by the platform and a price $a'$ per traffic unit that is uploaded to its ISP. Above we assumed that an average traffic $\omega$ is downloaded from a CP to a user, so that we can denote by $a = a'\omega$ the price per user that is charged to the CP. If the access ISP is allowed to apply a two-sided pricing mechanism, this will add an additional fee $c = c'\omega$ per user that the access ISP will charge to the CP.

The CP derives a stand-alone benefit $r_c$ from the combined platform-ISPs service. And it gets an advertising revenue $\gamma$ per user. Since the number of subscribers is $n_u$, this additional revenue is $\gamma n_u$, so that we can interpret $\gamma$ as the intensity of the cross-group network effects that the user side exerts on the CPs.

Putting all the above modeling decisions together, the expression for the profit that a CP obtains if joins to the combined service is:

$$\Pi_c = r_c + \gamma n_u - \alpha - (a + c)n_u = r_c - \alpha + (\gamma - c - a)n_u \qquad (3)$$

Again, note that the above expression has similarities with a setting where the CPs are charged both a participation fee $\alpha$ and a transaction fee $a + c$.

Finally, since the outside option $\Pi_0$ of each CP is uniformly distributed in the unity interval, the number of CPs that will join to the combined service $n_c$ can be computed as:

$$\frac{n_c}{N_c} = \text{Prob}\{\Pi_0 \leq \Pi_c\} =$$

$$= \text{Prob}\{\Pi_0 \leq r_c - \alpha + (\gamma - c - a)n_u\}$$

$$= \begin{cases} 0 & \text{if } r_c - \alpha + (\gamma - c - a)n_u < 0 \\ r_c - \alpha + (\gamma - c - a)n_u & \text{if } 0 \leq r_c - \alpha + (\gamma - c - a)n_u \leq 1 \\ 1 & \text{if } 1 < r_c - \alpha + (\gamma - c - a)n_u \end{cases} \qquad (4)$$

## 2.3 Platform's Decisions

The platform charges a fee $\beta$ to each subscriber and a fee $\alpha$ to each joined CP, so that it gets a revenue equal to

$$\Pi_p = \alpha n_c + \beta n_u. \qquad (5)$$

We neglect the variable costs incurred by the platform, so that the platform will set the two-sided price $\{\alpha, \beta\}$ in order to maximize $\Pi_p$.

If the platform is absent, then fees $\beta$ and $\alpha$ are set to zero.

## 2.4 ISP's Decisions

We assume that the ISP providing acces to the CPs is not an active agent in our model, so that we take $a$ as a parameter, and therefore its benefits are set to $an_c$.

As regards the access ISP, if a non neutral two-sided pricing is allowed, its revenue will be given by:

$$\Pi_u = (bn_c)n_u + (cn_u)n_c = (b + c)n_u n_c, \qquad (6)$$

and the access ISP will set the pair $\{b, c\}$ in order to maximize $\Pi_u$.

If the access ISP is instead under net neutrality regulation, which enforces $c = 0$, the access ISP will only set $b$ in order to maximize $\Pi_u = bn_u n_c$.

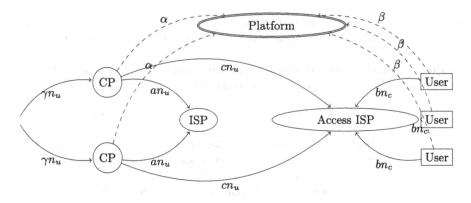

**Fig. 2.** Platform and ISPs payment flow model

## 3  Analysis

Figure 2 summarizes the payments flow described above.

We assume the following sequence of decisions:

1. The access ISP sets $\{c, b\}$
2. The platform sets $\{\alpha, \beta\}$
3. The users and the CPs decide whether to subscribe/join or not.

We therefore assume that the pricing decision by the access ISP is taken before the corresponding decision by the platform, under the assumption that the ISP's price decision is usually taken on a longer time frame that the pricing decision by a platform.

We do not restrict neither the platform nor the access ISP to set positive prices, so that they can set negative prices in one the side that creates stronger cross-network effects.

Furthermore, once prices are set by the access ISP and the platform, the subscription decision by users and CPs are modeled under the assumption of a fulfilled-expectations equilibrium, where agents (users or CPs) from one side form the same expectations on the participation of the agents of the other side and these expectations turn out to be correct. That is, the number of subscribers $n_u$ and joined CPs $n_c$ will be the solution $\{n_u, n_c\}$ to the system of the two equations (2) and (4) [1, p.83].

To sum up: the platform sets $\{\alpha, \beta\}$ anticipating $\{n_u, n_c\}$, and the access ISP sets $\{c, b\}$ anticipating the platform decision and the resulting $\{n_u, n_c\}$.

## 4  Results

We discuss the results in terms of ISP profits (Fig. 3 and Fig. 10), platform profits (Fig. 4 and Fig. 11), number of subscribers (Fig. 5 and Fig. 12), number

**Table 1.** Scenario comparison

|              | pnn     | pn      | ann     | an      |
|--------------|---------|---------|---------|---------|
| Access ISP   | 2nd-3rd | 2nd-3rd | 1st     | 4th     |
| Platform     | 1st-2nd | 1st-2nd | 3rd-4th | 3rd-4th |
| Users        | 1st-4th | 1st-4th | 1st-4th | 1st-4th |
| CPs          | 2nd-4th | 2nd-4th | 2nd-4th | 1st     |
| Social welfare | 1st-3rd | 1st-3rd | 1st-3rd | 4th   |

of joined CPs (Fig. 6 and Fig. 13), users/consumers' surplus (Fig. 7 and Fig. 14), CP surplus (Fig. 8 and Fig. 15) and social welfare (Fig. 9 and Fig. 16).

The Consumers' and CPs' surpluses are respectively computed as follows:

$$CS \equiv N_u \int_0^u u\,1\,du_0 = N_u u^2 \tag{7}$$

$$CPS \equiv N_c \int_0^{\Pi_c} \Pi_c\,1\,d\Pi_0 = N_c \Pi_c^2. \tag{8}$$

An the Social Welfare is the sum of the surpluses of all agents:

$$SW = CS + CPS + \Pi_p + \Pi_u. \tag{9}$$

The parameters used are $N_u = 10$, $N_c = 1$, $r_u = 0.9$, $r_c = 0.9$, $\delta = 2$, $\gamma = 4$ and $a = 0.5$ if not stated otherwise.

We conduct below comparative statics, that is, we characterize the equilibrium of the three-stage game described above as one parameter is varied across a range of values. Specifically, we analyze the effect of parameter $\delta$, which characterizes how intense the CP cross-network effect is; and of parameter $\gamma$, which quantifies the per subscriber advertising revenue for the CP.

We analyze the results comparatively between four possible scenarios according whether the access ISP is subject to net neutrality regulation or not; and whether the platform is present or absent:

- the platform is present and the ISP is non-neutral (*pnn* scenario);
- the platform is present and the ISP is neutral (*pn* scenario);
- the platform is absent and the ISP is non-neutral (*ann* scenario);
- the platform is absent and the ISP is neutral (*an* scenario)

The results will show that, for an intermediate range of $\delta$ and $\gamma$ values, the order of preference of the scenarios for each agent is the one shown in Table 1. These results can be summarized as follows:

- The users are indifferent between the four scenarios. And the CPs strictly prefer the scenario where there is no platform and a neutral ISP is operating, since this means not paying to neither the platform nor the access ISP. And finally, the social welfare is the same and greater in all scenarios but the one where the platform is absent and the ISP is neutral.

– When a non-neutral ISP is operating, the presence of the platform is not relevant for the CPs; however, when a neutral ISP is operating, the presence of the platform worsens the situation for the CPs. One can conjecture that the strategical interaction between the platform and the access ISP is more beneficial for the CPs when the play field is level (i.e., both platform and access ISP can adjust the same number of strategies, one price at each side).
– Trivially, the access ISP prefers to apply two-sided pricing and that the platform is absent.
– Finally, the platform prefers to be present than to be absent, but it is indifferent between interacting with a non-neutral and with a neutral ISP. This means that the platform pricing is so flexible that it can capture the same value against a non-neutral ISP as against a neutral ISP.

### 4.1   Comparative Statics: $\delta$

The parameter $\delta$ varies between 1 and 2.5. The results confirm that, for all $\delta$ values, the order of preference of the scenarios is the one shown in Table 1. Additionally, as $\delta$ increases, which means that the network effect that the CPs exert on the user side strengthens, the access ISP is able to capture the value associated with this increase (Fig. 3), but the platform cannot (Fig. 4), and therefore high values of $\delta$ are the preferred ones by the access ISP.

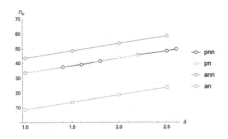

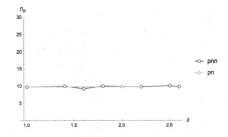

**Fig. 3.** Access ISP's profit as a function of $\delta$

**Fig. 4.** Platform's profit as a function of $\delta$

### 4.2   Comparative Statics: $\gamma$

The parameter $\gamma$ varies between 0.5 and 4.5. The results confirm that, for $\gamma$ values larger than 3, the order of preference of the scenarios is the one shown in Table 1. Additionally, as $\gamma$ is forced to have low values, which means that the revenue per user that each CP gets is reduced, the users cannot be retained at the full participation level, and this is specially so for the scenarios with platform present, which switch from 1st-3rd option to the 3rd-4th option as far as $\Pi_u$, $CS$ and $SW$ are concerned.

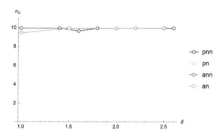

**Fig. 5.** Number of subscribers as a function of $\delta$

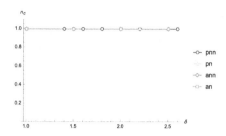

**Fig. 6.** Number of joined CPs as a function of $\delta$

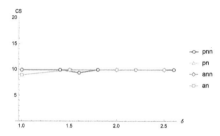

**Fig. 7.** Consumers' surplus as a function of $\delta$

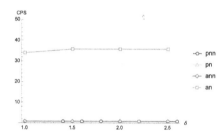

**Fig. 8.** CPs surplus as a function of $\delta$

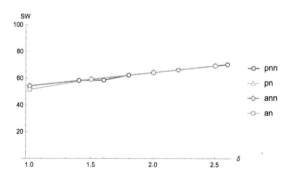

**Fig. 9.** Social welfare as a function of $\delta$

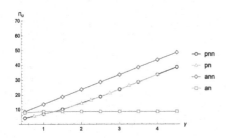

**Fig. 10.** Access ISP's profit as a function of $\gamma$

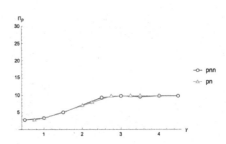

**Fig. 11.** Platform's profit as a function of $\gamma$

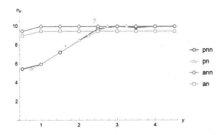

**Fig. 12.** Number of subscribers as a function of $\gamma$

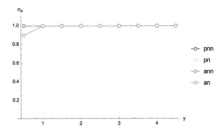

**Fig. 13.** Number of joined CPs as a function of $\gamma$

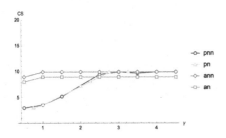

**Fig. 14.** Consumers' surplus as a function of $\gamma$

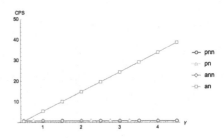

**Fig. 15.** CPs surplus as a function of $\gamma$

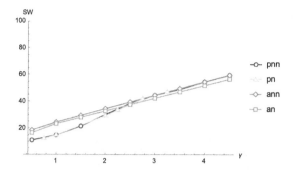

**Fig. 16.** Social welfare as a function of $\gamma$

# 5 Conclusions

We conclude that the presence of a platform does not modify the incentives of the CPs when the ISP is not subject to net neutrality regulations. The social welfare is unaffected by the platform presence. Nevertheless, when the ISP is subject to such regulation, the presence of a platform makes the CPs worse off, and the social welfare is also unaffected by the platform presence.

These conclusions reveal the fact that the platforms are extracting surplus from the CPs under the current net neutrality regime for the ISP, and that the platforms would not be able to do so under the counter-factual situation where the ISPs could apply two-sided prices.

**Acknowledgments.** This work has been conducted during a research stay in Summer 2023 at the Weizenbaum Institut, Berlin, Germany, hosted by the Research Group *Digital Economy, Internet, Ecosystems and Internet Policy* thanks to Dr. Stocker's invitation. Financial support is acknowledged from Grant PID2021-123168NB-I00, funded by MCIN/AEI, Spain/10.13039/ 501100011033 and the European Union A way of making Europe/ERDF and Grant TED2021-131387B-I00, funded by MCIN/AEI, Spain/ 10.13039/501100011033 and the European Union NextGenerationEU/ RTRP.

**Disclosure of Interests.** The authors have no competing interests to declare that are relevant to the content of this article.

# References

1. Belleflamme, P., Peitz, M.: The Economics of Platforms. Cambridge University Press (2021)
2. Economides, N., Tåg, J.: Network neutrality on the internet: a two-sided market analysis. Inf. Econ. Policy **24**(2), 91–104 (2012)
3. Rochet, J.C., Tirole, J.: Two-sided markets: a progress report. Rand J. Econ. **37**(3), 645–667 (2006)
4. Stocker, V., Lehr, W.: Regulatory policy for broadband: a response to the ETNO report's proposal for intervention in Europe's internet ecosystem. SSRN (2022)

# How to Accommodate Network Slicing and Network Neutrality?

Yassine Hadjadj-Aoul[1][ID], Patrick Maillé[2]([✉])[ID], and Bruno Tuffin[3][ID]

[1] University Rennes, IRISA, Inria, CNRS, 35000 Rennes, France
yassine.hadjadj-aoul@irisa.fr
[2] IMT Atlantique, IRISA, UMR CNRS 6074, 35000 Rennes, France
patrick.maille@imt.fr
[3] Inria, University Rennes, CNRS, IRISA, 35000 Rennes, France
bruno.tuffin@inria.fr

**Abstract.** Network slicing has emerged, with 5G mobile networks, as a response to the increasing networks' complexity and the inherent scaling limitations of traditional methods. That technological building block allows, in fact, a very agile orchestration of services, bringing dynamicity, differentiation, and most importantly the fulfillment of various service constraints.

Slicing is therefore seen as a key characteristic of 5G-and-beyond networks, however it seems in contradiction with neutrality principles promoted worldwide. We detail the two contradictory but considered compulsory notions, and discuss how they can be accommodated.

**Keywords:** Net neutrality · Regulation · Slicing · 5G · Quality of Experience · Specialized Services · Network Operators

## 1 5G and Network Slicing

5G stands for the latest generation of wireless networks, coming (as any new network generation) with new capabilities. That fifth generation is in particular expected to increase throughput by a factor up to 100 with respect to 4G, and to allow to connect enormous numbers of devices, from phones to cars and any type of object all over the world. What's more, 5G enables the support of a broad range of services, even the most demanding ones, including real-time interactivity, such as autonomous driving. As of June 2022, around 70 countries had already implemented a 5G network, and it is believed that in 2025, at least 3.6 billion 5G connections will be active. While the first phases of deployment are currently limited to access networks, 5G is designed to go far beyond that, with the ability to provide on-demand guaranteed end-to-end services. This feature is made possible with the adoption of a new concept in 5G and beyond networks, named *network slicing*.

Network slicing consists in creating multiple dedicated logical and virtualized networks over several domains, cutting the infrastructure into "slices" managed

© The Author(s), under exclusive license to Springer Nature Switzerland AG 2025
M. Naldi et al. (Eds.): GECON 2024, LNCS 15358, pp. 94–99, 2025.
https://doi.org/10.1007/978-3-031-81226-2_9

independently (see Fig. 1). That approach provides flexible and scalable resource provisioning for applications and services in order to align resources with needs for quality in terms of throughput, latency, reliability and other metrics, by appropriately dimensioning the slices. Slicing allows to simultaneously and efficiently manage heterogeneous traffic and offer tailored solutions to customers and industries, some being demanding such as telemedicine, online gaming, or augmented reality.

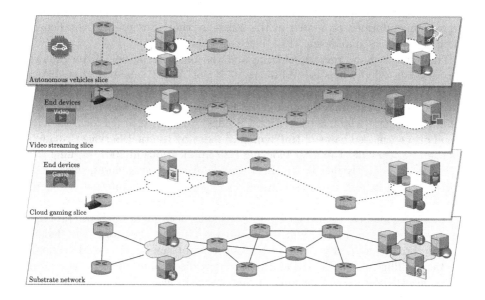

**Fig. 1.** Typical network slicing architecture

There are several reasons for the adoption of network slicing in 5G mobile networks. One is obviously the support of services with heterogeneous constraints, as described above. In fact, this is an opportunity for Network Operators (NOs) to get more value out of the transport of services, by being part of the content distribution value chain. Indeed, NOs currently have very limited control over their own infrastructure rental revenues, which are currently being determined by national regulators. Network slicing is also seen as one of the most important building blocks for network automation, as it brings more agility in the management of services. It also helps to deal with the growing complexity of networks. For all these reasons, we believe that network slicing will continue to be part of the next cellular network standards.

## 2  Network Neutrality

On the other hand, telecommunication networks have been under the scrutiny of regulators concerning neutrality issues. Network neutrality is the principle that traffic should be treated equally, without discrimination, restriction or interference, independently of the sender, receiver, type, content, device, service or application [7,10]. Due to the historic nature of a free and open Internet, the move to a commercial network ignited fears and threats that some services would not be available to all and/or that some would receive a degraded treatment. According to the rule currently in place in the EU [1], no differentiation is allowed, with exceptions *i)* in case of a legal action; *ii)* to ensure the security and integrity of the network if confronted to attacks; *iii)* in case of temporary congestion if no commercial consideration is taken into account. Those guidelines are in line with the recommendations promoted in the 2010s by the US regulator, the Federal Communications Commission (FCC); see for example [2].

The debate about revenue sharing and the business model of the Internet was raised in 2005 when Ed Whitacre, CEO of AT&T, claimed that distant content providers used the AT&T network for free in order to reach end users, and that architecture maintenance could not be economically sustained if those content providers (who make significant profits) were not charged for that. That period also witnessed cases of traffic management by Internet Service Providers, like the USA provider Comcast blocking P2P applications in 2007, arguing that P2P content is mostly illegal. All this raised a lot of concerns and protests from content providers and user associations, worried about the Internet not being open anymore and about the impact on service innovation if access was not free.

As a consequence, the neutrality principle has been highly debated and laws have been passed in most countries worldwide [7]. But the story (the debate) has not come to an end yet due to the outbreak of new services and economic practices falling in "grey areas" and raising new discussions, such as zero rating and sponsored data[1]; and network slicing seems to also fall into this category. Neutrality rules have even been recently repealed in the USA under the Trump administration [3] to allow more economic freedom, indicating that the regulatory environment is still moving.

## 3    Contradictions Between the Two Notions and Traditional Propositions

There seems to be a contradiction between the notions of neutrality, now a pillar of the Internet and telecommunication networks, particularly in Europe, and of slicing, a pillar of 5G networks: how to conciliate equal treatment among flows, with reserved resources for *some* traffic flows?

To address that question, regulators such as ARCEP in France or BEREC in Europe are proposing to define some services, called *specialized services*, which could be excluded from neutrality constraints. This would concern services with strict quality of service requirements, services usually not supported by the Internet network. Typical examples are video on demand, online gaming, autonomous

---

[1] In those practices, for some (favored) applications the operator does not count the corresponding data volume in the data cap, or the data cost is covered by the application provider, respectively.

vehicles or telemedicine [4]. The regulation would then allow allocating slices to each of these services, hence guaranteeing a sufficient quality, but potentially at the expense of other "regular" services.

The notion of specialized service and their management open some breaches to the implementation of neutrality principles. Indeed, the definition of a specialized service is vague: what prevents a new service and even an existing one from claiming the "specialized service" label? It would also be tempting for an NO to consider its own services (VoIP for example) as specialized ones in order to obtain a competitive advantage.

This raises a series of key questions: What are then the objective and clear criteria to be part of that category and to define the quality associated to each slice? Who chooses the relevance of pertaining to a slice, and the service levels associated with that slice? Who will ask for a service to be of this particular class? The Service or Content Provider (SCP), the NO? If it is the NO, isn't there a risk to favor commercial partners? What if an NO does not warrant a request from an SCP? How to proceed without economic considerations, which could constitute incentives to favor some services over others, even between slices and specialized services, something excluded by neutrality principles? Those open questions need some clear answers.

The definition of specialized services is therefore surrounded by many grey areas still to be sorted out, otherwise complaints are expected to pop up.

## 4   An Accommodation Proposition

Given the many unanswered questions, our aim in this section is to propose some high-level guidelines for a solution that could accommodate network slicing and network neutrality. The idea is to define a procedure that is as objective and automated as possible, limiting the holes and antagonist principles between slicing and neutrality.

What we propose is made of the following steps (see Fig. 2).

1. First, analyze the traffic flows, their requirements and constraints, and classify them into different "types", or classes. Classification can be either derived from information given by the service provider, or based on packet-level information, through deep packet inspection, or performed using statistical approaches [8], the latter case being possible even with encrypted traffic [6].
2. Define slices, one per traffic type, in terms of a given level of quality of experience (QoE) [9]. QoE "explains" the users' perceived quality for a given service, in general related to quality of service parameters (packet loss, delays, jitter, ...) but in an extremely complex way. Quantifying the QoE has been the topic of an extensive research activity during the past couple of decades [5].
3. If congestion and consequent degradation of quality of service occurs, differentiate service among slices to offer sufficient or satisfying QoE for each slice as much as possible, while treating all flows equally within each slice (which may imply interrupting service for a whole slice–or several, or uniformly selected flows–if resources are insufficient).

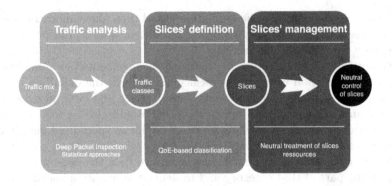

**Fig. 2.** Methodology.

Proceeding this way, flows with similar quality requirements and perceptions will be treated neutrally, and differentiation will be made possible at the benefits of end users. Users and service providers will be served in an optimal way according to the conditions, and NOs will be allowed to manage services.

Of course, this requires monitoring from regulators to verify that the behavior of actors corresponds to what is expected, here in terms of sufficient QoE. Specific procedures have to be designed toward that goal.

The proposed method allows to respect a new vision of neutrality, oriented toward classes of service, but aiming simultaneously at offering the best possible experience to users, at providing a sufficient quality to SCPs, and at leaving flexibility to NOs. It seems to us a reasonable trade-off for accommodating slicing and neutrality. This obviously requires some knowledge about service requirements and the ability to measure quality of experience, whether flows are encrypted or not. In an over-provisioned system, the operator will have the ability to meet the targeted quality criteria.

In the case of an under-provisioned system, the proposed slicing technique presents some challenges. First, what is the share of resources to be dedicated per class of service? Once we have partitioned the resources, how do we guarantee the quality of the supported services? What incentive is there for a network operator to set up several solutions (i.e., traffic classification, QoE measurement, service monitoring, etc.)? The answers to these questions are not necessarily unique, but several directions and accommodations exist to achieve these goals while respecting the principles of neutrality.

On the issue of resource sharing, there is the simple possibility of fixed sharing, prior to service deployment and which might be up to the preference of the operators and their interest in favouring one slice or another. But a better solution could be, instead, to have a dynamic sharing of resources that maximizes the satisfaction of the users belonging to the different slices. This would remove a bit of decision power from ONs, but seems to use a balanced solution to let them perform differentiation.

To guarantee the quality of the flows in a particular slice, there is a clear need to monitor the traffic of that slice in order to provide a fair intra-slice resource sharing (i.e., offering the same QoE). In the case where resources are insufficient to reach the minimum QoE, we can include an admission controller, that could act by randomly selecting some flows which will be blocked on this slice to reach the QoE objectives for those served. The selection would be according to a uniform law to ensure a form of neutrality/fairness.

Finally, the proposed solution allows the NOs to offer differentiation in their network, an option they do not have today, even if depriving them from differential control within a slice.

**Acknowledgement.** The authors acknowledge the support from France 2030 program, operated by the Agence Nationale de la Recherche (ANR), under the grant ANR-22-PEFT-0002.

# References

1. BEREC: BEREC guidelines on the implementation by national regulators of European net neutrality rules. Document number: BoR (16) 127 (2016). https://berec.europa.eu/eng/document_register/subject_matter/berec/regulatory_best_practices/guidelines/6160-berec-guidelines-on-the-implementation-by-national-regulators-of-european-net-neutrality-rules
2. Federal Communications Commission: Protecting and promoting the open internet (2015). https://www.federalregister.gov/documents/2015/04/13/2015-07841/protecting-and-promoting-the-open-internet
3. Federal Communications Commission: Restoring internet freedom (2018). https://docs.fcc.gov/public/attachments/FCC-17-166A1.pdf
4. IETF: Network slicing use cases: network customization and differentiated services (2017). https://tools.ietf.org/id/draft-netslices-usecases-00.html
5. Khokhar, M.J., Ehlinger, T., Barakat, C.: From network traffic measurements to QoE for internet video. In: 2019 IFIP Networking Conference (IFIP Networking), pp. 1–9. IEEE (2019)
6. Liu, C., He, L., Xiong, G., Cao, Z., Li, Z.: FS-Net: a flow sequence network for encrypted traffic classification. In: IEEE INFOCOM 2019 - IEEE Conference on Computer Communications, pp. 1171–1179. IEEE (2019). https://doi.org/10.1109/INFOCOM.2019.8737507
7. Maillé, P., Tuffin, B.: From Net Neutrality to ICT Neutrality. Springer, Verlag (2022)
8. Nguyen, T.T., Armitage, G.: A survey of techniques for internet traffic classification using machine learning. IEEE Commun. Surv. Tutorials **10**(4), 56–76 (2008). https://doi.org/10.1109/SURV.2008.080406
9. Rehman Laghari, K., Connelly, K.: Toward total quality of experience: a QoE model in a communication ecosystem. IEEE Commun. Mag. **50**(4), 58–65 (2012). https://doi.org/10.1109/MCOM.2012.6178834
10. Wu, T.: Network neutrality, broadband discrimination. J. Telecommun. High Technol. (2003)

# PricingTheCloud: A Pricing Estimator for an Informed Cloud-Migration Process

Ines Raissa Djouela Kamgang[1], Abdessalam Elhabbash[2], and Yehia Elkhatib[3(✉)]

[1] Department of Computer Engineering, Faculty of Engineering and Technology, University of Buea, Buea, Cameroon
`ines.djouela@ubuea.cm`
[2] School of Computing and Communications, Lancaster University, Lancaster, UK
`a.elhabbash@lancaster.ac.uk`
[3] School of Computing Science, University of Glasgow, Glasgow, UK
`yehia.elkhatib@glasgow.ac.uk`

**Abstract.** One of the main challenges facing businesses migrating to the cloud is getting an estimate of their costs in advance. The estimators available to date allow companies to compare the different virtual machine offerings from each operator, but only venture very slightly into estimating the overall cost, which includes operational and network costs. Existing estimators include operational costs in their estimates, but almost no one considers the network cost, which is a complex but far from negligible component. In this paper, we seek to address this issue by proposing a new estimator called *PricingTheCloud*. It is an estimator that enables companies to have an accurate estimate of their costs in advance. Unlike other estimators, *PricingTheCloud* considers network costs in the cost estimation. Its evaluation shows an average accuracy of 86.73% for compute costs and 65.44% for network costs in different AWS-to-AWS scenarios as compared to AWS invoices and shows the effectiveness of the proposed estimator compared to three other cloud costs estimators namely, Cloudorado, Holori, and Vantage.

**Keywords:** Cloud computing · Cost calculation · Pricing models · AWS · Compute costs · Network costs · Infrastructure as a Service (IaaS)

## 1 Introduction

Cloud computing has grown at an unprecedented rate and has become the de facto choice for obtaining highly available computing resources. More and more organizations and businesses are accelerating their transition from self-hosted to cloud-hosted systems that have the advantages of being more cost-effective, secure, flexible, reliable, and sustainable [4]. However, a number of questions acutely arise: Which cloud service provider (CSP) should the company choose? What type of virtual machines (VMs) or instances should be selected? Which

© The Author(s), under exclusive license to Springer Nature Switzerland AG 2025
M. Naldi et al. (Eds.): GECON 2024, LNCS 15358, pp. 100–111, 2025.
https://doi.org/10.1007/978-3-031-81226-2_10

VM configuration will match the needs of the enterprise? Which VMs offer the most cost-effective solutions for a specific workload and usage patterns? This final question is the one we aim to answer here. However, the answer to this and similar questions can be quite complex for the three main reasons.

*First, there are many CSPs on the market.* Three CSPs lead the pack of public cloud services with 65% of the market share [10, 16], namely Amazon Web Services-AWS (33%), Microsoft Azure (22%), and Google Cloud Platform-GCP (10%). Other CSPs include Alibaba, Digital Ocean, IBM, and Oracle to name a few. *Second, the number and heterogeneity of Infrastructure as a Service (IaaS) instances offered by CSPs continually increase.* Each of the above-mentioned providers offers different types of cloud instances, each with its specific features and properties. As a result, the number and type of cloud instances developed and released each year are constantly growing [15]. For instance, the number of Linux-based instance types has almost doubled between 2015 and 2022 [8, 18]. *Third, providers offer various pricing strategies.* Every CSP has its own pricing strategy that involves a bespoke calculation of how VMs are being used and how much network traffic is being transferred.

Thus, making the best choice for a given customer means choosing the best CSP, the type of instances that suitably match their needs, and the regions and availability domain/zone (AD/AZ) where the selected instances will be deployed.

While CSPs publish their pricing structures and some even offer proprietary cost calculators, accurately estimating the total cost of cloud resources remains a complex task due to the intricate and often opaque specifics of each provider's pricing model. Notably, these CSP-backed cost calculation tools often present a significant user burden due to their extensive input requirements.

In addition to the proprietary tools offered by CSPs, industry-based estimators have been developed to address these issues. However, the main function of these estimators is to compare the offerings of different CSPs without providing an accurate estimate of the total cost of the cloud resource used. Those that do, provide an erroneous estimate of the total cost, as they consider the prices related to computing and storage resources but neglect those generated by the network traffic between entities. This cost is far from negligible and is a point of misunderstanding for many customers.

To address these concerns, this paper makes the following contributions:

1. A new flexible, transparent, and low-complexity estimator to help companies have a complete cost estimate of their systems, regardless of their architectural structure.
2. An accurate total cost computation model that considers not only compute, but also network parameters.
3. An accuracy assessment of the values generated by the proposed estimator as compared to ground truth values obtained from real AWS deployments.
4. An assessment of the efficiency of our generated results in comparison to three other estimators.

The remainder of this article is organized as follows. Section 2 summarizes relevant related work in cloud service provider estimation and costing. The cost function used to implement the estimator is presented in Sect. 3. Section 4 details the different algorithms used in the implementation. Section 5 evaluates and validates the accuracy and the efficiency of the proposed estimator compared to real results generated by AWS invoices and other estimators. Section 6 details limitations and threats to validity and Sect. 7 concludes the study.

## 2  Related Works

Many approaches have been proposed to handle the complexity of computing and estimating total cloud costs. Those approaches are divided into two main categories, which are industry-based approaches and research-based approaches. In this section, we present relevant existing work in each category.

### 2.1  Industry Solutions

Most industry-based approaches rely on the development of estimator engines. From these, we focus on Helix BMC [3], Cloudorado [1], and Holori [2], highlighting their added values and shortcomings compared to our proposed approach.

The *Helix BMC* simulator helps companies in their migration process by estimating the monthly cost of replicating a given on-premise architecture in the cloud. The demo version, which is free of charge, allows the user to enter only three VMs in the system. However, it presents two main shortcomings. First, the simulator does not allow the user to choose the geographical location of the VM that the user wants whereas, in all the providers' offerings, the cost of a VM is highly dependent on its geographical location. As a result, the computational cost estimates are not realistic. Second, the total cost estimated at the end of the simulation process does not consider network costs since it does not allow the user to enter the amount of data transferred in and out of each VM.

*Cloudorado* is an estimator engine that compares IaaS cloud offerings between three CSPs: AWS, Azure, and GCP. The aim is to help companies make an informed migration process. The comparison occurs at three levels: server hosting, storage, and providers. However, even though the simulation interface seems more comprehensive than that of Helix BMC (e.g. it gives the possibility to enter network cost requirements such as inbound and outbound transfers), the estimator still presents a major shortcoming: it only compares offerings from different providers, but it does not give an estimation of the total cost

Finally, the *Holori* simulation platform functions similarly to Cloudorado but supports more than three CSPs. However, like Cloudorado, this estimator does not take network costs into account and does not calculate the total cost.

Overall, we observe that all industry estimators fall short in providing efficient total cost calculation engines that consider all strategic elements (compute, storage, and network costs), even within the architecture of a single cloud provider.

## 2.2   Academic Efforts

Several studies have highlighted the lack of transparency and certainty in estimating the costs of cloud computing services [9,11,13,17]. Research approaches to cloud cost estimations often rely on mathematical models. Kratzke [12] and Brumec et al. [6] present considerations for estimating cloud costs and express this mathematically. They propose algorithms for cost estimation including computing, storage, networking, and database costs. Aldossary et al. [5] present an energy-based cost model for VMs in the cloud, aiming to express the total cloud costs with a focus on energy savings. However, their cost estimation is limited to computing parameters and does not account for network cost parameters. Cho and Bahn [7] present a real-time cost estimation model for IaaS resources by monitoring resource usage, but leaves out network costs. It also assumes a linear relationship between resource usage and cost, which is not necessarily true.

For the aforementioned reasons, there is a need for an estimator that considers all relevant parameters, including compute and network costs, when estimating total costs, ultimately aiming to simplify the experience for cloud users.

## 3   Problem Formulation

To formally model the cloud cost estimation problem, we begin by defining the fundamental components of our cloud cost model, namely the operational compute and network costs, as well as the architecture on which they depend.

Let $G = (N, L)$ be a directed graph representing the architecture for which a user would like to estimate the costs after migration to the cloud. $N$ represents the set of VMs in the architecture, and $L$ the set of links between the VMs. Each VM is characterized by its CPU, memory, hourly rate, location, CSP, and processing time. The location consists of the triplet continent, region, and availability domain/zone.

The global expression of the total cost $(TC)$ is given by Eq. 1, where $Total\_OPCost$ is the total operational cost and $Total\_NCost$ is the total network cost.

$$TC = Total\_OPCost + Total\_NCost \qquad (1)$$

The total operational cost paid for hiring compute resources is expressed by:

$$Total\_OPCost = \sum_{VM \in N} processTime(VM) * hourrate(VM, location) \qquad (2)$$

where $processTime(VM)$ is the processing time of the considered VM and $hourrate$ its hourly rate. Note that a VM's hourly rate depends on its provider and location. For example, a VM launched in US-Ohio will not have the same price as one with the same characteristics launched in Asia Pacific-Tokyo.

The total network cost represents the cost for the volume of traffic exchanged between the VMs of a given architecture. This is expressed as follows:

$$Total\_NCost = \sum_{l \in L} dataRate(l) * cost\_per\_dataRate \qquad (3)$$

where $dataRate(l)$ is the volume of traffic exchanged on a unidirectional link $l$ separating two VMs of the graph, and $cost\_per\_dataRate$ is its data rate cost.

While Eq. 3 presents a fundamental formula for calculating network cost, the actual computation process is considerably more nuanced. The cost per data rate associated with each link in the cloud architecture is not a static value; rather, it fluctuates based on a confluence of factors. These factors include the specific CSPs that host the VMs at each end of the link, as well as the geographical distribution of these VMs across continents, regions, and availability zones. Moreover, in scenarios where communication occurs between VMs hosted by different CSPs, the volume of traffic exchanged becomes an additional factor that influences the cost per data rate.

This intricate interplay of variables, combined with the inherent complexity of network pricing structures, has led to the omission of network costs in a substantial number of existing cloud cost estimation tools. This omission, however, is a significant oversight, given the substantial impact that network costs can have on the overall financial outlay associated with cloud infrastructure. In contrast, our proposed estimator seeks to bridge this gap by incorporating a meticulous and comprehensive analysis of network cost invoicing practices employed by CSPs.

## 4  *PricingTheCloud* Implementation

Leveraging the aforementioned pricing specifics, we have formulated a generalized cost model and developed the requisite algorithms for our cloud cost estimator. The core engine of the estimator comprises three primary algorithms: total operational cost computation, total network cost computation, and total cost aggregation. The design of these algorithms has been guided by a thorough analysis of the unique pricing characteristics associated with major cloud providers, as discussed previously. These algorithms are described in detail below.

Algorithm 1 computes the total operational cost. Its input is a list of all the desired VMs along with their specified parameters. These parameters include CPU, memory, execution time, and CSP. Furthermore, each VM is associated with a dictionary detailing all its linked VMs and their respective data rates. The initial step involves matching the user's desired VM to the VMs available in the CSP database (line 5). It is important to note that the AWS CSP database, at the time of extraction, contained over 8,000 VM instance types across various regions, each with its distinct pricing characteristics. After filtering, the selected VM is added to a list of chosen VMs named *VMlist_afterDbSearch*. The list of chosen VMs is then taken as the input of the operational function to generate for each VM of the new list its operational cost following Eq. 2 (line 9). The result is summed up and the total operational cost is returned (line 11).

Algorithm 2 calculates the total network cost. It takes as input the list of VMs of the previous algorithm. For each VM, it retrieves all connections, and determines for each connection to which provider the two constitutive endpoints belong. Thus, depending on whether the two endpoint VMs belong to the same provider or not, the function encompassing the corresponding logic is called for

---

**Algorithm 1:** Total Operational Cost Computation Algorithm

---

**Data:**

$VM\_list$ : list of all the VMs of the desired architecture and their corresponding parameters;

$VMlist\_afterDbSearch$ : list of all the VMs after the pre-processing stage;

**Result:**

Total_OPCost : The total operational cost;

1 Begin

2 Total_OPCost = 0

3 $VMlist\_afterDbSearch = []$

4 **for** $(VM \in VM\_list)$ **do**

5     $chosen\_VM = findTheBestVm\_fromDb()$

6     $VMlist\_afterDbSearch+ = chosen\_VM$

7 **end**

8 **for** $(VM \in VMlist\_afterDbSearch)$ **do**

9     $VM\_OPCost = VM.hourrate * VM.processTime$

     Total_OPCost+ $= VM\_OPCost$

10 **end**

11 **return** Total_OPCost

---

execution and a network cost for that specific case is generated. The function getNCost_AWS_to_AWS() (line 5) is called if the two endpoint VMs belong to AWS, and getNCost_AWS_to_overseas() (line 7) if only the egress VM resides in AWS. Finally, the network costs computed at each level are aggregated.

The algorithm that computes the total cost is quite simple and will not be explicitly represented. It takes as input the results of algorithms 1 and 2 and generates the total cost by summing up those results following Eq. 1.

## 5 Evaluation

To evaluate *PricingTheCloud*, we benchmark its compute and network cost estimates against ground truth values derived from AWS invoices and against state-of-the-art commercial estimators *Cloudorado* [1], *Holori* [2], and *Vantage* [19]. It is worth mentioning that to the best of our knowledge, no other research paper has developed such an estimator for us to use as a baseline.

### 5.1 Accuracy Assessment Against AWS Invoices

A study we conducted allowed us to point out the fact that the cost of the assessed architecture also varies depending on the geographical position of the VMs in the architecture. Specifically, the network cost will then vary if the VMs are in the same region or not. The accuracy assessment needed to consider these potential variations to be efficient. For this purpose, our accuracy assessment is

---

**Algorithm 2:** Total Network Cost Computation Algorithm

---

**Data:**

$VM\_list$ : list of all the VMs of the graph and their corresponding parameters;

$link\_list$ : list of all the links between VMs and their corresponding data rate;

$VM_a$: the VM initiating the traffic (egress VM)

$VM_b$: the VM terminating the traffic (ingress VM)

**Result:**

NC : The total network cost;

1  Begin

2  $NC = 0$

3  **for** $(link \in link\_list)$ **do**

4  |    **if** $vm_a.CSP$ = "AWS" and $vm_b.CSP$ = "AWS" **then**

5  |    |    $NCost+ = getNCost\_AWS\_to\_AWS()$;

6  |    **else if** $vm_a.CSP$ = "AWS" and $vm_b.CSP$ != "AWS" **then**

7  |    |    $NCost+ = getNCost\_AWS\_to\_overseas()$ ;

8  |    **else**

9  |    |    print ("No such provider in our database")

10 |    **end**

11 **end**

12 **return** NCost

---

conducted following two different scenarios on the AWS platform. The first scenario evidences intra-regional intra-AD costs, and the second scenario evidences inter-regional costs. We hereafter present the two scenarios.

**Scenario 1: Intra-region, Intra-availability Domain.** In this first scenario, we concentrate all the tests in *us-east-1*, an AWS region in USA Ohio. We launch two VMs in the same availability domain (AD) called *us-east-2b*. The two VMs are *t2.micro* with 1v CPU, and 1GB memory. Each VM is launched with default storage capabilities (GP3 with 8 GB storage, 125 Mbps throughput, and 3000 IOPS), and runs Amazon Linux. To evaluate the network cost, we send traffic between the launched VMs using Iperf 3 [14]. This provided an estimate of the data rates required as input for *PricingTheCloud*. In this experiment, we transferred 46.7 GB of data at 111 Mbps for one hour between the client and server VMs, and then reversed the direction of the transfer for a similar duration.

**Scenario 2: Inter-region.** We launched two VMs, one in east coast USA ((us-east-2) called "VM_us_ohio", and the second in the UK (eu-west-2 ) called "VM_europe_london". Both VMs are t2 micro with default characteristics (1v CPU, 1 memory, 8 GB storage). Given the observed asymmetry in network pricing based on traffic origin, we evaluated network costs in both directions: USA to UK and vice versa. This assessment comprised two experimental steps:

**Table 1.** A summary of the results for estimating compute costs in USD ($). *PricingTheCloud* is the most accurate for the intra-region configuration, while Cloudorado offers better results for the inter-region configuration.

| Scenario | Element | AWS Invoices | Pricing TheCloud | Cloudorado | Holori | Vantage |
|---|---|---|---|---|---|---|
| **Scenario 1 Intra-Region** | VM_ohio_1 | 0.0100 | 0.0100 | 0.0900 | 0.0110 | 0.0116 |
| | VM_ohio_2 | 0.0100 | 0.0100 | 0.0900 | 0.0110 | 0.0116 |
| | **Total ($)** | 0.0200 | 0.0200 | 0.1800 | 0.0220 | 0.0232 |
| **Scenario 2 Inter-Region** | VM_ohio | 0.0563 | 0.0300 | 0.0900 | 0.0348 | 0.0396 |
| | VM_london | 0.0600 | 0.0400 | 0.0500 | 0.0396 | 0.0396 |
| | **Total ($)** | 0.1163 | 0.0700 | 0.1400 | 0.0744 | 0.0792 |

**Table 2.** A summary of the results for estimating network costs in USD. *PricingTheCloud* is the most accurate, while Cloudorado is the only other solution that offers network cost estimation but it is disproportionate.

| Scenario | Source | Destination | AWS Invoices | Pricing TheCloud | Cloudorado | Holori | Vantage |
|---|---|---|---|---|---|---|---|
| **Scenario 1 Intra-AD** | VM1_Ohio | VM2_Ohio | 0 | 0 | 4.455 | – | – |
| | VM2_Ohio | VM1_Ohio | 0 | 0 | 4.455 | – | – |
| | | **Total ($)** | 0 | 0 | 8.910 | – | – |
| **Scenario 3 Inter-Region** | VM_London | VM_Ohio | 0.9600 | 0.9300 | 8.9100 | – | – |
| | VM_Ohio | VM_London | 1.4900 | 1.4300 | 4.4100 | – | – |
| | | **Total ($)** | 2.4500 | 2.3600 | 13.3200 | – | – |

1. From UK London to US Ohio: "VM_europe_london" is configured as the client, and "VM_us_ohio" as the server. We send 45.7 GB of traffic during 1 h at 109 Mbps bitrate from "VM_europe_london" to "VM_us_ohio".
2. From US Ohio to UK London: At the end of the previous experiment, "VM_europe_london" becomes the server and "VM_us_ohio" becomes the client. We now send 71.5 GB of traffic at 85.3 Mbps bitrate. This second experiment is run for 2 hours.

The performance obtained from the above two scenarios is summarized in Tables 1 and 2. Specifically, Table 1 presents compute costs results obtained at the end of each scenario while Table 2 presents the network costs, against the real values obtained from AWS invoices in each case.

We can observe that for scenario 1, the compute costs for each VM involved in the represented architecture are similar. This is because the VMs are in the

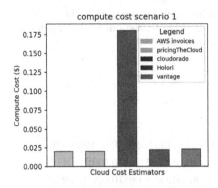

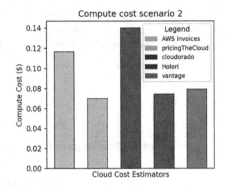

**Fig. 1.** Compute cost scenario 1          **Fig. 2.** Compute cost scenario 2

same region and run for the same duration. Moreover, we observe that the total compute costs generated by *pricingTheCloud* are similar to AWS costs because apart from launching the VMs, no other configuration is required. Concerning the network cost, we note that no network costs were generated throughout this experiment by either AWS or *pricingTheCloud* as neither charge for intra-availability domain traffic. In conclusion, our estimator is 100% accurate in predicting compute and network costs for intra-AD configurations.

Results obtained from scenario 2 show that compute costs generated by the AWS invoices are slightly higher ($0.1163) than those generated by *pricingThe-Cloud* ($0.07). This difference in prices can be explained by the fact that before launching the information exchange process between the two VMs involved in an inter-regional scenario, some configuration need to be applied such as creating a peering connection, configuring IP addresses, setting up a security group, etc. These phases are completed when the VMs are already launched, and thus the compute cost increases slightly due to the time taken for these configurations. In this specific case, *PricingTheCloud* is 60% accurate in predicting the compute costs. Concerning network costs, we observe a difference of $0.09 between AWS-generated network cost value and *pricingTheCloud*-generated value. Our estimator is then 96% accurate in predicting network costs in this case.

The above-presented results show that the developed estimator is 87% accurate on average in predicting compute costs for the two scenarios and 65% accurate on average in predicting network costs. In the following section, we compare the results of our estimator with three state-of-the-art estimators.

## 5.2   Efficiency Assessment: Comparison of *PricingTheCloud*'s Generated Results with Other Estimators

Figures 1, 2, 3 and 4 depict how *PricingTheCloud* performs as compared to three state-of-the-art commercial estimators, namely Cloudorado, Vantage, and Holori. The figures respectively show the total compute costs and the total network costs for each of the aforesaid scenarios.

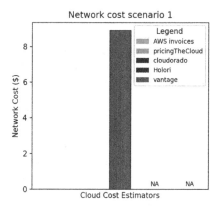
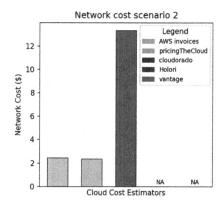

**Fig. 3.** Network cost scenario 1          **Fig. 4.** Network cost scenario 2

As far as total compute costs are concerned, we observe that *PricingTheCloud*, Holori and Vantage generate very similar results for scenario 1, with accuracies of 100%, 90%, and 84%, respectively, when compared to AWS invoices. However, Cloudorado generates a wildly inflated compute cost. For scenario 2 (inter-regional costs), the values generated by Cloudorado, Holori and Vantage are closer to that in AWS invoices.

Specifically, Cloudorado estimates compute cost with an accuracy of 80%, Holori with 64% and Vantage with 68%. However, *PricingTheCloud*'s costs are only 60% accurate and is thus less effective at computing compute costs in the inter-regional scenario.

Turning to network costs, Holori and Vantage are not able to produce any estimates as they do not take this functionality into account. Their missing values are denoted as "–" in the table and "**NA**" in the graphs. Cloudorado's estimates are grossly inflated, similar to its compute costs in scenario 1. *PricingTheCloud* is the most effective at predicting network costs with an accuracy of 100% in scenario 1 and 96% in scenario 2

## 6    Limitations and Threats to Validity

### 6.1    Limitations

Our experiments have demonstrated the accuracy and potential of *PricingTheCloud* as a tool for estimating cloud costs. However, like any nascent research, this study has limitations that deserve discussion.

First, we acknowledge that our evaluation focused exclusively on on-demand VMs from AWS, excluding other providers and pricing models. Specifically, we have not yet considered dynamic pricing options such as Spot instances, sustained use discounts, committed resources, or upfront payments. Thus, our current model reflects the specific pricing structures in effect at the time of this study, which may evolve and necessitate updates to the underlying codebase.

Despite these limitations, our work represents a significant step forward in accurate cloud cost estimation, particularly in the crucial area of network costs, which are often neglected by existing tools as shown by our research. Further research will expand the model's scope and enhance its robustness to pricing fluctuations, ultimately providing a more comprehensive and adaptable solution for cloud resource planning.

### 6.2   Threats to Validity

We now discuss potential threats to the validity of our study, particularly in terms of generalizability and trustworthiness.

**Construct.** The study focused on a specific set of workloads. The estimator's accuracy for workloads with different resource requirements might vary. Future work should investigate a broader range of workloads. Additionally, as discussed under limitations, the study evaluated the estimator on one major CSP. Since cost structures and pricing models can vary significantly across providers, further research is needed to assess generalizability to other cloud platforms.

**Internal.** The accuracy of the cost estimates depended on invoice data, which serves as the ground truth, ensuring minimal risk of inaccuracy or bias.

**External.** Similar to any other study, our work has certain limitations, including application architectures. These may not have captured the full spectrum of cloud computing usage scenarios, which could somewhat limit the generalizability of our findings.

## 7   Conclusion

We have proposed a new estimator to enable companies to estimate their costs before migrating to the cloud. The proposed estimator allows CSPs to have a clear estimate of their costs before migrating to the cloud. Experiments to date have been satisfactory, with an average accuracy of 86.73% for compute costs and 65.44% for network costs in different AWS-to-AWS scenarios. Furthermore, experiments show that the estimator is more efficient than three other available estimators in predicting costs in different scenarios. For future work, we plan to develop the estimation for inter-availability domain network costs and improve storage estimates. We also plan to experiment with other CSPs such as Azure and Google, and explore multi-cloud deployments.

## References

1. Cloud Computing Price Comparison — Cloudorado - Find Best Cloud Server from Top Cloud Computing Companies. https://www.cloudorado.com/
2. Holori - End-to-end multi cloud management platform. https://holori.com/
3. Use the BMC Helix Cloud Migration Simulator - BMC Software. https://www.bmc.com/forms/helix-cloud-migration-simulator-trial.html

4. Al Hadwer, A., Tavana, M., Gillis, D., Rezania, D.: A systematic review of organizational factors impacting cloud-based technology adoption using technology-organization-environment framework. Internet Things **15**, 100407 (2021). https://doi.org/10.1016/j.iot.2021.100407

5. Aldossary, M., Djemame, K.: Energy-based cost model of virtual machines in a cloud environment. In: 5th International Symposium on Innovation in Information and Communication Technology (ISIICT), pp. 1–8 (2018). https://doi.org/10.1109/ISIICT.2018.8613288

6. Brumec, S., Vrček, N.: Cost effectiveness of commercial computing clouds. Inf. Syst. **38**(4), 495–508 (2013). https://doi.org/10.1016/j.is.2012.11.002, special section on BPM 2011 conference

7. Cho, K., Bahn, H.: A cost estimation model for cloud services and applying to PC laboratory platforms. Processes **8**(1) (2020). https://doi.org/10.3390/pr8010076

8. Elhabbash, A., Samreen, F., Hadley, J., Elkhatib, Y.: Cloud brokerage: a systematic survey. Comput. Surv. **51**(6), 119:1–119:28 (2019). https://doi.org/10.1145/3274657

9. Elkhatib, Y., Samreen, F., Blair, G.S.: Same same, but different: a descriptive intra-IaaS differentiation. In: 19th IEEE/ACM International Symposium on Cluster, Cloud and Grid Computing (CCGrid), pp. 690–695 (2019). https://doi.org/10.1109/CCGRID.2019.00089

10. FLEXERA: State-of-the-cloud report 2022 (2022). https://info.flexera.com/CM-REPORT-State-of-the-Cloud

11. Khan, A.Q., Matskin, M., Prodan, R., Bussler, C., Roman, D., Soylu, A.: Cloud storage cost: a taxonomy and survey. World Wide Web **27**(4), 36 (2024). https://doi.org/10.1007/s11280-024-01273-4

12. Kratzke, N.: Cloud computing costs and benefits. In: Ivanov, I., van Sinderen, M., Shishkov, B. (eds.) CLOSER 2011. SSRISE, pp. 185–203. Springer, New York (2012). https://doi.org/10.1007/978-1-4614-2326-3_10

13. Makhlouf, R.R.M.: Cloud computing: developing a cost estimation model for customers. Ph.D. thesis, BTU Cottbus - Senftenberg (2023). https://doi.org/10.26127/BTUOpen-6284

14. Mortimer, M.: iperf3 (2018). https://github.com/thiezn/iperf3-python

15. Nicolas, R., Pat, M.: EC2 instance timeline. https://instancetyp.es/

16. RENO, N.: cloud infrastructure services market. Tech. rep., SGR (2022). https://www.srgresearch.com/

17. Samreen, F., Blair, G.S., Elkhatib, Y.: Transferable knowledge for low-cost decision making in cloud environments. Trans. Cloud Comput. **10**, 2190–2203 (2022). https://doi.org/10.1109/TCC.2020.2989381

18. Tian, J., Elhabbash, A., Elkhatib, Y.: Predicting cloud performance using real-time VM-level metrics. In: International Conference on High Performance Computing and Communications (HPCC). IEEE (2022). https://doi.org/10.1109/HPCC-DSS-SmartCity-DependSys57074.2022.00184

19. VNTG Inc.: Vantage: understand your cloud costs. https://www.vantage.sh/

# Innovating Letter-of-Credit Mechanisms: The Integration of RSA-Encrypted NFTs for Enhanced Security and Efficiency

L. K. Bang[1]($\boxtimes$), H. V. Khanh[1], M. N. Triet[1], N. N. Hung[1], T. N. Vinh[2], H. N. Kha[1], V. N. Minh[1], and K. T. N. Ngan[2]

[1] FPT University, Can Tho, Vietnam
{banglkce160155,khanhce171115,hungnnce171478,minhnvce171866}@fpt.edu.vn,
{nganntkpc06789,KhanhVH}@fe.edu.vn
[2] FPT Polytechnic, Can Tho, Vietnam
{vinhntce171035,nganntkpc06789}@fpt.edu.vn

**Abstract.** This paper presents a groundbreaking approach to modernizing the Letter-of-Credit (L/C) process in trade finance by integrating RSA-Encrypted Non-Fungible Tokens (NFTs). Addressing the prevalent challenges of fraud, privacy concerns, and operational inefficiencies in traditional L/C mechanisms, our research proposes a robust, transparent, and efficient framework. Building upon the advancements in blockchain technology and smart contracts, we introduce a dual-layered security strategy combining RSA encryption with the unique characteristics of NFTs. This integration ensures the secure encryption of trade documents, accessible only to authorized parties, and leverages blockchain's immutability to create a transparent, tamper-evident record of document ownership and verification. Our approach not only enhances the security and privacy aspects of trade finance but also introduces significant improvements in efficiency through the automation of verification and settlement processes via smart contracts. This paper discusses how our innovative framework sets a new standard in international trade finance, promising a more secure, efficient, and reliable L/C transaction.

**Keywords:** International trade · Blockchain · Smart contract · RSA-Encrypted NFT, Ethereum · Fantom · BNB Smart Chain

## 1 Introduction

Trade finance is undergoing a transformative phase, propelled by advancements in blockchain technology and smart contracts. The need for secure, transparent, and efficient mechanisms in international trade, especially within the letter-of-credit (L/C) framework, has never been more pronounced. Current methodologies, while robust, present several challenges, including fraud risk, privacy concerns, and operational inefficiencies. In light of this, our paper titled "Innovating Letter-of-Credit Mechanisms: The Integration of RSA-Encrypted NFTs

© The Author(s), under exclusive license to Springer Nature Switzerland AG 2025
M. Naldi et al. (Eds.): GECON 2024, LNCS 15358, pp. 112–122, 2025.
https://doi.org/10.1007/978-3-031-81226-2_11

for Enhanced Security and Efficiency" seeks to address these challenges by introducing a novel integration of RSA-encrypted Non-Fungible Tokens (NFTs) into the L/C process.

Building on this narrative, Ha et al. [5] introduced a decentralized marketplace mechanism that negates the need for a trusted third party, thus enhancing the trust and privacy in commercial transactions. Their work is a testament to the potential of blockchain technology in mitigating privacy risks and points of failure associated with traditional intermediaries. In the broader context of e-commerce, the SSSB system proposed by Quoc et al. [13] addresses the problems of transportation reliability and information latency, while also providing dispute resolution mechanisms—an essential feature for cross-border trade.

The pursuit of efficiency and reliability in e-commerce and delivery systems has also been explored by Madhwal et al. [10], who delve into the use of smart contracts for the management of Proof of Delivery processes. Their insights on the potential for transaction cost reduction and the need for blockchain systems to handle off-chain transactions pave the way for our proposed solution, which aims to streamline the L/C process further. Drawing inspiration from these seminal works, our research contributes to the field by not only emphasizing the efficiency and transparency afforded by blockchain and smart contracts but also by significantly bolstering the security aspect. The integration of RSA-Encrypted NFTs in the L/C process ensures the confidentiality and integrity of trade documents, mitigating the risks of unauthorized access and document tampering. This dual-layered security approach—combining RSA encryption with the inherent benefits of NFTs on the blockchain—provides an innovative leap forward in the realm of trade finance, setting a new standard for security and privacy in international trade transactions.

Our contribution to the field of trade finance is a pioneering framework that enhances the Letter-of-Credit (L/C) process with the integration of RSA-Encrypted Non-Fungible Tokens (NFTs), targeting the enduring challenges of security and privacy. By employing RSA encryption, our model ensures that trade documents are securely encrypted, making them accessible solely to entities with the corresponding decryption keys, thus addressing privacy concerns. The encapsulation of these documents within NFTs leverages blockchain's immutability, providing a transparent and tamper-evident ledger of document verification and ownership. This integration not only fortifies the trustworthiness of the L/C process but also streamlines it, as smart contracts automate and expedite the verification and settlement stages.

## 2 Related Work

### 2.1 Blockchain in Cash-on-Delivery Systems

The domain of smart contracts in trade finance has seen significant development aimed at enhancing transaction security and reliability. Son et al. [14] propose a blockchain-based smart contract mechanism to protect the seller's interests in cash-on-delivery systems, which are prevalent in cash-based economies [3].

Their system is designed to enforce specific delivery times, costs, and mortgage money, ensuring accountability for all parties. Similarly, Le et al. [9] introduce a double smart contract framework to assure non-fraudulent transactions in cash-on-delivery scenarios, mitigating risks by requiring both shippers and buyers to place a mortgage. This approach prevents fraudulent activities and safeguards sellers' interests by imposing penalties to deter buyers from unjustly refusing commodities and shippers from tampering with goods in transit. Addressing the challenges of creating highly trustworthy cash-on-delivery systems, Ha et al. [5] present an innovative decentralized marketplace mechanism that incentivizes honest behavior without a trusted third party and incorporates access control protocols to protect user privacy. Ngamsuriyaroj [12] and Hasan [7] further enhance COD systems and package delivery by leveraging blockchain technology to improve data integrity and user verification through decentralized proof of delivery systems using Ethereum smart contracts, offering tamper-proof solutions for tracking the delivery of physical assets and ensuring accountability and integrity throughout the delivery process. These studies collectively contribute to the development of secure and reliable trade finance mechanisms via smart contracts, reflecting a shift towards more decentralized, transparent, and accountable commercial transactions.

## 2.2    Blockchain and Smart Contracts in E-Commerce

In the realm of e-commerce and delivery systems, security, trust, and transparency are paramount. Quoc et al. [13] introduce the Safe Seller Safe Buyer (SSSB) system, a smart contract-based approach that leverages blockchain technology to address issues like transportation reliability and information latency in cross-border trade transactions. The SSSB framework establishes clear rules and policies during order and package creation, aiding in dispute resolution and enforcing penalty fees for contract violations. Ha et al. [6] further scrutinize trust and transparency in cash-on-delivery systems, proposing a blockchain-based system using Hyperledger Composer to eliminate the need for a trusted third party and reduce costs. Madhwal et al. [10] extend blockchain technology to Proof of Delivery (PoD) processes, developing an open-source system to enhance delivery efficiency and reliability, applying Transaction Costs theory to highlight potential cost reductions. Collectively, these studies underscore the potential of blockchain and smart contracts to enhance e-commerce and delivery system trustworthiness and efficiency. Our work advances this field by incorporating RSA encryption with NFTs to fortify the Letter-of-Credit process against fraud and privacy breaches, addressing crucial security gaps while maintaining transactional efficiency. The exploration of blockchain and smart contracts in e-commerce encompasses various dimensions and applications. Blockchain solutions to the letter-of-credit problem highlight innovations in trade finance, enhancing transparency and efficiency in e-commerce transactions [2]. A systematic literature review provides a comprehensive overview of existing applications, addressing identity verification and transaction management [8]. The impact of blockchain on e-commerce is assessed, showcasing its transformative potential in enhancing trust and operational efficiency [4]. In logistics, blockchain-based smart contracts offer significant improvements in transparency, security, and sustainability, crucial for e-commerce supply chains [1]. Additionally, decentralized reputation systems enabled by smart contracts aim to mitigate fraudulent activities and build trust among stakeholders in e-commerce environments [11].

## 3   Approach

### 3.1   Letter-of-Credit (L/C) Traditional Model

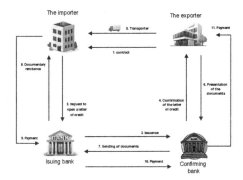

**Fig. 1.** Traditional Letter-of-Credit Transaction Process

Figure 1 presents a comprehensive depiction of the traditional letter-of-credit transaction process, which serves as a critical financial instrument in international trade. This process is designed to reduce the risk between trading partners or counterparts, namely the importer and exporter, and involves multiple steps facilitated primarily through two banking institutions.

At the inception of the transaction, we have the importer and exporter agreeing on a contract (1), signifying their intent to engage in the trade of goods or services. This contractual agreement lays the foundation for the subsequent financial interactions and is a pivotal point that necessitates a high level of trust between the two parties. Following the contract agreement, the importer initiates the process by applying for a letter of credit at their bank, known as the issuing bank (2). This application signifies the importer's request for the bank to guarantee payment to the exporter, provided that the terms stipulated in the letter of credit are met. Upon the importer's request, the issuing bank proceeds to open a letter of credit (3), which is then forwarded to the exporter's bank, referred to as the confirming bank. The confirmation of the letter of credit (4) by the confirming bank assures the exporter that payment will be received under the terms of the credit. This assurance is crucial as it mitigates the risk the exporter bears in sending goods to the importer without any guarantee.

Subsequently, the goods are dispatched by the exporter via a transporter (5), and upon shipment, the exporter presents the necessary shipping documents to the confirming bank (6). These documents are evidence that the goods have been sent as per the agreement, and it is imperative that they match the terms of the letter of credit to ensure that the payment obligation is triggered. The confirming bank reviews the documents for compliance and, once satisfied, sends the documents to the issuing bank (7). This transfer is known as documentary remittance (8) and is a critical step in ensuring that the issuing bank has all the necessary paperwork to authorize payment. Upon receipt and verification of the documents, the issuing bank releases the payment to the confirming bank (9), which in turn makes the payment to the exporter (10). Finally, the exporter receives the payment (11), concluding the transaction. The letter-of-credit process not only facilitates the smooth execution of payment upon fulfillment of the contractual obligations but also instills confidence in the international trade ecosystem by reducing the risk of non-payment and non-receipt of goods. This traditional model, while effective, involves several intermediary steps and parties, each of which introduces potential delays and costs, highlighting the opportunity for innovation and improvement through technologies such as blockchain (Fig. 2).

## 3.2   Phase 1: Contract Initiation and Digital Synchronization

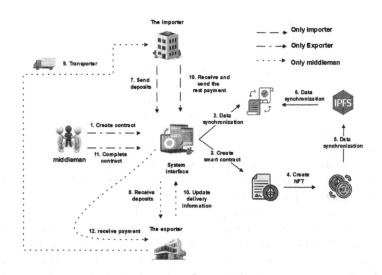

**Fig. 2.** Decentralized Trade Finance Model Utilizing Blockchain and NFTs.

The figure illustrates a cutting-edge decentralized model for trade finance that leverages blockchain technology, smart contracts, and Non-Fungible Tokens (NFTs) to streamline traditional processes. This proposed architecture offers a solution to the current system's inefficiencies by introducing a seamless, transparent, and secure mechanism for conducting trade transactions.

In this model, the initiation of a trade deal commences with the creation of a digital contract by the intermediary, which is subsequently synchronized with the system interface (1, 2). This synchronization ensures that all parties, including the importer and the exporter, have real-time access to the contract terms. The creation of a smart contract (3) is pivotal as it encapsulates the trade agreement's conditions and executes automatically upon the fulfillment of predefined criteria, thereby minimizing the need for manual intervention and reducing the potential for disputes. Furthermore, the innovative use of NFTs to digitize trade documents (4) introduces an unparalleled level of security and authenticity to the transaction process. These NFTs, stored on the blockchain, are immutable and easily verifiable, ensuring that documents cannot be tampered with or replicated fraudulently. Data synchronization steps (5, 6) across the blockchain network facilitate the real-time updating and verification of transaction information, allowing all parties to monitor progress and maintain transparency.

The importer and exporter interact with the system through deposits and payments (7, 8, 10, 12), with the blockchain providing a secure and efficient medium for the transfer of funds. This minimizes the dependency on traditional banking channels, reducing transaction times and costs. The transporter, integral to the physical movement of goods, is also integrated into the system (9), with delivery updates reflected in the blockchain, thus enabling dynamic updating of delivery information (10). Upon the successful delivery and verification of goods, the smart contract triggers the final settlement (11, 12). This automated process ensures that the exporter receives payment swiftly and securely, closing the loop on the transaction. The entire process is underpinned by the IPFS, which provides a distributed storage solution to host the transaction data, enhancing accessibility and durability.

### 3.3    Phase 2: Secure Exchange of RSA-Encrypted NFT Mechanism

The Fig. 3 illustrates the sophisticated RSA-Encrypted NFT architecture, a significant component in the second phase of a blockchain-based trade finance solution. This phase encapsulates the secure exchange of contractual agreements between the importer and exporter, facilitated through a series of cryptographic transactions that ensure both the confidentiality and the integrity of the trade documents. At the core of this system lies the use of RSA encryption, a public-key cryptosystem that is widely recognized for its security, which encrypts the sale contract document. Public keys, labeled as A and B in the diagram, correspond to the respective parties—the importer and the exporter. When the sale contract is created, it is encrypted with the exporter's public key (public key B). This encrypted document can only be decrypted by the corresponding private key, which is securely held by the exporter, ensuring that only the intended recipient can access the sensitive contract details. Subsequent to the encryption, the sale contract is linked to an NFT, creating an indelible record of the contract's issuance and its terms on the blockchain. This NFT, acting as a digital certificate

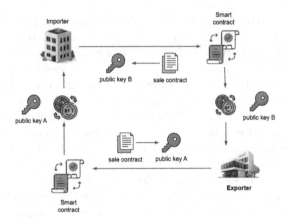

**Fig. 3.** Decentralized Trade Finance Model Utilizing Blockchain and NFTs.

of authenticity, ensures that the contract cannot be altered without detection, as each modification would require a new transaction on the blockchain, which is a transparent and tamper-evident process.

The smart contract, which is another crucial element of the architecture, acts autonomously to facilitate, verify, or enforce the negotiation or performance of the contract. It carries out pre-programmed instructions dependent on certain conditions, such as the confirmation of payment or receipt of goods, and is instrumental in reducing the need for intermediaries, thereby streamlining the transaction process. Once the NFT representing the sale contract is created and stored on the blockchain, it undergoes a synchronization process with the smart contract. This synchronization ensures that the terms encoded in the smart contract reflect the agreement detailed within the NFT-encrypted sale contract. Through this mechanism, the smart contract is effectively 'aware' of the contractual obligations and can execute the respective clauses upon the satisfaction of the agreed-upon terms.

## 4   Evaluation

### 4.1   Evaluating of the RSA-Encrypted NFT Framework

To evaluate the performance of our RSA-Encrypted NFT framework, we conducted experiments focusing on three key processes: generating RSA keys, encrypting, and decrypting. The tests were performed for two different scenarios: encrypting a 120 KB image and encrypting the text "Hello, RSA encryption!" The results, presented in tables, provide insights into the efficiency and effectiveness of our encryption and decryption mechanism.

For the image encryption scenario, the time taken for generating RSA keys varied, with an average of approximately 2537 milliseconds (ms). The encryption process showed a faster performance, averaging around 1136 ms. However, the decryption process took the longest time, with an average of around 3387 ms. The variation in times for key generation and decryption processes suggests that the complexity and size of the image significantly influence the performance (Table 1).

**Table 1.** Performance Metrics for RSA Key Generation, Encryption, and Decryption in Image Processing Scenario

| RSA with image(ms) | 1 | 2 | 3 | 4 | 5 | 6 | 7 | 8 | 9 | 10 |
|---|---|---|---|---|---|---|---|---|---|---|
| Generating RSA key | 2330 | 2206 | 2750 | 2314 | 2480 | 2218 | 2526 | 3790 | 2773 | 2378 |
| Encrypting image | 1436 | 848 | 913 | 890 | 1141 | 1422 | 1025 | 1036 | 1397 | 1355 |
| Decrypting image | 3234 | 3946 | 3337 | 3796 | 3379 | 3360 | 2449 | 3174 | 3830 | 3267 |

In the text encryption scenario, the RSA key generation times were slightly more consistent, averaging around 2453 ms, showing a comparable performance to the image scenario. The encryption times for the text were generally faster, averaging around 1161 ms. The decryption times for text were also high (around 3480 ms), which is consistent with the trend observed in the image scenario (Table 2).

**Table 2.** RSA Encryption Process Times for Text Data Across Multiple Trials

| RSA with Text(ms) | 1 | 2 | 3 | 4 | 5 | 6 | 7 | 8 | 9 | 10 |
|---|---|---|---|---|---|---|---|---|---|---|
| Generating RSA key | 2332 | 2257 | 2368 | 2259 | 2866 | 2736 | 2442 | 1947 | 2689 | 2151 |
| Encrypting Text | 1496 | 933 | 1363 | 1523 | 888 | 781 | 1483 | 825 | 1030 | 1520 |
| Decrypting Text | 3172 | 3810 | 3269 | 3218 | 4246 | 3483 | 4075 | 3228 | 3281 | 3329 |

Analyzing these results, it is evident that the RSA encryption process is more efficient for smaller data sizes, as seen in the text encryption scenario. However, the decryption process is consistently the most time-consuming step in both scenarios. This could be attributed to the computational complexity involved in decrypting data encrypted using RSA, which tends to increase with the size and complexity of the data. The key generation process, while relatively time-consuming, is a one-time process and does not significantly impact the overall efficiency of the system in real-world applications where keys can be reused. The encryption times are reasonably efficient, demonstrating the feasibility of our approach for real-time applications.

In conclusion, our RSA-Encrypted NFT framework shows promising results in terms of performance, particularly for smaller data sizes. The longer decryption times indicate a need for optimization, especially for larger data sets. However, considering the enhanced security and privacy this framework offers, the trade-off in decryption time could be acceptable in scenarios where security is of paramount importance. Future work could focus on optimizing the decryption process and exploring the scalability of the system for larger data sets to enhance its applicability in a broader range of trade finance scenarios.

## 4.2 Cost-Effectiveness in Deploying RSA-Encrypted NFTs

In our study, we evaluated the deployment of smart contracts on several leading Ethereum Virtual Machine (EVM)-compatible platforms known for their cost-effectiveness and blockchain prowess. Platforms such as Binance Smart Chain (BNB Smart Chain), Polygon, Fantom, and Celo were selected for their unique balance of compatibility, cost efficiency, and network innovation. These platforms provide an ideal testing ground for our RSA-encrypted NFT framework, specifically tailored for the nuanced requirements of Letter-of-Credit transactions in the global trade finance sector.

Our research primarily focused on the deployment of smart contracts and their subsequent operations, including transaction creation, NFT minting, and transfer processes, within the context of Letter-of-Credit transactions. Such operations are critical to the integrity and practical application of our encrypted NFTs in real-world trade finance scenarios.

Considering the economic implications is essential when integrating blockchain technologies into commercial applications, especially within the Letter-of-Credit framework. We conducted an exhaustive comparative analysis of the costs associated with deploying smart contracts and executing their primary functions across the selected blockchain platforms. This economic analysis is a cornerstone in evaluating the financial sustainability of implementing our RSA-encrypted NFT mechanism across various blockchain infrastructures.

**Table 3.** Transaction fee

|  | Contract Creation | Create NFT | Transfer NFT |
|---|---|---|---|
| BNB Smart Chain | 0.027311 BNB ($8.33) | 0.00109162 BNB ($0.33) | 0.00056991 BNB ($0.17) |
| Fantom | 0.0095767 FTM ($0.003) | 0.000405167 FTM ($0.000127) | 0.0002380105 FTM ($0.000075) |
| Polygon | 0.0068405000328344 MATIC($0.01) | 0.000289405001273382 MATIC($0.00) | 0.000170007500748033 MATIC($0.00) |
| Celo | 0.00709722 CELO ($0.004 ) | 0.0002840812 CELO ($0.000 ) | 0.0001554878 CELO ($0.000 ) |

Through this meticulous evaluation, we identified Fantom as the most economically viable platform for our purposes (Table 3). The transaction fees on Fantom were significantly lower than those on the other platforms, as detailed in our comparative findings. This economical advantage makes Fantom an attractive option for facilitating Letter-of-Credit transactions via our smart contract framework, given the need for frequent and cost-effective operations in trade finance.

# 5   Conclusion

In conclusion, our paper contributes in the field of trade finance. By integrating RSA-Encrypted NFTs into the L/C process, we address longstanding issues in security and privacy, bringing a much-needed transformation to traditional trade finance mechanisms. Our solution leverages the strengths of blockchain technology, including its transparency and immutability, and combines them with the robust security offered by RSA encryption. The resultant framework not only secures sensitive trade documents but also enhances the overall efficiency and reliability of the L/C process. This innovative approach paves the way for a new era in trade finance, marked by heightened security, improved operational efficiency, and reinforced trust among international trade participants. Our work demonstrates the potential of combining cutting-edge technologies like blockchain and encryption to revolutionize traditional financial processes, setting a benchmark for future innovations in the domain of international trade finance.

# References

1. Chauhdary, S.H., Saleem, S.: Use of blockchain-based smart contracts in logistics and supply chains. Electronics **12**, 1340 (2023)
2. Doe, J., Smith, J.: Blockchain solutions to the letter-of-credit problem. J. Blockchain Res. (2023)
3. Duong-Trung, N., et al.: Multi-sessions mechanism for decentralized cash on delivery system. Int. J. Adv. Comput. Sci. Appl. **10**(9), 553–560 (2019)
4. Green, M., White, L.: The impact of blockchain on e-commerce. E-Commerce Technol. Rev. **48**, 101054 (2021)
5. Ha, X.S., et al.: DeM-CoD: novel access-control-based cash on delivery mechanism for decentralized marketplace. In: 2020 IEEE 19th International Conference on Trust, Security and Privacy in Computing and Communications (TrustCom), pp. 71–78. IEEE (2020)
6. Ha, X.S., Le, T.H., Phan, T.T., Nguyen, H.H.D., Vo, H.K., Duong-Trung, N.: Scrutinizing trust and transparency in cash on delivery systems. In: Wang, G., Chen, B., Li, W., Di Pietro, R., Yan, X., Han, H. (eds.) SpaCCS 2020. LNCS, vol. 12382, pp. 214–227. Springer, Cham (2021). https://doi.org/10.1007/978-3-030-68851-6_15
7. Hasan, H.R., Salah, K.: Blockchain-based proof of delivery of physical assets with single and multiple transporters. IEEE Access **6**, 46781–46793 (2018)
8. Johnson, A., Brown, B.: A systematic literature review of blockchain and smart contract applications. Int. J. Blockchain Appl. **174**, 110891 (2022)
9. Le, N.T.T., et al.: Assuring non-fraudulent transactions in cash on delivery by introducing double smart contracts. Int. J. Adv. Comput. Sci. Appl. **10**(5), 677–684 (2019)
10. Madhwal, et al.: Proof of delivery smart contract for performance measurements. IEEE Access **10**, 69147–69159 (2022)
11. Kugblenu, C., Vuorimaa, P., Keller, B.: Smart contract enabled decentralized reputation system for E-Commerce reviews. In: Koucheryavy, Y., Balandin, S., Andreev, S. (eds.) NEW2AN/ruSMART -2021. LNCS, vol. 13158, pp. 22–34. Springer, Cham (2022). https://doi.org/10.1007/978-3-030-97777-1_3

12. Ngamsuriyaroj, S., et al.: Package delivery system based on blockchain infrastructure. In: 2018 Seventh ICT International Student Project Conference (ICT-ISPC) (2018)

13. Quoc, K.L., et al.: Sssb: An approach to insurance for cross-border exchange by using smart contracts. In: Awan, I., Younas, M., Poniszewska-Marańda, A. (eds.) Mobile Web and Intelligent Information Systems: 18th International Conference, vol 13475. pp. 179–192. Springer, Cham (2022). https://doi.org/10.1007/978-3-031-14391-5_14

14. Son, H.X., et al.: Towards a mechanism for protecting seller's interest of cash on delivery by using smart contract in hyperledger. Int. J. Adv. Comput. Sci. Appl. **10**(4) (2019)

# Enhancing Transparency and Ethical Sourcing in Handicraft Supply Chains Through Blockchain, Smart Contracts, NFTs, and IPFS Integration

P. H. T. Trung[1(✉)], N. N. Hung[1], T. D. Khoa[1], H. G. Khiem[1], N. T. Anh[1], V. C. P. Loc[1], T. B. Nam[1], and N. T. K. Ngan[2]

[1] FPT University, Can Tho, Vietnam
{Trungpht,hungnnce171478,khoatdce160367,KhiemHGCE160922,anhntce16023, locvcpce16030,namtbce161036}@fe.edu.vn
[2] FPT Polytecnic, Can Tho, Vietnam
nganntkpc06789@fe.edu.vn

**Abstract.** This paper discusses a framework for supply chain management in the handicraft industry, aiming to address the challenges of transparency and ethical sourcing. We introduce a system that integrates blockchain technology, smart contracts, Non-Fungible Tokens (NFTs), and the InterPlanetary File System (IPFS) to enhance the traceability and integrity of handicraft supply chains from creation to consumer. The study reviews related work that demonstrates the importance of blockchain for trust and transparent practices within supply chains. Our methodology was tested across multiple EVM-compatible platforms, examining the operational performance and economic feasibility of the system. The results of these tests inform our analysis of the system's functionality in terms of transaction speed, cost efficiency, and reliability in data management. Our findings indicate that the proposed framework can significantly contribute to the handicraft industry by providing a transparent, reliable, and efficient approach to supply chain management.

**Keywords:** Handicrafts Supply Chain · Blockchain · Smart Contracts · NFTs · IPFS

## 1 Introduction

The handicraft industry, characterized by its diverse and intricate supply chains, often encounters challenges in maintaining transparency and ethical sourcing due to the lack of complete traceability [13,20]. Traditional supply chain structures, extending from artisan creation to consumer purchase, frequently struggle to provide the necessary visibility and assurance required to uphold ethical standards [7,8]. The implementation of blockchain technology, along with the strategic use of smart contracts, Non-Fungible Tokens (NFTs), and the InterPlanetary File

© The Author(s), under exclusive license to Springer Nature Switzerland AG 2025
M. Naldi et al. (Eds.): GECON 2024, LNCS 15358, pp. 123–133, 2025.
https://doi.org/10.1007/978-3-031-81226-2_12

System (IPFS), presents a potential framework for addressing these issues [17]. By integrating these technologies, we aim to construct a supply chain management system specifically for the handicraft sector, which is designed to bolster transparency and ensure the integrity of data throughout the entire chain of custody.

Research by Le et al. and Ha et al. has shed light on the capacity of blockchain to bolster trust and facilitate transparent practices, which are critical to the integrity of supply chains and the principle of fair trade [9,12]. Work by Dietrich et al. and Shahid et al. expands on these findings, illustrating how smart contracts can reduce risks and improve traceability, a feature that is particularly relevant to the intricacies of handicraft production. The concept of integrating 'virtual operations' into supply chain management, as explored by Dolgui et al., and the convergence of blockchain with IoT for monitoring by Hasan et al., have been identified as progressive steps toward more dynamic and transparent supply chain systems. Collectively, these studies highlight the promise of blockchain and related technologies in transforming the management of supply chains by enhancing transparency and trust among stakeholders.

Our approach is designed to cater to the specificities of the handicraft supply chain, employing smart contracts, NFTs, and IPFS to build a cohesive management system. This system is engineered to document and safeguard the integrity and transparency of the data from the artisan's workspace to the end-user. It addresses the particular challenges of the handicraft sector, with a strong focus on traceability and ethical sourcing. By integrating IPFS with blockchain, our system ensures the durability and fidelity of supply chain records, overcoming the challenges of scalability and data integrity highlighted by Pawar et al. and enhancing trust and authenticity in line with the findings of Hawashin et al. [11,15]. Anchored by distributed ledger technology, the platform serves as a dependable ledger for all recorded transactions, providing stakeholders with consistent and accurate data, thereby fostering a transparent, responsive, and fair supply chain environment.

Our system was subjected to rigorous testing on several EVM-compatible platforms, including Binance Smart Chain, Polygon, Fantom, and Celo, to assess its capability to support the handicraft supply chain. During these tests, we focused on critical functions such as recording supply chain information, minting NFTs for product traceability, and transferring NFTs for secure data circulation. The findings provided us with a comprehensive understanding of how the system performs in terms of transaction speed, resource utilization, and overall reliability. A review of the transaction costs associated with each platform also offered insight into the economic aspects of the system, highlighting the potential for reducing expenses and enhancing the efficiency of supply chain operations within the handicraft industry.

# 2   Related Work

## 2.1   Sustainable Supply Chain and Transparency

The significance of blockchain technology in advancing sustainable supply chain management is well-documented in recent research. Saberi et al. delve into how blockchain can bolster trust and authenticate sustainable practices across supply chains, underscoring its role in enhancing transparency [18]. In a similar vein, Yoo et al. examine the mechanisms for transparent pricing within supply chains, which are vital for the verification of fair trade practices, further highlighting the utility of blockchain in ensuring fairness and transparency in supply chain operations [21].

The application of smart contracts within blockchain frameworks is explored by Dietrich et al., who argue that such technology can significantly reduce supply chain risks, thereby contributing to the overall sustainability of these networks [5]. This notion is echoed in the work of Shahid et al., who present a blockchain-based model specifically tailored for the agri-food sector, aimed at achieving traceability from the point of production to the end consumer [19]. Further contributions to this field include Alvarado et al., who view blockchain as a pivotal technology for achieving greater transparency in supply chains, a factor that is critical for enhancing sustainable practices [2]. Similarly, Bai et al. propose a methodological framework to assess the impact of blockchain on creating supply chains that are not only transparent but also sustainable, indicating the broad potential of blockchain technology in redefining supply chain management [3].

## 2.2   Blockchain and Smart Contracts for Supply Chain Management

Blockchain technology and smart contracts are being thoroughly investigated for their potential to improve supply chain management. Dolgui et al. integrate the concept of 'virtual operations' into smart contracts to synchronize the physical and digital aspects of supply chains [6]. Hasan et al. present a blockchain framework that combines smart contracts with IoT to monitor shipments in real-time, allowing for an immediate response to logistical changes [10]. Agrawal et al. examine the use of blockchain for resource sharing within business networks, ensuring data integrity through smart contracts [1]. Li et al. address the issues of information asymmetry and collaboration efficiency by standardizing information exchange via smart contracts, thus securing supply chain data [14]. Putri et al. explore the educational application of blockchain in agricultural supply chains through a serious game that simulates transactions using smart contracts [16], while Chang discusses the role of blockchain in re-engineering supply chains, highlighting the automation benefits provided by smart contracts [4] (Fig. 1).

## 3   Approach

### 3.1   Foundations and Functions: The Classical Architecture of Academic Knowledge Management

The architecture depicted in the flowchart represents a traditional supply chain model for handicrafts, a sector that is characterized by the labor-intensive creation of goods often imbued with cultural significance. This model outlines the sequential progression of a product from its inception by artisans to its eventual acquisition by consumers, delineating the key stages and entities involved in the supply chain. At the very foundation of this supply chain are the artisans, skilled individuals or groups engaged in the crafting of handicrafts. Their craftsmanship is not merely a means of livelihood but often a preservation of cultural heritage. The initial stage involves the artisans creating the handicrafts, which are then subject to certification. This certification process serves as a preliminary quality and ethical sourcing check, intended to assure that the products adhere to certain standards before they are introduced into the broader market.

**Fig. 1.** Traditional Supply Chain Management Architecture for Handicrafts

Following this, the certified handicrafts are conveyed to suppliers. These suppliers act as the intermediaries between the artisans and the market, playing a crucial role in the scaling of distribution. They are responsible for acquiring and amassing various handicrafts from multiple artisans, thereby aggregating supply to meet market demand. A subsequent critical juncture in the supply chain is the involvement of an inspection organization. This entity is tasked with a thorough examination of the handicrafts, ensuring that they meet specific standards that may include but are not limited to, quality, safety, and ethical sourcing. Issuing a certificate post-inspection provides a formal assurance that the handicrafts have been scrutinized and deemed compliant with the required standards.

The certified handicrafts are then distributed to retailers, the agents who provide the necessary infrastructure for the handicrafts to reach the consumer market. Retailers play a vital role in this architecture as they facilitate the transition of handicrafts from being a product available at a specific location to one that is accessible to a broad consumer base. It is at this stage that the products are made available for purchase, thereby entering the commercial mainstream. The final link in this traditional supply chain is the consumer, the end-user of the handicraft. Upon purchase, consumers have the opportunity to provide feedback regarding their experience with the product. This feedback can be instrumental in shaping future production, distribution, and certification processes, potentially influencing the entire supply chain (Fig. 2).

## 3.2  Implementing Blockchain, Smart Contracts, NFTs, and IPFS for Supply Chain Integrity in the Handicrafts Sectors

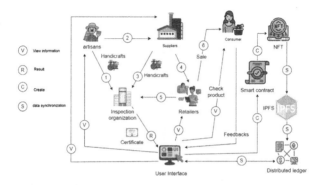

**Fig. 2.** Blockchain-Enabled Management Model in the Handicraft Supply Chain

The diagram illustrates a structured approach to managing supply chain transparency for handicraft products through the integration of blockchain, smart contracts, non-fungible tokens (NFTs), and the InterPlanetary File System (IPFS). This model delineates a sequence of interactions between various stakeholders and technologies that collectively contribute to an enhanced visibility and verification mechanism within the supply chain.

Artisans, at the beginning of the supply chain, are responsible for creating the handicrafts. Once a product is completed, its information is logged and verified by an inspection organization, which then issues a certificate indicating compliance with predefined standards. This certificate, along with detailed product information, is subsequently recorded on a blockchain, creating an immutable ledger entry that accompanies the product through the supply chain.

The blockchain serves as a foundational layer in this architecture, ensuring that each transaction and certification associated with the handicraft is securely and permanently recorded. Smart contracts automate the verification process at each transfer point, executing predefined rules that must be met before the product can proceed to the next stage. These contracts facilitate a trustless system where compliance with ethical sourcing and quality standards can be enforced without the need for intermediary verification at each step.

In parallel, each handicraft is associated with a unique NFT. This digital representation on the blockchain provides a singular, verifiable identity for the physical product, enabling clear ownership tracking and provenance tracing from the artisan to the consumer. The utility of NFTs extends to encapsulating the product's lifecycle information, providing buyers with a comprehensive background check capability. Additionally, IPFS is employed to store the associated data of each handicraft, including certificates of authenticity and ethical sourcing. This decentralized storage solution ensures that the data is not only tamper-resistant but also accessible across the network without reliance on centralized servers, thus enhancing the robustness of the system.

Feedback from consumers, gathered post-sale, is also recorded on the blockchain, providing a feedback loop that can inform and potentially improve future production practices. The user interface acts as a portal for the various stakeholders to interact with the system, view product information, and confirm certifications.

## 4    Evaluation

To adequately assess the capability of our system in the context of handicraft supply chain management, we plan to deploy our smart contracts on a selection of EVM-compatible platforms, namely Binance Smart Chain, Polygon, Fantom, and Celo. These platforms have been chosen for their distinct characteristics and performance metrics, which will be scrutinized to ascertain their suitability for our application. In tandem with the blockchain component, we will be using the IPFS for storing certification and related data, with Pinata providing the necessary gateway to this distributed network. The integration of Pinata is aimed at streamlining the management of information within the handicraft supply chain in a decentralized and structured fashion (Fig. 3).

### 4.1    Environment Simulation

The framework presented here constructs a blockchain network specifically designed to assess the functionality of NFTs and IPFS within the domain of a handicraft supply chain. This network is composed of interconnected nodes, each fortified by a unique set of cryptographic keys, ensuring secure transactions and interactions within the blockchain. The nodes symbolize different supply chain stakeholders, such as artisans, quality inspectors, and retailers, utilizing their public keys for transactional activities while relying on their private keys for authentication purposes.

In this environment, the nodes are assigned responsibilities crucial to the management of the handicraft supply chain. They oversee the creation and distribution of NFTs, engage with smart contracts, and facilitate the storage of data on IPFS. The network is equipped with a sufficient allocation of ether to support operations without the limitations often encountered due to resource scarcity. This test network aims to methodically investigate how NFTs and IPFS can

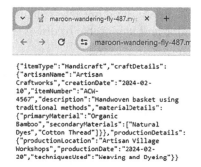

**Fig. 3.** IPFS Stored Metadata Viewed in a Web Browser

**Fig. 4.** JSON Structure for Handicraft Item Metadata

be effectively applied to document management and validation processes within the handicraft sector. By simulating the dynamics of an actual supply chain, the network enables an evaluation of the system's efficacy in a risk-free, controlled setting, thus avoiding the uncertainties associated with deploying new technologies in an operational market environment.

## 4.2   Implementing IPFS for Handicrafts Supply Chain Management

In the process of generating an NFT and uploading it to IPFS, Fig. 4 represents the initial step, which involves creating a JSON structure that encompasses all the relevant metadata for a handicraft item. This JSON file includes details such as the type of item, the artisan's name, the date of creation, and material specifics. This metadata forms the core of the NFT, encapsulating the unique attributes and the provenance of the handicraft, which are essential for future verification and tracking in the supply chain.

Following this, as depicted in Fig. 5, the smart contract responsible for handling the NFT is executed within a test environment. The result shown verifies the successful execution of the smart contract function, specifically confirming the proper setting of an unlock time parameter. This step is critical to ensure that the smart contract operates as intended, managing the NFT lifecycle events like creation, transfer, and access control based on predefined rules.

Figure 6 displays the successful upload of the metadata JSON file to Pinata, a service that interfaces with IPFS. The screenshot confirms that the metadata file has been uploaded and assigned a unique content identifier (CID), which acts as a reference point for accessing the file on the IPFS network. This step is crucial as it ensures the metadata is stored in a decentralized manner, enhancing the durability and accessibility of the data associated with the NFT.

Through these sequential steps, we can see the practical aspects of creating a digital representation of a handicraft item in the form of an NFT and ensuring its metadata is securely stored and accessible on IPFS. This process not only adds a layer of security and transparency to the supply chain but also enhances trust among all participants by providing a reliable and immutable record of the item's data.

### 4.3   Testing on EVM-Supported Platforms

In this study, we utilize the Ethereum Virtual Machine (EVM) to facilitate the implementation of smart contracts on a selection of compatible platforms, including Binance Smart Chain, Polygon, Fantom, and Celo. These platforms were selected to evaluate their capabilities in managing a transparent supply chain for handicrafts. We concentrated on fundamental operations such as recording supply chain events, generating Non-Fungible Tokens (NFTs) for product identification and lineage, and executing NFT transfers to maintain a secure chain of custody. Our assessment focused on transaction processing efficiency, cost-effectiveness, and the usability of the interface, all of which are critical for professionals managing supply chain activities. The intent of this examination is to discern the suitability of each platform for reinforcing a supply chain that is both transparent and operates seamlessly, with an emphasis on secure and dependable NFT-based transactions.

**Fig. 5.** Test Result for Smart Contract Execution

**Fig. 6.** Pinata Cloud Storage Confirmation for Metadata File

Table 1 presented outlines the transaction costs associated with various blockchain platforms, an essential factor in evaluating the financial practicality of employing blockchain in the management of supply chains for handicrafts. These transaction fees contribute significantly to the operational expenditures of the blockchain infrastructure. The table also captures the market values of the respective platform tokens as of January 27, 2024, at 7:00 AM UTC, providing a snapshot of the economic landscape within these blockchains operate. This information serves to inform stakeholders of the current financial implications of utilizing these networks in supply chain applications. On the Binance Smart Chain, initiating a transaction is listed with a fee of 0.0273134 BNB, approximately valued at $8.27. The creation of an NFT on this chain costs 0.00109162 BNB, or $0.33, while an NFT transfer requires a fee of 0.00057003 BNB, which translates to $0.17. These figures suggest that while Binance Smart Chain offers

**Table 1.** Transaction fee

|  | Transaction Creation | Create NFT | Transfer NFT |
|---|---|---|---|
| BNB | 0.0273134 BNB ($8.27) | 0.00109162 BNB ($0.33) | 0.00057003 BNB ($0.17) |
| Fantom | 0.00957754 FTM ($0.00) | 0.000405167 FTM ($0.00) | 0.0002380105 FTM ($0.00) |
| Polygon | 0.006840710032835408 MATIC ($0.01) | 0.000289405001852192 MATIC ($0.00) | 0.000170007501088048 MATIC ($0.00) |
| Celo | 0.007097844 CELO ($0.005) | 0.0002840812 CELO ($0.000 ) | 0.0001554878 CELO ($0.000 ) |

a robust environment for transaction processing, the costs associated might be higher compared to other platforms.

Fantom's transaction fee for the creation of a new transaction is 0.00957754 FTM, with no significant dollar value attributed, indicating a negligible cost. Similarly, creating and transferring an NFT on Fantom's network incurs fees of 0.000405167 FTM and 0.0002380105 FTM, respectively, both also reflecting minimal dollar value amounts. This implies a cost-effective platform for supply chain transactions, particularly for operations involving NFTs. For transactions on Polygon, the cost to create a transaction is noted at 0.006840710032835408 MATIC, or $0.01. Creating an NFT on Polygon is even less expensive, at 0.000289- 405001852192 MATIC, and transferring an NFT costs 0.000170007501088048 MATIC, both carrying essentially no dollar value, which demonstrates a very low-cost structure for supply chain operations on this platform. Lastly, Celo's transaction fee for creating a new transaction stands at 0.007097844 CELO, equivalent to $0.005. NFT creation and transfer on Celo are also cost-effective, with fees of 0.0002840812 CELO and 0.0001554878 CELO, respectively, both translating to less than a cent. These fees point to Celo being a financially viable platform for managing transactions within a handicraft supply chain.

## 5 Conclusion

The exploration of blockchain technology in the handicraft supply chain has revealed a pathway to enhanced transparency and the assurance of ethical sourcing practices. The framework we have developed integrates smart contracts, NFTs, and IPFS into the supply chain management process, creating a system that not only promotes transparency but also supports the integrity and traceability of handicraft items. Testing on multiple blockchain platforms has shown that our approach is both viable and effective, suggesting that it could lead to improvements in the economic and operational aspects of supply chain management for handicrafts. The deployment of this technology could represent a significant step forward for the industry, providing stakeholders with a reliable record of transactions and item histories, and ultimately fostering a supply chain that is accountable, transparent, and equitable. Our research indicates that the application of these technologies has the potential to reshape supply chain practices, making them more aligned with the current demands for sustainability and fair trade in the handicraft sector.

# References

1. Agrawal, T.K., et al.: Demonstration of a blockchain-based framework using smart contracts for supply chain collaboration. Int. J. Prod. Res. **61**, 1497–1516 (2022)
2. Alvarado, J., et al.: New era in the supply chain management with blockchain. Research Anthology on Blockchain Technology in Business, Healthcare, Education, and Government (2021)
3. Bai, C., et al.: A supply chain transparency and sustainability technology appraisal model for blockchain technology. Int. J. Prod. Res. **58**, 2142–2162 (2019)
4. Chang, S.E., et al.: Supply chain re-engineering using blockchain technology: a case of smart contract based tracking process. Technol. Forecasting Soc. Change **144**, 1–11 (2019)
5. Dietrich, F., Turgut, A., Palm, D., Louw, L.: Smart contract-based blockchain solution to reduce supply chain risks. In: Lalic, B., Majstorovic, V., Marjanovic, U., von Cieminski, G., Romero, D. (eds.) APMS 2020. IAICT, vol. 592, pp. 165–173. Springer, Cham (2020). https://doi.org/10.1007/978-3-030-57997-5_20
6. Dolgui, A., et al.: Blockchain-oriented dynamic modelling of smart contract design and execution in the supply chain. Int. J. Prod. Res. **58**, 2184–2199 (2020)
7. Duong-Trung, N., et al.: Multi-sessions mechanism for decentralized cash on delivery system. Int. J. Adv. Comput. Sci. Appl **10**(9), 553–560 (2019)
8. Ha, X.S., Le, H.T., Metoui, N., Duong-Trung, N.: DeM-CoD: novel access-control-based cash on delivery mechanism for decentralized marketplace. In: 2020 IEEE 19th International Conference on Trust, Security and Privacy in Computing and Communications (TrustCom), pp. 71–78. IEEE (2020)
9. Ha, X.S., Le, T.H., Phan, T.T., Nguyen, H.H.D., Vo, H.K., Duong-Trung, N.: Scrutinizing trust and transparency in cash on delivery systems. In: Wang, G., Chen, B., Li, W., Di Pietro, R., Yan, X., Han, H. (eds.) SpaCCS 2020. LNCS, vol. 12382, pp. 214–227. Springer, Cham (2021). https://doi.org/10.1007/978-3-030-68851-6_15
10. Hasan, H., et al.: Smart contract-based approach for efficient shipment management. Comput. Ind. Eng. **136**, 149–159 (2019)
11. Hawashin, D., et al.: Using composable NFTS for trading and managing expensive packaged products in the food industry. IEEE Access **11**, 10587–10603 (2023)
12. Le, H.T., et al.: Introducing multi shippers mechanism for decentralized cash on delivery system. Int. J. Adv. Comput. Sci. Appl. **10**(6), 590–597 (2019)
13. Le, N.T.T., et al.: Assuring non-fraudulent transactions in cash on delivery by introducing double smart contracts. Int. J. Adv. Comput. Sci. Appl. **10**(5), 677–684 (2019)
14. Li, J., et al.: Design of supply chain system based on blockchain technology. Appl. Sci. **11**, 9744 (2021)
15. Pawar, M.K., et al.: Secure and scalable decentralized supply chain management using Ethereum and IPFS platform, pp. 1–5 (2021)

16. Putri, A.N., et al.: Supply chain management serious game using blockchain smart contract. IEEE Access **11**, 131089–131113 (2023)

17. Quoc, K.L., et al.: SSSB: an approach to insurance for cross-border exchange by using smart contracts. In: Awan, I., Younas, M., Poniszewska-Marańda, A. (eds.)Mobile Web and Intelligent Information Systems: 18th International Conference, vol. 13475, pp. 179–192. Springer, Cham (2022). https://doi.org/10.1007/978-3-031-14391-5_14

18. Saberi, S., et al.: Blockchain technology and its relationships to sustainable supply chain management. Int. J. Prod. Res. **57**, 2117–2135 (2018)

19. Shahid, A., et al.: Blockchain-based agri-food supply chain: a complete solution. IEEE Access **8**, 69230–69243 (2020)

20. Son, H.X., et al.: Towards a mechanism for protecting seller's interest of cash on delivery by using smart contract in hyperledger. Int. J. Adv. Comput. Sci. Appl. **10**(4) (2019)

21. Yoo, M., et al.: A study on the transparent price tracing system in supply chain management based on blockchain. Sustainability **10**, 4037 (2018)

# Edge Computing and Energy Awareness

# Scheduling Energy-Aware Multi-function Serverless Workloads in OpenFaaS

Raulian Chiorescu[ID] and Karim Djemame[✉][ID]

School of Computing, University of Leeds, Leeds LS2 9JT, UK
{sc19ric,k.djemame}@leeds.ac.uk

**Abstract.** The paper investigates the prediction capabilities of a Machine Learning model in real-time scheduling applications on Kubernetes in a serverless computing environment with the aim to achieve a degree of energy efficiency. A highly pluggable framework for integrating a learning-based model into the Kubernetes scheduler is proposed and evaluated in a serverless setup on OpenFaaS. The experimental results in a cloud-native deployment demonstrate that, while maintaining Quality of Service for the application, an overall 8% in power reduction is achieved at a minimal performance loss.

**Keywords:** Serverless computing · Power consumption · Kubernetes · Machine Learning

## 1 Introduction

In the current climate, cloud computing plays a vital role in sustaining various aspects of our digital lives, from social media to large-scale data analysis. As the demand for these services continues to skyrocket, so does the need for more cloud data centres, which in turn increases overall energy consumption worldwide. As a consequence, energy efficiency has become an imperative issue for cloud computing service providers to lower costs as well as minimise the energy consumption impact on the environment.

Serverless computing is an architectural paradigm that enables developers to focus on application functionality rather than the underlying infrastructure. By abstracting away the underlying servers, serverless computing allows for automatic scalability, flexibility, and potential cost reductions, as users only pay for the number of invocations of their specific functions. This paradigm shift has transformed how applications are developed and deployed, leading to its widespread adoption in the cloud computing industry. On the other hand, as with any relatively novel technology, new challenges are introduced in the field. One of these challenges is to measure and potentially optimise energy usage in a cloud environment, as users do not have access to the underlying infrastructure. Moreover, a serverless function is essentially a proxy for energy usage as a unit of (serverless) compute and therefore a cost, making functions instantiation and orchestration significantly energy and resource efficient [4].

© The Author(s), under exclusive license to Springer Nature Switzerland AG 2025
M. Naldi et al. (Eds.): GECON 2024, LNCS 15358, pp. 137–149, 2025.
https://doi.org/10.1007/978-3-031-81226-2_13

OpenFaaS [13] is an open-source serverless platform that provides a framework for building serverless functions by allowing developers to package any process or container as a function facilitating their deployment without requiring extensive adaptation. OpenFaaS relies on Kubernetes for scheduling containers that run the serverless functions and is considered as an attractive serverless engine due to Kubernetes's extensibility. The evaluation of OpenFaas has revealed superior power efficiency as compared to a Docker containers setting [1]. As Machine Learning (ML) has gained increased traction and is being adopted in some critical areas of resource scheduling, planning and control, this paper addresses the question of whether the integration of a ML-based model into the Kubernetes scheduler can achieve *better* power efficiency as compared to the default scheduler. A change at the function or scheduler level must therefore be made in order to achieve energy-aware serverless functions.

The paper makes the following contributions:

- we propose a highly pluggable framework for integrating a learning-based model into the Kubernetes scheduler;
- we evaluate the performance of the proposed scheduler extension against the default Kubernetes Scheduler;
- we demonstrate that significant power efficiency is gained by integrating a learning-based model into the Kubernetes scheduler.

The paper is structured as follows: Sect. 2 reviews the related work and looks into the research landscape surrounding scheduling functions on serverless computing platforms. The design addressing the framework for integrating a learning-based model into the Kubernetes scheduler is presented in Sect. 3. The experimental environment setup and the results of the evaluation of the custom scheduler are described in Sect. 4. Section 5 concludes with a summary of the research findings and suggestions for future work.

## 2    Related Work

There have been a multitude of research investigations in the area of energy consumption in the serverless space. Alhindi et al. [1] investigate the difference in power usage between OpenFaaS and Docker across four scenarios, in a on-premises hardware, virtual machine-based experimental setup: standalone Docker containers, OpenFaaS with faasd, a lightweight runtime of OpenFaaS that runs on containerd directly under the hood, OpenFaaS on Kubernetes and Docker containers on Kubernetes. They discovered that OpenFaaS with faasd tends to consume less power on a memory-heavy benchmark than its Kubernetes counterpart with a decrease of 58%, which is expected, as the runtime is more lightweight.

Jia and Zhao [10] propose a mechanism for energy-aware resource allocation in a serverless context to minimise power consumption named RAEF. An agent running at the function level is proposed, constructed of four components, where the most important are the predictor and the resource explorer. The findings show that the proposed solution can reduce energy consumption anywhere from a noticeable 9.7% to a significant 21.2% across different workloads. Moreover, the control-plane components of OpenFaaS consumes an insignificant amount of power compared to the function runtime plane. Rocha et al. [15] implement a Kubernetes scheduler extension based on multiple linear regression models in order to predict energy and performance based on the workload, CPU and memory requirements. The approach includes a user set weight between 0 and 1 in decimal increments, that determines the desired balance between energy and performance. 7.1% improvement in terms of energy is achieved at the detriment of ~10% performance, while their maximum performance setting improves runtime by ~20% at a 5% energy increase. Toka et al. [16] propose a Kubernetes scaling engine that makes the auto-scaling decisions apt for handling the actual variability of incoming requests. Four different approaches to a learning-based solution are devised auto-regressive (AR), unsupervised (HTM), deep learning (LSTM) and reinforcement learning, to determine which one performs better by letting them compete against each other via a scoring mechanism based on past predictions. The experimental results show that at a slight increase in resource usage (2–9%) the system manages to decrease the loss in requests from 22% at the lowest to 72% percent at the highest. The work of Das et al. [3] focuses on cost efficient execution of multi-function serverless applications on hybrid cloud deployments based on OpenFaaS and AWS Lambda. A framework named Skedulix is proposed based on a greedy solution to scheduling after it was modelled into a Mixed Integer Linear Program (MILP). Serverless applications are modelled as directed acyclic graphs (DAGs), in which each node represents a different function. The goal of the scheduler is to speed up processing at the lowest cost possible, by maximising the use of the private cluster and offloading any incompletable work to the public cloud in cases where the deadline cannot be met. Fan and He [6] target the all too well-known issue of cold start by devising a new scheduling strategy that allows creating multiple pods at a time instead of the default pod-by-pod approach that Kubernetes adopts as it has to traverse each node to compute the score that determines the most beneficial placement which can cause a slowness in start-up latency. Essentially, they propose a simple algorithm based on Mixed Integer Programming (MILP), that divides pods into groups and schedules a group at a time when it passes a set overload threshold and achieves sizeable reduction in latency in simulation, ranging from ~20–60% depending on the number of pods that need to be scheduled.

In summary, work has addressed scheduler-level optimisations in Kubernetes, although none seem to consider energy consumption in a serverless context. Most are centred around performance but none considers the public cloud in their experiments. In terms of approach and workload, to the best of our knowledge no work targets a multi-function workload while considering energy efficiency. This work is aimed at an image processing pipeline on OpenFaaS and uses a learning-based approach for performing scheduling decisions. While RAEF focuses on function-level adjustments [10], this paper explores possibilities at the scheduler level, although similarly it aims to thread the needle between Quality of Service (QoS) provision boundaries in order to minimise power consumption.

## 3    System Design

The principal research question addressed in this paper is: *Following the integration of a ML-based model into the Kubernetes scheduler, are results reliable in presenting a realistic trade-off between performance and energy consumption?* This concludes if, following an evaluation of the custom Kubernetes scheduler, the results do illustrate a clear trade-off between energy consumption and performance, and if the reduction in energy is worthwhile in the sense that it maintains an acceptable QoS.

### 3.1    Architecture

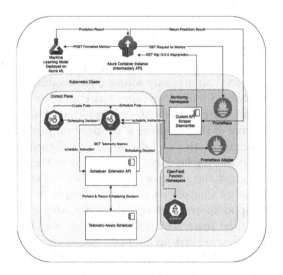

**Fig. 1.** Flow and Architecture

Figure 1 illustrates the architectural design and flow of our proposed implementation of the system. The flow is initiated with an agent situated on the monitoring stack of the solution. It invokes an endpoint part of an interim component between the ML model and the Kubernetes Cluster. Following the invocation, the container API retrieves resource usage metrics from the monitoring infrastructure Prometheus [14] and forwards them to the model to retrieve a prediction, sending it back to the agent which stores on each node their own version of the prediction result, being either schedulable or unschedulable at a specific point in time. Then, an adapter for Prometheus formats the result of the prediction, and passes it to the control plane of the cluster via the API server component. Finally, the custom scheduler implementation processes the formatted scheduling instruction metric and schedules new pods on the predicted nodes accordingly.

The core component of the system is a custom variation of Intel's *Telemetry Aware Scheduler* [8]. Essentially it is used to perform scheduling decisions based on various metrics. The manner in which it operates is based on files designated as telemetry policies. The user can define multiple scheduling strategies based on the desired metrics that should take part in scheduling decisions. Every metric can be assigned one of three operators, *Equals, LessThan* and *GreaterThan*. In our case this is signified by the *schedule_ instruction* metric, a pre-formatted prediction result, based on which the custom solution performs scheduling decisions.

### 3.2   Machine Learning Model

For the machine learning model Scikit-learn's Random Forest Classifier was employed [11]. This was chosen for its ability to handle a large number of features and its robustness against over-fitting. CPU and the memory are the most important resources to be considered in terms of performance and power consumption in the context of applications execution [5]. Resource consumption metrics (CPU and Memory Usage, Power, Pod Count) were collected from Prometheus on each node over multiple load experiments to serve as training and validation data. These experiments involved varying the load on the Kubernetes cluster in a controlled manner and collecting metrics at regular intervals.

The model provides predictions in the form *k8s_ worker_ [NODE_ ID]*, which represent the node that would be the most appropriate to schedule a new pod on based on the current metrics that are fed into it.

The model was deployed on Azure Machine learning [12], a comprehensive machine learning platform that supports language model fine-tuning and deployment. It exposes a REST endpoint that can be accessed with a POST request with the required usage data in order to output a prediction. This way of utilising the capabilities of Azure ML and Azure Container Instances is what makes the proposed solution highly-pluggable as models are trivial to interchange, and any of the metrics that are desired for the model to make a prediction require simple modifications at the level of the API running as the Container Instance.

### 3.3   Research Hypotheses

As a result of the architectural design and implementation of the proposed solution, a total of three hypotheses are formulated as predictions for the experimental outcomes. As such, experiments will test those hypotheses and the results of each experiment will prove or disprove them.

**H1**. *The ML solution will be reliable in scheduling pods, with little added delay between scheduling decisions.* This hypothesis is based on research publications that used a learning-based approach in building custom scheduling solutions for Kubernetes.

**H2**. *Towards the latter end of the experiments, where resource usage is high both solutions will perform similarly.* This is based on the fact that if all the compute resources in the cluster are needed, there will not be any technique that will consistently schedule pods differently. Simply the cluster would be filled up with all CPU cores being pinned close to 100%.

**H3**. *The default scheduler will outperform the custom scheduler in every scenario in terms of throughput.* This hypothesis is based on previous literature in terms of energy and performance trade-offs, where in seldom cases you can have both. The added overhead of custom scheduling decisions will likely impact the scaling capabilities of the cluster.

## 4 Experiments and Results

### 4.1 Experimental Setup

As the path of experimentation in this paper is to evaluate a chain-function setup, a CPU and Memory intensive workload was chosen, namely, image processing. The pipeline consists of four serverless functions: 1) Director Function, a design pattern in multi-function setups as it only requires the client to submit a single HTTP request to fully process an image instead of individual requests to each serverless function. Its purpose is to call all the other functions; 2) Image Resize Function (Upscaling); 3) Image Transform Function (Rotation), and 4) Image Recolour Function (RGB Manipulation).

The benchmarking client is a Standard_8s_v5 Virtual Machine in Azure configured with accelerated networking to allow for high request throughput. This size was chosen to ensure the reliability of running hundreds of concurrent clients that send web requests to the director functions deployed onto the Kubernetes cluster. Apache JMeter [2] is chosen as the primary load testing tool due to its high configurability of flows and easy extensibility when it comes to benchmarking different function deployment scenarios with varying amounts of initial replicas. The test plan employs a multi-threaded approach, simulating a large number of virtual users to stress-test the system. To measure power, the proposed power model in Fan et al. [7] is adopted as it is deemed more reliable than, e.g. a tool such as PowerTop [9], in a virtualised environment. This model applies the Thermal Design Power (TDP) values of the processors running within the cluster which are Intel Xeon Platinum 8730C, featuring 32 cores and 64 threads with a TDP of 270W. In our system, there are 40 vCores (Virtual Cores) worth processing power which is equivalent to 40 threads.

Experiments are run over a varying amount of initial function deployments, in order to observe the differences in resource usage metrics and power consumption between them. Five runs of each scenario are run for consistency and validity of results, each deployment is tested on the custom ML-agent based scheduler as well as Kubernetes default scheduler. The runs are broken down as follows: 1) 10 deployments per function (40 pods total with a theoretical maximum of 200 pods); 2) 20 deployments per function (80 pods total with a theoretical maximum of 400 pods); 3) 30 deployments per function (120 pods total with a theoretical maximum of 600 pods); 4) 40 deployments per function (160 pods total with a theoretical maximum of 800 pods), and 5) 50 deployments per function (200 pods total with a theoretical maximum of 1000 pods).

## 4.2 ML Model Performance

The model was trained on a dataset comprised of features extracted every 2 min from the Kubernetes cluster while being under load for a total of 6 h resulting in a total of approximately 3000 data points. The evaluation metrics were computed using a test set, 20% of the entire dataset, that was not part of the training data. The confusion matrix was constructed to capture the true positives, true negatives, false positives, and false negatives for each class. Table 1 illustrates the performance metrics achieved for the ML model, broken down into accuracy, precision, recall and F1 Score.

**Table 1.** Performance Metrics of the Random Forest Classifier

| Accuracy | Precision | Recall | F1 Score |
|----------|-----------|--------|----------|
| 94.59% | 95.80% | 94.59% | 94.79% |

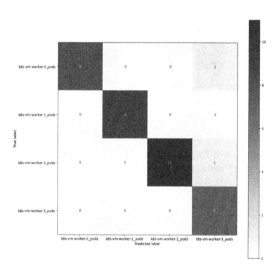

**Fig. 2.** Confusion Matrix of Test Set Predictions of the Random Forest Classifier

Figure 2 presents the confusion matrix generated following training and validation. The matrix is comprised of two categories, predicted label and true label,

with the main diagonal representing true values and the corners signifying false
predictions.

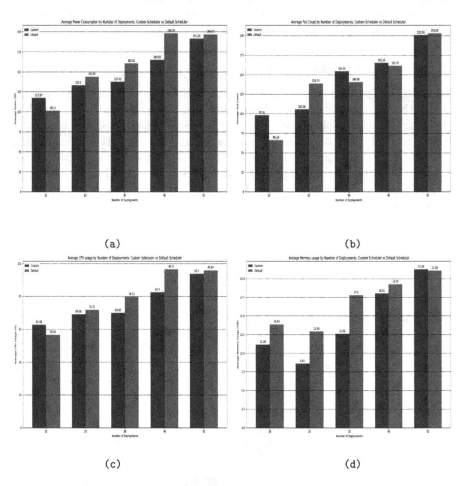

**Fig. 3.** Metrics by Number of Deployments. (a) Average Power Usage. (b) Average Pod
Count. (c) Average CPU Usage. (d) Average Memory Usage.

### 4.3 Custom Scheduler Evaluation

Figure 3(a) shows the breakdown of average power usage at varying levels of
deployments between the two scheduling solutions. At 10 deployments, the custom scheduler consumes approximately 15.7% more (Watt) power (117.07W)
than the default scheduler (101.2W). However, as the number of deployments
increases, the custom scheduler tends to become more power-efficient. At 20
deployments, the custom scheduler consumes about 9.6% less power (130.01W)

compared to the default (143.84W). At 30 deployments, the power saving increases to 14.5% (137.41W for custom vs. 160.62W for default). The trend continues at 40 deployments with a 16.7% reduction (164.95W for custom vs. 198.08W for default). Finally, at 50 deployments, the custom scheduler consumes approximately 2.8% less power (191.26W vs. 196.67W for default). At 50 deployments, the CPU usage is pinned towards 100% signifying that the hardware limitations of the cluster is reached. If further testing were to be conducted on a larger cluster, we would most likely observe a similar pattern to the 20,30 and 40 deployment's power values.

The number of pods metric in Fig. 3(b) provides insights into container orchestration efficiency as well as how many pods per function are needed for the functions to execute at an acceptable rate. At 10 deployments, the custom scheduler uses about 31.8% fewer pods (97 vs. 66 for default). At 20 deployments, the default scheduler uses a significant 31.4% more pods (138 vs. 105 for custom). However, at 30 deployments, the custom scheduler uses about 10% more pods (154 vs. 140 for default). At 40 and 50, the gap closes, with custom scheduler uses about 2.5% more pods (165 vs. 161 for default) and respectively, 1.5 % more (200 vs. 203 for default).

Figure 3(c) presents the average CPU usage, which is directly proportional to 3(a) as power estimations are directly based on CPU. At 10 deployments, the custom scheduler uses about 10.7% more CPU (62.68% vs. 56.56% for default). However, at 20 deployments, the CPU usage is nearly identical, with the custom scheduler using about 2.8% less CPU (69.06% vs. 71.72% for default). At 30 deployments, we see a marginal increase in CPU, although, the custom scheduler uses 12.7% less CPU (69.82% vs. 79.73% for default). The gap widens at 40 deployments, where the custom scheduler uses 14.6% less CPU (82.5% vs. 96.51% for default). Finally, at 50 deployments, the difference narrows to about 2.1% less CPU usage for the custom scheduler (93.7% vs. 95.84% for default). As mentioned in the presentation for power usage, the CPU tends to be pinned close to maximum with 50 deployments, not allowing a varied placement of pods on the nodes when essentially each node is maxed out in usage.

In Fig. 3(d), memory consumption tends to be lower for the custom scheduler in small deployments with an outlier at the minimum number of 10. The main consumer of memory is the resize serverless function, which upscales the chosen image to a $1920 \times 1080$ resolution, and the values suggest that the performance of the resize function, should in theory, be similar. At 10 deployments, the custom scheduler uses about 15% less memory (11.16 GiB vs. 13.85 GiB for default). At 20 deployments, the memory saving is significant at 38% (8.61 GiB for custom vs. 12,91 GiB for default). However, at 30 deployments, the custom scheduler uses about 29% less memory (12.61 GiB vs. 17.8 GiB for default). At 40 deployments, the memory usage is almost identical, with the custom scheduler using about 5% less memory (18.01 GiB vs. 19.26 GiB for default). Finally, at 50 deployments, both schedulers use virtually the same amount of memory (21.26 and 21.08 GiB).

Tables 2 and 3 present the average, median, 90, 95 and 99th percentiles response times of requests in all the deployments evaluated. With this knowl-

**Table 2.** Request Execution Times (ms) - Custom Scheduler

| No. | Avg. | Med. | 90th | 95th | 99th | Err% | Thr/s |
|-----|------|------|------|------|-------|--------|-------|
| 10 | 1167 | 445 | 3056 | 5548 | 9119 | 41.18% | 36.2 |
| 20 | 4885 | 5079 | 9103 | 9575 | 9943 | 39.9% | 41.5 |
| 30 | 4785 | 4719 | 8906 | 9474 | 9933 | 44.14% | 50.4 |
| 40 | 6834 | 7263 | 9536 | 9795 | 9993 | 62.74% | 33.8 |
| 50 | 7423 | 7716 | 9624 | 9844 | 10015 | 72.25% | 29.3 |

**Table 3.** Request Execution Times (ms) - Default Scheduler

| No. | Avg. | Med. | 90th | 95th | 99th | Err% | Thr/s |
|-----|------|------|------|------|-------|--------|-------|
| 10 | 1450 | 270 | 6064 | 8176 | 9672 | 53.44% | 24.3 |
| 20 | 3965 | 3614 | 8066 | 8974 | 9820 | 29.47% | 56.6 |
| 30 | 6299 | 6551 | 9344 | 9693 | 9972 | 45.86% | 50.0 |
| 40 | 7193 | 7453 | 9551 | 9802 | 10004 | 58.11% | 45.5 |
| 50 | 7089 | 7316 | 9538 | 9798 | 10005 | 69.68% | 31.6 |

edge, a comparison of the custom and the default schedulers is performed with the aim to conclude if an acceptable QoS has been achieved by custom scheduler through observing the energy vs performance trade-off. Note that the metrics displayed are only for successful (200 OK) requests and not errors (500 Internal Server Error).

**Throughput (Thr/s)** : the custom scheduler generally shows higher throughput in lower numbers of deployments (36.2 vs. 24.3 at 10 deployments). However, as the number of deployments increases, the default scheduler starts to outperform the custom one, which is expected, and especially noticeable at 20 deployments (41.5 vs. 56.6), considering the previous comparison in power consumption.

**Average Execution Latency (Avg.)** : the custom scheduler starts with a lower average latency at 10 deployments (1167 vs. 1450 ms). Although, as the number of deployments grows, the custom scheduler's average latency becomes competitive or even better than the default scheduler, particularly noticeable at 20 and 30 deployments.

**Percentile Execution Latencies (90, 95, 99th)** : Both schedulers show increasing latencies as we move from the median to the 99th percentile, which is expected. The custom scheduler generally has higher 99th-percentile latencies, indicating that it may be less reliable under heavier loads.

The error rates are notably high for both schedulers but are generally higher for the custom scheduler across all numbers of deployments. These values in error rate can be attributed to the limitations of the OpenFaaS Gateway scaling capabilities.

## 4.4 Research Hypotheses Evaluation

**H1** . *The ML solution will be reliable in scheduling pods, with little added delay between scheduling decisions.* This has proven to be true, with the proposed model achieving a 94.59% accuracy at predicting nodes on the test set. The accuracy metric is given by how similar the output of the model is to that of the default scheduler i.e. effectively the node label that a pod was scheduled on by the default scheduler. In the real-world deployment, it has added negligible overhead in terms of scheduling latency. If the logs of the scheduling extension are inspected, decisions are made in less than a second, deeming the solution reliable for real-time scheduling.

**H2** . *Towards the latter end of the experiments, where resource usage is high both solutions will perform similarly.* This hypothesis has proven to be entirely true as towards 50 deployments, the resources in the cluster were completely saturated, and both scenarios performed similarly across the board with a difference 1–3%, in terms of all the metrics considered, including performance. The results do truly show that scheduling decisions do not matter all that much when there is a lack of resources present.

**H3** . *The default scheduler will outperform the custom scheduler in every scenario in terms of throughput.* This hypothesis has proven to be partially true. We were intrigued by the results in the case of the two outliers in this experiment at 10 and 30 deployments. At 10 deployments the increase in performance directly correlates with the resources used in our custom scheduler scenario. However, the most intriguing result was at 30 deployments. Despite the custom scheduler consuming significantly less power, it managed to achieve a throughput of 50.4, essentially on par with the default scheduler's 50.0. The custom scheduler was able to deliver nearly identical throughput while being more power-efficient by 14.5%. This performance was consistent across multiple runs of the experiment though.

## 4.5 Summary

Apart from a couple outliers, the results do show a realistic trade-off between performance and power consumption. If all the scenarios to calculate an average in power reduction are considered, an 8% decrease in power consumption is achieved. With the outliers at 10 deployments and 30 deployments removed, the total average savings are 10.7%. In terms of performance loss the average, median, 90, 95 and 99th percentile values tend to be rather close to each other when comparing the two solutions. Finally, to answer the main research question, the proposed custom scheduler can provide an acceptable QoS depicted by the differences of error rate and throughput, while the implementation does pose higher values for dropped requests and lower for throughput in most cases. The reduction in power consumption can be considered worthwhile as the losses are an expected outcome when trying to save power and they situate themselves in the same realm to those of the default scheduler.

## 5     Conclusion

This paper has presented an energy-efficient pluggable solution to scheduling in Kubernetes in a serverless computing environment through the integration of a learning-based model into the scheduler. In terms of overall metrics this solution achieved 8% reduction in energy consumption at the cost of a directly correlated loss in performance, thus maintaining the application QoS. Future work will include the generalisation of the proposed model to other workloads such as data analytics and video processing, and scaling the experiments to encompass larger clusters and diverse cloud environments, thereby validating the scalability and robustness of the proposed solution. Moreover, it will consider experimentation with other solutions for scheduling in Kubernetes, e.g. investigate the use of Deep Learning-based schedulers, Mixed-Integer Linear Programming (MILP), or other optimisation techniques for scheduling tasks in Kubernetes. Investigating additional machine learning models could yield further insights and possibly superior performance outcomes.

**Acknowledgments.** The authors would like to thank the European Next Generation Internet Program for Open INTErnet Renovation (NGI-Pointer 2) for supporting this work under contract 871528 (EDGENESS Project).

**Disclosure of Interests.** The authors have no competing interests to declare that are relevant to the content of this article.

## References

1. Alhindi, A., Djemame, K., Banaie, F.: On the power consumption of serverless functions: an evaluation of openfaas. In: Proc. of the 15th IEEE/ACM International Conference on Utility and Cloud Computing (UCC), pp. 366–371. IEEE, Vancouver, USA (Dec 2022)
2. Apache Software Foundation: Apache jmeter (2023). https://jmeter.apache.org/
3. Das, A., Leaf, A., Varela, C., Patterson, S.: Skedulix: Hybrid cloud scheduling for cost-efficient execution of serverless applications. In: 2020 IEEE 13th International Conference on Cloud Computing, pp. 609–618. IEEE, Beijing, China (2020)
4. Djemame, K.: Energy efficiency in edge environments: a serverless computing approach. In: Tserpes, K., Altmann, J., Bañares, J., Agmon Ben-Yehuda, O., Djemame, K., Stankovski, V., Tuffin, B. (eds.) Economics of Grids, Clouds, Systems, and Services, pp. 181–184. Springer International Publishing, Cham (2021)

5. Djemame, K., Parker, M., Datsev, D.: Open-source serverless architectures: an evaluation of apache openwhisk. In: Proceedings of the IEEE/ACM 13th International Conference on Utility and Cloud Computing (UCC), pp. 329–335. IEEE, Leicester, UK (2020)
6. Fan, D., He, D.: A scheduler for serverless framework base on kubernetes. In: Proceedings of the 2020 4th High Performance Computing and Cluster Technologies Conference & 3rd International Conference on Big Data and Artificial Intelligence, pp. 229–232. HPCCT & BDAI '20, ACM, NY, USA (2020)
7. Fan, X., Weber, W., Barroso, L.: Power provisioning for a warehouse-sized computer. In: Proceedings of the 34th Annual International Symposium on Computer Architecture, pp. 13–23. ACM, NY, USA (2007)
8. Intel: Telemetry aware scheduling (Nov 2021). https://www.intel.com/content/www/us/en/developer/articles/technical/telemetry-aware-scheduling.html
9. Intel: Powertop (2023). https://wiki.archlinux.org/title/powertop
10. Jia, X., Zhao, L.: Raef: Energy-efficient resource allocation through energy fungibility in serverless. In: 2021 IEEE 27th International Conference on Parallel and Distributed Systems, pp. 434–441. IEEE, Los Alamitos, CA, USA (Dec 2021)
11. Kramer, O.: Scikit-Learn. In: Machine Learning for Evolution Strategies. SBD, vol. 20, pp. 45–53. Springer, Cham (2016). https://doi.org/10.1007/978-3-319-33383-0_5
12. Microsoft: Azure machine learning (2023). https://azure.microsoft.com/en-gb/products/machine-learning
13. OpenFaaS: Serverless functions, made simple (2023). https://openfaas.com/
14. Prometheus: From metrics to insight (2023). https://prometheus.io/
15. Rocha, I., Göttel, C., Felber, P., Pasin, M., Rouvoy, R., Schiavoni, V.: Heats: heterogeneity-and energy-aware task-based scheduling. In: 27th Euromicro International Conference on Parallel. Distributed and Network-Based Processing (PDP), pp. 400–405. IEEE, Pavia, Italy (2019)
16. Toka, L., Dobreff, G., Fodor, B., Sonkoly, B.: Machine learning-based scaling management for kubernetes edge clusters. IEEE Trans. Netw. Serv. Manage. **18**(1), 958–972 (2021)

# Efficient Placement of Interdependent Services in Multi-access Edge Computing

Shuyi Chen[1,2] , Panagiotis Oikonomou[3] , Zhengchang Hua[1,2] ,
Nikos Tziritas[3] , Karim Djemame[2] , Nan Zhang[1] ,
and Georgios Theodoropoulos[1(✉)] 

[1] Southern University of Science and Technology, Shenzhen, China
{chensy8,huazc,zhangn2019}@mail.sustech.edu.cn, theogeorgios@gmail.com
[2] University of Leeds, Leeds, UK
k.djemame@leeds.ac.uk
[3] University of Thessaly, Lamia, Greece
{paikonom,nitzirit}@uth.gr

**Abstract.** The rise of 5G fuels multi-access edge computing (MEC), a transformative computing paradigm that leverages edge resources for low-latency mobile access and complex service execution. Deploying services across geographically distributed edge nodes challenges providers to optimize performance metrics like latency and resource efficiency, impacting user experience, operational cost, and environmental footprint. In the context of service scheduling with data flow dependencies, we propose heuristic-based service placement algorithms that balance minimizing latency and maximizing resource efficiency. Our algorithms, evaluated in a simulated environment using state-of-the-art workload benchmarks, achieve significant energy consumption improvements while maintaining comparable latency.

**Keywords:** Service placement · Multi-access edge computing · Task dependency graph

## 1 Introduction

Driven by the advent of fifth generation (5G) network, multi-access edge computing (MEC) emerges as a transformative paradigm by leveraging network and computing resources at the network edge. This proximity offers low-latency access for mobile subscribers and facilitates the execution of complex, computationally intensive applications [9]. However, effectively managing custom applications in MEC requires strategic task offloading. This involves strategically assigning tasks to the most suitable computing nodes, balancing the demands of both users (low latency) and providers (resource efficiency). Jobs submitted by users may surround IoT data processing, healthcare, Augmented Reality(AR)-based experiences or financial services. The offloading process considers the application's underlying requirements, and allocates sufficient resources at the edge to ensure their successful execution.

© The Author(s), under exclusive license to Springer Nature Switzerland AG 2025
M. Naldi et al. (Eds.): GECON 2024, LNCS 15358, pp. 150–164, 2025.
https://doi.org/10.1007/978-3-031-81226-2_14

Quality of Service (QoS), a measure of service effectiveness, is paramount for service providers in MEC. Delivering optimal QoS involves meeting multiple objectives such as latency, bandwidth, and availability. Providers achieve this by meticulously coordinating network and computing resources, down to individual task allocation [10]. Beyond QoS, profitability remains a key concern. Minimising server rental costs and power consumption directly impact profits and contribute to a more sustainable industry. However, achieving these goals often involves trade-offs [15]. Striking a balance between user satisfaction (low latency) and provider needs (cost efficiency) presents a multi-objective optimization problem. While existing research offers solutions for various scenarios, they may lack the necessary universality and flexibility required for the dynamic nature of MEC environments and complex applications.

Beyond managing the distributed nature of MEC resources, the placement of services presents an additional challenge. In real-world applications, numerous interdependent components frequently collaborate [16]. Each component executes a specific task such as data extraction, transformation, loading, or integration. The optimal placement of these components has to fulfil the requirements of each component with dependency guarantees.

Existing service placement strategies in edge computing struggle to effectively handle these complex, dependency-aware applications. Traditional methods often overlook the inter-dependencies of application modules, or leverage a specific architecture or model. To address this gap, we propose service placement approaches specifically designed for Cloud-MEC environments, aiming at efficiently allocate resources for complex service execution and fulfill both user and provider demands. Offloading occurs at edge nodes located close to user devices, where computational tasks are transferred to reduce latency. Computation-intensive tasks may also be offloaded to powerful cloud data centers.

This work addresses the service placement problem with precedence constraints among service applications. Our objective is to improve quality of service (QoS), specifically minimizing latency, and optimize resource efficiency, measured by energy consumption. The inherent complexity of considering these multiple factors motivates our development of two novel heuristic-based placement algorithms. These algorithms strive to achieve a balance between minimizing user-experienced latency and energy consumption. Our contributions in this work are twofold:

- Dependency-aware Service Placement Algorithms: We propose two novel service placement algorithms specifically designed for the multi-access edge computing (MEC) environment. These algorithms consider precedence constraints between service components to optimize both end-to-end latency and dynamic energy consumption.
- YAFS Platform Extension: To support the evaluation of our algorithms, we developed an extension[1] to the YAFS simulation platform [6]. This extension enables the modeling of sequential task processing, a crucial aspect of service execution in MEC.

---

[1] https://github.com/Sukiiichan/YAFS_MEC.

The remainder of this paper is organized as follows. Section 2 briefly summarizes existing approaches and identifies the research gap. Section 3 describes the system models and problem formulation. Section 4 proposes our two algorithms in detail. Simulation results are presented in Sect. 5, and the paper concludes in Sect. 6.

## 2   Related Work

The multi-objective placement problem has attracted significant research attention, with solutions targeting diverse deployment scenarios and optimization goals. For example, [3] solves the joint user association and service function chain (SFC) placement problem in 5G networks, [5] proposed resource management schemes for Industrial IoT applications in Cloud-Edge networks. Thorough survey of literature surrounding the placement problem in various computing paradigms can be seen in [10]. However, many existing work differ from ours in the underlying assumptions and granularity of problem-solving. For instance, the aforementioned approaches leverage a Kubernetes-based architecture that limits its applicability. Consequently, their application to our context is not feasible. Existing task offloading research often investigates coarse-level abstractions of applications and overlook the task dependencies, which may be sufficient for jobs with less stringent latency requirements, while a number of approaches employ fine-grained service placement strategies that account for inter-service dependencies and allow more precise control for latency-sensitive applications. [7] extracts the function-level dependencies from the application using analysis tools. [8] studies the offloading of sub-tasks with dependencies and the allocation of communication resources in unmanned aerial vehicles assisted MEC systems. The approaches mentioned above either reduces a single metric, or incorporate specific strategies such as service replication. While in our work, we aim to reduce both the total energy consumption and latency throughout application execution without resorting to service replicas.

Service placement solutions typically target various objectives, including minimising end-to-end latency [2,3], reducing costs [16], lowering energy consumption [4], and improving resource utilization [13]. In the context of multi-objective optimization problems, researchers have employed a diverse set of approaches, including heuristics, meta-heuristics, and deep reinforcement learning, to achieve a balance between different objectives. For example, [17] proposes a joint placement algorithm for non-scalable services, balancing latency and deployment cost. Our proposed algorithms aim at optimising both user experience and energy efficiency. We strive to minimise end-to-end latency and reduce the dynamic energy consumption caused by computations. Several prior studies have explored optimisation objectives that converge with those targeted by our proposed approach. While work like [15] explore the energy-delay trade-off using monolithic task scheduling, it lacks dependency awareness. More recently, [16] presents a task offloading scheme for dependent tasks, jointly optimising latency and energy. However, their focus is on local execution vs. edge offloading, while ours leverages both Multi-access Edge Computing (MEC) and cloud resources. Similarly, regarding the energy consumption optimisation in dependency-aware placement strategies, [8,12] primarily focus on minimising energy consumption at the user device level.

Our work departs from the existing literature by considering a more realistic and intricate scenario that incorporates Cloud-MEC network characteristics and inter-service dependencies, and optimising energy consumption across the entire system comprehensively. We propose two heuristic-based algorithms designed for fast execution. These algorithms optimise user-experienced latency and minimise the overall energy consumption associated with task execution, allowing for a holistic optimization of both QoS and environmental sustainability.

## 3  System Model and Problem Formulation

### 3.1  MEC Network Model

Our work considers a multi-tier Cloud-MEC network infrastructure (Fig. 1) where micro datacenters (MDCs) act as resource pools at the edge, residing at interconnected mobile stations. Within each MDC, two key entities exist: edge **computing servers** available for service deployment and execution, and **data sources** that provide data flow from databases, sensors, and IoT devices without performing computations locally. Query-requests from various **user devices** can be concurrently handled by the MEC. The multi-access edge network is connected to a resource-rich cloud data center (Cloud DC).

We model the Cloud-MEC network topology as a graph: $G = (M, L)$. $M = \{m_1, m_2, ...m_n\}$ refers to the set of $n$ MDCs and Cloud DC, and $L = \{l_1, l_2, ...l_p\}$ represents the set of network connections between the DCs. The set of computing servers maintained by MDC $m_i$ can be expressed as $S_i = \{s_{i,1}, s_{i,2}, ...s_{i,m}\}$, while $D_i = \{d_{i,1}, d_{i,2}, ...d_{i,k}\}$ indicates the data sources connected to the local network of $m_i$. Server specifications of each $s_i \in S$ are given by $\{\gamma_{s_i}, \mu_{s_i}, f_{s_i}\}$, representing respectively the memory capacity, storage capacity and CPU frequency. For every network link $l \in L$, the two MDCs connected through it are expressed as $(l^{src}, l^{dst})$. The link bandwidth of $l$ is denoted by $b_l$, and the propagation delay of $l$ is a constant value $prop_l$.

### 3.2  Application Model

from each source to the corresponding service module. We use the directed acyclic graph (DAG) to establish the application model. The application $A$ that the user equipment (UE) requests to execute can be represented in the form of a DAG $A = (V, E)$. $V = \{D, O\}$ is the set of nodes composing the application, and $E$ is the directed edge set representing dataflow dependencies between the modules. We let $D = \{d_1, d_2, ...d_m\}$ to represent the data sources involved in the application, and use $O = \{o_1, o_2, ...o_n\}$ to indicate the set of service modules that are responsible for dataflow processing operations. The end user is denoted by $U$.

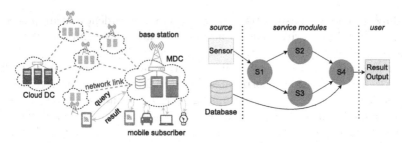

**Fig. 1.** An example Cloud-MEC network and an example app.

Each service module $o_i \in O$ represents a processing operator or function, with a set of properties $\{\alpha_{o_i}, \theta_{o_i}, \omega_{o_i}\}$ denoting the memory, storage and CPU cycles it requires to process each task. Modules with no predecessors that require input from outer data sources are called entry modules. Similarly, we refer to the modules without successor nodes as exit modules. The outputs of all exit nodes will be directed to the end user. Each edge $e$ in the set $E = \{e_1, e_2, ...e_o\}$ has an attribute $\delta_e$ representing the size of each packet transmitted. The start node $e^{start}$ of the directed edge $e$ is the source module sending data packets through the edge, and the end node $e^{end}$ is the destination. Our processing model adheres to the following assumptions: (i) a service is triggered only when it has received inputs from all its predecessors, (ii) each task represents the minimal unit of work and is indivisible, and (iii) each service node sends results to its successors only after finishing its task processing.

### 3.3   Problem Formulation

**Communication and Computation Model.** The communication time $T_{e,l}^{comm}$ for a data packet corresponding to DAG edge $e$ to be transmitted through network link $l$ can be calculated by summing up the data transmission time (packet size $\delta_e$ divided by bandwidth $b_l$) and the propagation delay, as expressed in Eq. 1 The deployment plan of a service module $o$ is denoted by $P(o)$, which is a mapping from service module $o$ to server $s$. For a DAG edge $e$ and its two vertices $o_{start}$, $o_{end}$, we assume these two modules are offloaded to servers $s_i$ and $s_j$ respectively. We use $path(s_i, s_j) = \{l_1, l_2...l_n\}$ to denote the routing path from server $s_i$ to $s_j$. When the predecessor module $o_{start}$ sends a data packet to the successor $o_{end}$, the communication delay is calculated by summing up the transmission delay and propagation delay along the routing path. Therefore, the total communication delay is obtained by Eq. 2 Additionally, between two services deployed in the same MDC, we assume a constant network delay.

$$T_{e,l}^{comm} = \delta_e/b_l + prop_l \quad (1) \quad T_{e,s_i s_j}^{comm} = \sum_{l}^{path(s_i,s_j)} (\frac{\delta_e}{b_l} + prop_l) \quad (2)$$

Assume that any computing server $s_i$ runs at a constant frequency $f_{s_i}$ when processing tasks, given the workload required by a service module $o$ to process a data packet requiring $\omega_o$ CPU cycles, the execution time can be calculated by Eq. 3

$$T_{o,s_i}^{exec} = \frac{\omega_o}{f_{s_i}} \quad (3) \qquad\qquad T_{o|n}^{exec} = T_o^{exec} * K(n) \quad (4)$$

For multiple service modules operating concurrently on the same server, the overhead caused by resource contention among the services is introduced by an overhead function $K$. $K(n)$ denotes the overhead coefficient for the multi-tenancy scenario of $n$ service modules deployed on one server. When $n$ service modules including $o$ are deployed on the same server and sharing resources, the task processing time of $o$ is calculated by Eq. 4

According to Sect. 3.2, for service modules with multiple predecessor nodes, the service module will not start the task execution until data packets from all the predecessors have arrived. The waiting time caused during this process affects the user-experienced delay. Therefore, for a service module $o$, the earliest time it starts processing tasks is decided by its most time-consuming predecessor. For $o$ with its predecessors $pred(o)$, we obtain its *Earliest Start Time (EST)* by:

$$EST(o) = \max_{o_i \in pred(o)} \left\{ EST(o_i) + T_{o_i}^{exec} + T_{o_i,o}^{comm} + T_{o_i,o}^{prop} \right\} \quad (5)$$

Thus the end-to-end latency experienced by user $U$ is $EST(U)$.

**Energy Consumption Model.** We drive the dominant, dynamic energy consumption of each server by calculating its dynamic power consumption over time. According to [15] and Eq. 3 assuming the supply voltage of the CMOS circuits and CPU operating frequency are linearly dependent, for a server running a service module $o$, the dynamic energy consumption during the processing period of a task is approximated by $EC_{dynamic} = \beta f^2 \omega_o$, where $\beta$ represents a device related factor.

**Placement Problem Formulation.** The objective of the present problem is to minimise the user-experienced latency and reduce overall dynamic energy consumption. The solution should be an appropriate mapping from the service nodes to the servers. We call a placement plan valid only if all the service modules are assigned to servers with sufficient resources and all the constraints are met. In light of this, we formulate the conditions that make a placement plan valid: (i)Given the set of service modules $O$ to place and the set of available servers in the Cloud-MEC environment $G$, each service in O should be mapped to a server in $G$. We formulate such a progress as a mapping function $P$, let S denote the set of all servers in the network, then $P : O \to S$ indicates a complete deployment of all services. (ii)The summation of resource occupancy for all assigned modules should not violate the capacity of the server.

$$\left. \begin{array}{l} \Phi_s = \{o \mid o \in O, P(o) = s\} \\ \forall s \in S \end{array} \right| \Rightarrow \begin{cases} \sum_{o \in \Phi_s} \theta_o \leq \mu_s \\ \sum_{o \in \Phi_s} \alpha_o \leq \gamma_s \end{cases} \quad (6)$$

(iii) Aside from these basic conditions, various optimisation goals may exist. In this work, our focus is to minimise user-experienced latency and overall energy consumption, therefore the multi-objective optimisation problem can be formulated as: **Opt** : $min\ EST(U), min\ \sum_{s \in S} EC_s$.

## 4    Energy-and-Latency-Aware Placement Algorithms

### 4.1    Energy-Aware Delay-Experienced Minimisation Algorithm

The proposed service placement algorithm, Energy-aware delay-experienced Minimisation (EDEM), adopts a two-stage approach to achieve a balance between latency minimisation and energy consumption reduction. In the first, coarse-grain stage, EDEM determines a service-to-MDC deployment plan that prioritises reducing end-to-end latency. Subsequently, the fine-grain stage refines the server deployment plan within each MDC, focusing on optimising energy consumption without affecting the overall latency. **Coarse-grain scheduler:** The critical-path-based coarse-grain scheduler seeks a balanced configuration with minimal transmission latency and maximized processing efficiency, leading to the lowest overall end-to-end latency. The pseudo-code of the coarse-grain scheduler is presented in Algorithm 1. We use $S(A)$ to denote the state space of services in application $A$, consisting all service-to-MDC placement options. The scheduler explores $S(A)$ by post-order traversing all placement options of the service modules in $A$. According to Eq. 5, the calculation of $EST$ for any service $v$ rely on the $EST$ value of all its predecessor modules $v.predecessors$. Following such rule, the scheduler can estimate the $EST$ for each service, paving the way for critical-path selection.

The critical path selection works in a greedy and optimistic fashion. Starting from the bottom, for each visited service $v$, given the set of available MDCs $M$, the value of $EST(v)$ will be estimated assuming $v$ resides at the least-loaded server $m.leastloaded$ in each MDC $m \in M$. For each predecessor $v.pred$ of $v$, knowing its estimated EST values $[EST(v.pred, m_1), EST(v.pred, m_2), ...]$, the pair $(v.pred, m)$ that produces the minimum estimated EST will be selected. Among all the selected predecessor-MDC pairs, the one with the maximum EST value will be chosen and marked as a critical node, and the criticality of non-critical modules becomes the EST value difference between it and the critical node in the same hierarchy. Such operation will be repeated until the exit node is reached. Thus we get the critical path reflecting the MDC allocation plan for the critical modules, while non-critical modules remain unassigned. At this stage, the load status of the MDCs involved in the MDC allocation plan will be updated, so is the least-loaded server $m.leastloaded$ of each MDC $m \in M$. Then the max-min procedures will be resumed for the non-critical modules, until their MDC allocation plan is decided. **Fine-grain scheduler:** Having the service-to-MDC placement plan decided in the coarse-grain stage, for each MDC involved, a fine-grain scheduler runs to drive the module-to-server placement solution. The fine-grain scheduler tries to place modules on less power-consuming servers, under the premise that the end-to-end latency of critical nodes will not be affected. Critical modules will take priority in placement, followed by non-critical modules. The pseudo-code of the fine-grain scheduler is presented as Step 3 in Algorithm 1. Similar to the design of the coarse-grain scheduler, all service-to-server placement options will be considered. The scheduler estimates the earliest start time of every service module regarding each available server in the local MDC. Holding the rule that the $EST$ value of modules on non-critical branches should not exceed the $EST$ of critical modules on the same hierarchy, for each possible placement option $(v, s)$, we calculate the value of $EST(v, s)$, and remove the ones that violate the rule. The remaining placement options are marked as 'valid', and the one with the minimum energy consumption $EC(v, s)$ will be chosen and added to the placement plan. The energy consumption will be approximated according to 3.3. Once a service placement decision is finalised, the load status of the server involved will be updated, and the estimated $EST$ of affected placement options will be recalculated. Such process will be repeated until all the service modules are mapped to exact servers.

---

**Algorithm 1: EDEM**

---

**Data**: App. $A = (V, E)$, MEC $G = (M, L)$
**Result**: Server placement map $P : O \to S$
*1. Coarse-grain stage:*
Initiate $S(A)$ $\forall v \in V, \forall m \in M$; $CP = \emptyset$;
Explore $S(A)$ using post-order traversal:
**for** $v.pred \in v.prdecessors$ **do**
    **for** $m \in M$ **do**
        Compute $EST(v.pred, m)$;
    **end**
    Select $(v.pred, m)$ with $min$
    $EST(v.pred, m)$;
**end**
$CP \leftarrow (v.pred, m)$ with $max(EST(v.pred, m))$;
Compute $Criticality(v)$;
*2. Fine-grain stage:*

**for** $(v, m) \in critical\_path$ **do**
    Initiate $S(V)$ $\forall s \in m.servers$;
    **for** $s \in m.servers$ **do**
        **if** $EST(v, s) \leq Criticality(v)$ **then**
            Compute $EC(v, s)$;
    **end**
    Assign $v$ to $s$ with $min$ $EC(v, s)$;
    Update load status of $s$;
**end**
**for** $(v, m) \notin critical\_path$ **do**
    Initiate $S(V)$ $\forall s \in m.servers$;
    **for** $s \in m.servers$ **do**
        **if** $EST(v, s) + T_{comm}(v, v.succ) \leq$
        $Criticality(v.succ)$ **then**
            Compute $EC(v, s)$;
    **end**
    Assign $v$ to $s$ with min $EC(v, s)$;
    Update load status of $s$;
**end**

---

## 4.2 Delay-aware Energy Minimisation Algorithm (DEM)

DEM prioritizes energy efficiency by first seeking an energy-saving server placement plan. Unlike EDEM, which prioritizes latency first, DEM focuses on minimizing energy consumption in the initial stage. This is followed by a refinement stage that fine-tunes the placement plan to optimize latency without exceeding the established energy constraints. DEM can be broken down into the 3 steps:

***Step 1:*** All available servers in the MEC network are sorted by the device-related energy consumption coefficient, in ascending order. Then a level-order traversal of the application graph starts from the entry modules. At each layer, modules are randomly assigned resources from the pre-ranked server list. After the assignment, DEM estimates the $EST$ value for each module, using Eq. 5.

*Step 2:* While *Step 1* prioritizes energy-efficient servers, it might not guarantee minimal total energy consumption. This is because geographically distant placements of dependent modules can lead to longer data transmission times and increased server idle energy usage while waiting for packets. To address this, a refinement stage iteratively explores alternative placements for each service module. For each module, all unexplored MDCs (excluding its current location) are considered. Within each unexplored MDC, the least power-consuming server is evaluated for potential reassignment. The algorithm estimates the total energy consumption $EC$ after each potential reassignment and updates the placement plan if a more energy-efficient configuration is found. Finally, the refined placement's overall latency $EST(U)$ and total energy consumption $\sum_{s \in S} EC(s)$ are calculated and stored for the next stage.

*Step 3:* Building upon the refined resource allocation (*Step 2*), DEM also focuses on improving user-experienced latency. Similar to EDEM's fine-tuning, it identifies critical modules through the application's critical path. For each critical module, it explores reassignment to alternative servers intending to reduce the critical path's estimated latency. After each reassignment, the critical path is recalculated to reflect potential latency improvements. This iterative process continues until no further latency reduction is possible. The resulting placement plan, balancing energy efficiency and latency, is then used to generate the final module-to-server mapping. The pseudo-code of DEM is presented in Algorithm 2.

---

**Algorithm 2: DEM**

---

**Data:** Application $A = (V, E)$, MEC network $G = (M, L)$
**Result:** Server placement map $P : O \rightarrow S$
*1. Server sorting and initial service assignment:*
Sort all servers $s \in G$ by $coeff(s)$;
$curServerIdx \leftarrow 0$;
Group service from level $n$ to $0$ and shuffle each set $S_n, ... S_0$
**for** *service* $v \in S_n, ..., S_0$ **do**
    Assign $v$ to server with index $curServerIdx$; $curServerIdx++$;
**end**
**for** $v \in V$ **do**
    Compute $EST(v,P(v))$ using Eqs;
**end**
*2. Energy-aware reassignment:*

**for** $v \in V$ **do**
    **for** $m \in M$ **do**
        **if** $P(v) \notin m$ **then**
            $s = \arg\min_{s' \in m.servers} coeff(s')$;
            **if** $EST(v,s) < EST(v,P(v))$ **then**
                Assign server $s$ to $v$;
        **end**
    **end**
Compute $EST(U)$ using Eqs;
Sum up $EstimatedEC(v,P(v)) \; \forall \; v \in V$;
*3. Latency-aware reassignment:*
Identify $critical\_path$ of A under placement $P$;
**for** $(v, P(v)) \in critical\_path$ **do**
    **for** $s \in P(v).mdc.servers$ **do**
        **if** $EST(U) > EST(U|P(v) = s)$ **then**
            Assign server $s$ to $v$;
            Re-identify $critical\_path$ of $A$;
    **end**
**end**

---

# 5   Experimental Evaluation

## 5.1   Performance Indicators and Setup

We employed simulation to evaluate the performance of the proposed algorithms (DEM and EDEM). The YAFS fog simulator [6] was used and extended to support sequential processing of dependent tasks. Network topologies were created using the NetworkX library[2]. These topologies consisted of up to 20 datacenters, one acting as the cloud and the others as micro edge datacenters. Each datacenter housed up to 5 computing servers. Details regarding the specific MEC network configurations are provided in Table 1. Three different random graph generation models were utilized: Barabasi-Albert (B-A) [1], Watts-Strogatz (W-S) [14], and ring topology.

To achieve more general results, real-world workloads were utilized from the Alibaba[3] cluster trace dataset. This dataset provides Directed Acyclic Graph information of production batch workloads from a large-scale cluster. Jobs composed of computing and algorithm services as well as statistical and data processing services, were submitted by users. We filtered applications exceeding 10 modules and selected 10 for evaluation (Table 2). Module resource requirements were configured based on the provided traces. For each experiment set, system events were simulated for 20,000 global timestamps and repeated 5 times with identical configurations to generate statistically significant averages. The simulations were conducted on a server with 4x Intel Xeon Gold 6230N CPU, 256GB of RAM and Ubuntu 20.04 operating system.

The proposed algorithms (DEM and EDEM) were evaluated based on four key metrics: i) Overall Energy Consumption ($EC$): This metric represents the total power consumed by all servers during the execution period, estimated from CPU usage data according to 3.3. ii) Average User-Experienced Latency ($LT$): This metric is the mean response time of user requests, calculated from raw timestamps recorded by the simulator during network transmissions. iii) Edge prioritization ($EP$): This metric reflects the percentage of services deployed at the Edge, iv) Algorithm Execution Time ($ET$): This metric indicates the time required for the algorithm to generate a placement, i.e. the wall clock time for executing each algorithm. The performance of DEM and EDEM was compared

**Table 1.** Configurations

|  | Cloud | MDC |
|---|---|---|
| CPU frequency (GHz) | [3,5] | [1,2] |
| RAM (GB) | [32,64] | [1,4] |
| Propagation Delay (ms) | 8 | 1 |
| Bandwidth (Gbps) | 10 | 2 |

**Table 2.** Application characteristics

| id | $\|V\|$ | $\|E\|$ | Max degree | Average transfer volume | Average workload |
|---|---|---|---|---|---|
| 0 | 12 | 9 | 3 | 39.33 | 9.50 |
| 1 | 16 | 17 | 6 | 29.00 | 257.88 |
| 2 | 16 | 17 | 7 | 23.63 | 40.50 |
| 3 | 17 | 17 | 5 | 42.82 | 13.53 |
| 4 | 16 | 17 | 3 | 46.06 | 35.75 |
| 5 | 12 | 11 | 6 | 38.67 | 8.17 |
| 6 | 10 | 10 | 4 | 44.30 | 14.40 |
| 7 | 10 | 9 | 5 | 35.60 | 7.10 |
| 8 | 16 | 16 | 2 | 47.19 | 1.00 |
| 9 | 10 | 9 | 4 | 43.40 | 32.70 |

---

[2] https://networkx.org/.

[3] https://github.com/alibaba/clusterdata.

against four existing algorithms: Response Time Aware (RTA) [2], Genetic Algorithm (GA) [11], Maximize Reliability Offloading (MROA) [12] and Energy-Makespan Multi-objective Optimization(EM-MOO) [4]. We selected these algorithms for their varying complexity, computational overhead, and optimization goals, providing a broader assessment of DEM and EDEM's efficiency.

## 5.2  Performance Assessment

In total, we conducted 8100 experiments, consisting of 5 experiments for each of the 6 algorithms and for each of the 10 applications. We varied the number of MDCs (denoted by $n$) between [5, 10, 20], and the number of servers (denoted by $m$) within each MDC to [2, 4, 8]. Also, we utilized three different network topologies. All figures presented in this section demonstrate the normalized performance of both $EC$ and $LT$ metrics. We set the source data emission interval to 100ms and the simulated time to 100 s and plot the performance of the proposed algorithms in terms of the aforementioned metrics. In Fig. 2, we show the normalized energy consumption for all algorithms. It can be seen that during the experiments using varied applications and under varied network typology, the DEM algorithm achieves significantly lower energy consumption compared to other algorithms, while RTA and MROA reaches the highest energy consumption. This is because RTA merely searches for the placement plan that may shorten the end-to-end latency, therefore less energy-efficient servers are chosen, and the overall energy consumption is sacrificed; MROA focuses merely on lowering the energy consumption of the user equipment, rather than that of the servers involved in task offloading, therefore the total energy consumed for task processing is rather high. DEM, on the contrary, tends to allocate services to edge servers with higher energy efficiency. Following DEM, EDEM also achieves energy consumption levels comparable to those of the GA and EM-MOO. Across diverse network topologies, DEM and EDEM maintain stable performances in terms of normalised energy consumption, while EM-MOO falter under the Watts–Strogatz network model. This proves that DEM and EDEM are robust to network variations.

Figure 3 demonstrates the normalized latency. We can observe that RTA, EDEM and MROA reach the lowest latency under all the scenarios. It should be highlighted that RTA and MROA sacrifice energy efficiency to achieve their performance, whereas EDEM maintains metrics. GA tends to demonstrate the worst performance for all network topologies while EDEM excels in certain applications. Specifically, in the ring topology, EDEM provides better latency performance which is crucial when network latency poses a significant bottleneck. Combining the results from Fig. 2 and Fig. 3, we can state that, compared to existing works, DEM and EDEM hold different degrees of preference for reducing energy consumption and lowering latency. EDEM effectively balances overall energy consumption and latency. On the other hand, DEM prioritizes energy-saving placement plans, potentially sacrificing latency to some extent.

Figures 4, 6 reveal that for the EC metric, the DEM and GA algorithms show the most significant improvements and efficiency when increasing either the number of MDCs or servers, while MROA consistently underperforms. EMMOO shows a slight decrease in energy consumption as the number of resources increases. Although EDEM is not the best choice, it demonstrates stable performance, making it a reasonable option. For the LT metric, RTA, EMMOO, and DEM perform better when increasing the number of MDCs, with EDEM following closely behind (Fig. 5). GA and MROA struggle with scalability in reducing latency as the system becomes more complex. In Fig 7, we observe that increasing the number of servers generally worsens latency performance for most algorithms. Although GA shows some improvement as the number of servers increases, it still cannot effectively optimize latency as the system scales up, compared to the other algorithms. EDEM, similar to its performance with the EC metric, remains stable, making it the best candidate when the number of servers exceeds four.

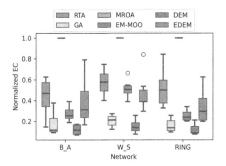

**Fig. 2.** $EC$, $n=20$ $m=4$

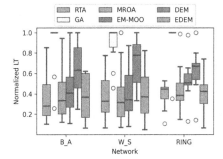

**Fig. 3.** $LT$, $n=20$ $m=4$

Table 3 offers a breakdown of service deployment across edge servers and the cloud. The number shown in the table represents the percentage of services deployed at the edge. The results of MROA align with our analysis: it greedily selects non-local, powerful machines. Consequently, around 40% of the services are offloaded to the cloud, resulting in the highest energy consumption observed. RTA and EDEM have similar preferences in adopting resources. Around 75–85% of the services are deployed at edge facilities, with the remaining tasks executed on the cloud. Such approach achieves a well-balanced outcome in terms of both latency and energy consumption: performing most computations at the edge helps to reduce transmission and energy costs, while offloading a select few, computationally intensive tasks to the cloud minimises processing time. By deploying over 95% of services at the edge, DEM, EMMOO and GA demonstrate the strongest tendency to utilise edge resources. Prioritising edge placement leads to the lowest energy consumption, but as a consequence of the energy-latency trade-off, the task execution time may not be as low as cloud execution, potentially sacrificing user-experienced latency.

The execution time of each algorithm is presented in Table 4. As expected, GA exhibit the longest execution times ($\sim$4 s), followed by EMMOO ($\sim$1 s), due

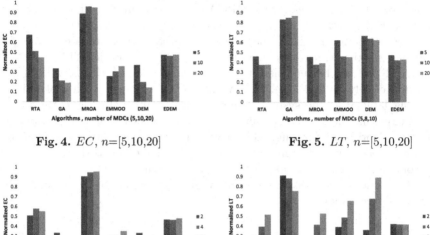

**Fig. 4.** $EC$, $n$=[5,10,20]

**Fig. 5.** $LT$, $n$=[5,10,20]

**Fig. 6.** $EC$, $m$=[2,4,8]

**Fig. 7.** $LT$, $m$=[2,4,8]

**Table 3.** Edge prioritization, $EP$

|       | RTA   | GA    | MROA  | EMMOO | DEM   | EDEM  |
|-------|-------|-------|-------|-------|-------|-------|
| B-A   | 85.86 | 97.75 | 58.52 | 98.80 | 98.24 | 85.70 |
| RING  | 76.61 | 89.79 | 57.90 | 99.66 | 95.19 | 84.24 |
| W-S   | 76.85 | 89.69 | 60.40 | 99.13 | 94.04 | 84.46 |

**Table 4.** Execution time (ms), $ET$

|       | RTA   | GA      | MROA | EMMOO   | DEM    | EDEM   |
|-------|-------|---------|------|---------|--------|--------|
| B-A   | 45.35 | 4110.22 | 3.13 | 1077.88 | 224.91 | 138.63 |
| RING  | 42.79 | 4475.50 | 3.37 | 1066.64 | 315.66 | 173.59 |
| W-S   | 45.96 | 4407.99 | 3.15 | 1064.44 | 290.66 | 161.51 |

to their population-based search and iterative nature, respectively. Conversely, MROA achieves the fastest execution times across all topologies because its operations related to latency and energy consumption limitations are skipped when no deadline constraints are set. RTA achieves the second fastest execution times across all topologies as it focuses solely on a single objective. EDEM and DEM demonstrate execution times comparable to RTA, thus can be adopted to respond in real-time and time-sensitive applications at the MEC. We also conducted an additional set of experiments to assess the impact of a MEC environment. In these experiments, we assumed a setup with 4 MDCs, 1 Cloud DC, and a BA topology. The results show that, on average, latency is reduced by 46.8% and energy consumption by 32.9% when scheduling decisions select resources from the edge-cloud continuum instead of relying solely on cloud resources.

# 6   Conclusions and Future Work

This paper introduces EDEM and DEM, two algorithms for service module placement in MEC networks that consider dependencies between service modules. EDEM prioritizes energy efficiency while maintaining low latency impact on users. DEM, on the other hand, achieves significant energy reductions by allowing for a more flexible trade-off with increased latency. Factors like the queuing of queries from different users that can impact the overall transmission delay, will be addressed in the next step. Future work will also incorporate user mobility into the design for better real-world applicability. Additionally, we aim to develop online versions of EDEM and DEM, enabling dynamic service rescheduling based on changing resource availability in MEC networks.

**Acknowledgments.** This work was supported in part by the Research Institute of Trustworthy Autonomous Systems (RITAS), and in part by the Shenzhen Science and Technology Program (project No. GJHZ20210705141807022).

# References

1. Barabási, A.L., Albert, R.: Emergence of scaling in random networks. Science **286**(5439), 509–512 (1999)
2. Cai, X., Kuang, H., Hu, H., Song, W., Lü, J.: Response time aware operator placement for complex event processing in edge computing. In: Pahl, C., Vukovic, M., Yin, J., Yu, Q. (eds.) Service-Oriented Computing: 16th International Conference, ICSOC 2018, Hangzhou, China, November 12-15, 2018, Proceedings, pp. 264–278. Springer International Publishing, Cham (2018). https://doi.org/10.1007/978-3-030-03596-9_18
3. Harutyunyan, D., Shahriar, N., Boutaba, R., Riggio, R.: Latency and mobility-aware service function chain placement in 5g networks. IEEE Trans. Mob. Comput. **21**(5), 1697–1709 (2020)
4. Ijaz, S., Munir, E.U., Ahmad, S.G., Rafique, M.M., Rana, O.F.: Energy-makespan optimization of workflow scheduling in fog-cloud computing. Computing **103**, 2033–2059 (2021)
5. Kaur, K., Garg, S., Kaddoum, G., Ahmed, S.H., Atiquzzaman, M.: Keids: Kubernetes-based energy and interference driven scheduler for industrial Iot in edge-cloud ecosystem. IEEE Internet Things J. **7**(5), 4228–4237 (2019)
6. Lera, I., Guerrero, C., Juiz, C.: Yafs: A simulator for iot scenarios in fog computing. IEEE Access **7**, 91745–91758 (2019)
7. Mo, J., Liu, J., Zhao, Z.: Exploiting function-level dependencies for task offloading in edge computing. In: IEEE INFOCOM 2022-IEEE Conference on Computer Communications Workshops (INFOCOM WKSHPS), pp. 1–6. IEEE (2022)
8. Nguyen, L.X., Tun, Y.K., Dang, T.N., Park, Y.M., Han, Z., Hong, C.S.: Dependency tasks offloading and communication resource allocation in collaborative uavs networks: A meta-heuristic approach. IEEE Internet of Things Journal (2023)
9. Oikonomou, P., Karanika, A., Anagnostopoulos, C., Kolomvatsos, K.: On the use of intelligent models towards meeting the challenges of the edge mesh. ACM Comput. Surv. (CSUR) **54**(6), 1–42 (2021)
10. Salaht, F.A., Desprez, F., Lebre, A.: An overview of service placement problem in fog and edge computing. ACM Comput. Surv. (CSUR) **53**(3), 1–35 (2020)
11. Sarrafzade, N., Entezari-Maleki, R., Sousa, L.: A genetic-based approach for service placement in fog computing. J. Supercomput. 1–22 (2022). https://doi.org/10.1007/s11227-021-04254-w

12. Shang, Y., Li, J., Wu, X.: Dag-based task scheduling in mobile edge computing. In: 2020 7th International Conference on Information Science and Control Engineering (ICISCE), pp. 426–431. IEEE (2020)
13. Skarlat, O., Nardelli, M., Schulte, S., Borkowski, M., Leitner, P.: Optimized iot service placement in the fog. SOCA **11**(4), 427–443 (2017)
14. Watts, D.J., Strogatz, S.H.: Collective dynamics of 'small-world'networks. nature **393**(6684), 440–442 (1998)
15. Zhang, G., Zhang, W., Cao, Y., Li, D., Wang, L.: Energy-delay tradeoff for dynamic offloading in mobile-edge computing system with energy harvesting devices. IEEE Trans. Industr. Inf. **14**(10), 4642–4655 (2018)
16. Zhang, Y., Chen, J., Zhou, Y., Yang, L., He, B., Yang, Y.: Dependent task offloading with energy-latency tradeoff in mobile edge computing. IET Commun. **16**(17), 1993–2001 (2022)
17. Zhao, X., Shi, Y., Chen, S.: Maesp: mobility aware edge service placement in mobile edge networks. Comput. Netw. **182**, 107435 (2020)

# Optimal CPU Frequency Selection to Minimize the Runtime of Tasks Under Power Capping

Fanny Dufossé[1] and Rizos Sakellariou[2]([✉])

[1] University Grenoble Alpes, Inria, CNRS, Grenoble, France
fanny.dufosse@inria.fr
[2] The University of Manchester, Manchester, UK
rizos@manchester.ac.uk

**Abstract.** Data centers are increasingly becoming significant energy consumers worldwide. To reduce the amount of electricity they consume, power capping may be used to set a limit to the maximum power they can use at some given point in time. In this situation, an interesting problem is how to make best use of the available power by throttling the CPU frequency of different servers. As different tasks assigned to each of these servers may not be impacted the same way when changing a server's CPU frequency, one problem that arises is how to select CPU frequencies for each of the servers running tasks with specific characteristics in such a way that the total execution time of all these tasks is minimized while the overall power cap for all the servers is respected. The paper presents an approach that models this problem as an optimization problem and shows how to find an optimal solution in different cases. This work can provide the basis to find economical solutions to operate large data centers under power capping efficiently.

**Keywords:** Data Centers · Power Capping · DVFS · CPU frequency selection

## 1 Introduction

Energy consumption has become a serious concern for computing in recent years. Mechanisms such as *power capping* or *Dynamic Voltage Frequency Scaling* (DVFS) set limits to control power consumption: power capping sets an upper bound for the maximum power that can be consumed at any point in time, while DVFS scales down voltage and CPU frequency, hence power. Both mechanisms have the potential to lead to energy savings, however, there are various aspects and trade-offs that have to be considered for this to happen, also to avoid any adverse effects on performance and system Quality of Service [10,12,20]. In general, there appears to be a consensus that such techniques need to be carefully managed if they are to lead to energy savings.

In this paper, we present work that considers a set of DVFS-enabled servers which operate in an environment where a global power cap needs to be met. This

© The Author(s), under exclusive license to Springer Nature Switzerland AG 2025
M. Naldi et al. (Eds.): GECON 2024, LNCS 15358, pp. 165–174, 2025.
https://doi.org/10.1007/978-3-031-81226-2_15

could be, for instance, the servers of a cluster, a cloud provider or a data center, where the total power consumption of the cluster, provider or data center, respectively, should not exceed a certain limit. Each of the servers has been allocated some tasks, with specific CPU and I/O requirements; these tasks cannot be reallocated and must be executed on the servers they have been allocated to. The problem that we address is how to choose frequencies for each of the servers in a way that the overall execution time of the tasks is minimized, yet the global power cap for all the servers is met. The key property to take into account is the task requirements: the execution time of tasks with high CPU requirements is affected most by a CPU frequency reduction whereas the execution time of tasks with high I/O requirements is affected less.

The rest of the paper describes the fundamentals of an approach to solve the problem. Section 2 provides some background and related work. Section 3 formulates the problem. Section 4 presents a solution along with an example of how this solution can be applied. Finally, Sect. 5 concludes the paper.

## 2   Background and Related Work

There has been lots of work in the literature that considers DVFS-enabled resources where the objective is to select appropriate CPU frequencies often to minimize energy consumption [1,2,11,14,16,19]. Other work has also considered how to optimize performance in the presence of a power cap [5,6,18]. In general, finding an appropriate configuration of frequencies to meet a power cap without overly damaging performance is not a trivial problem. Besides the optimization aspects, there are various trade-offs between power (hence CPU frequency too), energy and performance, which may also be affected by the characteristics of the specific applications that are running; see, for example, Figures 1–3 in [15].

Yet, as also noted in [13,14], some cloud providers price compute resources in terms of CPU frequency too, in such a way that a low CPU frequency costs less than a high CPU frequency. This means that cloud users would need to select CPU frequencies that optimize their use of cloud resources: clearly, going for the cheapest CPU frequency, which is the lowest, may not necessarily be a good option as, in this case, applications will take longer to complete. Furthermore, following the observations in [15], it is not the case that the same CPU frequency would be ideal for different sorts of tasks (applications). Generally, CPU-bound tasks (or tasks that do lots of CPU processing) would be affected more than I/O-bound tasks (or tasks that spend lots of time doing input-output and less time on the CPU) if they run at a lower CPU frequency. In other words, the performance drop of CPU-bound tasks would be more noticeable than the performance drop of I/O-bound tasks when running at a lower CPU frequency. Thus, as users typically have a maximum budget for the cloud resources they use, the problem is how to use their budget to select CPU frequencies appropriately in a way that optimizes the performance of a set of tasks with different characteristics that they need to execute on a cloud platform. It is this problem that motivated the work in this paper.

Assuming that CPU frequencies are priced linearly, the answer to this problem from the user's point of view is equivalent to finding an answer to the following practical question: *Given a cloud provider or a data center that should not exceed a certain power consumption limit (power cap), how this provider/center can lower frequencies of individual servers, each of which has been allocated a specific task with different CPU and I/O characteristics for execution, so that the provider/center's power cap is not exceeded while the total execution time of all these tasks is minimized?*

The model that we develop in the paper to answer this question relies on two key sub-problems that have a significant history in the literature. The first is how to model power consumption in relation to CPU frequency. Generally, it is assumed that power consumption is proportional to frequency cubed [17], a relation that is generalized [2–4] to:

$$P_f = P_0 \cdot f^\alpha, \tag{1}$$

where $P_0$ and $\alpha > 1$ are hardware-dependent characteristics and $P_f$ is the power consumption at frequency $f$. In this paper, we adopt Eq. (1) to model power.

The second sub-problem is how the reduction in frequency affects the execution time of a task. Adopting an approach initially proposed in [9] and also used in [7,8], we estimate the runtime $RT(i, f)$ of a task $i$ at frequency $f$, as follows:

$$RT(i, f) = \left( \beta_i \cdot (\frac{f_{max}}{f} - 1) + 1 \right) \cdot RT(i, f_{max}), \tag{2}$$

where $RT_{f_{max}}$ is the task runtime when running at the maximum CPU frequency $f_{max}$ and $\beta_i$ is a task-specific parameter that captures a task's CPU-boundedness, takes values between 0 and 1 and can be estimated through profiling [7,8]. Tasks with lots of CPU requirements have a value close to 1 whereas tasks with lots of I/O have a value close to 0.

## 3   Problem Formulation

We consider a problem with $n$ tasks allocated on $m$ identical machines. An allocation function *Alloc* indicates for each task $i$, the machine $Alloc_i$ on which it is allocated. In the following, we will use the notation $S_j = \{i, Alloc_i = j\}$, the set of tasks allocated on machine $j$. Each machine can operate at a frequency $f$ between bounds $f_{min}$ and $f_{max}$. The frequencies are fixed once and for all on each machine, before beginning the execution of the tasks. The objective is thus to determine these frequencies in a way that minimizes runtime without exceeding a total power cap. We consider that each task consists of a part of I/O exchanges, and a part of pure CPU computation. The periods of I/O exchanges are not affected by CPU frequency. Both power consumption and runtime are correlated with CPU frequency, as shown in Eqs. (1) and (2). Thus, the runtime of tasks allocated on machine $j$ is

$$RT_j(f) = \sum_{i \in S_j} RT(i, f). \tag{3}$$

For the sake of simplicity, we denote $C_j = \sum_{i \in S_j} \beta_i f_{\max} RT(i, f_{\max})$ the amount of computation of the tasks of $S_j$ and $CT_j = \sum_{i \in S_j} (1 - \beta_i) RT(i, f_{\max})$ its I/O duration. Equation (3) can thus be written:

$$RT_j(f) = \frac{C_j}{f} + CT_j. \tag{4}$$

We consider a power capping constraint $P$ for the consumption of the $m$ machines. We make the hypothesis that $P \geq m \times P_0 f_{\min}^{\alpha}$, to guarantee the existence of a valid solution. The optimization criterion is the sum of the runtimes of all tasks. Then, the objective is to minimize the function:

$$RT = \min_{f_1, \ldots, f_m} \sum_{i=1}^{m} RT_j(f_j) \tag{5}$$

under the constraints:

$$\forall j, P_0 \sum_{j=1}^{m} f_j^{\alpha} \leq P, \tag{6}$$

and

$$\forall j, f_{\min} \leq f_j \leq f_{\max}. \tag{7}$$

Without loss of generality, we will consider in the following $P_0 = 1$.

### 3.1   Example

We consider as an example the execution of 5 tasks with the following parameters $(C_j, CT_j)$: $[(1,5), (6,6), (7,3), (8,2), (40,20)]$. We consider the frequency limits $f_{min} = 2$ and $f_{max} = 5$ and $\alpha = 3$. This means that the minimum power consumption is 40 with resulting runtimes $[5.5, 9, 6.5, 6, 40]$; the sum of runtimes equals 67. The maximal power consumption is 625, with runtimes $[5.2, 7.2, 4.4, 3.6, 28]$ and sum of runtimes 48.4.

We consider a power cap of 200. A first possibility is to run the longest tasks at maximum frequency and the shortest tasks at minimum frequency. We may for example run tasks 1,2 and 3 at frequency 2, and task 5 at frequency 5; the remaining power 51 is for task 4 that can run at frequency $^3\sqrt{51} \sim 3.7$. With this allocation, we obtain a runtime $\sim 53.2$. A second possibility is to use the same frequency for all tasks. We then run all tasks at frequency $^3\sqrt{40} \sim 3.4$. Then, we obtain a runtime of around 54.1.

The optimal frequency values proven in Sect. 4 obtain a sum of runtimes around 53.1.

## 4   An Optimal Algorithm to Select Frequencies

### 4.1   Solution Without Frequency Bounds

We first consider the problem where frequencies have no bounds, that is, there is no constraint as defined in Eq. (7).

**Lemma 1.** *Optimal frequencies with no bounds If no constraints are given for frequencies values, then, the minimum total runtime is reached for*

$$f_i = \left( \frac{P \cdot C_i^{\frac{\alpha}{1+\alpha}}}{\sum_{j=1}^m C_j^{\frac{\alpha}{1+\alpha}}} \right)^{\frac{1}{\alpha}}.$$

*The corresponding total runtime is then*

$$RT = P^{-\frac{1}{\alpha}} \left( \sum_{j=1}^m C_j^{\frac{\alpha}{1+\alpha}} \right)^{\frac{\alpha+1}{\alpha}} + \sum_{j=1}^m CT_j.$$

*Proof.* We demonstrate this lemma by induction on $m$. This property is trivially true for $m = 1$.

Suppose the result holds for $m - 1$, let us prove it for $m$. We denote $P_1$ the power consumed by the $m - 1$ first machines. By induction, we know that for $i$ between 1 and $m - 1$, $f_i = \left( \frac{P_1 \cdot C_i^{\frac{\alpha}{1+\alpha}}}{\sum_{j=1}^{m-1} c_j^{\frac{\alpha}{1+\alpha}}} \right)^{\frac{1}{\alpha}}$. In addition, it remains $P - P_1$ power available for machine $m$, thus $f_m = (P - P_1)^{\frac{1}{\alpha}}$.

We obtain:

$$RT = \min_{P_1} \left( \sum_{i=1}^{m-1} \frac{C_i}{\frac{P_1^{\frac{1}{\alpha}} \cdot c_i^{\frac{1}{1+\alpha}}}{\left( \sum_{j=1}^{m-1} c_j^{\frac{\alpha}{1+\alpha}} \right)^{\frac{1}{\alpha}}}} \right) + \frac{C_m}{(P-P_1)^{\frac{1}{\alpha}}} + \sum_{j=1}^m CT_j$$

$$= \min_{P_1} P_1^{-\frac{1}{\alpha}} \left( \sum_{j=1}^{m-1} c_j^{\frac{\alpha}{1+\alpha}} \right)^{\frac{1}{\alpha}} \left( \sum_{i=1}^{m-1} \frac{C_i}{C_i^{\frac{1}{1+\alpha}}} \right) + \frac{C_m}{(P-P_1)^{\frac{1}{\alpha}}} + \sum_{j=1}^m CT_j$$

$$= \min_{P_1} P_1^{-\frac{1}{\alpha}} \left( \sum_{i=1}^{m-1} C_i^{\frac{\alpha}{1+\alpha}} \right)^{\frac{\alpha+1}{\alpha}} + \frac{C_m}{(P-P_1)^{\frac{1}{\alpha}}} + \sum_{j=1}^m CT_j$$

We define the function $f(x) = x^{-\frac{1}{\alpha}} \left( \sum_{i=1}^{m-1} C_i^{\frac{\alpha}{1+\alpha}} \right)^{\frac{\alpha+1}{\alpha}} + \frac{C_m}{(P-x)^{\frac{1}{\alpha}}}$.

Then, $f'(x) = -\frac{1}{\alpha x^{\frac{\alpha+1}{\alpha}}} \left( \sum_{i=1}^{m-1} C_i^{\frac{\alpha}{1+\alpha}} \right)^{\frac{\alpha+1}{\alpha}} + \frac{C_m}{\alpha(P-x)^{\frac{\alpha+1}{\alpha}}}$. $f'(x)$ is an increasing function between 0 and P, that tends to $-\infty$ in 0 and $+\infty$ in P, so $f(x)$ is first decreasing then increasing, and its minimum is obtained in $x_{opt}$ with $f'(x_{opt}) = 0$. Thus,

$$\frac{1}{\alpha x_{opt}^{\frac{\alpha+1}{\alpha}}} \left( \sum_{i=1}^{m-1} C_i^{\frac{\alpha}{1+\alpha}} \right)^{\frac{\alpha+1}{\alpha}} = \frac{C_m}{\alpha(P-x_{opt})^{\frac{\alpha+1}{\alpha}}}$$

$$\left( \sum_{i=1}^{m-1} C_i^{\frac{\alpha}{1+\alpha}} \right)^{\frac{\alpha+1}{\alpha}} (P - x_{opt})^{\frac{\alpha+1}{\alpha}} = C_m x_{opt}^{\frac{\alpha+1}{\alpha}}$$

$$\left( \sum_{i=1}^{m-1} C_i^{\frac{\alpha}{1+\alpha}} \right) (P - x_{opt}) = C_m^{\frac{\alpha}{1+\alpha}} x_{opt}$$

$$x_{opt} = P \frac{\sum_{i=1}^{m-1} C_i^{\frac{\alpha}{1+\alpha}}}{\sum_{i=1}^m C_i^{\frac{\alpha}{1+\alpha}}}$$

The optimal value for $P_1$ is, therefore, $P_1 = x_{opt}$. We can easily deduce the result for all values $f_i$ and RT.

In the following, we denote

$$f(i,j,k,P) = \left( \frac{P \cdot C_i^{\frac{\alpha}{1+\alpha}}}{\sum_{l=j}^{k} C_l^{\frac{\alpha}{1+\alpha}}} \right)^{\frac{1}{\alpha}}$$

## 4.2   Main Problem Resolution

We now focus on the main problem with frequencies bounded between $f_{\min}$ and $f_{\max}$. First note that if frequencies given by Lemma 1 are all in the good interval defined in Eq. (7), the solution is optimal. We consider without loss of generality that machines are ordered by increasing $C_i$, that is $C_1 \leq C_2 \leq \cdots \leq C_n$. We first prove the following result.

**Lemma 2.** *For two machines $i$ and $j$, if $C_i \leq C_j$, then in the optimal solution $f_i \leq f_j$.*

*Proof.* If we just consider the run times of machines $i$ and $j$, we obtain $x = \frac{C_i}{f_i} + \frac{C_j}{f_j} + CT_i + CT_j$. By optimality, exchanging frequencies of $i$ and $j$ has lower runtime and same power consumption. Thus, if $C_i < C_j$,

$$\frac{C_i}{f_i} + \frac{C_j}{f_j} + CT_i + CT_j \leq \frac{C_i}{f_j} + \frac{C_j}{f_i} + CT_i + CT_j$$
$$\frac{C_i}{f_i} + \frac{C_j}{f_j} \leq \frac{C_i}{f_j} + \frac{C_j}{f_i}$$
$$\frac{C_j - C_i}{f_j} \leq \frac{C_j - C_i}{f_i}$$
$$f_i \leq f_j$$

If $C_i = C_j$, Lemma 1 states that the optimal frequencies are equal for same duration tasks.

We can conclude that in the optimal solution, the frequencies $f_j$ are of increasing values of $j$. We define $j_{\min}$ and $j_{\max}$ as the last index of a machine at frequency $f_{\min}$ (0 if no machine is at $f_{\min}$) and the first index of a machine at $f_{\max}$ ($n+1$ if no machine is at $f_{\max}$). Then, the machines from 1 to $j_{\min}$ run at frequency $f_{\min}$, the machines from $j_{\max}$ to $m$ run at frequency $f_{\max}$, and the machines between $j_{\min}+1$ and $j_{\max}-1$ operate at a frequency defined by Lemma 1. More precisely, for $j_{\min} < j < j_{\max}$, the optimal frequency of machine $j$ is $f_j = f(j, j_{\min}+1, j_{\max}-1, P_{bound})$ with $P_{bound} = P - j_{\min} \cdot f_{\min}^\alpha - (m - j_{\max} + 1) \cdot f_{\max}^\alpha$. This corresponds to an optimal solution of the problem for this subset of machines.

In such a solution, the runtime can be computed as follows:

$$RT = \frac{\sum_{k=1}^{j_{\min}} C_k}{f_{\min}} + P_{bound}^{\frac{1}{\alpha}} \left( \sum_{k=j_{\min}+1}^{j_{\max}-1} C_k^{\frac{\alpha}{\alpha+1}} \right)^{\frac{\alpha+1}{\alpha}} + \frac{\sum_{k=j_{\max}}^{m} C_k}{f_{\max}} + \sum_j CT_j$$

We denote $S_{\min} = \sum_{k=1}^{j_{\min}} C_k$, $S_{\max} = \sum_{k=j_{\max}}^{m} C_k$, $S_{RT} = \sum_{k=j_{\min}+1}^{j_{\max}-1} C_k^{\frac{\alpha}{\alpha+1}}$ and $CT = \sum_j CT_j$. Thus, we obtain:

$$RT = \frac{S_{\min}}{f_{\min}} + P_{bound}^{\frac{1}{\alpha}} S_{RT}^{\frac{\alpha+1}{\alpha}} + \frac{S_{\max}}{f_{\max}} + CT$$

The problem now is to determine the optimal values for $j_{\min}$ and $j_{\max}$. The main constraint for these values corresponds to frequency bounds. The frequencies computed by Lemma 1 need to be contained in the bounds of Eq. (7). Formally,

$$\forall j_{\min} < j < j_{\max}, f_{\min} \leq f(j, j_{\min} + 1, j_{\max} - 1, P_{bound}) \leq f_{\max} \qquad (8)$$

As $C_j$ are in increasing order, we can simply verify

$$f(j_{\min} + 1, j_{\min} + 1, j_{\max} - 1, P_{bound}) \geq f_{\min} \qquad (9)$$

and

$$f(j_{\max} - 1, j_{\min} + 1, j_{\max} - 1, P_{bound}) \leq f_{\max} \qquad (10)$$

With the current notation, we have :

$$f(j_{\min} + 1, j_{\min} + 1, j_{\max} - 1, P_{bound}) = \left( \frac{P \cdot C_{j_{\min}+1}^{\frac{\alpha}{1+\alpha}}}{S_{RT}} \right)^{\frac{1}{\alpha}} \text{ and}$$

$$f(j_{\max} - 1, j_{\min} + 1, j_{\max} - 1, P_{bound}) = \left( \frac{P \cdot C_{j_{\max}-1}^{\frac{\alpha}{1+\alpha}}}{S_{RT}} \right)^{\frac{1}{\alpha}} .$$

**Input:** $f_{min}, f_{max}, \alpha, [(C_1, CT_1), \cdots (C_m, CT_m)]$
1  $MinRT = +\infty$; $S_{total} = \sum_{i=1}^{m} C_i$; $S_{\min} = 0$; $S_{\max} = S_{total}$; $S_{RT} = 0$;
2  **for** $j_{\min} = 0$ *to* $m$ **do**
3  $\qquad S_{\max} = S_{total} - S_{\min}$; $S_{\min}{+}{=} C_{j_{\min}}$; $S_{RT} = -C_{j_{\min}}^{\frac{\alpha}{\alpha+1}}$;
4  $\qquad$ **for** $j_{\max} = j_{\min} + 1$ *to* $m + 1$ **do**
5  $\qquad\qquad S_{\min}{-}{=} C_{j_{\max}-1}$; $S_{RT}{+}{=} C_{j_{\max}-1}^{\frac{\alpha}{\alpha+1}}$;
6  $\qquad\qquad P_{bound} = P - j_{\min} * f_{\min}^{\alpha} - (m - j_{\max} + 1) * f_{\max}^{\alpha}$;
7  $\qquad\qquad$ **if** $P_{bound} \geq 0$ **and** $f(j_{\min} + 1, j_{\min} + 1, j_{\max} - 1, P_{bound}) \geq f_{\min}$ **and** $f(j_{\max} - 1, j_{\min} + 1, j_{\max} - 1, P_{bound}) \leq f_{\max}$ **then**
8  $\qquad\qquad\qquad RT_{current} = \frac{S_{\min}}{f_{\min}} + P_{bound}^{\frac{1}{\alpha}} S_{RT}^{\frac{\alpha+1}{\alpha}} + \frac{S_{\max}}{f_{\max}}$;
9  $\qquad\qquad\qquad$ **if** $RT_{current} < MinRT$ **then**
10 $\qquad\qquad\qquad\qquad MinRT = RT_{current}$;
11 $\qquad\qquad\qquad$ **end**
12 $\qquad\qquad$ **end**
13 $\qquad$ **end**
14 **end**
15 Return $MinRT$;

**Algorithm 1:** Algorithm for optimal frequencies without allocation

We check all possibilities for $j_{\min}$ and $j_{\max}$ between 1 and $m$, as described in Algorithm 1, which enumerates all possible values for $j_{\min}$ between 0 and $m$, and for $j_{\max}$ between 1 and $m+1$. For each of these values, it updates the values of $S_{\min}$, $S_{\max}$ and $S_{RT}$ (lines 3–5). Then, line 7 verifies if the current values $j_{\min}$ and $j_{\max}$ constitute a valid solution for constraints (6), (9) and (10). The last lines (8-11) compute the corresponding runtime and update the objective value $MinRT$ if necessary. The algorithm has a quadratic complexity $O(m^2)$, due to the constant time to update variables $S_{\min}$, $S_{\max}$ and $S_{RT}$.

### 4.3    An Example

We use again the example in Sect. 3.1, with 5 tasks with parameters $(C_j, CT_j)$: $[(1,5), (6,6), (7,3), (8,2), (20,20)]$, global parameters $f_{min} = 2$, $f_{max} = 5$ and $\alpha = 3$, and a power cap of 200. Obtaining optimal values according to Sect. 4.1 leads to frequency values between 2.05 and 4.33 that is valid for frequency limits. It corresponds to a total runtime of 47.4. This property holds for a power cap ranging between 186.8 (in which case the optimal frequency for task 1 is 2) and 308.6, with an optimal frequency for task 5 of 5. Below a power cap of 186.8, the optimal frequency for task 1 will be $f_{min} = 2$ and above a power cap of 308.6, the frequency of task 5 will be fixed at 5. If we consider a variant with task parameters $C_j$: $[1, 6, 7, 8, 30]$, the optimal frequency for the first task without frequency limits is 1.96, below $f_{min}$. Applying frequency limits, this task will run at minimum frequency, and the remaining tasks will follow Lemma 1 applied on the 4 remaining tasks with power 192.

Using parameters $C_j$: $[1, 6, 7, 8, 40]$ and a power cap of 235, the optimal frequency values without bounds range from 1.99 to 5.01. The optimal solution in the general problem is then obtained with task 1 running at frequency 2 and task 5 at frequency 5.

## 5    Conclusion

This paper has presented a model and a solution to select CPU frequencies for a set of servers belonging to a cloud provider or a data center so that a global power cap constraint can be met while the execution time of the tasks allocated to these servers is minimized. To achieve this, the paper relies on modelling tasks in terms of their CPU boundedness and exploiting the fact that CPU-bound tasks are more impacted by any frequency reduction than I/O-bound tasks. The preliminary work in this paper suggests that there is potential in producing energy-efficient solutions that could be used in practice to find economical solutions to operate large data centers under power capping. Additional work could evaluate our approach in real-world environments while it could evaluate and model the CPU-boundedness of tasks in different workloads more elaborately.

# References

1. Arroba, P., Moya, J.M., Ayala, J.L., Buyya, R.: Dynamic Voltage and Frequency Scaling-aware dynamic consolidation of virtual machines for energy efficient cloud data centers. Concurrency Comput. Pract. Exp. **29**(10), e4067 (2017). https://doi.org/10.1002/cpe.4067

2. Bansal, N., Chan, H.L., Pruhs, K.: Speed scaling with an arbitrary power function. In: Proceedings of the 2009 Annual ACM-SIAM Symposium on Discrete Algorithms (SODA), pp. 693–701. https://doi.org/10.1137/1.9781611973068.76

3. Bansal, N., Kimbrel, T., Pruhs, K.: Dynamic speed scaling to manage energy and temperature. In: 45th Annual IEEE Symposium on Foundations of Computer Science, pp. 520–529. IEEE (2004). https://doi.org/10.1109/FOCS.2004.24

4. Chen, J.J., Kuo, T.W.: Multiprocessor energy-efficient scheduling for real-time tasks with different power characteristics. In: 2005 International Conference on Parallel Processing (ICPP 2005), pp. 13–20. IEEE (2005). https://doi.org/10.1109/ICPP.2005.53

5. Conoci, S., Di Sanzo, P., Pellegrini, A., Ciciani, B., Quaglia, F.: On power capping and performance optimization of multithreaded applications. Concurrency Comput. Pract. Exp. **33**(13), e6205 (2021). https://doi.org/10.1002/cpe.6205

6. Costero, L., Igual, F.D., Olcoz, K.: Dynamic power budget redistribution under a power cap on multi-application environments. Sustain. Comput. Inf. Syst. **38**, 100865 (2023). https://doi.org/10.1016/j.suscom.2023.100865

7. Etinski, M., Corbalan, J., Labarta, J., Valero, M.: Optimizing job performance under a given power constraint in HPC centers. In: Proceedings of the International Green Computing Conference, pp. 257–267. IEEE (2010). https://doi.org/10.1109/GREENCOMP.2010.5598303

8. Etinski, M., Corbalan, J., Labarta, J., Valero, M.: Understanding the future of energy-performance trade-off via DVFS in HPC environments. J. Parallel Distrib. Comput. **72**(4), 579–590 (2012). https://doi.org/10.1016/j.jpdc.2012.01.006

9. Hsu, C.H., Kremer, U.: The design, implementation, and evaluation of a compiler algorithm for CPU energy reduction. ACM SIGPLAN Notices **38**(5), 38–48 (2003). https://doi.org/10.1145/780822.781137

10. Katal, A., Dahiya, S., Choudhury, T.: Energy efficiency in cloud computing data centers: a survey on software technologies. Clust. Comput. **26**(3), 1845–1875 (2022). https://doi.org/10.1007/s10586-022-03713-0

11. Lin, W., Luo, X., Li, C., Liang, J., Wu, G., Li, K.: An energy-efficient tuning method for cloud servers combining DVFS and parameter optimization. IEEE Trans. Cloud Comput. **11**(4), 3643–3655 (2023). https://doi.org/10.1109/TCC.2023.3308927

12. Petoumenos, P., Mukhanov, L., Wang, Z., Leather, H., Nikolopoulos, D.S.: Power Capping: what Works, What Does Not. In: IEEE 21st International Conference on Parallel and Distributed Systems (ICPADS), pp. 525–534 (2015). https://doi.org/10.1109/ICPADS.2015.72

13. Pietri, I., Sakellariou, R.: Cost-efficient CPU provisioning for scientific workflows on clouds. In: Altmann, J., Silaghi, G.C., Rana, O.F. (eds.) Economics of Grids, Clouds, Systems, and Services, pp. 49–64. Springer International Publishing, Cham (2016). https://doi.org/10.1007/978-3-319-43177-2_4

14. Pietri, I., Sakellariou, R.: A Pareto-based approach for CPU provisioning of scientific workflows on clouds. Futur. Gener. Comput. Syst. **94**, 479–487 (2019). https://doi.org/10.1016/j.future.2018.12.004

15. Rauber, T., Rünger, G.: A scheduling selection process for energy-efficient task execution on DVFS processors. Concurrency Comput. Pract. Exp. **31**(19), e5043 (2019). https://doi.org/10.1002/cpe.5043

16. Rizvandi, N.B., Taheri, J., Zomaya, A.Y., Lee, Y.C.: Linear combinations of DVFS-enabled processor frequencies to modify the energy-aware scheduling algorithms. In: 10th IEEE/ACM International Conference on Cluster, Cloud and Grid Computing, pp. 388–397 (2010). https://doi.org/10.1109/CCGRID.2010.38

17. Sundriyal, V., Sosonkina, M.: Modeling of the CPU frequency to minimize energy consumption in parallel applications. Sustain. Comput. Inf. Syst. **17**, 1–8 (2018). https://doi.org/10.1016/j.suscom.2017.12.002

18. Zhang, H., Hoffmann, H.: Maximizing performance under a power cap: a comparison of hardware, software, and hybrid techniques. SIGPLAN Notices **51**(4), 545–559 (2016). https://doi.org/10.1145/2954679.2872375

19. Zhang, W., Zhang, Z., Zeadally, S., Chao, H.C., Leung, V.C.M.: Energy-efficient workload allocation and computation resource configuration in distributed cloud/edge computing systems with stochastic workloads. IEEE J. Sel. Areas Commun. **38**(6), 1118–1132 (2020). https://doi.org/10.1109/JSAC.2020.2986614

20. Zhao, D., et al.: Sustainable supercomputing for AI: GPU power capping at HPC Scale. In: Proceedings of the 2023 ACM Symposium on Cloud Computing, pp. 588–596. SoCC 2023, Association for Computing Machinery, New York, NY, USA (2023). https://doi.org/10.1145/3620678.3624793

# Energy-Efficient Task Offloading in Edge Computing: A Survey of Deep Reinforcement Learning Approaches

Eleftheria Papageorgiou[1], Theodoros Theodoropoulos[1,2] (iD),
and Konstantinos Tserpes[2(✉)] (iD)

[1] Harokopio University of Athens, Kallithea, Greece
{csi23310,ttheod}@hua.gr
[2] National Technical University of Athens, Zografou, Greece
tserpes@mail.ntua.gr

**Abstract.** In edge computing, task offloading involves transferring computational tasks from the "far-edge", which includes end-user devices or less powerful edge devices, to the "near-edge", comprising more capable edge servers, or to the 'core' cloud infrastructure. This practice optimizes performance, reduces latency, and enhances overall efficiency. Energy efficiency in particular has recently become a high-priority criterion for task offloading. A prominent technique for making offloading decisions in edge computing environments is Deep Reinforcement Learning (DRL), known for its ability to adapt to complex environments and excel in multi-objective optimization tasks in terms of decision quality and speed. This paper explores the details of DRL approaches, providing an overview of recent research developments in this field. To simplify the literature analysis, we classify DRL approaches for energy-efficient task offloading between two "computing continua": the far/near-edge continuum, and the (far-)edge-cloud continuum.

**Keywords:** Green Computing · Efficient Computing · Deep Reinforcement Learning · Edge Computing · Edge-Cloud · Energy Efficiency

## 1 Introduction

At a conceptual level, Cloud computing concentrates the execution of the larger part of applications into virtual computing "silos" in which resources are connected with nearly zero communication latency. This trend is now revised in favor of the incorporation of devices into the resource pool that may present an increased latency to the existing silos but reduced latency with regards to the data sources and end users. The tradeoff is: reduced latency across application components Vs reduced latency between application Edges (data sources, end users) and application components.

The growing dependency on data has shifted this "Edge Computing" paradigm to further extremes, with the incorporation of heterogeneous, resource-constrained devices into the resource pool, especially in IoT-based applications.

© The Author(s), under exclusive license to Springer Nature Switzerland AG 2025
M. Naldi et al. (Eds.): GECON 2024, LNCS 15358, pp. 175–184, 2025.
https://doi.org/10.1007/978-3-031-81226-2_16

The IoT-Edge-Cloud continuum [21] refers to a spectrum of computing resources ranging from centralized Cloud servers to decentralized Edge devices, with varying degrees of proximity to end-users and data sources. As IoT-Edge-Cloud Computing gradually becomes the dominant execution paradigm, energy efficiency becomes a key challenge to overcome in the complete range of the IoT-Edge-Cloud continuum.

The potentially resource-constrained nature of devices, especially in an IoT-Edge-Cloud context, underscores the imperative to judiciously harness the available Edge resources for optimal performance [30]. Given the inherent limitations in processing and storage capacities of those devices, it becomes crucial to design and implement efficient algorithms and resource management strategies that make the most out of the constrained environment. Additionally, the challenge is exacerbated by the fact that Edge devices often operate with restricted energy autonomy, necessitating a delicate balance between computational efficiency and energy conservation. Addressing these challenges is pivotal to unlocking the full potential of Edge computing in meeting the stringent requirements of next-generation applications while ensuring sustainability in the face of energy constraints.

Task offloading [16] is one of the distinguishing operations in IoT-Edge-Cloud computing, enabling the system to select the appropriate resource across the continuum where to deploy an appropriate application component instant. The objective of this operation is to optimize resource utilization and meet QoS/QoE requirements. Task offloading algorithms typically make optimization decisions on factors like latency, bandwidth, and resource utilization. This process enhances responsiveness, and improves overall system efficiency by processing data closer to the point of generation or consumption.

The relevant scientific literature, refers to two primary paradigms for energy-efficient task offloading in resource-constrained Edge devices. The first paradigm focuses on offloading tasks from one Edge device to more suitable Edge resources, such as Edge devices, and servers. We refer to this practice as "far/near-edge continuum offloading". The second paradigm involves offloading tasks from an Edge device to a broader range of computing resources across the computing continuum, which includes both Edge resources and centralized Cloud data centers. We refer to this practice as "far-edge to cloud continuum offloading"or simply"edge-cloud continuum offloading".

Furthermore, the literature promotes Deep Reinforcement Learning (DRL) [1] as a prominent technique to enable energy efficient offloading. DRL is a machine learning algorithm where an agent learns to make decisions by interacting with an environment to achieve certain goals. In the context of task offloading, DRL can assist in decision-making by dynamically determining which tasks should be processed locally on Edge devices or Cloud resources to be processed [26]. Through continuous learning and using feedback from the environment, DRL algorithms optimize task allocation based on factors such as network conditions, device capabilities, QoS requirements and most recently -and importantly- based on energy efficiency requirements.

Recognizing the importance of the contribution of DRL in task offloading, we performed a review on contemporary solutions that are based on the use of DRL algorithms for energy efficient task offloading across the two compute continua. The analysis follows the following structure: Section 2 briefly describes various contemporary DRL algorithms that shall be explored within the frame of this work. Section 3 showcases various DRL solutions for energy efficient task offloading within the frame of exclusive Edge resources (far/near-edge continuum). Section 4 showcases various DRL solutions for energy efficient task offloading at the edge-cloud continuum. Finally, Sect. 5 summarizes the merits and findings of this work, and proposes potential future research directions.

# 2  Background: Deep Reinforcement Learning Algorithms

## 2.1  Deep Q-Network (DQN)

Deep Q-Network (DQN) [20] combines Q-learning with deep neural networks to approximate Q-values, which represent the expected cumulative rewards for actions in given states. DQN trains a neural network to predict Q-values directly from raw inputs, enabling learning of complex behaviors in high-dimensional environments. It uses experience replay and target networks to stabilize training and improve efficiency, learning from past experiences to mitigate issues of correlated data and non-stationarity. By iteratively interacting with the environment and updating network parameters via gradient descent, DQN optimizes decisions to maximize expected cumulative rewards over time.

## 2.2  Double Deep Q-Network (DDQN)

Double Deep Q-Network (DDQN) [28] enhances DQN by addressing the overestimation bias in traditional Q-learning. DDQN uses two neural networks—the online and target networks—to decouple action selection and value estimation. The online network selects actions, while the target network estimates their values, reducing bias and stabilizing learning. DDQN also uses experience replay and target network updates to further improve stability and sample efficiency, enabling robust learning of optimal policies in complex environments with discrete action spaces.

## 2.3  Deep Deterministic Policy Gradient (DDPG)

Deep Deterministic Policy Gradient (DDPG) [24] is a model-free, off-policy algorithm for continuous action spaces. It uses neural networks to approximate both the policy (actor) and value function (critic), combining policy gradient methods and Q-learning in an actor-critic framework. DDPG employs target networks and experience replay to mitigate issues like non-stationarity and correlated data, learning effectively from past experiences. By updating policy parameters in the direction of the estimated gradient of expected cumulative rewards, DDPG generates actions that maximize long-term rewards, facilitating complex behaviors in challenging environments.

## 2.4   Multi-agent Deep Reinforcement Learning (MADRL)

Multi-Agent Deep Reinforcement Learning (MADRL) [12] extends DRL to scenarios with multiple agents interacting with each other and the environment. MADRL trains neural network-based agents to learn individual policies and strategies for cooperation or competition. It addresses challenges like non-stationarity and mixed interactions among agents. MADRL typically uses decentralized training with centralized execution, where agents share information during training but maintain decentralized control during execution. This approach enables agents to develop sophisticated behaviors and strategies for achieving collective goals in dynamic environments.

Multi-Agent Deep Deterministic Policy Gradient (MADDPG) [9] extends DDPG to multi-agent environments. MADDPG uses centralized training with decentralized execution, where each agent has its own actor and critic networks. During training, critics have access to all agents' observations and actions, enhancing coordination and learning of optimal policies. Decentralized execution allows agents to operate independently based on their observations during testing. MADDPG uses experience replay and target networks to stabilize learning, improve efficiency, and handle continuous action spaces, enabling robust learning in complex multi-agent environments.

## 3   Task Offloading in Far/Near-Edge Compute Continuum

Task offloading in the far/near-edge compute continuum involves the delegation of computational tasks from resource-constrained Edge devices to more powerful computing resources located in nearby Edge servers or to other Edge devices. This process aims to optimize performance, reduce latency, and conserve energy by distributing computing tasks strategically across the available resources. Task offloading decisions are typically based on factors such as the computational requirements of the task, the availability of resources, network conditions, and user preferences. Offloading decisions can be made dynamically in real-time using various algorithms and heuristics, ensuring efficient utilization of Edge resources while meeting the quality-of-service requirements of applications.

### 3.1   DQN

In Mobile Edge Computing (MEC), mobile terminals can offload tasks to nearby Edge servers for computational offloading. A DQN algorithm can be employed to determine the optimal task offloading and resource allocation strategy, ensuring proper resource allocations via MEC [15]. Here, each potential outcome is represented as a state space, and transitions between states are considered actions. Utilizing the DQN approach reduces both energy consumption and task delay costs.

In wireless-powered MEC, multiple wireless devices connect to the same network and follow a binary offloading policy, either executing computation tasks locally or remotely on a MEC server [19]. The Deep Reinforcement learning-based Online Offloading (DROO) [14] algorithm maximizes the weighted sum computation rate in these networks, significantly reducing computational complexity by avoiding combinatorial optimization problems, especially in large networks. An adaptive procedure is proposed to automatically adjust DROO algorithm parameters, enhancing the algorithm's learning from past experiences to improve offloading actions. This leads to reduced computation time per task and lower system energy consumption. Unlike the TADPG agent that runs on each mobile device, DROO operates a single agent for all wireless devices.

In vehicular Edge computing, deciding whether computation tasks should be executed locally or on Edge servers in nearby vehicles is crucial. A DQN-based algorithm incorporating Bayesian inference, leveraging prior distributions and statistical data, addresses this need [25]. By offloading tasks to vehicular Edge servers, the overall delay and energy costs are minimized.

## 3.2  DDQN

In 5G networks, MEC enables user equipment to offload tasks requiring substantial computation resources and energy to nearby MEC servers. The goal is to minimize energy consumption in a dynamic multi-user MEC system through joint optimization of computation offloading and resource allocation, considering task delay and requirements constraints. A study explores Q-learning and DDQN solutions [32]. The Q-learning agent learns optimal behaviors independently over time, whereas DDQN uses DNNs to estimate Q-learning's action-value function, separating action selection and evaluation. Both methods effectively reduce energy consumption and achieve desirable average task delays.

## 3.3  DDPG

Using the DDPG paradigm, a Temporal Attentional Deterministic Policy Gradient (TADPG) approach [4] addresses computation offloading and resource allocation. Each mobile device runs a TADPG agent for dynamic partial task offloading and resource allocation decisions. The TADPG agent features a temporal feature extraction network, consisting of an attentional LSTM [23] and a 1-dimensional convolution residual block, along with a rank-based priority experience replay to prioritize significant experiences. This approach speeds up training and improves stability, reducing task completion time and energy consumption.

In MEC, IoT devices offload intensive computations to Edge servers to achieve low latency and reduced energy consumption. When multiple devices are connected, computing delays can occur. This issue can be addressed with a DDPG approach, training a centralized policy to optimize local computing CPU frequencies and offloading policies, minimizing energy consumption and average computing delay [18].

## 3.4  MADRL

In the Intelligent Internet of Things (IIoT) paradigm, each smart device is an agent, known as a machine-type agent (MTA). In factories, MTAs communicate, generating large datasets that increase communication costs. A MADRL algorithm optimizes offloading policies [5], deciding whether to offload computations based on channel conditions and past data to minimize delay and interference, enhancing channel access success and reducing costs and energy consumption.

As IIoT evolves, multi-access MEC offloads Cloud services to Edge clients, often leading to high energy consumption. In dynamic network environments, intelligent task offloading strategies are challenging due to limited battery capacity [3]. The multi-agent deep deterministic policy gradient (MA2DDPG) computation offloading framework addresses this, using centralized training and distributed execution for optimal resource allocation and minimizing energy consumption and transmission latency [11]. This framework features in-layer optimization for resource allocation and outer-layer modules for task scheduling, energy transmission, and channel interference management.

# 4  Task Offloading in the Edge-Cloud Compute Continuum

Task offloading in the IoT-Edge-Cloud continuum [6] involves the strategic allocation of computing tasks across the spectrum of computing resources. This approach aims to optimize performance, reduce latency, and conserve energy by dynamically distributing tasks based on factors such as computational requirements, network conditions, and user preferences. Tasks can be offloaded from Edge devices to nearby Edge servers for low-latency processing or to the Cloud for high-complexity computations. Offloading decisions are made dynamically in real-time, considering the trade-offs between latency, bandwidth, and resource availability, to ensure efficient utilization of both Edge and Cloud resources while meeting application requirements.

## 4.1  DQN

Vehicle Ad Hoc Networks (VANETs) enable vehicles to communicate within smart city infrastructure. With the increasing number of vehicles, risks arise when offloading tasks through mobile devices like roadside base units. Blockchain and smart contracts ensure system safety, while a DRL algorithm [31] using extended DQN addresses the offloading problem by finding the optimal strategy for each vehicle, considering data amount, MEC processing power, throughput, and bandwidth. Blockchain-based access control efficiently identifies and prevents unauthorized offloading, ensuring security and privacy.

A DRL-driven optimization scheme for resource allocation in IoT-Edge-Cloud environments includes intelligent content caching and request aggregation mechanisms. A DQN solution addresses asymmetrical control and multi-layer heterogeneous resource allocation problems by optimizing content distribution [10].

The DQN algorithm enhances content caching and task scheduling based on past user requests and available resources, improving bandwidth and resource use, reducing energy consumption, and enhancing environmental sustainability.

The Internet of Vehicles (IoV) connects vehicles to their environment, providing efficient, low-latency transmission services [22]. Dynamic vehicle environments impact communication, causing latency-sensitive services to face limitations. A cooperative IoT-Edge-Cloud content-delivery scheme uses a DQN approach [7] to optimize computing, caching, and communication resources, minimizing network latency and improving content distribution and QoS in asymmetrical IoV environments. Furthermore, Vehicle Edge networks, consisting of Cloud servers, roadside units, and moving vehicles, constitute an optimization problem in computational offloading and resource allocation. A distributed DQN learning algorithm [17] with parallel DNNs is capable of solving this problem, minimizing system costs in terms of time and energy.

## 4.2  DDQN

In [29], DDQN is proposed as an offloading algorithm for multi-user computing offloading in Cloud-assisted mobile Edge computing environments [13]. Multiple devices offload tasks simultaneously, evenly distributing wireless bandwidth. The optimal strategy found by the algorithm allows MEC and Cloud computing to collaborate, reducing delay and energy consumption effectively.

## 4.3  DDPG

5G beyond involves leveraging the capabilities of end devices, Edge servers, and the Cloud for computation-intensive and delay-sensitive applications. Thus, the decision-making process for computation offloading is quite complex. In [8], a DDPG algorithm is proposed to minimize system energy consumption. The DDPG algorithm solves joint computation offloading and resource allocation problems using an Actor-Critic framework, where the Actor generates actions and the Critic guides the Actor. Action refinement in DRL supports joint offloading and resource allocation, minimizing system energy consumption.

## 4.4  MADRL

The GreenKube framework [27] employs the MADRL concept to address latency issues and enhances computational infrastructure using AI methodologies like Deep Learning, Deep Reinforcement Learning, and Graph Neural Networks. Intelligent, Monitoring, and Forecasting Agents interact with the Kubernetes[1] platform to predict QoS metrics, guide strategies for Autoscaling, Self-Healing, and Task Offloading. These strategies ensure efficient use of computing power, minimize costs and energy consumption, and reduce latency for sensitive tasks. The framework aims to improve container orchestration by meeting QoS requirements and minimizing energy consumption using AI methodologies.

---

[1] https://kubernetes.io/.

**Table 1.** Related Work Taxonomy

| Related Work | Algorithm | Domain |
|---|---|---|
| [15] | DQN | far/near-Edge |
| [14] | DQN | far/near-Edge |
| [25] | DQN | far/near-Edge |
| [32] | DDQN | far/near-Edge |
| [4] | DDPG | far/near-Edge |
| [18] | DDPG | far/near-Edge |
| [5] | MADRL | far/near-Edge |
| [3] | MADRL | far/near-Edge |
| [31] | DQN | Edge-Cloud |
| [10] | DQN | Edge-Cloud |
| [7] | DQN | Edge-Cloud |
| [17] | DQN | Edge-Cloud |
| [2] | DDQN | Edge-Cloud |
| [29] | DDQN | Edge-Cloud |
| [8] | DDPG | Edge-Cloud |
| [27] | MADRL | Edge-Cloud |

## 5   Conclusion

In summary, this paper investigates multiple solutions for optimizing task offloading in the Edge-Cloud compute continuum. We distinguish the works to those that promote edge to edge resource task offloading (Far/Near-Edge compute continuum) and those that promote edge to cloud resource offloading (Edge-Cloud compute continuum). The solutions proposed are based on DRL algorithms, like DQN, DDQN, DDPG, and MADRL, for optimizing task offloading while considering the system's energy efficiency. A related work taxonomy based on the findings of this work is showcased in Table 1. As technology advances, the integration of innovative DRL algorithms with the Edge computing environment is essential so that the full potential of next-generation applications can be experienced by the users and simultaneously to tackle sustainability issues in the face of energy limitations.

**Acknowledgments.** This project has received funding from the Horizon Europe Framework Programme under Grant agreement No 101135775 (PANDORA). This paper reflects only the authors' view and the Commission is not responsible for any use that may be made of the information it contains.

# References

1. Arulkumaran, K., Deisenroth, M.P., Brundage, M., Bharath, A.A.: Deep reinforcement learning: a brief survey. IEEE Signal Process. Mag. **34**(6), 26–38 (2017)
2. Nguyen, D.C., Pathirana, P.N., Ding, M., Seneviratne, A.: Secure computation offloading in blockchain based IoT networks with deep reinforcement learning. IEEE Trans. Netw. Sci. Eng. **8**(4), 3192–3208 (2021)
3. Cao, B., Zhang, L., Li, Y., Feng, D., Cao, W.: Intelligent offloading in multi-access edge computing: a state-of-the-art review and framework. IEEE Commun. Mag. **57**, 56–62 (2019)
4. Chen, J., Xing, H., Xiao, Z., Xu, L., Tao, T.: A DRL agent for jointly optimizing computation offloading and resource allocation in MEC. IEEE Internet Things J. **8**, 17508–17524 (2021)
5. Chen, X., Jiao, L., Li, W., Fu, X.: Efficient multi-user computation offloading for mobile-edge cloud computing. IEEE/ACM Trans. Netw. **24**, 2795–2808 (2015)
6. Chourlias, A., Theodoropoulos, T., Violos, J., Leivadeas, A., Tserpes, K., Zalachoris, C.K.: A brief review of population-based methods for task offloading in cloud-to-edge continuum. In: 2023 IEEE 12th International Conference on Cloud Networking (CloudNet), pp. 448–453. IEEE (2023)
7. Cui, T., Yang, R., Fang, C., Yu, S.: Deep reinforcement learning-based resource allocation for content distribution in IoT-edge-cloud computing environments. Symmetry **15**(1), 217 (2023)
8. Dai, Y., Zhang, K., Maharjan, S., Zhang, Y.: Edge intelligence for energy-efficient computation offloading and resource allocation in 5g beyond. IEEE Trans. Veh. Technol. **69**(10), 12175–12186 (2020)
9. Du, J., et al.: MADDPG-based joint service placement and task offloading in MEC empowered air-ground integrated networks. IEEE Internet Things J. **11**(6), 10600–10615 (2024)
10. Fang, C., et al.: A DRL-driven intelligent optimization strategy for resource allocation in cloud-edge-end cooperation environments. Symmetry **14**(10), 2120 (2022)
11. Gong, Y., et al.: Decentralized edge intelligence-driven network resource orchestration mechanism. IEEE Netw. **37**(2), 270–276 (2023)
12. Gronauer, S., Diepold, K.: Multi-agent deep reinforcement learning: a survey. Artif. Intell. Rev., 1–49 (2021). https://doi.org/10.1007/s10462-021-09996-w
13. Hortelano, D., et al.: A comprehensive survey on reinforcement-learning-based computation offloading techniques in edge computing systems. J. Netw. Comput. Appl. **216**, 103669 (2023)
14. Huang, L., Bi, S., Zhang, Y.J.: Deep reinforcement learning for online computation offloading in wireless powered mobile-edge computing networks. IEEE Trans. Mob. Comput. **19**, 2581–2593 (2019)
15. Huang, L., Feng, X., Zhang, C., Qian, L., Wu, Y.: Deep reinforcement learning-based joint task offloading and bandwidth allocation for multi-user mobile edge computing. Digit. Commun. Netw. **5**, 10–17 (2018)
16. Islam, A., Debnath, A., Ghose, M., Chakraborty, S.: A survey on task offloading in multi-access edge computing. J. Syst. Architect. **118**, 102225 (2021)
17. Khayyat, M., Elgendy, I.A., Muthanna, A., Alshahrani, A.S., Alharbi, S., Koucheryavy, A.: Advanced deep learning-based computational offloading for multilevel vehicular edge-cloud computing networks. IEEE Access **8**, 137052–137062 (2020)
18. Liu, R., Liu, X., Wang, S., Yin, C.: Deep deterministic policy gradient based computation offloading in wireless-powered MEC networks. In: 2020 IEEE Globecom Workshops (GC Wkshps, pp. 1–6 (2020)

19. Mao, Y., You, C., Zhang, J., Huang, K., Letaief, K.: A survey on mobile edge computing: the communication perspective. IEEE Commun. Surv. Tutorials **19**, 2322–2358 (2017)
20. Roderick, M., MacGlashan, J., Tellex, S.: Implementing the deep q-network. arXiv preprint arXiv:1711.07478 (2017)
21. Rosendo, D., Costan, A., Valduriez, P., Antoniu, G.: Distributed intelligence on the edge-to-cloud continuum: a systematic literature review. J. Parallel Distrib. Comput. **166**, 71–94 (2022)
22. Singh, P.K., Nandi, S.K., Nandi, S.: A tutorial survey on vehicular communication state of the art, and future research directions. Veh. Commun. **18**, 100164 (2019)
23. Staudemeyer, R.C., Morris, E.R.: Understanding LSTM–a tutorial into long short-term memory recurrent neural networks. arXiv preprint arXiv:1909.09586 (2019)
24. Tan, H.: Reinforcement learning with deep deterministic policy gradient. In: 2021 International Conference on Artificial Intelligence, Big Data and Algorithms (CAIBDA), pp. 82–85. IEEE (2021)
25. Tang, D., Zhang, X., Li, M., Tao, X.: Adaptive inference reinforcement learning for task offloading in vehicular edge computing systems. In: 2020 IEEE International Conference on Communications Workshops (ICC Workshops), pp. 1–6 (2020)
26. Tang, M., Wong, V.W.: Deep reinforcement learning for task offloading in mobile edge computing systems. IEEE Trans. Mob. Comput. **21**(6), 1985–1997 (2020)
27. Theodoropoulos, T., Makris, A., Korontanis, I., Tserpes, K.: GreenKube: towards greener container orchestration using artificial intelligence. In: 2023 IEEE International Conference on Service-Oriented System Engineering (SOSE), pp. 135–139 (2023)
28. Van Hasselt, H., Guez, A., Silver, D.: Deep reinforcement learning with double q-learning. In: Proceedings of the AAAI Conference on Artificial Intelligence, vol. 30 (2016)
29. Wang, Y., Ge, H., Feng, A., Li, W., Liu, L., Jiang, H.: Computation offloading strategy based on deep reinforcement learning in cloud-assisted mobile edge computing. In: 2020 IEEE 5th International Conference on Cloud Computing and Big Data Analytics (ICCCBDA), pp. 108–113 (2020)
30. Zhang, J., Hu, X., Ning, Z., Ngai, E.C.H., Zhou, L., Wei, J., Cheng, J., Hu, B.: Energy-latency tradeoff for energy-aware offloading in mobile edge computing networks. IEEE Internet Things J. **5**(4), 2633–2645 (2017)
31. Zheng, X., Li, M., Chen, Y., Guo, J., Alam, M., Hu, W.: Blockchain-based secure computation offloading in vehicular networks. IEEE Trans. Intell. Transp. Syst. **22**(7), 4073–4087 (2021)
32. Zhou, H., Jiang, K., Liu, X., Li, X., Leung, V.C.M.: Deep reinforcement learning for energy-efficient computation offloading in mobile-edge computing. IEEE Internet Things J. **9**(2), 1517–1530 (2022)

# Edge Energy Orchestration

Vijay Kumar[1], Nima Valizadeh[1]([✉]), Ioan Petri[2], Omer Rana[1], Ambarish Nag[3], Sagi Zisman[3], Charles Tripp[3], and Shuva Paul[4]

[1] School of Computer Science and Informatics, Cardiff University, Cardiff, UK
`{kumarv14,ValizadehN,RanaOF}@cardiff.ac.uk`
[2] School of Engineering, Cardiff University, Cardiff, UK
`PetriI@cardiff.ac.uk`
[3] Computational Science Center, National Renewable Energy Lab (NREL), Colorado, USA
`{ambarish.nag,sagi.zisman,charles.trip}@nrel.gov`
[4] Energy Security and Resilience Center, National Renewable Energy Lab (NREL), Colorado, USA
`shuva.paul@nrel.gov`

**Abstract.** Edge computing devices have increased in number and capability over recent years. The ability to process data and execute machine learning in proximity to data generation and collection sources provides several advantages over using cloud- based data centers. We describe an orchestration mechanism that enables edge devices to make more effective use of energy resources in their proximity – a technique we refer to as "edge energy orchestration". A software "orchestrator" can take account of renewable generation to alter how task execution on edge devices is carried out. An application scenario is used to illustrate the use of the orchestrator in practice, followed by a discussion about how this approach can be generalized to a broader set of applications

**Keywords:** energy efficiency · renewable energy use · edge-cloud continuum · resource management

## 1 Introduction

An edge resource, positioned nearer to the data source, process data locally, thus reducing latency and bandwidth consumption. It acts as an intermediary, delivering faster response times and localized computing power. Ensuring continuous and efficient operation of the edge presents unique challenges and opportunities, especially in cases where edge devices are powered using renewable energy sources such as solar power, hydrogen fuel cells, and wind power. Renewable energy sources, while environmentally beneficial, are inherently variable and depend on factors such as weather conditions and time of day. This variability necessitates adaptive strategies to manage power consumption effectively. The primary goals are to maximize the utilization of edge energy, minimize reliance

© The Author(s), under exclusive license to Springer Nature Switzerland AG 2025
M. Naldi et al. (Eds.): GECON 2024, LNCS 15358, pp. 185–194, 2025.
https://doi.org/10.1007/978-3-031-81226-2_17

on cloud computation and data transmission to the cloud, and make the most efficient use of the computational capabilities of edge resources.

We explore three primary use cases at the edge: (i) the edge devices function primarily as a data aggregator, collecting data from various endpoints and transmitting it to the cloud for processing. This approach minimizes energy consumption at the edge of the network by offloading computational tasks to the cloud. However, energy consumption will depend on the size of the data transfer and will require a high network bandwidth depending on the quantity of data to be transferred; (ii) the edge devices perform all necessary data processing locally, providing rapid responses and minimizing the need for data transfer to the cloud. This use case leverages computational capabilities to maximize edge computing while relying on renewable energy sources; (iii) a hybrid approach balancing the computational load between the cloud and the edge. By dynamically partitioning tasks based on real-time energy availability and computational demand, this strategy aims to optimize both energy use and processing efficiency, striving to minimize cloud computation and data transmission.

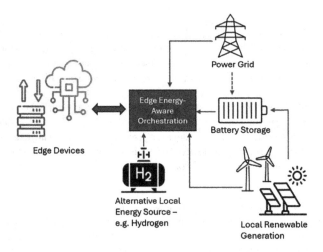

**Fig. 1.** Application execution using an orchestration engine that takes account of renewable edge energy sources

As illustrated in Fig. 1, we describe an energy-aware orchestrator able to use locally available energy sources to schedule applications on edge resources. Such an orchestration mechanism aims to maximize the use of locally available energy sources before connecting to a power grid. Three types of energy resources are considered: (i) local renewable generation, which can have variable frequency and availability. This edge energy source enables devices to directly connect to these sources, and task execution on edge devices can be scheduled based on availability; (ii) a local battery which can be charged through renewable sources. The battery can remove fluctuations in generation from local renewable generation and provide a more reliable source of (local) energy. Specifying the size of the battery needed within a given context and monitoring its state-of-charge variation are two requirements when such a source is used; (iii) alternative local sources of (more expensive) energy may also be available, such as hydrogen, as an alternative. The orchestrator needs to create a schedule for data collection and task execution on available edge resources based on user requests and energy availability. The orchestrator can have several utility functions to influence its operations, such as maximizing the use of locally sourced energy, achieving a throughput target for task execution, and maximizing the use of renewable energy sources rather than the battery of the power grid. We investigates methods for adjusting power consumption at the edge to align with the availability of renewable energy. Identifying how a balance can be established between computational demand and energy availability, contributing to the development of more resilient and sustainable computing infrastructures, is a key contribution. This aspect is covered from two perspectives: (i) monitoring local renewable energy resources to assess their stability and availability profile over a predefined time window; this aspect is covered in Sect. 2. An accurate estimation enables direct use of local energy resources; (ii) adaptive use of renewable energy at the edge, smoothing out fluctuations in generation using battery storage, covered in Sect. 3.

## 2   Condition Monitoring of Renewable Energy Resources

The production of renewable energy depends on a complex interplay of factors, including the natural variability of resources and weather conditions. Beyond these external influences, the quality and operational condition of renewable energy infrastructure and storage systems are crucial for determining energy output. The efficiency and reliability of solar panels, wind turbines, and large battery storage systems are pivotal. Any faults or degradation in these technologies can cause significant fluctuations and reductions in energy production. Therefore, maintaining high standards in the construction, upkeep and monitoring of renewable energy infrastructure and storage is essential to ensure a stable and reliable energy supply. Schenato et al. [10] describe real time insights, conditional monitoring of renewable energy resources, optimizing distribution networks, enhancing building energy efficiency, and efficiently managing EV charging infrastructure.

Wind energy could benefit from edge processing by improving monitoring systems, reducing downtime and enabling predictive maintenance. Xu et al. [14] have devised an embedded multi-sensor architecture to detect incipient short-circuit in wind turbine electrical generators, that is robust to both false positives and negatives, and enables the testing of five different sensor settings in three feature extraction methods and four classifiers. Abdelmoula et al. [2] proposed a novel framework for monitoring decentralized photovoltaic systems within a smart city infrastructure – using edge computing to overcome challenges associated with costly processing via remote cloud servers.

## 3    Renewable Energy at the Edge

Lowering of the carbon footprint of edge computing systems in a sustainable way requires both energy efficiency techniques to save power consumption and the use of renewable energy (green energy) as the primary power supply and brown energy (fossil fuel-based energy) as the secondary energy supply. The relatively small energy demand of edge computing systems positions them to make effective use of renewable energy. Utilising a microgrid, distributed renewable energy sources in the same area can be effectively integrated to supply power to local users with less power loss due to transmission and distribution infrastructure and match the dynamic local demand with local supply in a more convenient way. Li et al. [5] proposed an energy management framework that systematically integrates edge computing and the microgrid so that these two systems can cooperate and complement each other to enhance the effectiveness and utilization of energy resources while still satisfying the requirements of IoT applications. The proposed integration methodology reinforces the sustainability of both microgrid and edge computing, by virtue of being tightly coupled with a renewable energy management workflow that enables efficient interaction and collaboration between the systems. For devices operating at the edge, (i) they may be run by single-use (non-rechargeable) batteries, (ii) they may be run by rechargeable batteries that store renewable energy or, (iii) they may be directly connected to the electric grid. However, the most energy-efficient scenario might be determined by a pareto-style optimization, where a linear combination of these three different options might turn out to be optimal.

Sustainable edge servers can also utilize photo-voltaic (PV) panels or micro wind turbines to harvest solar or wind energy from the surrounding environment to enable the scaling and sustainability. Recent experimental results indicate that when the solar power density reaches $600\,\mathrm{W/m^2}$ or the wind speed reaches $11\,\mathrm{m/s}$ (24.6 mph), a $2\,\mathrm{m^2}$ PV panel with 20% energy conversion efficiency, or a $12\,\mathrm{kg}$ wind turbine with $1.2\,\mathrm{m^2}$ rotor-swept area can generate more than $170\,\mathrm{W}$ of power, which suffices to drive high-performance processors, such as AMD EPYC 7501 and Intel Xeon Gold 6328HL. Given this ability for energy harvesting, edge servers can be deployed outside the coverage of electric grids. A SES (sustainable edge server) needs to dynamically update its computing power based on the energy harvesting rate to achieve the best computational performance, since solar and wind-based energy production are not consistent but highly variable with time. Luo at al. [15] have proposed an optimal computing power management strategy to maximize the average computing power of the solar-powered SES in dynamic renewable energy environments. An energy harvesting model that supports a feedback loop between power consumption to energy generation of the SES is developed.

Edge computing can reduce energy consumption by cloud providers, as data transfer from edge devices and computation at a data center can be minimized. The pervasive nature of edge devices also allows workload balancing, enabling excess tasks to be offloaded to or from a cloud platform. Such mechanisms help coordinate resources and associated tasks by providing more intelligent access to distributed edge resources.

## 4  Power-Aware Edge Implementation

Edge devices can offload computation to centralized servers to enhance user experience. However, this migration incurs energy costs. Jiang et al. [4] discuss offloading strategies, such as local execution, partial offloading [12], and full offloading [4]. Mao et al.,introduce dynamic computation offloading for mobile-edge computing with energy harvesting devices. This approach adapts offloading decisions based on the energy availability of devices. By leveraging energy harvesting information, it optimizes the trade-off between local execution and offloading, ensuring energy-efficient task execution [7]. Wang et al. propose a reinforcement learning-based algorithm, in which mobile users learn from network states and historical behaviors to find optimal energy consumption point and resource allocation policies [13]. By planning offloading base stations for user devices, they achieve a 28% reduction in total energy consumption while ensuring balanced traffic management across base stations [6].

These algorithms aim to strike a balance between energy efficiency and system performance. In another interesting work, Sun et al., propose a joint offloading and computing optimization approach in wireless powered mobile-edge computing systems. By considering both computation offloading and resource allocation, their strategy aims to maximize system throughput while minimizing energy consumption. It dynamically allocates resources to edge nodes, striking a balance between computation tasks and energy availability [11]. Furthermore, in another work by Ahvar et al., which underscores the energy efficiency of distributed computing architectures utilizing foundational energy model and evaluates the consumption of cloud-related architectures, including edge computing [1], our proposed edge energy orchestration mechanism aims to further optimize energy utilization by dynamically aligning task execution with renewable energy availability, which leads to enhancing the the sustainability of edge computing infrastructures. Additionally, the empirical analysis by Mocnej et al. on the impact of edge computing on IoT energy consumption [8] aligns with our objective to enhance energy efficiency, providing a case study that exemplifies the potential for edge computing to extend the operational lifespan of IoT devices through improved energy management.

Energy efficiency in computing devices can be enhanced using various hardware and software modifications, e.g.: (i) underclocking the CPU to reduce the CPU clock speed; (ii) disabling HDMI output when it is not in use; (iii) turning off onboard LEDs to conserve power. Utilizing an efficient power supply and disconnecting unnecessary peripherals, such as USB devices and external drives, further contributes to lower power consumption. Software optimizations involve employing a lightweight operating system to decrease system load, e.g. using Raspbian Lite on a Raspberry Pi can reduce power usage. Power management tools like `powertop` can identify and mitigate power-hungry processes and settings.

Devices can be configured to reduce their CPU clock speed based on the remaining battery power, thereby optimizing energy consumption. This process involves utilizing battery monitoring tools such as `upower` or `acpi` to continuously track the battery level. Software optimizations play a crucial role in enhancing energy efficiency. Utilizing built-in power modes is a primary strategy. For instance, the `nvpmodel` tool on devices like Jetson Nano allows for switching between different power modes, such as setting the device to a 5W mode (mode 1) to reduce power consumption. Similarly, the Jetson AGX Xavier provides more granular control over power consumption through various power modes that can be selected using the `nvpmodel` tool. Enabling Dynamic Voltage and Frequency Scaling (DVFS) on these devices dynamically adjusts the voltage and frequency of the processor according to the workload, optimizing energy usage. Additionally, disabling unused CPU cores and services can significantly reduce power consumption by ensuring that only necessary components are active. Employing power management tools such as `tegrastats` enables the monitoring of power consumption and resource usage, helping to identify and optimize power-hungry processes.

## 4.1   Power-Aware Orchestration

An edge resource orchestrator (EO) is a software component that dynamically determines the placement and scheduling of user applications to: (i) improve utilisation of resources that are in proximity to a user; (ii) meet overall application execution constraints such as deadline, network latency and security. We consider the EO to be hosted on a network component (e.g. the first hop router to a user) to undertake this process. The EO may: (i) schedule tasks on locally available edge resource(s), or forward tasks to a cloud system; (ii) aggregate/divide tasks prior to forwarding these to a cloud system, described in [9]. An EO able to take account of local energy resources is illustrated in Fig. 1 – connecting computational devices at the network edge with energy sources. This component harnesses data from energy generation and storage, in proximity to edge devices, to influence scheduling of tasks, making most effective use of such energy. An EO in this instance is able to:

- Approximate task deployment based on resource proximity, as edge resources are identified based on geographical proximity facilitating advantages related to cost, latency and security.
- Reduce cost by deploying tasks efficiently: an edge orchestrator can find low cost edge resources where the overall execution is still compliant with a quality of service requirement identified by a user, whilst meeting an energy usage profile.
- Maximize performance: an edge orchestrator can reduce latency associated with data transfer based on existing placement requirements, i.e. when quality-of-solution is important, the edge orchestrator can search for high throughput resources.

# 5   Edge AI Use-Cases

We provide a number of scenarios using different types of energy resources – and associated orchestration.

**Edge Devices with Single-Use (Non-rechargeable) Batteries**: The Internet of Things (IoT) enables citizens to take informed actions based on data. IoT-generated data can be categorized into logical layers based on where it is generated, how it is used, and the evolving roles of data collectors and users: personal, built environment, district and urban. At the personal level, wearable devices embedded with sensors, like activity trackers, utilize edge AI to gather and analyse data on various physical activities, e.g. counting steps, estimating calorie expenditure, tracking sleep patterns, and recording elevation changes, aiding individuals in monitoring their health. These wearable sensors also leverage edge AI to detect indicators of critical health events such as strokes or traumatic brain injuries (TBI) in patients. Moreover, sensors installed on surfaces (such as battery-powered sofas, chairs, beds) monitor metrics such as heart rate, respiratory signals, movement activity during sleep, and sleep quality – offering sleep analysis and detecting sleep-related issues and identify and prevent poor body postures that may negatively affect health and lead to discomfort and other complications. In these applications, sensors have their own battery that powers data collection. Data collection occurs at limited time intervals, minimising the amount of energy consumption of the device.

Edge Devices with Rechargeable Batteries: recent support for AI/ML-based applications on the edge can make use of ultra-low-power devices with an energy cost below 1mW. This enables the development of many advanced applications in domains where edge computing is favored due to requirements such as high mobility, sustainability, low latency, privacy preservation, and continuous availability.

**Optimised LLMs:** TinyChat [3] provides an efficient and lightweight system for Large Language Models (LLM) deployment on the edge, that runs Meta's LLaMA-2 model at 30 tokens per second on NVIDIA Jetson Orin and can support different models and hardware. In this approach, direct embedding of LLMs into real-world systems, e.g. the copilot services (coding, smart reply and office) on laptops, in-car entertainment systems, vision-language assistants in robots or vehicular control interfaces enables users to instantly access responses and services without relying on a stable internet connection. Moreover, this approach often bypasses queuing delays associated with cloud services. Running LLMs on the edge not only improves user experience but also relieves privacy concerns, as sensitive data remains localized, which in turn, reduces the potential risk of breaches. A reduction in power can also lead to restricted memory bandwidth and limited peak computation throughput on the edge. Moreover, edge devices have restricted memory capacity. As an example, the NVIDIA Jetson Orin Nano, characterized by its 8GB DRAM, cannot accommodate even the most compact LLaMA-2 model in half precision. TinyChat provides a solution for weight quantization, enabling LLM inference on edge devices with limited memory.

**Urban Observatories: Building Level**: at a building level, electricity companies are implementing smart meters, enabling citizens to monitor their energy consumption at half-hourly, daily, monthly, and yearly intervals. This data aids in comprehending and itemizing electricity charges, pinpointing energy-intensive appliances by identifying electric usage signature at the edge using federated learning. Occupancy levels within buildings can now be accurately determined through innovative methods utilizing mobile phones and WiFi signals. Both domestic and non-domestic building require energy optimization that often involve deployment and execution of neural networks and genetic algorithms on edge devices. Additionally, depth-based cameras and edge AI analyse the functional movements of individuals, such as vulnerable individuals or patients and serve as alert mechanisms, capable of detecting potentially hazardous events like individuals on the verge of falling, monitoring walking patterns, and identifying specific types of dementia.

Edge Devices with Renewable Power Sources - Wind/Solar: At a district level, edge AI utilises the data available around the environment (air quality/temperature, wind speed/direction, traffic delays), location of EV charging points, car parking spots and availability to optimize traffic flow, manage waste collection, enhance public safety, and improve overall urban living conditions. Further, information about crime maps, neighborhoods, past activity can help to predict crime in near future.

At the urban level, the integration of edge AI technologies enhances the monitoring and management of environmental factors. Authorities often deploy a network of sensors equipped with edge AI capabilities to collect real-time data on air quality, temperature, humidity, and barometric pressure throughout the city and its surroundings. This advanced sensor network enables not only the identification of sources of air pollution, such as power plants, road transport, and industrial processes, but also the analyses of complex data patterns to predict air quality levels. By combining air pollution data with meteorological information authorities can accurately forecast air quality trends and understand how they are influenced by seasonal variations and weather conditions. Furthermore, edge AI-driven analytics provide insights into energy demand patterns by processing meteorological data, including rainfall and solar energy levels. This enables city councils to optimize energy management strategies and enhance the efficiency of household energy consumption.

City councils employ sensor technology, including cameras, microphones, and edge computing, to monitor street activities such as pedestrian and cyclist traffic in intersections and parks. This data helps authorities improve citizen services and manage crowds effectively, including coordinating with law enforcement when necessary. Thermal cameras near harbours and water bodies aid in detecting individuals at risk of falling into the water. Furthermore, data on vehicle purchases and ticketing for various modes of transportation enable transport authorities to analyse mobility patterns and optimize services, such as adding more trains to crowded stations. Automatic Plate Number Recognition (APNR) systems track vehicle movements at city borders and monitor the distribution of petrol, diesel, hybrid, and electric vehicles. This information informs efforts to address air pollution and gauge public acceptance of electric cars. Moreover, edge machine learning is utilized to enhance road infrastructure management, with applications like road damage detection improving productivity and reducing costs for city councils. This technology ensures safer road conditions by addressing issues such as faded lane markings and graffiti on street signs, thereby enhancing overall traffic safety.

**Decentralised AI and Variable (Decentralised) Energy Sources**: Edge computing can also enable decentralized operation of AI systems, thereby reducing the need for large-scale data centers. Decentralized AI systems lower the risk of downtime and improve the reliability and availability of AI systems – in addition to reducing power requirements of centralised data centers. In edge computing, the volume of data traversing the network can be reduced greatly, which in turn can free up bandwidth. This is more efficient from both time and energy perspective to work with the data on the edge and send the data to the cloud only if it is really needed there for aggregation and other manipulations. Moreover, bypassing the requirement for voluminous data storage lowers the demand for power-hungry data centers. Ait

## 6  Conclusion

The need for supporting an energy orchestrator at the edge of the network has been identified. The orchestrator is able to utilise energy generation and usage "signals" to influence how computational tasks can be scheduled and managed on edge devices. Whereas previous work has primarily focused on undertaking partitioning of tasks between edge and cloud resources to meet quality of service targets (such as latency, throughput, response time, etc.) – this work highlights the need to also maximise the use of energy generation in proximity to edge resources.

A number of application *classes* have been identified that make use of different types of energy sources: from non-rechargeable battery use for limited data acquisition and transmission/storage, to city-scale infrastructure that is able to harness power generation across a number of locations across a city, able to take account of various renewables and alternative forms of energy (such as hydrogen). The Urban Observatory is used as a common infrastructure to illustrate these different uses of edge resources. An orchestrator that is able to respond to varying needs of these application classes, and able to adapt its behaviour is a key requirement identified in this work.

## References

1. Ahvar, E., Orgerie, A.C., Lebre, A.: Estimating energy consumption of cloud, fog, and edge computing infrastructures. IEEE Trans. Sustain. Comput. **7**(2), 277–288 (2022). https://doi.org/10.1109/TSUSC.2019.2905900

2. Ait Abdelmoula, I., et al.: Towards a sustainable edge computing framework for condition monitoring in decentralized photovoltaic systems. Heliyon **9**(11), e21475 (2023). https://doi.org/10.1016/j.heliyon.2023.e21475, https://linkinghub.elsevier.com/retrieve/pii/S2405844023086838

3. Tang, H., Yang, S., Lin, J., Tang, J., Chen, W.M., Wang, W.C., Han, S.: TinyChat: large language model on the edge (2023). https://hanlab.mit.edu/blog/tinychat

4. Jiang, C., et al.: Energy aware edge computing: a survey. Computer Communications **151**, 556–580 (2020). https://doi.org/10.1016/j.comcom.2020.01.004, https://www.sciencedirect.com/science/article/pii/S014036641930831X

5. Li, W., et al.: On enabling sustainable edge computing with renewable energy resources. IEEE Commun. Mag. **56**(5), 94–101 (2018). https://doi.org/10.1109/MCOM.2018.1700888,https://ieeexplore.ieee.org/document/8360857/

6. Lv, X., Ge, X., Zhong, Y., Li, Q., Xiao, Y.: Energy consumption optimization for edge computing-supported cellular networks based on optimal transport theory. Sci. China Inf. Sci. **67**(2) (2024). https://doi.org/10.1007/s11432-023-3855-5

7. Mao, Y., Zhang, J., Letaief, K.B.: Dynamic computation offloading for mobile-edge computing with energy harvesting devices. IEEE J. Sel. Areas Commun. **34**(12), 3590–3605 (2016). https://doi.org/10.1109/JSAC.2016.2611964

8. Mocnej, J., Miskuf, M., Papcun, P., Zolotova, I.: Impact of edge computing paradigm on energy consumption in IoT. IFAC-PapersOnLine **51**(6), 162–167 (2018). https://doi.org/10.1016/J.IFACOL.2018.07.147

9. Petri, I., Rana, O.F., Zamani, A.R., Rezgui, Y.: Edge-cloud orchestration: Strategies for service placement and enactment. In: IEEE International Conference on Cloud Engineering, IC2E 2019, Prague, Czech Republic, 24–27 June 2019, pp. 67–75. IEEE (2019). https://doi.org/10.1109/IC2E.2019.00020

10. Schenato, R.: Empowering the Energy Sector; edge computing solutions for a sustainable future (2024). https://sixsq.com/blog/discover/2024/02/27/edge-computing-solutions-for-energy-sector.html

11. Sun, H., Zhou, F., Hu, R.Q.: Joint offloading and computation energy efficiency maximization in a mobile edge computing system. IEEE Trans. Veh. Technol. **68**(3), 3052–3056 (2019). https://doi.org/10.1109/TVT.2019.2893094

12. Tang, Q., Lyu, H., Han, G., Wang, J., Wang, K.: Partial offloading strategy for mobile edge computing considering mixed overhead of time and energy. Neural Comput. Appl. **32**(19), 15383–15397 (2020). https://doi.org/10.1007/s00521-019-04401-8, https://doi.org/10.1007/s00521-019-04401-8

13. Wang, Y., Dai, X., Wang, J.M., Bensaou, B.: A reinforcement learning approach to energy efficiency and QoS in 5G wireless networks. IEEE J. Sel. Areas Commun. **37**(6), 1413–1423 (2019). https://doi.org/10.1109/JSAC.2019.2904365

14. Xu, Y., et al.: Multi-sensor edge computing architecture for identification of failures short-circuits in wind turbine generators. Appl. Soft Comput. **101**, 107053 (2021). https://doi.org/10.1016/j.asoc.2020.107053, https://linkinghub.elsevier.com/retrieve/pii/S1568494620309911

15. Luo, Y., Pu, L., Liu, C.H.: Computing power and battery charging management for sustainable edge computing (2024). https://my.ece.msstate.edu/faculty/chliu/papers/journal/CompPower.pdf

# AI/Forecasting/Prediction Sales

# Towards Trustworthy Aircraft Safety: Explainable AI for Accurate Incident and Accident Predictions

Maryam Amin[1] ⓘ, Umara Noor[1(✉)] ⓘ, Manahil Fatima[1] ⓘ, Zahid Rashid[2] ⓘ, and Jörn Altmann[2,3,4] ⓘ

[1] Department of Software Engineering, Faculty of Computing and Information Technology, International Islamic University, Islamabad 44000, Pakistan
{maryam.phdcs190,umara.zahid,manahil.mscs1111}@iiu.edu.pk
[2] Technology Management Economics and Policy Program, College of Engineering, Seoul National University, Seoul, South Korea
rashidzahid@snu.ac.kr, jorn.altmann@acm.org
[3] Institute of Engineering Research (IOER), College of Engineering, Seoul National University, Seoul, South Korea
[4] Integrated Major in Smart City Global Convergence, Seoul National University, Seoul, South Korea

**Abstract.** Despite technological advancements, ensuring aircraft safety remains a challenge, however, Machine learning (ML)-based approaches for predicting future incidents play a crucial role in addressing flight safety. As ML models increase in complexity, their decision-making process becomes less transparent, posing significant challenges to trustworthiness. While simpler models demonstrate lower accuracy, more intricate models such as deep neural networks achieve higher accuracy but sacrifice interpretability. In this study, we enhance trustworthiness in aircraft safety prediction by leveraging a dataset of past accidents and incidents to prevent similar accidents from occurring in the future. To achieve this, we apply Random Forest and Extreme Gradient Boosting models to classify different categories of aircraft incidents. Additionally, we apply two powerful explainable artificial intelligence (XAI) techniques: Local Interpretable Model-Agnostic Explanations (LIME) and Shapley Additive exPlanations (SHAP) to provide insights into both local and global predictions made by the models. Notably, our results reveal high accuracy in these predictions while maintaining trustworthiness. This research contributes to the advancement of XAI and offers valuable insights for safety-critical applications and decision support systems.

**Keywords:** Aircraft Safety · Random Forest · Extreme Gradient Boosting (XGBoost) · Explainable Artificial Intelligence · Local Interpretable Model-Agnostic Explanations (LIME) · Shapley Additive exPlanations (SHAP)

© The Author(s), under exclusive license to Springer Nature Switzerland AG 2025
M. Naldi et al. (Eds.): GECON 2024, LNCS 15358, pp. 197–211, 2025.
https://doi.org/10.1007/978-3-031-81226-2_18

# 1  Introduction

Safety of aircraft is critical as it poses a significant risk of accidents and incidents, threatening aircraft operations and imposing substantial economic costs on the aviation industry. Aircraft incidents and accidents can have a profound impact, resulting in loss of life, severe injuries, and significant economic losses, as well as damaging the reputation of airlines and aircraft manufacturers and undermining public trust in the aviation industry. The annual safety report by the International Civil Aviation Organization revealed a global accident rate of 2.05 accidents per million departures in 2022, representing a 6.3% increase from the previous year's statistics [23].

As the fastest means of transportation, the aircraft industry is poised for significant expansion, with global demand expected to triple by 2050, thereby increasing the demand for aviation safety to meet the escalating requirements [25]. However, the dominant safety frameworks currently utilized by air traffic controllers are largely reactive, focusing on minimizing the impact of safety incidents after they happen. However, such systems are often criticized as a basic form of risk management, and during emergencies, they become less efficient and resource-intensive. Pilots and air traffic controllers rely on real-time data to make their safety-critical decisions, ensuring timely and effective responses to evolving situations in the flight.

There exist complex non-linear interactions and interdependencies between various factors such as mechanical, weather, human, and communication, coupled with their dynamic evolution over time, pose significant challenges in developing precise physical models that can accurately capture the complex relationships governing aircraft safety. Machine learning (ML) has demonstrated its ability to accurately model and predict intricate physical phenomena, leading to the widespread application of this technology especially for predicting the safety of complex systems. In the aviation industry, ML-based predictive safety approaches are important which prioritize risk prevention, anticipate hazards, and mitigate them before incidents occur. However, due to black-box nature of ML models, their decision-making process is difficult to interpret by humans, leading to a lack of transparency and subsequent trust issues.

In literature ML-based aircraft's safety prediction demonstrates impressive predictive capabilities but their opacity of decision-making processes undermines trust among airline stakeholders, thereby severely limiting their widespread adoption in real-world applications, where safety and trustworthiness are paramount. The safety prediction made by simpler models (e.g., linear regression, decision trees) demonstrates limited predictive accuracy while exhibiting strong power of prediction's interpretability, whereas more complex models (e.g., deep neural networks) achieve superior accuracy but offer low reasoning of the decision-making process [1]. Although some surveys and reviews have provided general guidelines for explanations of predictions made by ML models there exists a significant gap between theoretical advancements and practical implementation of integrating trustworthiness in aircraft safety predictions as only two research endeavors on it, one for aircraft failure diagnosis [15] and other for runway surface contamination [16]. Also, the relative importance of each feature and their impact in the decision-making process remain unexplored which poses a significant challenge in the pursuit of trustworthy ML models.

The main objective of this paper is to investigate the application of ML methods in the prediction of aircraft safety with higher accuracy and to demonstrate reasoning for the model's prediction to ensure trustworthiness. This is done for predicting different types of aircraft accidents such as accidents, incidents, criminal occurrence, hijacking, ground fire, sabotage, and other unknown occurrences, through developing two autoregressive-inspired time series ensemble approaches of Random Forest (RF) and Extreme Gradient Boosting (XGBoost) classification models which are known for their efficiency, speed, and accuracy on large datasets [22]. The models are trained on a vast collection of historical accident and incident records from around the world, providing a rich source of information that enables the models to learn from past experiences and improve their predictive capabilities. Similar to other ensemble methods, RF and XGBoost are inherently not interpretable, therefore, we utilize two powerful techniques: Local Interpretable Model-Agnostic Explanations (LIME) and SHapley Additive exPlanations (SHAP) to develop simplified models that provide both global and local explanations, enabling the understanding of the model's predictions and the contribution of individual features to the output. The performance of our ML models is evaluated and compared with other similar accident/incident prediction approaches. The results of this study reveal remarkable predictive accuracy while maintaining transparency and ensuring trustworthiness. Our findings contribute to advancing the field of XAI and provide valuable insights for safety-critical applications and decision support systems.

The following items state the main contributions of this research.

- The study's results exhibit outstanding predictive accuracy of RF (Random Forest) and XGBoost models in predicting aviation safety incidents, while maintaining a high degree of transparency and ensuring the trustworthiness of the models.
- XAI techniques like LIME and SHAP are demonstrated to provide clear local and global explanations of model predictions in aviation safety systems.
- The study's findings identified potential issues in aviation systems before they resulted in critical failures, fostering trust in AI systems, which is crucial for their adoption in safety-critical applications.

This research paper is organized into the following sections. Section 2 covers the literature review, Sect. 3 provides details of Methodology while the results and discussions are described in Sect. 4. Finally, the paper ends with concluding remarks in Sect. 5.

## 2 Literature Review

Aircraft safety prediction by using ML algorithms is a highly focused research area and many researchers have been contributing regarding different dimensions. The research in [2] applies data-mining and sequential deep-learning techniques to accident investigation textual reports published by the National Transportation Safety Board (NTSB) to get predictions regarding adverse events. Zeng et al. [3] introduce an innovative method combining the least absolute shrinkage and selection operator (LASSO) with long short-term memory (LSTM) for aviation safety prediction which demonstrates improved efficiency and robustness while maintaining excellent generalization ability. The study in [4] presents a novel deep learning technique based on auto-encoders and bidirectional gated recurrent unit networks to handle extremely rare failure predictions in aircraft predictive maintenance modeling. The authors of [5] introduce an analytical methodology which combines data cleaning, correlation analysis, classification-based supervised learning, and data visualization to identify critical parameters and remove extraneous factors. The research in [6] develops a methodology to identify and classify human factor categories from textual aviation incident reports by using semi-supervised Label Spreading and supervised Support Vector Machine (SVM). Silagyi in [7] applies SVM models to predict the severity of aircraft damage and personal injury during approach and landing accidents. The study in [8] investigates cognitive workload in aviation by applying a stacking ensemble machine learning algorithm (support vector machine, random forest, and logistic regression) on electroencephalogram (EEG) data collected from ten collegiate aviation students during live-flight operations in a single-engine aircraft.

Focusing on aircraft safety prediction, the research in [12] explores the value and necessity of XAI when using DNNs (Deep Neural Networks) for Predictive Maintenance in Aerospace Integrated Vehicle Health Management. Saraf et al. in [13] investigate the intersection of AI and aviation safety by exploring implications, possibilities, innovation capacity, skills development, and ethical regulation. The authors in [14] conduct a comprehensive literature review to explore the applications of AI in safety-critical domains by identifying Themes and Techniques, Future Research Directions, and Practical Implications. The research in [18] analyzes AI's usefulness within the aviation domain and synthesizes findings into a conceptual framework called the Descriptive, Predictive, and Prescriptive model.

Hernandez et al. in [17] focus trustworthiness of AI-based automated solutions in air traffic management and propose a novel framework which encompasses technical robustness, transparency, security, and safety. The practical challenges related to need of transparency and explainability, are also presented. The study in [15] addresses the challenge in aviation maintenance and proposes an XAI methodology, called Failure Diagnosis Explainability (FDE) which enhances transparency and enables checking whether a new failure aligns with expected diagnosis values. The research in [16] combines XGBoost models with the XAI technique SHAP to address the challenge of runway surface contamination (e.g., snow, ice, slush) during winter seasons, which reduces tire-pavement friction and poses safety risks for aviation.

In the existing literature, there are some research gaps. First, trustworthiness is often overlooked in the context of aircraft incident/accident predictions. Although ML models demonstrate strong predictive power but reliable, transparent, and safety are crucial for building trust among aviation professionals and passengers. Second, some models may sacrifice accuracy for interpretability striking the right balance between accuracy and interpretability remains a challenge. Third, there remains a gap between theoretical advancements and practical implementation of integrating trustworthiness in aircraft safety predictions as only two research endeavors on it for aircraft failure diagnosis [15] and runway surface contamination [16].

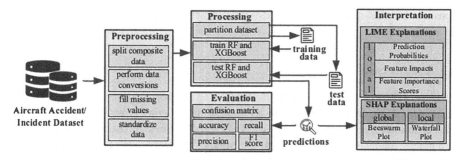

**Fig. 1.** The Proposed Methodology

# 3 Methodology

The methodology comprises of steps as shown in Fig. 1, each step is discussed in detail in the following subsections.

## 3.1 Dataset

The dataset selected for this research focuses on aviation safety and comprises a comprehensive collection of worldwide accidents, failures, and hijackings involving airliners, corporate jets, and military transport aircraft [24]. The dataset is selected because examining past accidents, researchers can determine the underlying causes and contributing factors, which can inform strategies to prevent similar accidents in the future. With 23519 data points and 23 features, this extensive dataset is contained in a single CSV file, covering incidents from 1919 to November 2, 2022, providing a valuable resource for analysis and insight into aviation safety trends and patterns. The dataset is obtained from kaggle which is a vast repository of publicly accessible datasets across various domains.

## 3.2 Preprocessing

Preprocessing plays a crucial role in ML as it ensures data correctness and consistency, and suitability for analysis. The selected dataset contains missing information, composite values and inconsistent data format which need completeness, splitting and standardization in order to improve its quality. A two-step preprocessing is performed; one by using MS Excel and other by using Python. In Microsoft Excel the data is split based on delimiter characters such as: '|', '/', ':' for instance the column Onboard_Crew contains composite data containing the number of 'Fatalities' and 'occupants' of an incident separated by '/' which is splitted into two columns 'Onboard_Crew_Fatalities' and 'Onboard_Crew_Occupants'. The data of date column such as Incident_Date is converted into timestamp. By using Python Null values in Object column are replaced by forward fill method (ffil) and question marks used as missing values in different columns were first replaced by NAN which are then replaced by 'unknown'. The Null values in integer columns are replaced with mean values and the dates in incident_date column are converted into dd-mm-yyyy format and the categorical data is converted into numerical data.

### 3.3 Feature Selection

RF extracts features in a recursive manner, selecting the most informative features at each node of the decision tree. The process is repeated multiple times, resulting in a collection of decision trees, each with their own set of extracted features. XGBoost extracts features in a greedy manner, selecting the most informative features at each node of the decision tree. The process is repeated multiple times, resulting in a collection of decision trees, each with their own set of extracted features. Therefore, both RF and XGBoost ensemble approaches reduce overfitting and improve generalization. Finally, columns containing text narratives, such as Incident_cause(es) and Incident_subcategory, from the dataset used in this study while these narratives could indeed provide valuable insights for explaining aircraft incident and accident predictions, we plan to explore these aspects in future work to enhance the comprehensiveness of our analysis.

### 3.4 Random Forest

This study builds prediction models that classify aviation events using the resilient Random Forest (RF) model by using dataset of past incidents. As an advancement of the bagging (Bootstrap Aggregating) technique, RF was created in 2001 and combines several decision trees to increase the model's robustness and accuracy [21]. It is renowned for its effectiveness, speed, and accuracy on big datasets with lots of variables and is utilized for both regression and classification problems. In a variety of industries, including finance, healthcare, and e-commerce, RF is used to predict risks.

Random Forest is chosen for its exceptional performance, offering a rare combination of speed, accuracy, and scalability. It efficiently processes large datasets with numerous features, minimizing bias and robustly handling missing values and outliers, making it an ideal algorithm for our analysis. To predict a new point x:

Classification: Let $\widehat{C}_b(x)$ be the class prediction of the bth random-forest tree. Then

$$\widehat{C}_{rf}^B(x) = majorityvote\{\widehat{C}_b(x)\}_1^B \tag{1}$$

### 3.5 eXtreme Gradient Boosting

Using a large dataset of historical incidents, this research builds prediction models that categorize aircraft incidents using the cutting-edge XGBoost algorithm. Since its release in 2014, XGBoost, a highly scalable and effective implementation of gradient boosting decision trees has gained a great deal of attention and praise. It has proven successful in machine learning competitions and has been used in a variety of transportation risk assessment applications across a range of industries, including road traffic, aviation, and shipping.

Because of XGBoost's exceptional performance, handling of big datasets, and speed of computation, it was chosen to train the airplane safety predictor. Furthermore, multicollinearity, a common problem in our data is successfully reduced using XGBoost's decision tree ensemble technique, guaranteeing reliable and accurate predictions. In real life, the model has to be trained on the data, which are often represented as an n-dimensional vector of outcomes (y) and a n times m matrix of input variables (X). A decision tree fk(x) is obtained at each iteration by minimizing an objective function.

$$obj(f_k(x)) = \sum_{i=1}^{n} L(y_i, \hat{f}(x_i)^{[k-1]} + f_k(x_i)) + \Omega(f_k(x)) \tag{2}$$

where $(x_i, y_i)$ is the i-th observation, $\sum_{i=1}^{n} L(y_i, \hat{f}(x_i)^{[k-1]} + f_k(x_i))$ is the empirical estimate of the loss, $\hat{f}(x_i)^{[k-1]}$ is the current estimate of the model(i.e., the model computed at the previous iteration k-1), and $\Omega(f_k(x))$ is a penalty term that penalized the tree complexity.

### 3.6 Experimental Setup

The experiment was conducted on a laptop equipped with a 12th Gen Intel® Core™ i5-1235U 1.30 GHz processor, 8.00 GB RAM, and a 64-bit Windows 10 operating system with an x64-based processor. The Python code was developed and executed within Jupyter Notebook to perform tasks such as data analysis and scientific exploration. This setup provided a robust environment for executing computational tasks efficiently, ensuring that the data analysis processes were both reliable and reproducible. The choice of Jupyter Notebook facilitated an interactive coding experience, allowing for real-time visualization and iterative development, which are crucial for thorough scientific investigation.

### 3.7 Models Training

Our goal is to predict aircraft safety based on previous accident/incident dataset and the features of the dataset are used to predict incident category. The types of incidents are labeled into six classes; *Accident* class with 19543 records (Label 0), *Criminal occurrence* (sabotage, shoot down) having 1256 entries (Label 1), *Hijacking* with 1092 (Label 2), *Incident* having 12 records (Label 3), *occurrence unknown* with 570 entries (Label 4) and *other occurrence* (ground fire, sabotage) with 1046 records (Label 5). The dataset is partitioned into eighty percent training (18815 records) and twenty percent test (4704 records) data frames. Since the categorical data is converted into numerical data therefore all six classes are labeled with numbers from 0 to 5. Both RF and XGBoost are trained on training data.

# 4 Results and Discussions

## 4.1 Performance of Models

On test dataset both models demonstrated an accuracy of 90.11% and 82.91% respectively. Considering the substantial imbalance in the dataset, where only 5.1% of cases belong to the incident class, relying solely on accuracy as a performance metric for classification in this research is inadequate. Accuracy may not accurately reflect the model's performance on the minority class. Therefore, the performance of the RF classification model is assessed using confusion matrices, which provide a detailed breakdown of True Positives (TP), True Negatives (TN), False Positives (FP), and False Negatives (FN) predictions. Table 1 displays the confusion matrix for RF model's predictions, with the columns representing predicted classes and the rows representing actual classes, offering a clear visualization of the model's performance. The high values of TP for class 0, 2 and 5 gives confidence in model's performance whereas the marginal scores of other classes and few zeros in case of class 3 are due to imbalance distribution of classes in dataset. The results of confusion matrix provide essential information about model's performance and help analyze misclassifications.

For evaluation we also apply precision, recall and F1 score for each classification class as shown in Table 2 which makes a weighted average precision, recall and F1 score as 0.89, 0.90 and 0.88 respectively. These promising scores reveal model's powerful predictive ability on unseen data and its performance beyond training data.

In Table 3 the effectiveness of our models is evaluated by comparing their performance to similar research endeavors, notably [15], which tackled aircraft failure diagnosis prediction, and [16], which addressed runway surface contamination prediction, providing a framework for evaluating our approach's efficacy. The results show that our research employs Random Forest and XGBoost machine learning models to forecast aircraft accidents and incidents worldwide, yielding high accuracy scores of 90.11% and 82.91%, respectively, demonstrating the effectiveness of our approach in predicting aviation safety risks.

**Table 1.** Confusion Matrix

|   | 0 | 1 | 2 | 3 | 4 | 5 |   |
|---|------|----|-----|---|----|-----|---|
| 0 | 3815 | 9  | 13  | 0 | 16 | 18  |   |
| 1 | 159  | 73 | 4   | 0 | 2  | 29  |   |
| 2 | 74   | 0  | 165 | 0 | 0  | 1   |   |
| 3 | 1    | 0  | 0   | 0 | 0  | 0   |   |
| 4 | 97   | 0  | 0   | 0 | 24 | 2   |   |
| 5 | 34   | 5  | 1   | 0 | 0  | 162 |   |

**Table 2.** Evaluation Metrics

| Class | Precision | Recall | f1-score |
| --- | --- | --- | --- |
| 0 | 0.91 | 0.99 | 0.95 |
| 1 | 0.84 | 0.27 | 0.41 |
| 2 | 0.90 | 0.69 | 0.78 |
| 3 | 0 | 0 | 0 |
| 4 | 0.57 | 0.20 | 0.29 |
| 5 | 0.76 | 0.80 | 0.78 |

**Table 3.** Comparison with Existing Work

| Ref | Dataset | Model Used | Accuracy | Explanation |
| --- | --- | --- | --- | --- |
| 15 | Netherland | RF | 81% | FDE |
| 16 | Norway | XGBoost | NA | SHAP |
| This work | Global | RF XGBoost | 90.11% 82.91% | SHAP and LIME |

## 4.2 Interpretation

The complexity of RF and XGBoost models, which aggregate scores from numerous decision trees (between 50 and 250) renders them challenging to interpret and comprehend. This opacity has contributed to the growing interest in Explainable Artificial Intelligence (XAI), as the increasing reliance on sophisticated black-box algorithms like XGBoost and deep neural networks necessitates a better understanding of their decision-making processes [16]. XAI refers to a set of processes and methods designed to enhance human understanding and trust in machine learning algorithms [27]. As AI models grow in complexity, their decision-making processes become increasingly opaque, posing challenges for interpretability. XAI techniques aim to illuminate these "black-box" models, making their predictions more transparent and reliable. XAI encompasses a range of techniques and methodologies aimed at demystifying the complex decision-making processes of black-box ML models, thereby rendering their predictions more comprehensible, trustworthy, and accountable, thereby fostering greater human understanding and confidence in AI-driven decision-making. XAI is actively used in diverse fields such as agriculture, games, information systems, smart cities, social media, sports, [19].

**SHapley Additive exPlanations (SHAP).** SHAP is a powerful framework for explaining the predictions of ML models [20]. SHAP (SHapley Additive exPlanations) is based on Shapley values, which have their roots in cooperative game theory. SHAP provides global as well as local explanations for predictions and can be used for tabular, text, image, and genomic data. It helps us understand why a specific instance received a particular prediction. SHAP treats any supervised learning model as a black box and calculates

Shapley values for each feature by evaluating all potential feature combinations and their respective contributions. This method assesses the impact of individual features on a model's predictions. It connects optimal credit allocation (determining how much each feature contributes) with local explanations.

For SHAP explanations the predictions made by XGBoost model is utilized. The goal of using shapley values is to distribute the prediction among variables. This makes Shapley values part of the additive feature attribution methods, which means they have an explanation model that is a linear function of binary variables:

$$g(z) = \varnothing_0 + \sum_{j=1}^{m} \varnothing_j z_j \tag{3}$$

where $z \in \{0,1\}m$ is a coalition vector giving the absence/presence of input variables in x and m is the number of variables in the original model. Methods with this explanation model assign an importance effect $\varnothing_j$ to each variable and summing the effects of all variables approximates the output of the original model.

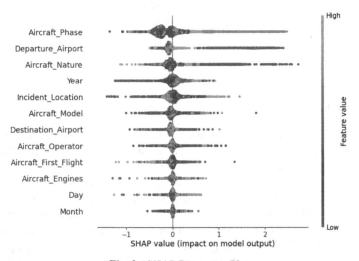

**Fig. 2.** SHAP Beeswarm Plot

SHAP values were intended for localized explanations, providing insights into individual predictions. However, Tree SHAP's high-speed estimations enable the generation of local explanations for entire datasets, facilitating a more extensive understanding of the model's overall performance. By plotting local explanations for a complete test set, we can amalgamate individual insights into a comprehensive global understanding of the model's behavior and decision-making processes.

Figure 2 shows a beeswarm plot of local SHAP values for each test sample, aggregated to form a global explanation of the classification model's overall performance, revealing how the model generates predictions for all instances in the test set. The plot displays the variables in decreasing order of importance, with increasing SHAP values (moving right on the x-axis) indicating a higher likelihood of accident class and negative values indicating a lower likelihood, with point density and color representing individual variable values.

First important observation from Fig. 2 is that globally the most impactful features in prediction of accident/incident are 'Aircraft-phase', 'departure_Airport' and 'Destination_Airport' which reveals that landing and takeoff flights at airport are most critical stages of a flight. Second, the 'Aircraft_Nature' and 'Aircraft_Model' are also impactful as they reveal the poor mechanical aspect of an aircraft are placed at the top. Third, since we have split 'date', 'day' and 'year' the season and weather at an instance also play a significant role in the safety prediction.

The waterfall plot in Fig. 3 focuses on explaining a single prediction (local) made by the model. It starts from the expected value of the model output (usually the average prediction) and shows how each feature's contribution (positive or negative) moves the prediction from the expected value to the actual model output for that specific instance. Each row in the waterfall plot represents a feature. The SHAP value of a feature reflects how much that feature's evidence influences the model's output. The plot uses color-coding: red for positive and blue for negative contributions that helps to understand which features are driving model's decision for specific prediction.

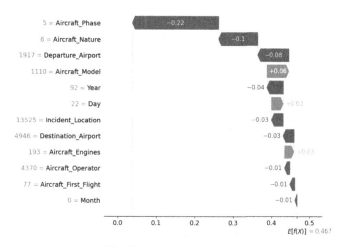

**Fig. 3.** SHAP Waterfall Plot

First important observation in Fig. 3 is that for a given prediction, positive SHAP values such as 'Aircraft_Model', 'Day' and 'Aircraft_Engines'. Second, negative values such as 'Aircraft_Phase', 'Aircraft_Nature' and 'Departure_Airport' contribute negatively to reach a prediction. However, the global explanation in Fig. 2 ranks these features contradictory as compared to Fig. 3. This contradiction can be explained that each prediction, SHAP determines how much each feature contributes to that specific prediction, known as local SHAP values. To derive global explanations, SHAP takes the average of the absolute local SHAP values for each feature across all data instances. So as a result this average indicates the overall significance of each feature in the model's predictions globally.

**Local Interpretable Model-Agnostic Explanations.** Local Interpretable Model-Agnostic Explanations (LIME) provides local, interpretable explanations for individual predictions made by any machine learning model [26]. It treats any supervised learning model as a black box, can be applied to various types of models. LIME focuses on explaining predictions within the vicinity of a specific data point. It samples data points around the instance being explained, creates a simpler surrogate model, and approximates the original model's behavior. For LIME explanations the predictions made by RF model is utilized.

Figure 4 displays a bar chart depicting prediction probabilities for six different classes; 0 indicates Accident, 1 represents Criminal occurrence, 2 shows Hijacking, 3 indicates Incident, 4 represents occurrence unknown and 5 shows other occurrence as described in Sect. 3.7. These probabilities represent the likelihood of different outcomes. The highest probability (0.75) of class 0 corresponds that the model classifies the given instance as 'Accident' whereas the other probabilities are 0.13, 0.10, and the lowest (0.01) for other classes. In Figs. 4 and 5 the horizontal bars use different colors to represent values of prediction probabilities, making it easy to visually compare the values.

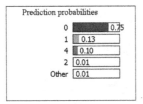

**Fig. 4.** LIME Prediction Probabilities

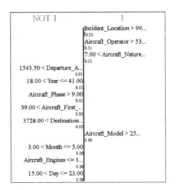

**Fig. 5.** LIME Feature Impacts

**Fig. 6.** LIME Feature Importance Scores

In Fig. 5, there's a list of features with corresponding weights. 'Incident_Location' has a strong positive weight (99%), meaning it significantly influences the prediction. Conversely, 'Departure_Aircraft' has a negative weight (-25%), reducing the likelihood of this outcome. The Fig. 6 lists several features on the right side. These features are likely input variables used by ML model such as "Incident Location," "Aircraft Operator," "Departure Airport," "Year," "Aircraft Phase," "Aircraft First Flight," "Aircraft Model," "Month," and "Day". Each feature has a corresponding value next to it. This value represents the importance or impact of that feature on the model's prediction. For instance, a high value 4881 of 'Destination_Airport' indicates that changing that feature significantly affects the model's output. In Fig. 6, the orange color indicates features that positively influence reaching a prediction label, while the gray color represents features that negatively impact achieving a prediction.

This is particularly significant when comparing these results with findings of prior research efforts in interpreting predictions for aircraft safety domain those have just focused on two aspects one for aircraft failure diagnosis [15] and other for runway surface contamination [16]. The study's findings focus on aircraft incident and accident predictions which reveal exceptional predictive accuracy for RF and XGBoost models, coupled with a high level of transparency and trustworthiness. Additionally, XAI techniques such as LIME and SHAP effectively offer clear local and global explanations for the model's predictions.

## 5  Conclusion

The research successfully accomplished its objectives, which centered on predicting aircraft accidents and incidents for safety-critical systems. By leveraging historical data, the study forecasted future accidents. The AI models RF and XGBoost both achieved remarkable accuracy in these predictions. Moreover, the research demonstrated the effective application of XAI techniques, specifically LIME and SHAP, to provide comprehensive explanations for both local and global predictions in order to enhance trustworthiness.

The study exhibits several limitations. Firstly, the results heavily rely on a publicly available dataset, which may introduce biases or inaccuracies. Additionally, the dataset suffers from imbalanced class distribution, missing values, and inconsistencies in data format. Secondly, the predictive features used are limited; incorporating environmental factors such as temperature, air pressure, and humidity could enhance accuracy. Thirdly, the research explored only two ML models, RF and XGBoost, warranting further investigation into more complex techniques like deep learning. Also currently we have provided both local and global explanations for predictions of XGBoost using SHAP, and interpretations of local predictions for RF using LIME. The application of both XAI frameworks to RF and XGBoost, could provide valuable insights for explaining aircraft incident and accident predictions to allow a more interesting direct comparison on the performance and level of explainability of the two frameworks. Lastly, to improve accuracy and interpretability, additional XAI methods should be considered.

While the airline industry frequently displays hesitance toward adopting novel technologies since safety is the top priority and new technologies are held to extremely high standards before they can be adopted. AI holds significant promise for enhancing safety and ensuring trustworthiness. In forthcoming studies, emphasizing feature engineering and enhancing model accuracy will be pivotal. Furthermore, ensuring the interpretability of predictions is essential for their effective adoption within the airline industry particularly in decision support system.

**Acknowledgments.** This work was supported by the National Research Foundation of Korea (NRF) grant funded by the Korea government, Ministry of Science and ICT (MSIT), with project No. NRF-2022R1A2C1092077, NRF-RS-2023–00302083 (as part of the EC-funded Swarmchestrate Project), and BK21 FOUR (Fostering Outstanding Universities for Research) funded by Korea's Ministry of Education (MOE) and the NRF of Korea.

# References

1. Myo, T., Ahmed, M. R., Al Hadidi, H., Al Baroomi, B.: Trends and Challenges of machine learning-based predictive maintenance in aviation industry. In: International Conference on Aeronautical Sciences, Engineering and Technology, pp. 362–368. Springer Nature, Singapore (2023). https://doi.org/10.1007/978-981-99-7775-8_39
2. Zhang, X., Srinivasan, P., Mahadevan, S.: Sequential deep learning from NTSB reports for aviation safety prognosis. Saf. Sci., 142 (2021)
3. Zeng, H., Guo, J., Zhang, H., Ren, B., Wu, J.: Research on aviation safety prediction based on variable selection and LSTM. Sensors **23**(1), 41 (2022)
4. Dangut, M.D., Jennions, I.K., King, S., Skaf, Z.: A rare failure detection model for aircraft predictive maintenance using a deep hybrid learning approach. Neural Comput. Appl. **35**(4), 2991–3009 (2023)
5. Lee, H., et al.: Critical parameter identification for safety events in commercial aviation using machine learning. Aerospace **7**(6), 73 (2020)
6. Madeira, T., Melício, R., Valério, D., Santos, L.: Machine learning and natural language processing for prediction of human factors in aviation incident reports. Aerospace **8**(2), 47 (2021)
7. Silagyi II, D.V., Liu, D.: Prediction of severity of aviation landing accidents using support vector machine models. Accident Anal. Prev., 187 (2023)
8. Taheri Gorji, H., Wilson, N., VanBree, J., Hoffmann, B., Petros, T., Tavakolian, K.: Using machine learning methods and EEG to discriminate aircraft pilot cognitive workload during flight. Sci. Rep. **13**(1) (2023)
9. Hassija, V., et al.: Interpreting black-box models: a review on explainable artificial intelligence. Cogn. Comput. **16**(1), 45–74 (2024)
10. Chamola, V., Hassija, V., Sulthana, A.R., Ghosh, D., Dhingra, D., Sikdar, B.: A review of trustworthy and explainable artificial intelligence (XAI). IEEE Access (2023)
11. Ali, S., et al.: Explainable Artificial Intelligence (XAI): what we know and what is left to attain Trustworthy Artificial Intelligence. Inf. Fus., 99 (2023)
12. Shukla, B., Fan, I.S., Jennions, I.: Opportunities for explainable artificial intelligence in aerospace predictive maintenance. PHM Soc. Eur. Conf. **5**, 11 (2020)
13. Saraf, A.P., Chan, K., Popish, M., Browder, J., Schade, J.: Explainable artificial intelligence for aviation safety applications. In: AIAA Aviation 2020 Forum (2020)
14. Sutthithatip, S., Perinpanayagam, S., Aslam, S.: (Explainable) Artificial intelligence in aerospace safety-critical systems. In: IEEE Aerospace Conference 2022, pp.1–12 (2022)
15. Zeldam, S.G.: Automated failure diagnosis in aviation maintenance using explainable artificial intelligence (XAI) (Master's thesis, University of Twente) (2018)
16. Midtfjord, A.D., De Bin, R., Huseby, A.B.: A decision support system for safer airplane landings: predicting runway conditions using XGBoost and explainable AI. Cold Regions Sci. Technol., 199 (2022)
17. Hernandez, C.S., Ayo, S., Panagiotakopoulos, D.: An explainable artificial intelligence (xAI) framework for improving trust in automated ATM tools. In: IEEE/AIAA 40th Digital Avionics Systems Conference (DASC), pp. 1–10 (2021)
18. Weber, P., Carl, K.V., Hinz, O.: Applications of explainable artificial intelligence in finance—a systematic review of finance, information systems, and computer science literature. Manage. Rev. Q. **74**(2), 867–907 (2024)
19. Degas, A., et al.: A survey on artificial intelligence (AI) and explainable AI in air traffic management: Current trends and development with future research trajectory. Appl. Sci. **12**(3) (2022)

20. Messalas, A., Kanellopoulos, Y., Makris, C.: Model-agnostic interpretability with Shapley values. In: 10th International Conference on Information, Intelligence, Systems and Applications, pp. 1–7. IEEE (2019)
21. Liu, Y., Wang, Y., Zhang, J.: New machine learning algorithm: random forest. In: $3^{rd}$ International Conference on Information Computing and Applicatizons, pp. 246–252. Springer Berlin Heidelberg, Chengde, China (2012). https://doi.org/10.1007/978-3-642-34062-8_32
22. Chen, T., Guestrin, C.: XGBoost: a scalable tree boosting system. In: 22nd ACM SIGKDD International Conference on Knowledge Discovery and Data Mining, pp. 785–794 (2016)
23. ICAO safety Report. http://www.icao.int/safety/Documents/ICAO_SR_2023_20230823.pdf. Accessed 25 Jun 2024
24. Aircraft Accidents, Failures & Hijacks Dataset. https://www.kaggle.com/datasets/deepcontractor/aircraft-accidents-failures-hijacks-dataset. Accessed 25 Jun 2024
25. Gössling, S., Humpe, A.: The global scale, distribution and growth of aviation: implications for climate change. Glob. Environ. Chang. **65**, 102194 (2020)
26. Zafar, M.R., Khan, N.: Deterministic local interpretable model-agnostic explanations for stable explainability. Mach. Learn. Knowl. Extract. **3**(3), 525–541 (2021)
27. Angelov, P.P., Soares, E.A., Jiang, R., Arnold, N.I., Atkinson, P.M.: Explainable artificial intelligence: an analytical review. Wiley Interdisc. Rev.: Data Min. Knowl. Discov. **11**(5), e1424 (2021)

# Trust and Trust-Building Policies to Support Cybersecurity Information Sharing: A Systematic Literature Review

Richard Posso[1]([envelope]) [iD] and Jörn Altmann[1,2] [iD]

[1] Technology Management, Economics and Policy Program College of Engineering, Seoul National University, Seoul, South Korea
richardposso@gmail.com, jorn.altmann@acm.org
[2] Integrated Major in Smart City Global Convergence, Seoul National University, Seoul, South Korea

**Abstract.** Cybersecurity threats information (CTI) sharing protects firms and stakeholders from cyberattacks and avoid security vulnerabilities. However, despite these benefits of CTI sharing, firms are still unwilling to share due to barriers and challenges related to a lack of trust. Some studies explored the significance of trust in sharing cyber security information, but further studies are required to determine what dimensions compose trust, which processes support trust, and what trust building policies have been enacted to foster the sharing of information in cybersecurity ecosystems, which is the main purpose of this review. The deliverables from this review present 25 trust dimensions, 6 main processes supporting trust, and 30 trust government policies enacted to foster trust and sharing in cybersecurity. These outcomes enable the creation of a framework for building trust in cybersecurity ecosystems and facilitating the cyberthreat information sharing.

**Keywords:** Trust · Cybersecurity · Information Sharing · Trust Dimensions · Trust Processes · Trust-Building Policies

## 1 Introduction

The widespread use of technology and digital platforms worldwide expanded cyberattacks to every organization and individuals [1]. In 2022, data breaches affected around 53 million people only in USA [2] costing approximately USD $4.35 million per data breach [3]. Due to increased cyber dangers, firms cannot afford to defend themselves isolated from the threat environment. Hence, threat information exchange is essential in cybersecurity domain [4]. Cybersecurity threats information sharing (CTI) helps stakeholders anticipate and avoid security vulnerabilities [5].

### 1.1 Trust Role in Cybersecurity

Despite the benefits of CTI sharing, companies are still unwilling to engage in sharing due to barriers and challenges [6], such as fear to personal information leakage, risk

© The Author(s), under exclusive license to Springer Nature Switzerland AG 2025
M. Naldi et al. (Eds.): GECON 2024, LNCS 15358, pp. 212–228, 2025.
https://doi.org/10.1007/978-3-031-81226-2_19

of exploitation, reputation loss [7], privacy and civil liberties (citizens' trust in governments), loss of customer trust [6], socio-cultural (trust and confidence), technological, legal and regulatory, operational [8], confidentiality, trust management, trust on information, risk assessments [9], legal, technological (lack of interoperability), collaborative (trust between firms), and organizational cost [10]. Among these challenges and barriers, lack of trust is one of the major ones [6] because of its fragility [11]. Previous studies explored the significance of trust in sharing prediction information [12], but further studies are needed to determine what parameters, processes, and trust building policies influence trust in cybersecurity. Conventional classification to study trust suggests two categories: service requesters (trustees) and service providers (trustors) [13, 14]. When addressing CTI, an alternative approach suggests three types: trust of partner to platform (TPP) [15–20], trust between partners (TBP) [15–18, 21], and trust of partner to information (TPI) [15, 17, 22]. This classification gives a thorough review of trust and suggests dimensions and correlations between and within trust kinds that must be explored.

### 1.2 Stakeholders and Trust Types in Cybersecurity Ecosystems

The key cybersecurity players in trust building and information exchange are service providers, insurance providers, security groups, security administrators, government, data source providers, information providers, standardization organizations, and end users. A stakeholder can play more than one role depending on the ecosystem's foundations. For this study, cybersecurity stakeholders are categorized as platform, partner, or information provider.

**Trust of Partners to Platform.** Trusting the platform provider enhances partner collaboration, because platform security supports cyber community participation [17]. Stakeholders with roles for this category are service providers or insurance providers.

**Trust between Partners.** This trust type is essential for CTI sharing because of its sensitivity [17]. Therefore, only the most trusted partners will receive secret information. Partners' trust and motivation to share falls, if free riders are included in the ecosystem. To improve dependability and incentivize CTI sharing between partners, reputation systems are suggested [15, 17]. Stakeholders belonging to this category are cybersecurity groups, administrators, government, and end users.

**Trust of Partners to Information.** Partners' trust in CTI is a major factor affecting the ecosystem. Cybersecurity teams must trust information to face threats. Thus, cybersecurity memberships require strong trust in CTI [17]. Stakeholders fitting into this category are data providers, information providers, and standardization organizations.

## 2  Methodology

### 2.1  Methodology Overview

This study adopted Okoli's (2015) standalone systematic literature review (SLR) methodology, to guarantee explicit and reproducible research. Figure 1 shows the process to carry out the SLR in 9 steps. Claiming SLR's main goal is conducted by identifying a broad research gap (step 1). The next step involves finding and evaluating review papers (step 2). This step supports research questions formulation and originality (step 3). The next step defines keywords to gather all the relevant papers (step 4). Four databases (Scopus, Web of Science, ACM Digital Library, IEEE Xplore) were chosen for the search, and customized search queries for each database were formulated (step 5). An initial number of 4790 articles were collected. By screening these articles and applying the inclusion and exclusion criteria (step 6), the number could be reduced to 490 articles. Quality appraisal of the article reduced the number to 87 articles (step 7). Data extraction is performed using Zotero version 6 (step 8), on which the analysis is performed (step 9).

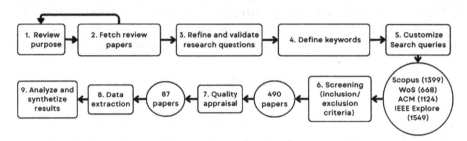

**Fig. 1.** Systematic Literature Review Steps

**Review Papers.** This step supports research gap and review relevance. Table presents the different topics that trust in cybersecurity review papers have addressed. Trust in data networks includes IoT [23, 24], wireless [25], mobile [26–29], P2P [30], and cloud computing [25, 31, 32]. Reviews also studied trust taxonomy [23, 24, 31, 32], trust management [25, 27, 28, 30], and trust evaluation [26, 29, 33]. In addition, researchers studied some trust dimensions such as similarity, timeliness [27], decentralization, privacy [28], asymmetry, sensitivity [24], and reputation [30].

**Research Gap.** Despite these efforts to disclose trust dimensions, more work is needed to describe how trust types in cybersecurity ecosystems are linked to trust dimensions and what interrelationships exist between them. Table 1 shows that some reviews studied processes such dissemination [25], maintenance [29], or transference [33], but no connection between them was researched. Trust management includes some processes, but it is unclear which processes maintain, build, or disseminate trust in cybersecurity ecosystems. Thus, additional studies are needed to unveil the processes that promote trust in cybersecurity. Moreover, reviews studied trust security policies [32] but focused only on internal security policies, excluding external regulations. Thus, studies of trust government policies and their interaction are needed.

**Research Relevance.** Table 1 also shows that no systematic evaluation has examined trust dimensions and their relationships, trust processes, and trust-building policies to leverage CTI. Understanding current research and emerging trust challenges and trends for these topics in cybersecurity ecosystems is relevant to face growing concerns about cyber threats and boost cybersecurity information sharing.

**Research Questions.** The literature reviews include trust taxonomy, management, and evaluation, but the relationship between cybersecurity trust dimensions remains unknown. So, RQ1 was formulated. What are the dimensions of trust required for building trust in cybersecurity information sharing ecosystems? Table 1 also illustrates that most review papers present trust processes scattered in different areas. Thus, RQ2 was formulated. What processes have been implemented to increase trust in cybersecurity information sharing ecosystem? Table 1 also shows that trust regulations in cybersecurity ecosystem are understudied. Thus, RQ3 is proposed. What government policies have been enacted to support trust and increase information sharing in cybersecurity ecosystems?

**Research Keywords.** As seen in Fig. 1, step 4 shows keyword sets created to find all relevant papers: trust* AND ("cybersecurity" OR "network security" OR "cyber-security" OR "security of data" OR "cyber security" OR "information security" OR "security of information") AND ("information" OR "data") AND ("sharing"). All these strings used cybersecurity, information, and the asterisk (*).

**Table 1.** Comparison of Review Articles on Trust in Cybersecurity

| Study | Focus of review | Trust for Security of Data Networks | | | | | Trust Taxonomy | Trust Management | Trust Evaluation | Trust Dimensions | Trust Processes | Trust Policies |
|---|---|---|---|---|---|---|---|---|---|---|---|---|
| | | IoT | Wireless | Mobile | Peer to Peer | Cloud Computing | | | | | | |
| [32] | Trust Architecture | | | | | ● | ● | | | | | ◖ |
| [23] | Remote attestation (IoT) | ● | | | | | ● | | | | | |
| [27] | Trust Factors (IoV) | | | ● | | | | ● | | ◖ | | |
| [25] | Models (WSN, IoT) | | ● | | | ● | | ● | | | ◖ | |
| [28] | Trust Models (VANET) | | | ● | | | | ● | | ◖ | | |
| [24] | Trust Classification (IoT) | ● | | | | ● | | | | ◖ | | |
| [29] | Trust models (MANET) | | | ● | | | | | ● | | ◖ | |
| [31] | Network Topology (WSCN) | | | | | ● | ● | | | | | |
| [30] | Reputation Issues (P2P) | | | | ● | | | | ● | ◖ | | |
| [33] | Trust Factors | | | | | | | | ● | | ◖ | |
| [26] | Trust Initialization (MAS) | | | ● | | | | | ● | | | |
| This Study | Sharing Information, Policies | | | | | | | | | ● RQ1 | ● RQ2 | ● RQ3 |

● Covered ◖ Partially covered

**Research Queries.** Step 6 presents the research queries. As shown in Table 2, the search queries are adjusted to the syntax of the each databases to get relevant results and avoid missing important articles. Scopus, Web of Science (WoS), ACM Digital Library, and IEEE Xplore were chosen, since they are key sources for citation scientific data in multidisciplinary domains, a strength for this study.

**Screening.** Step 6 involves screening and applying inclusion and exclusion criteria. Through this stage, 4740 articles were reduced to 490. Figure 2 summarizes this stage, which describes the technical and content criteria applied.

**Table 2.** Strings Queries Used in Databases

| Database | Query | No |
|---|---|---|
| SCOPUS | TITLE-ABS-KEY (trust* AND (cybersecurity OR cyber-security OR cyber security OR network security OR security of data OR security of information OR information security) AND (information OR data) AND (sharing)) | 1399 |
| WoS | trust* AND (cybersecurity OR cyber-security OR cyber security OR network security OR security of data OR security of information" OR "information security") AND (information OR data) AND (sharing) | 668 |
| ACM Digital Library | AllField:(trust*) AND AllField:(cybersecurity OR "cyber-security" OR "cyber security" OR "network security" OR "security of data" OR "security of information" OR "information security") AND AllField:("information" OR "data ") AND AllField:(sharing) | 1124 |
| IEEE Explore | trust* AND(cybersecurity OR"cyber-security" OR"cyber security"OR "network security" OR"security of data"OR "security of information" OR "information security")AND(informationORdata) AND(sharing) | 1549 |
| Total Number of Papers | | 4740 |

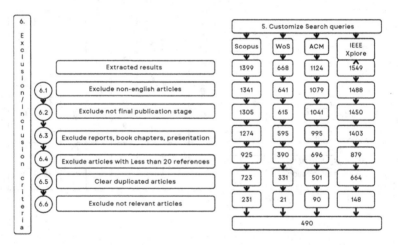

**Fig. 2.** Inclusion and Exclusion Criteria Applied

**Quality Appraisal.** Step 7 comprises the quality appraisal, to identify the most relevant and important papers. The criteria are based on a set of questions proposed by [34, 35] and a tool suggested by [36]. The questions are: Is the paper a research or a discussion based on expert opinion? Is there a clear statement of the research aims? Is there an adequate description of context, in which the research was carried out? Was the research method appropriate to address the aims of the research? Was the data analysis sufficiently rigorous? Is there a clear statement of findings? Is there a clear statement of limitations? Is the study of value for this research?

**Data Extraction.** The quality rating yields 87 research papers for data extraction (step 8). Zotero version 6 is used to arrange the retrieved study citations.

**Analysis of Results.** This stage of the systematic literature review is detailed in the next section.

# 3 Research Results

## 3.1 Descriptive Analysis

The descriptive analysis includes a keyword co-occurrence of the 87 articles using VOSViewer (version 1.6.18). Figure 3(a) shows 46 keywords in the selected articles that occurred at least three times, generating 3 clusters using Van Eck and Waltman's clustering algorithm [37, 38]. The 3 clusters represent trust dimensions (cybersecurity trust characteristics), trust processes, and trust policies in cybersecurity ecosystems. Additional analysis also included the top occurrences and the keyword link strength. The link strength is the number of articles with identical keywords [38]. Figure 3(b) shows that the top 13 co-occurring terms and their link strength. The terms are trust, information sharing, cyber security, cybersecurity policy, and data secrecy policy. It reveals the significance of these terms in cybersecurity information sharing ecosystems.

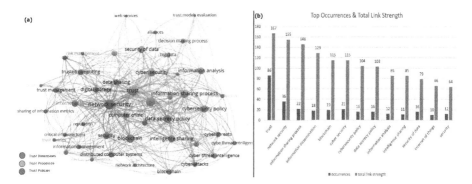

**Fig. 3.** (a) Keyword Co-occurrence Relations; (b) Top Occurrence and Keyword Link Strength

## 3.2 Trust Dimensions in Cybersecurity Information Sharing Ecosystems

As seen in Fig. 4(a), the research identified 25 trust dimensions that influence the three trust types and motivate CTI sharing.

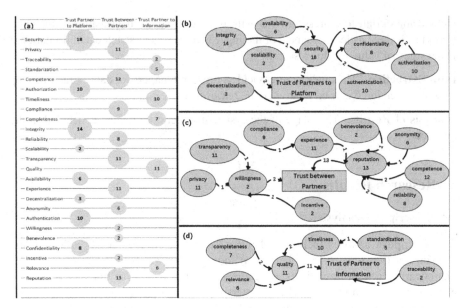

**Fig. 4.** (a) Trust Dimensions by Trust Types; (b) TPP; (c) TBP; and (d) TPI Relationships

**Trust of Partner to Platform (TPP).** Figure 4(a) shows that in TPP the most influential trust dimensions are security [17, 39–50] [51–55], integrity [17, 40, 46, 48, 50, 52, 56–63],authorization [15, 17, 20, 48, 50, 51, 61, 64–66], and authentication [15, 20, 22, 45, 48, 50, 56, 61, 66, 67]. The analysis also reveals that confidentiality [7, 17, 47, 48, 50, 59, 68, 69],availability [48, 50, 52, 62, 70, 71], decentralization [44, 65, 72], and scalability [18, 52] play a secondary role in the research of TPP (Fig. 4(b)). Some dimensions are influenced by others: integrity, authentication, authorizathion impact security [50]; also impacts security [50]; confidentiality impacts security [68]; authorization [48] and authentication [45] impact confidentiality.

**Trust between Partners (TBP).** Figure 4(a) also reveals that TBP is mostly influenced by dimensions such as reputation [18, 22, 30, 57, 63, 75–78], competence [18, 22, 52, 56, 78, 80], experience [18, 22, 30, 50, 53, 60, 71, 75, 81–83], transparency [17, 21, 30, 42, 47, 49, 61, 64, 81, 84, 85], and privacy [17, 20, 46, 51, 52, 55, 62, 64, 86–88]. Moreover, the analysis also shows secondary dimensions such as compliance [40, 49, 51, 52, 57, 65, 79, 89], reliability [17, 18, 44, 45, 52, 54, 75, 81], and anonymity [17, 18, 41, 51, 67, 72], incentive [40, 74], benevolence [13, 40], and willingness [18, 55]. Figure 4(c) summarizes the different relationships that exist in TBP. First, incentive [65], privacy [87], and transparency [64] have an impact on willingness to trust and share information. Compliance [71] impact experience; experience influences reputation [75], and benevolence [13], competence [75, 76], reliability [17, 75], and anonymity [41] impacts on reputation.

**Trust of Partner to Information.** TPI dimensions such as quality [17, 18, 46, 52, 58, 64, 71, 80, 88, 90, 91], and timeliness [17, 18, 52, 53, 75, 90–94] influence trust of partners to information (Fig. 4(a)). In addition, completeness [17, 60, 81, 90–93], relevance [17, 41, 54, 90, 92, 93], standardization [39, 52, 60, 89, 95], and traceability [61, 93] constituting secondary influences. As additional analysis shows (Fig. 4(d)), TPI quality is impacted by relevance [17, 90], timeliness [17, 90], completeness [17, 90], whereas standardization impacts on timeliness [44].

### 3.3 Processes to Increase Trust in Cybersecurity Ecosystems

Six processes and their subprocesses, which increase trust in cybersecurity ecosystems, have been identified (Fig. 5):

**Trust Setup Process.** This phase establishes trust connections for exchanging and transmission of threat information [86] (Fig. 5). The setup process is divided into three subprocesses, namely user registration [7, 65, 86], source validation [17, 56, 78, 80, 87, 91, 93], and building trust structure [42, 57, 86, 93, 95–97].

**Trust Gathering Process.** The gathered data is used to compute trust by qualitative or quantitative approach [75]. Gathering process is divided into four subprocesses named encryption [7, 17, 42, 86, 87, 98], authentication [14, 17, 20, 56, 59, 65, 69, 86, 87, 97], authorization [7, 20, 41, 44, 51, 61, 66, 69, 71, 94, 95, 99–101], and collection [14, 61, 75, 78, 82, 83].

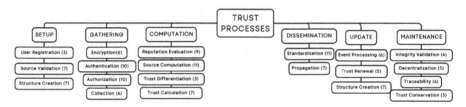

**Fig. 5.** Trust Processes and Subprocesses

**Trust Computation Process.** Statistical, probabilistic, or machine learning methods are used during computing [75]. The findings suggest dividing trust computation into four subprocesses: reputation evaluation [42, 44, 71, 76, 86, 90, 91, 95, 96], source computation [7, 17, 41, 46, 48, 65, 85, 87, 91, 93, 102], trust differentiation [44, 89, 93], and trust calculation [16, 44, 52, 56, 61, 75, 76].

**Trust Dissemination Process.** This process distributes the computed trust values to partners [7, 95]. Depending on the cybersecurity ecosystem, suitable trust scenarios will implement a centralized or distributed scheme for the dissemination [75]. This process should be divided in two subprocesses: standardization [44, 64, 67, 87, 93, 94, 97, 99, 101, 103, 104], and propagation [7, 83, 95] [52, 56, 75].

**Trust Update Process.** It is required to identify the events that trigger a trust update estimation process [75]. The result of this review suggest to partition into two distinct subprocesses: event processing [17, 52, 56, 57, 61, 71], and trust renewal [52, 71, 75, 76, 96].

**Trust Maintenance Process.** It not only determines how often trust information needs to be revised [75, 93] but also indicates how often to verify the information source [93]. The process should be partitioned into four distinct subprocesses: integrity validation [17, 46, 61, 87], decentralization [17, 41, 48, 61, 65], traceability [17, 61, 86, 87], and trust conservation [44, 75, 93].

### 3.4   Trust and Sharing Policies in Cybersecurity

As presented in Fig. 6, 30 government initiatives were discovered in primary papers to improve trust or information sharing. These policies also safeguard government, public, and private sector from growing cyberthreats [105].

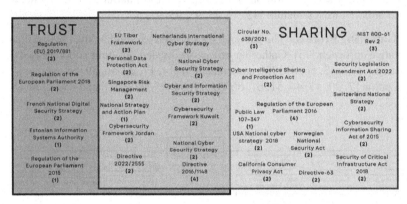

**Fig. 6.** Trust and Sharing Policies

## 4   Discussion

### 4.1   Opportunities

This research outlines opportunities to create trustful cybersecurity information sharing ecosystems by identifying trust dimensions, trust processes, and trust policies. So, every stakeholder participating in the ecosystem can get a common trust overview, and collaboration becomes easier with other members. The findings contribute to create a comprehensive cybersecurity information sharing ecosystems, where stakeholders, trust types, trust dimensions, trust processes, and trust policies can be measured to evaluate real trust impact on the ecosystem.

It is an opportunity to standardize and evaluate best practices for trust processes in cybersecurity. These processes can be used for the implementation, testing, and comparison of performance and efficiency between ecosystems. Trust and sharing policies not only provide an outlook about governments' regulations and efforts to promote trust but also frame the trust types relationships under legal boundaries and support trust dimensions enhancement. The results could disrupt traditional approaches for leveraging trust in cybersecurity and improve best practices and policies.

There is also opportunity to overcome trust barriers in cybersecurity ecosystems. Barriers demonstrate current flaws that impede collaboration and trust emerging in cybersecurity ecosystems. Thus, strategies may incorporate dimensions, processes, and policies to overcome barriers. For example, if the aim is to reduce the barrier of ambiguity in regulations, it requires standardization of concepts and clarification about what dimensions should be measured and how to measure them.

Technological solutions can increase the willingness and participation of partners in the proposed framework for trust in cybersecurity ecosystems. Therefore, there is research opportunity to analyze the relationship between incentives, rewards and incorporate the diversity of technologies, to evaluate which solution creates better trusted ecosystem involving trust dimensions, trust processes, and policies compliance. There is also an opportunity to analyze how digital transformation complies with regulations and with trust dimensions. So, the willingness of stakeholders to share information may be strengthened in cybersecurity ecosystems.

### 4.2 Challenges

One of the main challenges is addressing legal requirements, because regulations are different for each cybersecurity ecosystem. It is vital to adhere to local regulation, to standardize trust concepts, and to establish trust processes for facilitating trust in cybersecurity information sharing ecosystems. Another challenge to achieve the opportunities is to find appropriate real testing environments, in which trust dimensions, processes, and policies can be adjusted, to determine acceptable levels of performance and sustainable ecosystems that can be implemented. A permanent challenge is the gathering of reliable information, to support and validate the different hypothesis in the area. It is recommended to ask the experts in cybersecurity communities, to evaluate how accurate the information obtained from research is applicable to real scenarios.

## 5 Limitations and Future Research

Despite the systematic literature review and primary study selection, relevant papers or articles may not have been included. These articles may have affected the review's conclusions and comprehensiveness. It also focuses on trust dimensions, processes, and policies that directly affect cybersecurity ecosystem information exchange. This study ignored other cybersecurity aspects. However, evaluating dimensions, processes, and policies in a single setting might provide significant cybersecurity trust outcomes. Generalization may be difficult, since further study and verification may be needed to strengthen the evidence. Outcomes from a single element must be evaluated in numerous contexts, and further scenarios with distinct characteristics must be addressed.

**Acknowledgments.** This work was supported by the National Research Foundation of Korea (NRF) grant funded by the Korea government, Ministry of Science and ICT (MSIT), with project

No. NRF-2022R1A2C1092077, NRF-RS-2023–00302083 (as part of the EC-funded Swarmchestrate Project), and BK21 FOUR (Fostering Outstanding Universities for Research) funded by Korea's Ministry of Education (MOE) and the NRF of Korea. Institute of Engineering Research (IOER) of Seoul National University provided the research facility.

# References

1. Takahashi, T., Kadobayashi, Y.: Reference ontology for cybersecurity operational information. Comput. J. **58**, 2297–2312 (2015). https://doi.org/10.1093/comjnl/bxu101
2. Statista (2022a) Data breaches and individuals impacted U.S. 2022. In: Statista. https://www.statista.com/statistics/273550/data-breaches-recorded-in-the-united-states-by-number-of-breaches-and-records-exposed/. Accessed 3 Oct 2022
3. IBM (2022) Cost data breach 2022. https://www.ibm.com/reports/data-breach. Access 3 Oct 2022
4. Ali, H., Papadopoulos, P., Ahmad, J., Pitropakis, N., Jaroucheh, Z., Buchanan, W.J.: Privacy-preserving and trusted threat intelligence sharing using distributed ledgers. In: 14th International Conference on (SIN) (2021). https://doi.org/10.1109/SIN54109.2021.9699366
5. Rashid, Z., Noor, U., Altmann, J.: Economic Model for Evaluating Value Creation Through Information Sharing within the Cybersecurity Information Sharing Ecosystem (2021). https://doi.org/10.1016/j.future.2021.05.033
6. Pala, A., Zhuang, J.: Inf Sharing in Cybersecurity: A Review (2019). https://doi.org/10.1287/deca.2018.0387
7. Vakilinia, I., Tosh, D.K., Sengupta, S.: Attribute based Sharing in Cybersecurity Information Exchange Framework. In: 2017 International Symposium (SPECTS), pp. 1–6. IEEE, Seattle, WA, USA (2017)
8. Alkalabi, W., Simpson, L., Morarji, H.: Barriers and Incentives to Cybersecurity Threat Information Sharing in Developing Countries: A Case Study of Saudi Arabia (2021). https://doi.org/10.1145/3437378.3437391
9. Bernabe, J.B., Skarmeta, A.: Challenges in Cybersecurity and Privacy: The European Research Landscape. River Publishers (2019). https://doi.org/10.1201/9781003337492
10. Koepke, P.: Cybersecurity Information Sharing Incentives and Barriers. MIT, Working Paper CISL# 2017–13 (2017)
11. Höök, K.: Steps to take before intelligent user interfaces become real. Interact. Comput. **12**, 409–426 (2000). https://doi.org/10.1016/S0953-5438(99)00006-5
12. Özer, Ö., Zheng, Y., Chen, K.-Y.: Trust in forecast information sharing. Manag. Sci. **57**, 1111–1137 (2011). https://doi.org/10.1287/mnsc.1110.1334
13. Deljoo, A., van Engers, T., Gommans, L., de Laat, C.: Social Computational Trust Model (SCTM): A Framework to Facilitate Selection of Partners. 2018 IEEE/ACM (INDIS). Dallas, TX, USA, pp 45–54 (2018)
14. Wu, Z.: A Semantic Approach for Trust Information Exchange in Federation Systems. In: 2009 International Conference on Advanced Information Networking and Applications Workshops, pp. 25–30. IEEE, Bradford, United Kingdom (2009)
15. Latvala, O., et al.: Proof-of-concept for a granular incident management information sharing scheme. In: 2022 IEEE World AI IoT Congress. IEEE, Seattle, WA (2022)
16. Qin, X., Zhang, C., Lei, Q., Guo, Y.: A trust model for data-sharing in virtual communities. In: 2012 IEEE International Conference on Computer Science and Automation Engineering (CSAE). IEEE (2012)

17. Wu, Y., Qiao, Y., Ye, Y., Lee, B.: Towards Improved Trust in Threat Intelligence Sharing using Blockchain and Trusted Computing. In: 2019 Sixth International Conference on Internet of Things: Systems, Management and Security (IOTSMS), pp. 474–481. IEEE, Granada, Spain (2019)

18. Vance, A., Benjamin Lowry, P., Wilson, D.W.: Using Trust and Anonymity to Expand the use of anonymizing systems that improve security across organizations (2017). https://doi. org/10.1057/sj.2015.22

19. Din, I.U., Bano, A., Awan, K.A., Almogren, A., Altameem, A., Guizani, M.: LightTrust: Lightweight Trust Management for Edge Devices in Industrial Internet of Things (2023). https://doi.org/10.1109/JIOT.2021.3081422

20. Song, H., Yin, F., Han, X., Luo, T., Li, J.: MPDS-RCA: multi-level privacy-preserving data sharing for resisting collusion attacks based on an integration of CP-ABE and LDP. Comput. Secur. **112**, 102523 (2022). https://doi.org/10.1016/j.cose.2021.102523

21. Chen, P.-K., He, Q.-R., Chu, S.: Influence of Blockchain and Smart Contracts on Partners' Trust, Visibility, Competitiveness, and Environmental Performance (2022). https://doi.org/ 10.3846/jbem.2022.16431

22. Gao, Y., Li, X., Li, J., Gao, Y., Yu, P.: Info-Trust: A Multi-Criteria and Adaptive Trustworthiness Calculation Mechanism for Information Sources (2019). https://doi.org/10.1109/ACC ESS.2019.2893657

23. Johnson, W.A., Ghafoor, S., Prowell, S.: A taxonomy and review of remote attestation schemes in embedded systems. IEEE Access **9**, 142390–142410 (2021). https://doi.org/10. 1109/ACCESS.2021.3119220

24. Ahmed, A., Ab Hamid, S.H., Gani, A., Khan, S., Khan, M.: Trust and reputation for Internet of Things: Fundamentals, taxonomy, and open research challenges (2019). https://doi.org/ 10.1016/j.jnca.2019.102409

25. Fang, W., Zhang, W., Chen, W., Pan, T., Ni, Y.: Trust-based attack and defense in wireless sensor networks: a survey. Wir. Commun. Mob. Comput. **2020**, 1–20 (2020). https://doi.org/ 10.1155/2020/2643546

26. Lin, C., Varadharajan, V.: Modelling and Evaluating Trust Relationships in Mobile Agents Based Systems. In: Zhou, J., Yung, M., Han, Y. (eds.) Applied Cryptography and Network Security, pp. 176–190. Springer, Berlin Heidelberg, Berlin, Heidelberg (2003)

27. Siddiqui, S.A., Mahmood, A., Sheng, Q.Z., Suzuki, H., Ni, W.: A survey of trust management in the internet of vehicles. Electronics **10**, 2223 (2021). https://doi.org/10.3390/electronics1 0182223

28. Lu, Z., Qu, G., Liu, Z.: A Survey on Recent Advances in Vehicular Network Security, Trust, and Privacy (2019). https://doi.org/10.1109/TITS.2018.2818888

29. Ahmed, A., Abu Bakar, K., Channa, M., Haseeb, K., Khan, A.: A survey on trust based detection and isolation of malicious nodes in ad-hoc and sensor networks (2015). https:// doi.org/10.1007/s11704-014-4212-5

30. Selvaraj, C., Anand, S.: A survey on security issues of reputation management systems for peer-to-peer networks. Comput. Sci. Rev. **6**, 145–160 (2012). https://doi.org/10.1016/j.cos rev.2012.04.001

31. Xiang, M., Liu, W., Bai, Q., Al-Anbuky, A.: Avoiding the Opportunist: The Role of Simmelian Ties in Fostering the Trust in Sensor-Cloud Networks (2015). https://doi.org/10. 1155/2015/873941

32. He, Y., Huang, D., Chen, L., Ni, Y., Ma, X., Huo, Y.: A survey on zero trust architecture: challenges and future trends. Wirel. Commun. Mob. Comput. **2022**, 1–13 (2022). https:// doi.org/10.1155/2022/6476274

33. Luo, W., Najdawi, M.: Trust-building measures: a review of consumer health portals. Commun. ACM **47**, 108–113 (2004). https://doi.org/10.1145/962081.962089

34. Dybå, T., Dingsøyr, T.: Strength of Evidence in Systematic Reviews Sw Engin, pp 178–187 (2008b)
35. Kitchenham, B.A., Budgen, D., Brereton, P.: Evidence-Based Software Engineering and Systematic Reviews, 0 ed. Chapman and Hall/CRC (2015)
36. Okoli, C.: A guide to conducting a standalone systematic literature review. Commun. Assoc. Inf. Syst. 37 (2015). https://doi.org/10.17705/1CAIS.03743
37. Waltman, L., Van Eck, N.J., Noyons, E.C.M.: A unified approach to mapping and clustering of bibliometric networks. J. Informetr. 4, 629–635 (2010). https://doi.org/10.1016/j.joi.2010.07.002
38. Van Eck, N.J., Waltman, L.: VOSviewer (2023). https://www.vosviewer.com/features/highlights
39. Sun, N., et al.: Defining Security Requirements With the Common Criteria: Applications, Adoptions, and Challenges (2022). https://doi.org/10.1109/ACCESS.2022.3168716
40. Deljoo, A., VanEngers, T., Koning, R., Gommans, L., DeLaat, C.: Towards Trustworthy Information Sharing by Creating Cyber Security Alliances (2018)
41. Lorchat, J., Pelsser, C., Fontugne, R.: Collaborative Repository for Cybersecurity Data and Threat Information. In: 2014 Third International Workshop on (BADGERS), pp. 83–87. IEEE, Wroclaw (2014)
42. Wang, K., Dong, J., Wang, Y., Yin, H.: Securing data with blockchain and AI. IEEE Access 7, 77981–77989 (2019). https://doi.org/10.1109/ACCESS.2019.2921555
43. Hellwig, O., et al.: Challenges in structuring and institutionalizing CERT-communication. In: 2016 11th International Conference on (ARES). IEEE, Salzburg, Austria, pp. 661–667 (2016)
44. Steinberger, J., Kuhnert, B., Sperotto, A., Baier, H., Pras, A.: In Whom Do We Trust - Sharing Security Events. In: Badonnel R, Koch R, Pras A, pp. 111–124. Management and Security in the Age of Hyperconnectivity. Springer International Publishing, Cham (2016)
45. Wachter, S.: Normative challenges of identification in the Internet of Things: Privacy, profiling, discrimination, and the GDPR (2018). https://doi.org/10.1016/j.clsr.2018.02.002
46. Li, W., Tan, J., Wang, Y.: A Framework of Blockchain-Based Collaborative Intrusion Detection in Software Defined Networking. In: Kutyłowski, M., Zhang, J., Chen, C. (eds.) Network and System Security, pp. 261–276. Springer International Publishing, Cham (2020)
47. Sayed, A.I.E., Aziz, M.A., Azeem, M.H.A.: Blockchain Decentralized IoT Trust Management. In: 2020 International Conference on Innovation and Intelligence for Informatics, Computing and Technologies (3ICT), pp. 1–6. IEEE, Sakheer, Bahrain (2020)
48. Saha, S., Neogy, S., Paul, A., Sengupta, J.: Suitability of Different Cryptographic Approaches for Securing Data Centric Applications. In: 2017 IEEE International Conference on Power, Control, Signals and Instrumentation Engineering (ICPCSI), pp. 603–608. IEEE, Chennai (2017)
49. Teisserenc, B., Sepasgozar, S.: Adoption of Blockchain Technology through Digital Twins in the Construction Industry 4.0: A PESTELS Approach (2021). https://doi.org/10.3390/buildings11120670
50. Aarthi, S., Bharathi, N.: Analysis of Security and Privacy Issues over Vehicular Communication in Internet Of Vehicles. In: 2022 International Mobile and Embedded Technology Conference (MECON), pp. 500–505. IEEE, Noida, India (2022)
51. Hernandez, J., McKenna, L., Brennan, R.: TIKD: A Trusted Integrated Knowledge Dataspace for Sensitive Data Sharing and Collaboration. In: Curry, E., Scerri, S., Tuikka, T. (eds.) Data Spaces, pp. 265–291. Springer International Publishing, Cham (2022)
52. Aslam, M.J., Din, S., Rodrigues, J., Ahmad, A., Choi, G.: Defining service-oriented trust assessment for social IoT. IEEE Access 8, 206459–206473 (2020). https://doi.org/10.1109/ACCESS.2020.3037372

53. Wallis, T., Leszczyna, R.: EE-ISAC—practical cybersecurity solution for the energy sector. Energies **15**, 2170 (2022). https://doi.org/10.3390/en15062170
54. Colella, A., Castiglione, A., De Santis, A.: The Role of Trust and Co-partnership in the Societal Digital Security Culture Approach. In: 2014 International Conference on Intelligent Networking and Collaborative Systems, pp. 350–355. IEEE, Salerno (2014)
55. Li, G., Fang, C.-C.: Exploring factors that influence information resources sharing intention via the perspective of consensus perception of blockchain. Inf. Technol. Manag. **23**, 23–38 (2022). https://doi.org/10.1007/s10799-021-00338-4
56. Awan, K., Din, I., Almogren, A., Kim, A.: VTrust: an IoT-enabled trust-based secure wireless energy sharing mechanism for vehicular Ad Hoc networks. Sensors **21**, 7363 (2021). https://doi.org/10.3390/s21217363
57. Lodi, G., Baldoni, R., Elshaafi, H., Mulcahy, B.P., Csertan, G., Gonczy, L.: Trust Management in Monitoring Financial Critical Information Infrastructures. In: Chatzimisios, P., Verikoukis, C., Santamaría, I. (eds.) Mobile Lightweight Wireless Systems, pp. 427–439. Springer, Berlin Heidelberg, Berlin, Heidelberg (2010)
58. Wang, Y.: Design of trustworthy cyber–physical–social systems with discrete bayesian optimization. J. Mech. Des. **143**, 071702 (2021). https://doi.org/10.1115/1.4049532
59. Laufenberg, D., Li, L., Shahriar, H., Han, M.: Developing a Blockchain-Enabled Collaborative Intrusion Detection System: An Exploratory Study. In: Arai, K., Kapoor, S., Bhatia, R. (eds.) Advances in Information and Communication, pp. 172–183. Springer International Publishing, Cham (2020)
60. Habib, S.M., Vassileva, J., Mauw, S., Mühlhäuser, M.: Trust Management X: 10th IFIP WG 11.11 International Conference, IFIPTM 2016, Darmstadt, Germany, July 18–22, 2016, Proceedings. Springer International Publishing, Cham (2016)
61. Lahbib, A., Toumi, K., Laouiti, A., Laube, A., Martin, S.: Blockchain based Trust management mechanism for IoT. In: 2019 IEEE Wireless Communications and Networking Conference.Morocco, pp 1–8 (2019)
62. Al-Aswad, H., El-Medany, W.M., Balakrishna, C., Ababneh, N.: BZKP: Blockchain-based Zero-Knowledge Proof Model for Enhancing Healthcare Security (2021). https://doi.org/10.1080/25765299.2020.1870812
63. Hung, Y.-T.C., Dennis, A.R., Robert, L.: Trust in virtual teams: towards an integrative model of trust formation. In: 37th Annual Hawaii International Conference on System Sciences, 2004 (2004)
64. Fisk, G., Ardi, C., Pickett, N., et al.: Privacy Principles for Sharing Cyber Security Data. In: 2015 IEEE Security and Privacy Workshops. IEEE, San Jose, CA, pp. 193–197 (2015)
65. Nguyen, K., Pal, S., Jadidi, Z., Dorri, A., Juldak, R.: A blockchain-enabled incentivised framework for cyber threat intelligence sharing in ICS. In: 2022 IEEE International Conference on Pervasive Computing and Communications Workshops and other Affiliated Events IEEE, Pisa, Italy, pp 261–266 (2022)
66. Huang, H., Zhang, J., Hu, J., Fu, Y., Qin, C.: Research on Distributed Dynamic Trusted Access Control Based on Security Subsystem (2022). https://doi.org/10.1109/TIFS.2022.3206423
67. Tounsi, W., Rais, H.: A survey on technical threat intelligence in the age of sophisticated cyber attacks. Comput. Secur. **72**, 212–233 (2018). https://doi.org/10.1016/j.cose.2017.09.001
68. Mivule, K.: Data swapping for private information sharing of web search logs. Procedia Comput. Sci. **114**, 149–158 (2017). https://doi.org/10.1016/j.procs.2017.09.017
69. Palmo, Y., Tanimoto, S., Sato, H., Kanai, A.: A consideration of scalability for software defined perimeter based on the zero-trust model. In: 10th International Congress on Advanced Applied Informatics (2021)

70. Zhou, S., Zhang, G., Meng, X.: LocTrust: a local and global consensus-combined trust model in MANETs. Peer-Peer Netw. Appl. **15**, 355–368 (2022). https://doi.org/10.1007/s12083-021-01250-y
71. Elshaafi, H., McGibney, J., Mulcahy, B., Botvich, D.: Enhancement of critical financial infrastructure protection using trust management. In: Lee C, Seigneur J-M, Park JJ, Wagner RR (eds.) Secure and Trust Computing, Data Management, and Applications. Springer Berlin Heidelberg, Berlin, Heidelberg (2011)
72. Deshpande, V.M., Nair, M.K.: Towards trusted computing-a novel holistic policy based approach. In: 2018 3rd International Conference for Convergence in Technology. Pune, pp. 1–7 (2018)
73. Arachchilage, N.A.G., Namiluko, C., Martin, A.: A taxonomy for securely sharing information among others in a trust domain. In: 8th International Conference for Internet Technology and Secured Transactions (ICITST-2013), pp. 296–304. IEEE, London, United Kingdom (2013)
74. Quigley, K.: "Man plans, God laughs": Canada's national strategy for protecting critical infrastructure: Canada's Strategy for Protecting Critical Infrastructure (2013). https://doi.org/10.1111/capa.12007
75. Awan, K., et al.: RobustTrust A Pro-Privacy Robust Distributed Trust Management Mechanism for IoT (2019). https://doi.org/10.1109/ACCESS.2019.2916340
76. Ma, Z., Liu, L., Meng, W.: DCONST: Detection of Multiple-Mix-Attack Malicious Nodes Using Consensus-Based Trust in IoT Networks. In: Liu, J.K., Cui, H. (eds.) Information Security and Privacy, pp. 247–267. Springer International Publishing, Cham (2020)
77. Purohit, S., Calyam, P., Wang, S., Yempalla, R., Varghese, J.: DefenseChain: Consortium Blockchain for Cyber Threat Intelligence Sharing and Defense. In: 2020 2nd Conference on Blockchain Research & Applications for Innovative Networks and Services (BRAINS), pp. 112–119. IEEE, Paris, France (2020)
78. Latif, R.: ConTrust: a novel context-dependent trust management model in social Internet of Things. IEEE Access **10**, 46526–46537 (2022). https://doi.org/10.1109/ACCESS.2022.3169788
79. Chan, K., Cho, J.-H., Adali, S.: Composite Trust Model for an Information Sharing Scenario. In: 2012 9th International Conference on Ubiquitous Intelligence and Computing and 9th International Conference on Autonomic and Trusted Computing, pp. 439–446. IEEE, Fukuoka, Japan (2012)
80. Randall, R.G., Allen, S.: Cybersecurity Professionals Information Sharing Sources and Networks in the U.S. Electrical Power Industry (2021). https://doi.org/10.1016/j.ijcip.2021.100454
81. Panahifar, F., Byrne, P.J., Salam, M.A., Heavey, C.: Supply Chain Collaboration and Firm's Performance: The Critical Role of Information Sharing and Trust (2018). https://doi.org/10.1108/JEIM-08-2017-0114
82. Ebrahimi, M., Haghighi, M.S., Jolfaei, A., Shamaeian, N., Tadayon, M.: A Secure and Decentralized Trust Management Scheme for Smart Health Systems (2022). https://doi.org/10.1109/JBHI.2021.3107339
83. Hoque, M.A., Hasan, R.: A Trust Management Framework for Connected Autonomous Vehicles Using Interaction Provenance. In: ICC 2022 - IEEE, pp. 2236–2241. Korea, Republic of, Seoul (2022)
84. Fischer-Hübner, S., Angulo, J., Karegar, F., Pulls, T.: Transparency, Privacy and Trust – Technology for Tracking and Controlling My Data Disclosures: Does This Work? (2016)
85. Brignoli, M.A., et al.: Combining exposure indicators and predictive analytics for threats detection in real industrial IoT sensor networks. In: 2020 IEEE International Workshop on Metrology for Industry 4.0 & IoT. IEEE, Roma, Italy, pp. 423–428 (2020)

86. Dunnett, K., Pal, S., Jadidi, Z., Putra, G., Jurdak, R.: A Democratically Anonymous and Trusted Architecture for CTI Sharing using Blockchain. In: 2022 International Conference on Computer Communications and Networks (ICCCN), pp. 1–7. IEEE, Honolulu, HI, USA (2022)

87. Sadique, F., Bakhshaliyev, K., Springer, J., Sengupta, S.: A System Architecture of Cybersecurity Information Exchange with Privacy (CYBEX-P). In: 2019 IEEE 9th Annual Computing and Communication Workshop and Conference (CCWC), pp. 0493–0498. IEEE, Las Vegas, NV, USA (2019)

88. Liu, P., Chetal, A.: Trust-based secure information sharing between federal government agencies. J. Am. Soc. Inf. Sci. Technol. **56**, 283–298 (2005). https://doi.org/10.1002/asi.20117

89. Dunnett, K., Pal, S., Putra, G., Jadidi, Z., Jurdak, R.: A Trusted, Verifiable and Differential Cyber Threat Intelligence Sharing Framework using Blockchain (2022)

90. Mavzer, K.B., et al.: Trust and Quality Computation for Cyber Threat Intelligence Sharing Platforms. In: 2021 IEEE International Conference on Cyber Security and Resilience (CSR), pp. 360–365. IEEE, Rhodes, Greece (2021)

91. Gao, Y., Li, X., Li, J., Gao, Y., Guo, N.: Graph Mining-based Trust Evaluation Mechanism with Multidimensional Features for Large-scale Heterogeneous Threat Intelligence. In: 2018 IEEE International Conference on Big Data (Big Data), pp. 1272–1277. IEEE, Seattle, WA, USA (2018)

92. González, G., Faiella, M., Medeiros, I., Azevedo, G.S.: ETIP: An Enriched Threat Intelligence Platform for Improving OSINT Correlation (2021). https://doi.org/10.1016/j.jisa.2020.102715

93. Schaberreiter, T., et al.: A quantitative evaluation of trust in the quality of cyber threat intelligence sources. In: Proceedings of the 14th International Conference on Availability, Reliability and Security. ACM, Canterbury CA United Kingdom, pp. 1–10 (2019)

94. Pahlevan, M., Voulkidis, A., Velivassaki, T.-H.: Secure exchange of cyber threat intelligence using TAXII and distributed ledger technologies - application for electrical power and energy system. In: The 16th International Conference on Availability, Reliability, Security. Austria, pp. 1–8 (2021)

95. Zhang, F., et al.: Federated Learning Meets Blockchain: State Channel based Distributed Data Sharing Trust Supervision Mechanism (2021). https://doi.org/10.1109/JIOT.2021.3130116

96. Li, F., et al.: Wireless Communications and Mobile Computing Blockchain-Based Trust Management in Distributed IoT (2020). https://doi.org/10.1155/2020/8864533

97. Homan, D., Shiel, I., Thorpe, C.: A New Network Model for Cyber Threat Intelligence Sharing using Blockchain Technology. In: 2019 10th IFIP International Conference on New Technologies, Mobility and Security (NTMS), pp. 1–6. IEEE, CANARY ISLANDS, Spain (2019)

98. Shao, S., Gong, W., Yang, H., Guo, S., Chen, L., Xiong, A.: Data Trusted Sharing Delivery: A Blockchain Assisted Software-Defined Content Delivery Network (2021). https://doi.org/10.1109/JIOT.2021.3124091

99. Haque, M., Krishnan, R.: Toward automated cyber defense with secure sharing of structured cyber threat intelligence. Inf. Syst. Front. **23**, 883–896 (2021). https://doi.org/10.1007/s10796-020-10103-7

100. Štumpf, O., Bureš, T., Matěna, V.: Security and trust in data sharing smart cyber-physical systems. In: Proceedings of the 2015 European Conference on Software Architecture Workshops. ACM (2015)

101. Yuan, E., Wenzel, G.: Assured Counter-Terrorism Information Sharing Using Attribute Based Information Security (ABIS). In: 2005 IEEE Aerospace Conference, pp. 1–12. IEEE, Big Sky, MT (2005)

102. Suryotrisongko, H., Musashi, Y., Tsuneda, A., Sugitani, K.: Robust Botnet DGA Detection: Blending XAI and OSINT for Cyber Threat Intelligence Sharing (2022). https://doi.org/10.1109/ACCESS.2022.3162588

103. Wagner, C., Dulaunoy, A., Wagener, G., Iklody, A.: MISP: The Design and Implementation of a Collaborative Threat Intelligence Sharing Platform, pp. 49–56. ACM, Vienna Austria (2016)

104. Briliyant, O.C., Tirsa, N.P., Hasditama, M.A.: Towards an Automated Dissemination Process of Cyber Threat Intelligence Data using STIX, pp. 109–114. IEEE, Depok, Indonesia (2021)

105. Salomon, J.M.: Public-Private Partnerships and Collective Cyber Defence. In: 2022 14th International Conference on Cyber Conflict: Keep Moving! (CyCon), pp. 45–63. IEEE, Tallinn, Estonia (2022)

# Influencer Sales on TikTok: Forecasting Prominent Factors

Jiahao Liang[1], Simon Fong[1] (iD), Sandra Méndez-Muros[2] (iD),
and Antonio J. Tallón-Ballesteros[3]([⊠]) (iD)

[1] University of Macau, Macau, China
[2] University of Seville, Seville, Spain
[3] University of Huelva, Huelva, Spain
`antonio.tallon@diesia.uhu.es`

**Abstract.** The rapid growth of e-commerce, particularly on platforms that merge socializing and shopping functions like TikTok, has led to the rise of the influencer economy, where influencers drive significant sales through their online presence. This paper aims to forecast the prominent factors influencing influencer sales on TikTok, motivated by the need to better understand this evolving economic model. We establish an original dataset containing data from 100 influencers over a three-month period on TikTok's e-commerce platform. A comprehensive descriptive analysis is conducted to identify variations among influencers, followed by a data mining process to extract key characteristics based on their behavior across different levels, including daily activities, marketing strategies, and basic demographic information. A predictive model is developed to assess influencers' sales levels, revealing that the root mean square error (RMSE) of the model is close to 13. In particular, the study identifies the top 10 most influential sales features. These findings contribute to a deeper understanding of the factors driving influencer sales, offering valuable insights for both influencers and marketers in optimizing their strategies for success on TikTok.

**Keywords:** Influencer · Machine learning · TikTok · Data Mining · E-commerce

## 1 Introduction

The influencer role has emerged and consumer decisions are based on social media and currently prominent social network users are the reference model for other users [3]. In recent years, online shopping has surged in popularity, driven by the rapid advancements in information technology and the expansion of the Internet economy [10]. This trend has been further accelerated by the global spread of COVID-19, which led to the closure of physical stores and an increased demand for online shopping. Consequently, more companies, brands, and new retail platforms have entered the e-commerce market, contributing to its continuous growth. Between 2014 and 2022, the global retail e-commerce market nearly tripled in size. In 2021, global retail e-commerce sales reached approximately $5.2 trillion, and this figure is projected to grow by 56%, reaching around $8.1 trillion by 2026 (https://www.helpscout.com/blog/ecommerce-statistics/). According to

© The Author(s), under exclusive license to Springer Nature Switzerland AG 2025
M. Naldi et al. (Eds.): GECON 2024, LNCS 15358, pp. 229–243, 2025.
https://doi.org/10.1007/978-3-031-81226-2_20

the U.S. Department of Commerce, U.S. e-commerce sales increased from $1.040 trillion in 2022 to approximately $1.119 trillion in 2023, a 7.6% rise, while total retail sales grew from $4.904 trillion in 2022 to about $5.088 trillion in 2023, an increase of 3.8%. As Generation Z's purchasing power continues to grow, they are expected to become the dominant online consumers. The leading platforms in the global e-commerce market include Alibaba, Amazon, Jingdong, Pinduoduo, Apple, eBay, Samsung, Xiaomi, Coupang, and Walmart. In the U.S. and Canadian e-commerce markets, Amazon dominates in total visits. As of August 2023, Amazon's total visits in the U.S. and Canada reached 2.5 billion and 182 million, respectively. In second place is eBay, with 722 million total visits in the United States and Canada. Additionally, Walmart, Home Depot, and other e-commerce platforms are highly active in the North American market, with a comparable number of visits. The rise of China's "four little dragons" has intensified competition in the North American e-commerce market [9]. Temu, for example, quickly captured consumer interest with ultra-low prices after entering the overseas market; TikTok recently launched its TikTok Shop service for U.S. users; and SHEIN introduced its third-party platform model, SHEIN Marketplace, earlier this year.

As the market and user base expand, major social and e-commerce platforms are exploring new business models, continually refining their operations to grow their content ecosystems, and striving to build a diverse and high-quality ecosystem. Facebook, Instagram, and TikTok are the three most prominent social platforms globally, and for years, they have driven e-commerce sales by directing users to shopping sites via branded advertisements. Recently, however, these platforms have begun integrating stores and checkout features to allow consumers to complete transactions directly within the platform. In April 2023, Meta announced that stores on Facebook and Instagram would require in-platform checkout through Facebook. In August, TikTok announced plans to shut down its semi-closed-loop model in preparation for the rollout of TikTok Shop. TikTok officially launched TikTok Shop in the U.S. in September and celebrated its first Black Friday, offering discounts of up to 50%. By the end of the year, some of TikTok Shop's best-selling items had sold over 100,000 units per month. This new business model is largely fueled by the influencer economy. The influencer economy [7] refers to the phenomenon where influencers use the Internet and social platforms to independently select and promote products, guiding their followers toward consumption, thereby generating revenue and creating business opportunities. As live broadcasts, short videos, and other social platforms continue to evolve, the forms of Internet content consumption are becoming more diverse. Millions of original content creators on major online media platforms actively create content and participate in its dissemination. Many of these ordinary Internet users have attracted large followings through continuous content creation and sharing, transforming into influencers and giving rise to the influencer economy. For e-commerce platforms, combining shopping functions with live broadcasting, short videos, and self-media platforms can increase user engagement, improve order conversion and repurchase rates, and effectively maintain user loyalty. For brands and sellers, the conversion rate of orders generated by an influencer's private domain traffic is often higher than that of the platform's public domain traffic. According to Statista, the global influencer marketing market has grown significantly, from $6.5 billion in 2019 to $16.4 billion in 2022, more than doubling in size in under three years [2]. In 2023, influencer marketing was valued at over $21 billion, with more than 75% of brands investing in influencer marketing and over 11% spending more than $500,000 on it.

To address these developments, this paper examines the factors influencing influencer sales on TikTok. Our objectives are threefold: first, to gather primary data on influencers and their sales; second, to analyze the marketing behaviors of these influencers to uncover patterns and principles; and third, to build a machine learning model that combines influencers' behavioral features with basic characteristics to explore the relationship between these factors and sales levels. These studies offer insights into the new economic model of influencer marketing and assist influencers and their brokers in achieving precise market positioning. The model, which combines influencers and e-commerce, holds significant research value in the current context. Therefore, this paper begins by examining the rise and development of influencers, analyzing the current state of influencer marketing, and identifying the characteristics exhibited by influencer representatives over time. Finally, it provides rational suggestions aimed at offering theoretical guidance for influencer operations and assisting merchants in selecting the right partners. The remainder of this paper is structured as follows: Sect. 2 reviews key concepts related to the influencer economy and associated issues; Sect. 3 describes the data acquisition process; Sect. 4 introduces the proposed methodology; Sect. 5 presents the experimental results; and Sect. 6 concludes the paper.

## 2  Foundations

Influencers are individuals who gain fame either through a specific event or behavior that captures the attention of netizens in real or online life, or through the consistent and long-term sharing of their expertise. Their popularity arises from certain qualities that the Internet amplifies, resonating with the public's psychological preferences for aesthetics, entertainment, excitement, voyeurism, and other such traits. These qualities make them the focal point of online attention, leading them to become influencers, whether intentionally or unintentionally [8]. The modern concept of influencers did not originate with social media platforms but rather with mommy bloggers. The first wave of mommy bloggers began in 2002 when Melinda Roberts created The Mommy Blog.com, a site where she shared the highs and lows of motherhood [11]. Through her tips, product recommendations, and parenting experiences, she influenced how mothers around the world raised their children. The launch of Instagram in 2010 marked a significant shift in influencer culture. Instagram enabled users to connect, post pictures, and share their favorite products. Influencers quickly began using the platform to connect with followers on a deeper level, sharing their daily lives and the products they used. In 2013, Instagram introduced a paid advertising feature, making it easier for brands to collaborate with influencers, streamlining the process of selling products and enabling influencers to monetize their recommendations with a simple click. Twitch, founded in 2011, introduced a new dimension to social media through live gaming. It allowed gamers to connect, live stream their games, and interact with viewers in real time, giving rise to a new category of social media influencers known as gaming influencers. These gamers could now earn income by streaming their content and sponsoring various games. TikTok, launched in 2016, brought another unique approach to social media. Unlike other platforms, TikTok's content is tailored to individual users, offering a personalized and highly engaging experience through its "For You" page. The platform's constant stream of diverse content keeps users entertained, while influencers use it to grow their following and connect with audiences in innovative ways. TikTok also allows influencers to participate in trends, such as popular songs and dance challenges, and to create sponsored content. As influencer marketing continues to evolve, the forms of influencers have diversified. What started as individual content creation has expanded into various development models, including capital investment, platform-based operations, and the involvement of MCN (Multi-Channel Network) agencies.

E-commerce, a broad term for trading goods and services over the Internet, was defined by the International Chamber of Commerce (ICC) in 1997 as the process of digitally realizing entire transactions through technology. It transforms traditional brick-and-mortar stores into online establishments on the information superhighway. E-commerce can be categorized into three types based on the transaction platform: the first category includes franchised e-commerce platforms like Amazon, Taobao, and Jingdong; the second involves social media platforms, such as Facebook and Weibo, which promote e-commerce by attracting fans to shop on these platforms; and the third combines socializing and shopping functions, exemplified by platforms like Xiaohongshu and TikTok. Influencer marketing [6], which leverages individuals with significant social media followings, has become increasingly important for brands. This form of marketing involves partnering with influencers to promote a brand and drive consumers to purchase through the social media channels the influencers operate on. Unlike traditional marketing, where the seller communicates directly with the consumer, influencer marketing entrusts the influencer to deliver the brand's message, building trust with the audience by sharing their expertise and insights. It has the following four main features: a) Powerful Influence: Influencers usually have a large fan base and a solid social presence. Each of their tweets and videos can attract thousands of attention and interactions, which makes them ideal candidates to promote their products; b) Precise audience targeting: Different influencers have different fan bases and audience targeting. By choosing the right influencers to work with relevant to the merchant's product or brand, they can precisely deliver ads to their target audience and increase marketing efficiency; c) Highly interactive: Influencer marketing is usually presented in video, live streaming, social media, etc. This multimedia format is highly interactive. Consumers can interact with influencers by commenting, liking, sharing, etc., increasing user participation and brand attention and d) Image spokesperson effect: As influencers have unique personal images and styles, products cooperating with them can use their image spokesperson effect to give products a unique brand image and increase product recognition and reputation.

## 3  Data Acquisition

TikTok is the world's largest short-format video platform, with 1.56 billion active users in 2024. The platform is predominantly youthful, with 60% of its monthly active users aged between 16–24, and those aged 10–29 accounting for over 60% of all active users in the U.S. Generation Z (Gen Z) represents TikTok's most significant potential user base. Today, TikTok has become the preferred search engine for Gen Z, even surpassing older search engines. In early 2021, TikTok launched its e-commerce platform, TikTok

Shop, in Indonesia and the U.K., and within just one year, TikTok Shop generated approximately $5 billion in Gross Merchandise Value (GMV).

Unlike traditional shelf e-commerce platforms such as Amazon, Shein, and Temu, TikTok employs an interest-based e-commerce model with a one-stop shopping experience within the app. This dual-driven model combines content and shelf e-commerce. Traditional shelf e-commerce operates on the principle of users searching for specific products when they have a clear shopping need. In contrast, interest-based e-commerce involves actively presenting graphic or short video content to users through recommendation algorithms. TikTok, with its vast pool of highly engaged users, has successfully tested this interest-based e-commerce model through its domestic Douyin store. This emerging model is expected to become the mainstream approach in future e-commerce.

Given the significance of this model, this study focuses on a specific market segment, namely the TikTok platform. From an academic perspective, focusing on a specific segment can reduce the number of variables missed during analysis. By concentrating on a single platform, it is possible to effectively assess the commercial value of influencers within that segment, aiding merchants in quickly identifying the right influencers for their needs.

Due to TikTok's regulations, it is not possible to directly obtain influencers' marketing data from the platform. Therefore, we selected 110 influencers in the apparel category in the U.K. using the EchoTik platform to gather their marketing data and personal information over last three months of the previous year (01 October 2023 till 31 December 2023), resulting in a dataset of 2,750 records. In any case, EchoTik is a TikTok shop data analytics platform.

The data preprocessing in this study involved several key steps: a) removing records for influencers with missing marketing data, and b) standardizing the data to thousands of units. After cleaning the data, we obtained a final dataset of 2,610 records for 100 influencers.

### 3.1 Basic Information About the Influencers

In this study, we analyze the personal attributes of influencers to identify common characteristics, which will serve as the foundation for the subsequent quantitative analysis. On the TikTok platform, influencers can select up to five labels that help users quickly find influencers of similar types or receive recommendations tailored to their browsing preferences. Therefore, these labels can be considered representative of the influencers' attributes. Among the 100 influencers analyzed, 88% (88 influencers) chose the label "Professional Services". Other frequently selected labels include Government, Health, and Fashion & Style, all of which were chosen by more than half of the influencers. These attributes will be used as variables in the following study to explore the relationship between influencer attributes and sales performance.

Influencers capture the attention of their fans by posting content on TikTok, and they typically begin to monetize their influence once their follower count reaches a certain threshold. Thus, the role of followers is crucial for influencers. In this paper, we obtained follower data for 100 influencers, which were the top 100 over the year, and analyzed their follower counts. The average number of followers among these influencers is approximately 218,000, with the highest follower count being 2.9 million and the lowest being just 1,300. Statistically, 75% of the influencers have fewer than the average number of followers, with only a few top-tier influencers having significantly larger followings. Given the importance of followers, the frequency with which influencers publish content plays a vital role in attracting and retaining followers. Therefore, this paper examines the number of posts made by 100 influencers. The average number of posts per influencer is 1,081, though there is considerable variation. The influencer with the fewest posts has published 59, while the most prolific influencer has published 5,400. The relationship between the number of posts and sales performance will be analyzed in the following sections. The number of likes on an influencer's content is an indicator of popularity and content quality. However, since the number of posts varies between influencers, relying solely on the total number of likes to assess popularity can be misleading. To address this, we introduce two indirect metrics: the average number of likes per video and the likes-to-fans ratio. The average number of likes per video is calculated by dividing the total number of likes by the number of posts for each influencer. The likes-to-fans ratio is obtained by dividing the total number of likes by the number of followers. This ratio reflects the engagement level and content quality relative to the influencer's follower base.

In our analysis, we found significant variation in the quality of content and follower engagement among influencers. The likes-to-fans ratio, for instance, ranges from as low as 500 likes per fan to as high as 161,000 likes per fan, with an average of about 28,000 likes per influencer. Regarding the average number of likes per video, the influencers analyzed received an average of 10 million likes per post. The influencer with the lowest average likes per post garnered just 22,000 likes per post. These variations suggest that the quality of content differs greatly among influencers, and in this paper, we will use the number of likes and the likes-to-fans ratio as dependent variables to investigate their correlation with sales performance. In addition to likes, the number of views also serves as an indicator of an influencer's popularity. The number of views reflects the reach and appeal of the content, with higher view counts indicating broader attention and, potentially, higher popularity. In this paper, we analyze the total view counts for the content posted by 100 influencers. The analysis reveals a wide range of total views, with the lowest being 5,500 and the highest reaching 655 million, while the average is approximately 47 million views.

### 3.2 Influencer's Marketing Message Description

On the TikTok platform, influencers primarily earn money through selling goods. The typical process involves requesting free samples from sellers on the platform, awaiting the merchant's approval to ship the products, and then creating at least one short video featuring the samples to complete the transaction. In this study, we collected data on the video promotions of 100 TikTok influencers over the past three months, along with statistics on the retweets and likes of these videos. Given that fewer TikTok influencers opt for live streaming to promote products, video-based marketing is the sole marketing behavior examined in this paper. We analyzed the number of marketing videos posted by influencers within a three-month period. The minimum number of videos posted per month was two, while the maximum reached 564. On average, 60% of the videos posted by these influencers were marketing-related, with a few influencers dedicating all their videos to marketing. The number of items an influencer sells is often indicative of their popularity among merchants; only those who are highly reputable and effective at selling are consistently chosen to promote products for various stores. This paper examines the number of items sold by 100 influencers over three months. The analysis reveals that the average number of items sold is 138, with significant variation among influencers—ranging from as few as five items to as many as 979. However, a high number of items sold does not necessarily correlate with high sales volume. Therefore, the following section introduces the number of items sold by influencers over three months as a dependent variable to explore whether there is a correlation between this metric and sales volume. The average price of items promoted by influencers can reflect the purchasing power of their fan base to some extent, providing merchants with insight into whether their product prices align with the spending capacity of the influencers' followers. This paper examines the average price of items promoted by 100 influencers over three months. The analysis shows that the price range is relatively narrow, with the lowest price at £12.5, the highest at £49.2, and an average of £20. Approximately 60% of the influencers' average item prices hover around £20. Sales volume is frequently considered one of the most critical metrics for assessing an influencer's ability to sell products, as it often directly impacts the success of product promotions. This paper analyzes the sales volume of items sold by 100 influencers over three months. The findings indicate significant disparities in sales volume among influencers, with the lowest being 16 pieces and the highest reaching 100,000 pieces. The average sales volume for influencers stands at 7,246 pieces. In the subsequent section, we will explore whether sales volume is indeed the most important factor influencing overall sales performance.

# 4  Proposal

Selling products is a crucial aspect for influencers aiming to monetize their presence on TikTok, where most influencers opt to promote items through short videos. The number of marketing videos refers to the quantity of videos posted by influencers that include shopping cart links. The proportion of marketing videos is defined as the ratio of such videos containing shopping carts to the total number of videos posted by the influencer over the past three months. Additionally, variables like the average number of comments, likes, and retweets on marketing videos are also considered.

Before constructing the model, a correlation analysis was conducted to determine the relationship between each feature and sales. The correlation coefficient between an influencer's marketing features and their sales volume was calculated. Notably, the correlation coefficient between the number of sales and total sales volume is 0.731, indicating a strong relationship, which suggests that sales volume is a significant factor in influencing overall sales. The average number of likes and the average duration of marketing videos show moderate correlations with sales, with coefficients of 0.305 and 0.310, respectively, while other features exhibit weaker correlations.

Everyday videos, which do not include shopping carts, typically involve influencers sharing their daily lives or creating more narrative-driven content. These behaviors, classified as non-marketing behavioral characteristics, are important because they help influencers build trust and deepen the connection with their audience. This enhanced trust can increase the likelihood that followers will purchase the products recommended by the influencer. Therefore, variables representing these daily behaviors are included in the model construction.

The correlation analysis between influencers' daily characteristics and sales, as shown in Table 1, reveals that most of these characteristics are weakly correlated with sales. However, the average number of likes and views on daily videos are exceptions, showing moderate correlations with sales.

**Table 1.** Output of Correlation Coefficients

| Characteristic Classification | Eigenvalue | Correlation coefficient |
|---|---|---|
| Non-marketing Behavioral Characteristics | Number of daily videos | 0.082 |
| | Average number of comments on daily videos | 0.256 |
| | Average number of retweets on daily videos | 0.077 |
| | Average number of likes on daily videos | 0.307 |
| | Average number of daily video views | 0.334 |

User fan volume is a key indicator of an influencer's reach and influence. Most influencers have a fan base ranging from 500,000 to 2 million. To analyze how different levels of fan volume impact sales, influencers are categorized into five levels: fans lev1, fans lev2, fans lev3, fans lev4, and fans lev5. The criteria for these divisions and their correlation coefficients with sales are detailed in the following table. The correlation coefficients for fans lev1 and fans lev3 with sales are 0.354 and 0.383, respectively, indicating a moderate correlation. In contrast, the correlation coefficients for the other three levels show only a weak correlation with sales.

The number of videos published by an influencer is another important metric, reflecting their level of activity. This study categorizes influencers based on the number of videos they have posted, with the classification criteria and correlation test results compiled in the table below. However, it was found that all these characteristic quantities are only weakly correlated with sales.

Video views are indicative of an influencer's traffic and the popularity of their content. The views were divided into specific levels, and their division criteria along with the correlation test results are presented in the table below. The correlation coefficients for Views_lev1, Views_lev2, and Views_lev4 with sales are 0.344, 0.430, and -0.314, respectively, suggesting a moderate correlation, while the other two levels show a weak correlation with sales.

Additionally, other features such as influencer likes, the like-to-fan ratio, and the total number of items sold are also included as statistical quantities in this model evaluation, as shown in Table 2.

**Table 2.** Output of Correlation Coefficients

| Eigenvalue | Definition | Correlation coefficient |
| --- | --- | --- |
| Likes | Likes of Influencer Accounts | 0.179 |
| Likes to Fans Ratio | Likes-to-fans ratio of the influencer's account | 0.125 |
| Total Products | Total number of items of the influencer's account | 0.093 |

# 5  Experimental Results

We will now construct a machine learning model to explore further the relationship between influencers' behavioural characteristics and sales. This paper makes use of a visual tool [4] to cover tasks from Data Analytics (DA) [5] within Data Engineering. This section mainly introduces the grouping of the data and the division of the comparison experiments, which will be used to make the prerequisite assumptions for constructing the model in the following two sections. This paper will use decision trees, random forests, and k-NN models to conduct comparative experiments and predict the influencers' sales levels. Therefore, this section will divide the data into test and training sets. The ratio of the model training set and test set is 8:2, i.e., 80% of the original data is used to train the model, which is represented by the feature dataset X_train and the dependent variable set Y_train, respectively, and 20% of the data is used to test the model, which X_test and Y_test, respectively represent. The model predicts the features of the test data X_test to produce the prediction data set Y_pred and then evaluates the classification effect of the model by comparing the test result Y_pred with the actual data Y_test.

We explore the relationship between influencer sales and behavioural characteristics. The experiments in this paper are conducted through Rapidminer [1] and are categorized into the following five sets of comparison experiments: i) full-time full-feature model: All the features of influencers are put into the model classifier to investigate the influence of the overall features of influencers on the sales level, ii) personal attribute information feature model: Train the classification model using personal attribute information features to explore how personal attribute information features affect influencer sales level prediction, iii) non-marketing behavioural features model: Input influencers' non-marketing behavioural features and basic attribute information into the training classification model to explore the influence of influencers' daily behavioural features on their sales level prediction, iv) marketing behavioral features model: Input all the personal information characteristics of the influencers and the marketing characteristics of the last three months into the classification model to compare the prediction results of the full-time full-featured model, v) pure marketing feature model: In the classification model, only the corresponding amount of marketing features is inputted to compare the prediction results with the marketing behaviour feature model. Prediction results through a decision tree are shown in Table 3.

**Table 3.** Output of Decision Tree Model

| Norm | Full-time full-feature model | Personal attribute information features model | Non-marketing behavioral features model | Marketing behavioral features model | Pure marketing features mode |
|---|---|---|---|---|---|
| RMSE | 17.759 | 28.636 | 27.644 | 13.525 | 13.200 |
| Correlation | 0.814 | 0.571 | 0.540 | 0.913 | 0.896 |
| MAE | 12.693 | 22.645 | 20.6 | 10.150 | 10.041 |
| Spearman_rho | 0.684 | 0.657 | 0.638 | 0.882 | 0.898 |

From the evaluation indexes of the models, we can make the following observations:

I. From the comparison of the indicators, it can be found that the pure marketing characteristics model is optimal in all indicators; RSME and MAE are the lowest, while Correlation and Spearman_rho are 0.896 and 0.898, respectively, which indicate a strong correlation. The RMSE of the pure marketing characteristics model can reach 13.2 at the lowest, the RMSE of the marketing behaviour characteristics model is 13.525, which is second only to that of the pure marketing characteristics model, and the RSME of the two is very close to each other, which indicates that the influencer's marketing behaviours are more able to influence its sales level. However, the influencer's sales level is not only influenced by the marketing behaviours.

II. The RSME of the non-marketing behavioural characteristics model and the personal attribute information characteristics model is the highest among all models, which indicates that it is impossible to comprehensively measure the commercial value of an influencer by simply relying on the influencer's influence or simply relying on the influencer's daily behavioural characteristics while ignoring other behavioural manifestations.

III. The RSME of the marketing behavioural characteristics model is lower than that of the full-time full-featured model, which indicates that the marketing behavioural characteristics model is better than the full-time full-featured model, further reflecting that the influencer's daily behavioural characteristics are not the first factor we consider when we consider the influencer's sales ability.

As already mentioned, this paper uses Rapidminer to process the data with the Random Forest algorithm. In order to better validate the model performance, this paper will compare the evaluation of the model under different classifiers by using RMSE, Correlation, MAE, and Spearman_rho as the model performance metrics, and the output is shown in Table 4.

**Table 4.** Output of Random Forest Model

| Norm | Full-time full-feature model | Personal attribute information features model | Non-marketing behavioural features model | Marketing behavioral features model | Pure marketing features model |
|---|---|---|---|---|---|
| RMSE | 19.650 | 25.741 | 23.999 | 19.640 | 13.459 |
| Correlation | 0.835 | 0.510 | 0.591 | 0.855 | 0.892 |
| MAE | 16.185 | 23.204 | 20.829 | 16.527 | 10.286 |
| Spearman_rho | 0.830 | 0.571 | 0.573 | 0.857 | 0.872 |

From the evaluation indexes of the model models, we have the following observations: i) From the comparison of the indicators, we can find that the pure marketing feature model is optimal in all indicators, RSME and MAE are the lowest, while Correlation and Spearman_rho are the highest, the RMSE of the pure marketing feature model can reach 13.459 at the lowest level. The RMSE of the marketing behavioural feature model is 19.640, which is only second to the pure marketing The RMSE of the pure marketing feature model is lower than that of the marketing behavioural feature model, which indicates that the influencer's marketing behavioural features are more likely to affect their sales level. Meanwhile, the level of sales of influencers is mainly influenced by marketing behavior; ii) The RSME of the non-marketing behaviour feature model and the personal attribute information feature model is the highest among all models, so it is the same as the conclusion obtained from the decision tree model, i.e., the influencer's personal information or daily behaviours cannot be used as an indicator to judge the influencer's sales ability alone; iii) The RSME of the full-time, full-feature model and the marketing behaviour feature model are very close to each other, and the marketing behaviour feature model is slightly better than the full-time, full-feature model, which shows that the level of the influencer's sales is not only affected by personal information and marketing behaviour.

Random Forest ranks in the top 10 regarding the importance of feature quantity, as shown in Table 5. The top 10 features include five marketing behaviour features, two daily behaviour features, and three basic personal information features. The number of sales is ranked first and is the most crucial feature quantity, and in the correlation analysis above, we also learned that there is a strong correlation between the number of sales and sales, and here again, the importance of the number of sales on sales is demonstrated. The remaining four marketing characteristics indicate that the interactivity and popularity of the marketing video are also essential. Among the three personal characteristics of the influencer, the label represents the personal attributes of the influencer, the play count represents the popularity of the influencer's video, and the number of likes reflects not only the popularity of the video but also the stickiness of the fans, which indicates that the better the stickiness of the fans is, the higher the quality of the video, and it can also contribute to the level of sales to a certain extent. The evaluation results by means of a $K$-NN algorithm are reported in Table 6.

**Table 5.** Top 10 Importance Features

| Eigenvalue |
| --- |
| Sales volume |
| Hashtag |
| Views |
| Average comments(s) |
| Average likes(s) |
| Average view(s) |
| Average comment(d) |
| Likes |
| Average share(d) |
| Average video duration(s) |

**Table 6.** Output of *K*-NN Model

| Norm | Full-time full-feature model | Personal attribute information features model | Non-marketing behavioral features model | Marketing behavioral features model | Pure marketing features model |
| --- | --- | --- | --- | --- | --- |
| RMSE | 28.446 | 27.045 | 27.045 | 27.039 | 27.037 |
| Correlation | 0.422 | 0.516 | 0.516 | 0.517 | 0.517 |
| MAE | 22.942 | 22.473 | 22.470 | 22.506 | 22.506 |
| Spearman_rho | 0.523 | 0.532 | 0.532 | 0.532 | 0.532 |

From the evaluation metrics of the model outputs, the following are the observations: i) The overall performance of each group of comparison experiments in the K-NN algorithm is close to each other; the RMSE of the pure marketing feature model is still the lowest but higher than the prediction results of the decision tree and the random forest, and the RMSE of the marketing behaviour feature model is only second to that of the pure marketing feature model, which further illustrates that the marketing behaviour is the main factor influencing influencers' sales level; ii) The RMSE of the personal attribute information model and the non-marketing behavioural characteristics model is the same at 27.045, while the RMSE of the full-time full-feature model is the highest at 28.446. Comparing the marketing behavioural characteristics model and the full-time full-feature model further shows that the daily behavioural characteristics are not the primary factor we consider when considering the influencer's sales ability; iii) By comparing the RSME, MAE, Correlation and Spearman_rho of *K*-NN with those of Random Forest and Decision Tree, Random Forest and Decision Tree are more effective in this classification.

Figure 1 plots the experimentation summary related to test RMSE.

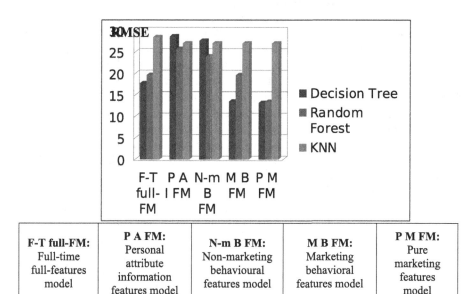

| **F-T full-FM:** Full-time full-features model | **P A FM:** Personal attribute information features model | **N-m B FM:** Non-marketing behavioural features model | **M B FM:** Marketing behavioural features model | **P M FM:** Pure marketing features model |
| --- | --- | --- | --- | --- |

**Fig. 1.** Test RMSE in Different Scenarios

## 6 Conclusions

This paper acquired, modeled, and analyzed influencers' data to assess the factors that influence their sales performance. The key research findings are divided into three parts: a) we identified a list of eligible influencers through data from a third-party platform, then collected their personal information and marketing data over the past three months as our primary research subject; b) we used the influencers' sales data from the past three months as the dependent variable, with the remaining influencer data serving as independent variables. Descriptive statistical analysis was conducted to demonstrate behavioral differences among influencers; c) we constructed marketing behavior characteristics, non-marketing behavior characteristics, and personal information characteristics by analyzing influencers' behaviors. Correlation analysis with sales was performed, and subsequently, we established a sales volume assessment model using decision tree, random forest, and K-NN algorithms, which were then evaluated.

The significance of this paper lies in the following contributions: first, we constructed distinct behavioral characteristics by analyzing influencers' behaviors, combined with personal information, and conducted descriptive statistical analysis and correlation tests with sales volume. These features were then used to build a model to predict influencers' sales levels. The predictive effectiveness of the model was assessed using machine learning classification metrics, and the importance of each feature was ranked. Specifically, i) through correlation analysis, we found that the number of sales and the sales volume are strongly correlated; the average number of likes, the average duration of market-ing videos, and the average number of views of daily videos are moderately correlated with sales. Fans lev1, fans lev3, Views_lev1, Views_lev2, and Views_lev4 also show moderate correlation with sales, while other behavioral characteristics are weakly cor-related. This indicates that the number of sales is the most critical factor influencing an influencer's success; ii) the decision tree, random forest, and K-NN algorithms were used to predict influencer sales based on behavioral data from the past three months. The results showed that the decision tree provided the best classification, followed by random forest and K-NN models. The consistent conclusion across all three algorithms is that marketing behavior is the primary factor in determining an influencer's sales capacity, while daily behavioral characteristics are less significant; iii) the random forest algorithm identified the top ten features in terms of importance, including five market-ing behavior features, two daily behavior features, and three basic personal information features. This underscores the greater impact of marketing behavior on influencer sales, with the label and the number of views among the three basic personal information features ranking second and third, respectively, indicating the importance of the influ-encer's label and content popularity. This study provides influencers with a means to evaluate their current performance. It also offers valuable insights for aspiring influ-encers, MCN organizations, and merchants seeking to collaborate with influencers. The practical significance of this paper is threefold: a) it provides a theoretical framework for empirical analysis in the field of influencer research; b) it quantitatively analyzes the impact of influencers' behavioral characteristics on e-commerce using machine learning modeling, thereby enriching quantitative analysis methods and empirical research in the influencer e-commerce domain; c) it offers a theoretical basis for MCN organizations and companies in optimizing their operations and selecting the right influencers for partnerships.

# References

1. Akthar, F., Hahne, C.: Rapidminer 5 operator reference. Rapid-I GmbH **50**, 65 (2012)
2. Aw, E.C.X., Agnihotri, R.: Influencer marketing research: review and future research agenda. J. Marketing Theory Pract., 1–14 (2023)
3. Barta, S., Belanche, D., Fernández, A., Flavián, M.: Influencer marketing on TikTok: the effectiveness of humor and followers' hedonic experience. J. Retail. Consum. Serv. **70**, 103149 (2023)
4. Cho, S.B., Tallón-Ballesteros, A.J.: Visual tools to lecture data analytics and engineering. In: International Work-Conference on the Interplay Between Natural and Artificial Computation (pp. 551–558). Springer, Cham (2017). https://doi.org/10.1007/978-3-319-59773-7_56
5. Dong, G., Liu, H.: Feature Engineering for Machine Learning and Data Analytics. CRC Press (2018)
6. Gillin, Paul: The new influencers: a marketer's guide to the new social media. Linden Publishing (2007)
7. Kubler, K.: Influencers and the attention economy: the meaning and management of attention on Instagram. J. Mark. Manag. **39**(11–12), 965–981 (2023)
8. Lou, C., Yuan, S.: Influencer marketing: how message value and credibility affect consumer trust of branded content on social media. J. Interact. Advert. **19**(1), 58–73 (2019)

9. Si, R.: China livestreaming e-commerce industry insights. Springer Singapore Pte. Limited (2021). https://doi.org/10.1007/978-981-16-5344-5
10. Wang, D., Guo, B.: Will online shopping lead to more brand loyalty than offline shopping? The role of uncertainty avoidance. J. Mark. Res. **61**(1), 92–109 (2024)
11. Zarrella, D.: The social media marketing book. Inc, O'Reilly Media (2009)

# Machine Learning Explainability as a Service: Service Description and Economics

Paolo Fantozzi[1]([✉])[ID], Luigi Laura[2][ID], and Maurizio Naldi[1][ID]

[1] Department of Law, Economics, Politics, and Modern Languages at LUMSA University, Via Pompeo Magno, 28, Rome 00192, Italy
{p.fantozzi1,m.naldi}@lumsa.it
[2] International Telematic University Uninettuno, Rome, Italy
luigi.laura@uninettunouniversity.net

**Abstract.** Explainability is a growing concern in many machine learning applications. Machine learning platforms now typically provide explanations accompanying their model output. However, this may be considered as just a first step towards defining explainability as a service in itself, which would allow users to get more control over the kind of explainability technique they wish to employ. In this paper, we first provide a survey of the current offer of machine learning platforms, observing their pricing models and the explainability features they possibly offer. In order to progress towards Explainability-as-a-Service (XaaS), we propose to base its definition on the REST paradigm, considering three major examples of explainability techniques, relying on either feature scoring, surrogate linear models, or internal state observation. We also show that XaaS is dependent on machine-learning model provisioning, and the two services are linked by a one-way essential complement relationship, where ML provisioning plays the role of the essential component and XaaS is the complement option. We also suggest that vertical integration is the natural arrangement for companies offering either service, given their mutual relationship.

**Keywords:** Explainability · XaaS · Pricing

## 1 Introduction

Explainability is becoming an unavoidable companion to all machine learning (ML) models. In many fields, providing the output of a machine-learning task, though exhibiting impressive performances, is not enough. An explanation of how the result was obtained and what contributed most to those results is required by both domain experts and people affected by those results and is typically attained by identifying the most relevant features to determine the output of the ML model.

The literature on explainability techniques is now so large that it includes hundreds of papers. In Sect. 2, we provide a brief review of the most relevant ones.

© The Author(s), under exclusive license to Springer Nature Switzerland AG 2025
M. Naldi et al. (Eds.): GECON 2024, LNCS 15358, pp. 244–253, 2025.
https://doi.org/10.1007/978-3-031-81226-2_21

A recent survey dedicated to a single category of machine learning architectures, namely transformers, counted roughly 150 papers [9].

Though explainability is an additional task with respect to building a machine-learning model, its growing relevance has led many machine-learning platforms (e.g., Azure or AWS) to include explainability parameters when showing the resulting ML model. Though bundling explainability information adds value to ML model building, we observe that it is lacking at least in two respects. First, explainability is provided on as as-is basis, denying users the possibility to specify the explainability technique they wish. Second, it does not extract the full value of the information that is provided alongside ML model results.

We claim that explainability should be considered as a service in itself, which the user can ask for and pay accordingly. Though introducing explainability as a service has been invoked in the literature, no further actions have been taken to fulfil that wish. In this paper, we wish to mark a first step in that direction through the following contributions: a) we review the current panorama of machine-learning platforms, highlighting their side explainability features (Sect. 3); b) we provide an initial description of the service, adopting the REST (Representational State Transfer) paradigm (Sect. 4); c) we show that Explainability-as-a-Service can be considered to be in a one-way essential complement relationship with the ML model service, with consequences on its pricing (Sect. 5).

## 2   Literature Review

Explainability-as-a-Service (XaaS for short) relies on the adoption of explainability methods and can be seen as an accompanying feature of ML models. In this section, we briefly survey the literature on explainability and then examine the (scarce) literature on XaaS, highlighting the research gap.

There are many ways to classify the explainability methods. Here, we adopt the classification into model-agnostic and model-aware techniques proposed in [2], based on the relationship to the model to be explained. In model-agnostic techniques, the model to be explained is considered as a black box, i.e., as a set of input-output tuples, and the explanation is derived just by analysing these tuples. On the other hand, in the model-aware family, the architecture of the model to be explained is known and can be exploited to gain insight into the way the model result is arrived at.

### 2.1   Model-Agnostic Techniques

In most model-agnostic methods, explanations are sought by perturbing the input and measuring the differences in the output. A major technique is Local Interpretable Model-agnostic Explanation (LIME) [14], where linear models are derived as surrogates for the actual ML model. It provides a local explanation with no guarantee about its capabilities outside a small neighbourhood. Another method providing a surrogate model is SHAP (SHapley Additive exPlanations) [11], which employs game theory based on the notion of Shapley values [17].

## 2.2  Model-Aware Techniques

Model-aware techniques are largely employed when the ML model to be explained employs neural networks. Such model-aware methods observe, e.g., the activations returned by layers in the neural network or the gradients computed by the learning algorithm. Methods dedicated to attention-based architectures, e.g., transformers, are achieving greater visibility [9].

A major activation-based method is Layer-wise Relevance Propagation (LRP) [3], where all layers of the neural network use ReLU activation, like in convolutional architectures (CNN). Neuron activations represent the relevance of the neuron. Many subsequent works extended LRP beyond the ReLU assumption, e.g., [8]. Further variations of LRP are Partial-LRP, applicable to transformers [18], and that proposed for images in [6]. A different approach dedicated to CNN architectures to classify images was Class Activation Mapping (CAM) [19], where a global average pool layer is included just before the fully connected last layer. The activation given by each filter of the last convolutional layer is multiplied by the weights matrix of the last fully connected layer to form scores for each super-pixel (a patch) of the image. Super-pixels are then reconciled with the original image to form a saliency map over the original pixels. Variations of this method were presented in [12] (based on Single Value Decomposition, in [16] (Grad-CAM) and in [5] (Grad-CAM++). Attention Rollout and Attention Flow were both presented in [1], using the attention weights as a proxy for explaining the output. By accumulating the attention scores over the layers (from last to first), a score can be computed for each input feature.

We have just offered a brief survey of the large body of literature dealing with explainability. The notion of configuring it as a service has not been explored as largely. One of the first attempts concerned a very specific application field, i.e., the use of explainable AI for robot planning, where an automated planner is called to justify its plans based on the user's constraints [4]. XaaS has been invoked as an approach to address biases and satisfy users' requirements in [10], where, however, no specific solutions are suggested. Further support for the introduction of XaaS was given in [13], where the abbreviation XaaS was also introduced, in the context of finance applications of AI, with third-party providers offering specialized tools and services for AI explainability, in particular surrogate linear models (namely LIME and SHAP). Again, no specific solutions are suggested for the service. The notion of XaaS was again put forward in [15], with, however, no specific description of the service architecture. What we see missing in the literature is a precise definition of a service architecture for XaaS.

## 3  Machine Learning Platforms

In addition to developing their own ML solutions via coding on their machines, researchers and practitioners may also exploit the services offered by ML platforms. Those platforms are to be given the problem and a dataset and allow the user to select an algorithm and proceed with model training, validation and deployment. In this section, we provide a brief description of those platforms.

Most of these platforms target non-technical users, so they offer a simple user interface to upload data of many different types (images, text, videos, etc.), guiding the user through preprocessing the data and labelling them. Also, the platforms we examine here focus on supervised learning techniques because they are easier to understand for a non-technical user.

The major machine-learning platforms are:

- Google Cloud AutoML (https://cloud.google.com/automl)
- AWS SageMaker (https://aws.amazon.com/sagemaker), which offers both no-code solutions (JumpStart, Canvas, etc.) and tools to train a model by coding.
- Azure AutoML (https://azure.microsoft.com/solutions/automated-machine-learning)
- IBM Watson Studio (https://www.ibm.com/products/watson-studio)
- BigML (https://bigml.com/)
- ObviouslyAI (https://www.obviously.ai/)

All these platforms offer some preprocessing tools, usually guided by visualizations produced through automatic data exploration, and also labelling tools, with many identifiable similarities with dedicated tools (such as Label Studio[1]).

Even though all the platforms offer the possibility to train a model from scratch, from simple regressions to more complex models such as (sequential) neural networks, only some allow us to exploit the so-called *Foundation Models*. Since foundation models are most often closed-source, the availability of these models inside a platform means that there exists a deal between the owner of the platform and the companies owning the models. Depending on the model, they can be used either by fine-tuning on the user data, or with a few-shots approach.

The implication of these deals between companies is that some models are provided only by some platforms. For instance, the only platform to provide access to OpenAI models is Azure AutoML, because of the exclusive deal signed by OpenAI and Microsoft[2]. For this reason, the differences between platforms are not limited to their functionalities and user interface, but may extend to the set of pre-trained models available. Although most online machine learning platform providers try to train their own foundation models to be used in their platforms, there exists a differentiation between providers. Some providers use their own models as their crown jewels (e.g., Google and IBM), while others focus on models developed by other companies (e.g., Microsoft and Amazon).

A further difference among providers is related to the provider's cloud ecosystem itself. Indeed, while small providers (e.g., BigML and ObviouslyAI) do not have a complete cloud ecosystem, big providers (e.g., Google, Amazon, Microsoft and IBM) offer a full set of services related to machine learning, e.g., data storage, which is critical for data-intensive applications and also for training ML models. Small providers tend to integrate as many services as possible to increase their services' attractiveness. On the other hand, big providers wish to turn customers away from competitors and have them switch to their services. They do

---

[1] https://labelstud.io/.
[2] https://blogs.microsoft.com/blog/2023/01/23/microsoftandopenaiextendpartner ship/.

so by providing integration with other providers just through favouring migration, leaving as a prerequisite that the data should be either uploaded directly to the ML service or integrated by using their data storage service.

All big providers offer an explainability service (among small providers, BigML offers explainability while ObviouslyAI does not). Furthermore, all big providers (which usually also offer PaaS services to train machine learning models) give the users the possibility to upload already-trained models built using standard frameworks (e.g., PyTorch or Tensorflow), so the platform can apply explainability even if models have been trained outside. Platforms tend to use well-known explainability methods, typically either model-agnostic post-hoc methods or post-hoc methods based on neural network architectures.

## 4    Explainability as a Service

In the previous sections, we examined current explainability solutions and ML platforms, where explainability is offered as a free companion to ML model building. We claim that explainability can now be offered as a separate service. A formal description of XaaS has not been provided yet. In this section, we wish to introduce a formal description of explainability as a web service, adopting REST (Representational State Transfer) as the tool of reference.

In order to describe the interactions between systems, we have chosen the OpenAPI standard instead of WSDL (Web Service Definition Language), due to its wide use in real-world applications and the availability of graphical tools to visualize and interact with APIs. Also, OpenAPI is mainly based on REST, which is the de-facto standard for web applications. Also, the stateless nature of REST makes users tend to build easier APIs that are also much easier to scale up because of the lack of critical sections intrinsic to the APIs themselves.

The platform should include a main service to run models for inference and the explainability service for the models loaded with the main service. In order to run a model for inference, we need a trained model in a well-known format and the amount of resources for the model. Ideally, the service should support all the file formats produced by the de-facto standard tools (just like PyTorch and TensorFlow), but it is not enough to be able to read and run the model file, since we also need the architecture used in the model (e.g., it is not easy to inspect a model to understand whether it is similar to an encoder-only transformer). We also need to size the hardware to run the model, which again is not obtainable by inspecting the model: the size of RAM needed to run a Mixture-of-experts model is not linearly dependent on the number of model parameters, because during inference only a fraction of the parameters are loaded into RAM. In Fig. 1, we show the OpenAPI code to load the model.

Besides the main service access point, we should also provide at least three different access points to explainability services. Depending on the model type (or architecture) to be explained, we could apply a subset of methods, e.g., the following three classes (whose OpenAPI code is in Figs. 2, 3 and 4):

```
"/load_model/": {
   "post": {
      "summary": "Load Model",
      "operationId": "load_model_load_model__post",
      "parameters": [{
         "name": "model_file_url", "in": "query", "required": true,
         "schema": { "type": "string", "format": "uri", "minLength": 1}
      }, {
         "name": "model_type", "in": "query", "required": true,
         "schema": {"$ref": "#ArchitectureType"}
      }, {
         "name": "resources_to_allocate", "in": "query", "required": true,
         "schema": {"type": "string", "title": "Resources To Allocate"}
      }],
      "responses": {
         "200": {
            "description": "Successful Response",
            "content": {
               "application/json": {
                  "schema": {"$ref": "#ModelAllocated"}
               }
            }
         },
         "422": {
            "description": "Validation Error",
            "content": {
               "application/json": {
                  "schema": {"$ref": "#HTTPValidationError"}
}}}}}},
```

**Fig. 1.** OpenAPI specification for load model API

**Features' scores**, including the methods providing an importance score for each input feature. A major method in this class is GradCAM, applicable to any CNN-based architecture and returning a matrix of scores to be projected on the input image to produce a saliency map, plottable as a heatmap showing the most important pixels in the input image. In order to apply this method, we first need to know the architecture used since the computation of the convolutional part is carried out separately from the classification (or regression) head mounted on the convolutional layers.

**Surrogate model**, including the methods providing a surrogate model (often a linear one) locally approximating the original model. The surrogate model obtained should roughly provide the same output as the original model, but its quality (its accuracy) degrades as we move away from the local neighbourhood for which the surrogate model was generated. A major method in this class is LIME, where the most important regressors in the linear model represent the most relevant features to explain the model. LIME is model-agnostic, so that we can dispense with the need to know the architecture of the ML model to be explained.

**Model internal observation**, including the methods that just plot the internal parameters of the models. For instance, for transformer-based architectures we could plot the attention weights learned in different layers of the model. The only computation performed in this case is the aggregation of multi-head attention weights. For this type of approach, we first need the model architecture and then check whether this architecture is supported by the observation methods provided by the platform.

```
"/model_inspect/": {
    "post": {
        "summary": "Model Inspect",
        "operationId": "model_inspect_model_inspect__post",
        "parameters": [{
            "name": "allocation_id", "in": "query", "required": true,
            "schema": {"type": "string"}
        }, {
            "name": "section_of_model_to_inspect", "in": "query", "required": true,
            "schema": {"type": "string"}
        }, {
            "name": "method", "in": "query", "required": false,
            "schema": {"type": "string", "default": "auto"}
        }],
        "requestBody": {
            "required": true,
            "content": {
                "application/json": {
                    "schema": {"$ref": "#Body_model_inspect_model_inspect__post"}
                }
            }
        },
        "responses": {
            "200": {
                "description": "Successful Response",
                "content": {
                    "application/json": {
                        "schema": {"$ref": "#SampleExplanationModelInspect"}
                    }
                }
            },
            "422": {
                "description": "Validation Error",
                "content": {
                    "application/json": {
                        "schema": {"$ref": "#HTTPValidationError"}
}}}}}},
```

**Fig. 2.** OpenAPI specification for model inspect API

```
"/features_scores/": {
    "post": {
        "summary": "Features Scores",
        "operationId": "features_scores_features_scores__post",
        "parameters": [{
            "name": "allocation_id", "in": "query", "required": true,
            "schema": {"type": "string"}
        }, {
            "name": "method", "in": "query", "required": false,
            "schema": {"type": "string", "default": "auto"}
        }],
        "requestBody": {
            "required": true,
            "content": {
                "application/json": {
                    "schema": {"$ref": "#Body_features_scores_features_scores__post"}
                }
            }
        },
        "responses": {
            "200": {
                "description": "Successful Response",
                "content": {
                    "application/json": {
                        "schema": {"$ref": "#SampleExplanationFeaturesScores"}
                    }
                }
            },
            "422": {
                "description": "Validation Error",
                "content": {
                    "application/json": {
                        "schema": {"$ref": "#HTTPValidationError"}
}}}}}},
```

**Fig. 3.** OpenAPI specification for features scores API

```
"/surrogate_model/": {
    "post": {
        "summary": "Surrogate Model",
        "operationId": "surrogate_model_surrogate_model__post",
        "parameters": [{
            "name": "allocation_id", "in": "query", "required": true,
            "schema": {"type": "string"}
        }, {
            "name": "method", "in": "query", "required": false,
            "schema": {"type": "string", "default": "auto"}
        }],
        "requestBody": {
            "required": true,
            "content": {
                "application/json": {
                    "schema": {"$ref": "#Body_surrogate_model_surrogate_model__post"}
                }
            }
        },
        "responses": {
            "200": {
                "description": "Successful Response",
                "content": {
                    "application/json": {
                        "schema": {"$ref": "#SampleExplanationFeaturesScores"}
                    }
                }
            },
            "422": {
                "description": "Validation Error",
                "content": {
                    "application/json": {
                        "schema": {"$ref": "#HTTPValidationError"}
}}}}}}
```

**Fig. 4.** OpenAPI specification for surrogate model API

## 5   Pricing Models

None of the ML platforms in Sect. 3 offers explainability as a separate service from ML provisioning. Rather, it is offered as a built-in feature of ML models, which is not priced separately. In this section, we first review the pricing models adopted by platform providers for ML provisioning and then examine the characteristics of a pricing model for XaaS.

The pricing policies adopted by the platforms can be classified again into two categories based on the platform providers themselves: big providers offering cloud services and small providers more devoted to the product.

For big providers, the main cost is linked to the amount of resources used during model training and inference, with a pay-as-you-go plan where either a little or no cost at all is added. For example, Azure offers a pay-as-you-go scheme where computing capacity is metered by the second, with no long-term commitments or upfront payments, and increasing or decreasing consumption on demand. However, a savings plan can be subscribed, where customers commit to spend a fixed hourly amount for 1 or 3 years. Similarly, Amazon's Sage-maker offers an On-Demand Pricing scheme (metered by the hour) with neither minimum fees nor upfront commitments, as well as Savings Plans. In Google's AutoML, a price per node hour is proposed based on the specific operation, e.g., Training, Deployment and online prediction, or Batch prediction. Small providers instead apply pricing policies based on a monthly fee covering all the services offered by the platform. BigML offers a set of plans differing for the size of datasets supported and parallel tasks. ObviouslyAI offers a single plan with higher costs and limitations on the number of predictions provided.

Since XaaS would require a dedicated pricing policy, how can we attach a price to explainability? Here, we do not provide specific indications, but we can describe some constraints based on the nature of XaaS. First, we notice that you cannot get an explanation if you do not set an ML model first, so the demand for XaaS cannot be greater than that for ML. We also envisage that the price of XaaS should be lower than that of ML model provisioning. In addition, we can consider XaaS as a complement of ML (rather than a substitute), so that the demand and prices of ML model provisioning and XaaS should be related. Precisely, we expect the demand for XaaS to be negatively impacted by the price of ML model provisioning as well as by its own price. Since ML modelling can take place without explainability, but not the reverse, we can classify the relationship between the two services as a one-way essential complement, where ML provisioning is essential while XaaS is optional [7].

As to the market structure, we have a case of natural vertical integration, where the providers of ML and XaaS coincide. When the value of the option (XaaS) is smaller than the essential service (ML) and marginal costs are zero, the provider would choose to price the option at zero (what the providers are doing today) [7]. The joint monopolist would give XaaS away and earn all its profits by selling ML provisioning. Providers offering ML would, therefore, include XaaS in a bundle package and compete on the quality and prices of ML provisioning.

## 6   Conclusions

We have set the case for adding explainability as a service to ML model provisioning. Currently, explainability is provided as a side output of ML provisioning. However, providing XaaS would allow users to cast specific requests and get the explainability they wish. Our description of the service relying on the OpenAPI standard can be employed as a first step in that direction. We have sketched the service primitives for three types of XaaS output, showing the variety of service features that users can get with respect to the current offer where XaaS is offered on an as-is basis. However, ML provisioning and XaaS are actually not two totally separate services, their relationship being that of one-way essential complementarity. This may have some effect on pricing. Though listing XaaS as a separate service would allow the provider to set separate prices, under certain conditions, the best option for the provider may be to include XaaS in a bundle package with ML and practically offer XaaS for free. We expect to examine the impact of XaaS bundle offer on competition in future works.

## References

1. Abnar, S., Zuidema, W.: Quantifying attention flow in transformers. In: Jurafsky, D., Chai, J., Schluter, N., Tetreault, J. (eds.) Proceedings of the 58th Annual Meeting of the Association for Computational Linguistics, pp. 4190–4197 (2020)
2. Adadi, A., Berrada, M.: Peeking inside the Black-Box: a survey on explainable artificial intelligence (XAI). IEEE Access **6**, 52138–52160 (2018)

3. Bach, S., Binder, A., Montavon, G., Klauschen, F., Müller, K.R., Samek, W.: On Pixel-Wise explanations for Non-Linear classifier decisions by Layer-Wise relevance propagation. PLoS ONE **10**(7), e0130140 (2015)
4. Cashmore, M., Collins, A., Krarup, B., Krivic, S., Magazzeni, D., Smith, D.: Towards explainable ai planning as a service. arXiv preprint arXiv:1908.05059 (2019)
5. Chattopadhay, A., Sarkar, A., Howlader, P., Balasubramanian, V.N.: Grad-CAM++: generalized Gradient-Based visual explanations for deep convolutional networks. In: 2018 IEEE Winter Conference on Applications of Computer Vision (WACV), pp. 839–847. IEEE (2018)
6. Chefer, H., Gur, S., Wolf, L.: Transformer interpretability beyond attention visualization. In: 2021 IEEE/CVF Conference on Computer Vision and Pattern Recognition (CVPR), pp. 782–791, June 2021
7. Chen, M.K., Nalebuff, B.J.: One-way essential complements. Technical report CFDP 1588, Cowles Foundation for Research in Economics (2006)
8. Ding, Y., Liu, Y., Luan, H., Sun, M.: Visualizing and understanding neural machine translation. In: Proc. of the 55th Annual Meeting of the Association for Computational Linguistics, vol. 1, pp. 1150–1159, Vancouver, Canada (2017)
9. Fantozzi, P., Naldi, M.: The explainability of transformers: current status and directions. Computers **13**(4), 92 (2024)
10. Jovanović, M., Schmitz, M.: Explainability as a user requirement for artificial intelligence systems. Computer **55**(2), 90–94 (2022)
11. Lundberg, S.M., Lee, S.I.: A unified approach to interpreting model predictions. In: Proceedings of the 31st International Conference on Neural Information Processing Systems, NIPS 2017, pp. 4768–4777, Red Hook, NY, USA (2017)
12. Muhammad, M.B., Yeasin, M.: Eigen-CAM: class activation map using principal components. In: 2020 International Joint Conference on Neural Networks (IJCNN), pp. 1–7. IEEE, July 2020
13. Rane, N., Choudhary, S., Rane, J.: Explainable artificial intelligence (xai) approaches for transparency and accountability in financial decision-making. Available at SSRN 4640316 (2023)
14. Ribeiro, M.T., Singh, S., Guestrin, C.: "Why should I trust you?": explaining the predictions of any classifier. In: Proc. of the 22nd ACM SIGKDD Intl Conf on Knowledge Discovery and Data Mining, pp. 1135–1144, New York, NY, USA (2016)
15. Samiei, S., Baratalipour, N., Yadav, P., Roy, A., He, D.: Addressing stability in classifier explanations. In: 2021 IEEE International Conference on Big Data (Big Data), pp. 1920–1927. IEEE (2021)
16. Selvaraju, R.R., Cogswell, M., Das, A., Vedantam, R., Parikh, D., Batra, D.: Grad-CAM: visual explanations from deep networks via gradient-based localization. In: 2017 IEEE Intl Conf on Computer Vision (ICCV), pp. 618–626 (2017)
17. Shapley, L.S.: A value for n-person games. In: Harold William Kuhn, A.W.T. (ed.) Contributions to the Theory of Games (AM-28), vol. II, pp. 307–318. Princeton University Press (1953)
18. Voita, E., Talbot, D., Moiseev, F., Sennrich, R., Titov, I.: Analyzing Multi-Head Self-Attention: Specialized heads do the heavy lifting, the rest can be pruned. In: Proc. of the 57th Annual Meeting of the Association for Computational Linguistics, pp. 5797–5808, Florence, Italy (2019)
19. Zhou, B., Khosla, A., Lapedriza, A., Oliva, A., Torralba, A.: Learning deep features for discriminative localization. In: 2016 IEEE Conference on Computer Vision and Pattern Recognition (CVPR). IEEE, June 2016

# Smart Mobility Solutions for Urban Transportation in ASEAN: A Bibliometric Study of Trends and Innovations

Dany Pambudi[1,2]([✉]) [iD] and Junseok Hwang[1,2]

[1] Technology Management Economics and Policy Program, College of Engineering, Seoul National University, 08826 Seoul, South Korea
{danypambudi,junhwang}@snu.ac.kr
[2] Integrated Major in Smart City Global Convergence, Seoul National University, 08826 Seoul, South Korea

**Abstract.** The ASEAN region faces unique challenges in urban transportation due to rapid urbanization, increasing population densities, and the growing demand for sustainable mobility solutions. This study does a thorough bibliometric analysis of the patterns and advancements in smart mobility, with the objective of tackling these difficulties between 2013 and 2023, focusing on 1,249 peer-reviewed publications. The analysis shows a consistent increase in research effort, with publications reaching their highest point in the past two years. The study identified six main research areas: Intelligent Transportation Systems, Public Transportation, Smart City, Urban Mobility, Autonomous Vehicle, and Advanced Mobility Technologies. The findings suggest a transition from conventional transportation systems to integrated, technologically enhanced solutions prioritizing sustainability and efficiency. The study emphasizes the importance of innovation in addressing urban transportation issues in ASEAN cities and proposes potential areas for further research, including incorporating emerging technology and analyzing socio-economic effects.

**Keywords:** Urban Transportation · ASEAN · Smart Mobility · Intelligent Transportation Systems · Bibliometric Analysis

## 1 Introduction

Urban transport management has become more difficult in the Association of Southeast Asian Nations (ASEAN) region as a result of the amazing urban development of recent decades. Using cutting-edge technology and data-driven methods to improve transportation networks, or smart mobility, has become a vital answer to these problems. The demand for efficient, enduring, and astute transportation systems is increasing alongside the development of Southeast Asian cities [1].

Smart mobility is one of the digital technology components that are integrated into the idea of smart cities to raise living standards, lessen environmental effects, and increase the effectiveness of urban services [2]. In the context of ASEAN, smart mobility goes beyond

© The Author(s), under exclusive license to Springer Nature Switzerland AG 2025
M. Naldi et al. (Eds.): GECON 2024, LNCS 15358, pp. 254–258, 2025.
https://doi.org/10.1007/978-3-031-81226-2_22

simple technical integration to include adjusting innovations to regional requirements and conditions, which differ greatly around the region [3].

The purpose of this bibliometric study is to examine, with an emphasis on urban transportation, the developments and trends in smart mobility particularly within the ASEAN area. Though smart cities have received more and more academic attention worldwide, thorough research that gather and summarize the development of smart mobility concepts specific to Southeast Asian cities is conspicuously lacking. This study will map out the scholarly terrain using bibliometric techniques, pointing up important patterns, foundational works, and new themes in the literature over the last ten years.

## 2 Literature Review

Smart mobility is the umbrella term for a variety of technologies and approaches intended to improve urban transportation by increasing its effectiveness, sustainability, and resident-responsiveness. Driven by developments in IoT, big data analytics, and artificial intelligence (AI), which are changing the way metropolitan transport networks function, this sector has grown significantly globally [4, 5].

A vital component of smart cities, mobility is necessary to lower carbon emissions, enhance air quality, and improve urban life [2]. Real-time traffic management systems, intelligent ticketing and payment systems, and mobile application integration of several transportation options are examples of smart mobility solutions [1].

Specializing on the ASEAN region, its varied socioeconomic and geographic environment creates a special fusion of problems and breakthroughs. Thuzar [6], for example, looks at how Southeast Asia's fast urbanization has increased pollution and traffic congestion, making the use of smart mobility solutions imperative. Particularly for Vietnam, the research by Nguyen & Mogaji [7], emphasizes how government policies support smart transportation networks in developing nations.

## 3 Methodology

The method used in this research is a quantitative method to identify trends and innovations in smart mobility solutions for urban transportation within the ASEAN region. Meanwhile, for data analysis and visualization, bibliometric analysis is used using R-Packages and Biblioshiny WebInterface software. There are five stages carried out in this research, namely determining keywords that are relevant to the research topic, searching for data according to the keywords, selecting articles, data validation, and data analysis. Bibliometric analysis, derived from conventional literature reviews [8] and systematic literature reviews, involves the statistical examination of published articles and their citations to assess their influence [9].

The papers included in this study are English language literature found in the Scopus and Web of Science databases. These papers contain specific keywords such as "smart mobility," "intelligent mobility," "connected mobility," "autonomous mobility," "future mobility," "innovative mobility," "urban mobility," "city mobility," "smart transportation," "urban transportation," "intelligent transportation," "city transportation," "public transportation," and "transportation system" in their title, abstract, or keywords. Additionally, the study focused on ASEAN Countries, specifically "Indonesia," "Malaysia," "Thailand," "Singapore," "Vietnam," "Philippines," "Brunei," "Cambodia," "Laos," and "Myanmar." The scope of our data collection method was limited to publications published between 2013 and 2023. The assessment exclusively focused on review papers, articles, and journals.

## 4  Results

### 4.1  Main Information

The publications that the author used in this research were publications from 2013 to 2023. The paper using only three types of documents, namely articles, review articles and journals. Using selected keywords, a search was conducted on the Scopus Database and Web of Science for a period of around ten years.

This search yielded a total of 1249 items. The article document type contains 1161 articles and the review article type contains 88 documents. The data on smart mobility trends and innovation in ASEAN reveals that the average yearly publishing rate is 4.05, with an average citation per document of 24.1 and a total of 8208 references.

### 4.2  Most Relevant Affiliates and Most Citations

Analysis of publication trends between 2013 and 2023 reveals annual variations. In ASEAN countries, the number of scholarly papers on smart mobility trends and innovations peaked in 2022 and 2023 with 232 and 255, respectively. 4.05% is the average growth rate of publication trends in ASEAN countries with the topic of smart mobility.

According to the analysis results, the affiliate with the highest number of publications is the National University of Singapore, with a total of 207 publications. Following closely behind is the Nanyang Technological University with 201 articles. In addition, the third and fourth highest number of publications were produced by Massachusetts Institute of Technology and University of Malaya, respectively, with a combined total of 55 publications. The remaining articles are in the range of 20–50.

### 4.3  Co-word Analysis

According to Fig. 4, this study has identified 6 clusters of primary theme issues that are significant, closely related to, and align with the study of Smart Mobility Solutions for Urban Transportation in ASEAN Countries. These 6 clusters are:

- Cluster 1 (Red) is about Intelligent Transportation Systems, related to intelligent transportation systems, vanet, optimization, big data, clustering, routing, intelligent transportation, mobility, traffic flow, intelligent transportation system (its), vehicular ad hoc networks, planning.
- Cluster 2 (Blue) is about Public Transportation, the keywords are public transportation, transportation, covid-19, autonomous vehicles, thailand, logistics, service quality.

- Cluster 3 (Green) is about Smart City, related to smart city, internet of things, blockchain, security, smart cities, smart mobility, internet of things (iot), privacy, sustainable development.
- Cluster 4 (Purple) is about Urban Mobility, related to urban mobility, sustainability, climate change.
- Cluster 5 (Orange) is about Autonomous Vehicle, the main keywords are public transport, traffic congestion, autonomous vehicle.
- Cluster 6 (Brown) is about Advanced Mobility Technologies, related to intelligent transportation system, deep learning, machine learning, artificial intelligence, deep reinforcement learning (Fig. 1).

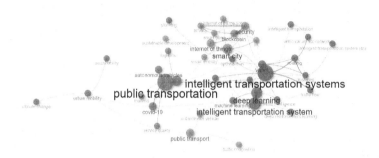

**Fig. 1.** Network Co-occurrence Map using Each Author's Keywords (Color figure online)

## 5 Conclusions

Research on smart mobility is growing strongly, as seen by the bibliometric analysis carried out over a ten-year period (2013–2023) using data from Scopus and Web of Science. Publications have increased significantly in the final two years of the study period. More specifically, in 2023 publishing peaked at 255 articles, indicating a growing interest and noteworthy progress in this area. The average rate of publication trend growth was 4.05%, indicating a consistent rise in academic interest in smart mobility among ASEAN nations.

With a sizable 207 articles, the National University of Singapore leads the study's results, suggesting a focused effort to progress smart mobility research in the area. Nanyang Technological University follows closely with 201 publications. The research produced by these universities not only emphasizes Singapore's important position in smart mobility research but also the city-state's dedication to being a leader in sustainable urban transportation options.

Six primary research clusters that offer a thorough picture of the breadth and depth of the topic were also identified by the theme analysis. The clusters include anything from "Intelligent Transportation Systems" with an emphasis on big data and optimization to "Advanced Mobility Technologies," which highlights the part artificial intelligence and machine learning play in developing transportation solutions. This multiplicity of topics suggests a multidisciplinary strategy to address the challenges related to urban mobility in fast changing urban settings.

**Acknowledgments.** This research was supported by the MSIP (Ministry of Science, ICT and Future Planning), Korea, under the Human Resource Development Project for Global R&DB Program (IITP-2019-0-01328) supervised by the IITP (Institute for Information & Communications Technology Planning & Evaluation). This work is also supported by Korea Ministry of Land, Infrastructure and Transport (MOLIT) as Innovative Talent Education Program for Smart City.

**Declaration of Competing Interest.** The authors affirm that they do not possess any identifiable personal relationships or competing financial interests that might have appeared to exert an influence on the research presented in this article.

# References

1. Benevolo, C., Dameri, R.P., D'Auria, B.: Smart Mobility in Smart City. In: Torre, T., Braccini, A.M., Spinelli, R. (eds.) Empowering Organizations, pp. 13–28. Springer, Cham (2016). https://doi.org/10.1007/978-3-319-23784-8_2
2. Caragliu, A., Bo, C.D., Nijkamp, P.: Smart Cities in Europe. In: Creating Smarter Cities, Routledge (2013)
3. Cocchia, A.: Smart and digital city: a systematic literature review. In: Dameri, R.P., Rosenthal-Sabroux, C. (eds.) Smart City: How to Create Public and Economic Value with High Technology in Urban Space, pp. 13–43. Springer, Cham (2014). https://doi.org/10.1007/978-3-319-06160-3_2
4. Batty, M., et al.: Smart cities of the future. Europ. Phys. J. Special Topics **214**, 481–518 (2012). https://doi.org/10.1140/epjst/e2012-01703-3
5. Kitchin, R.: The real-time city? Big data and smart urbanism. GeoJournal **79**, 1–14 (2014). https://doi.org/10.1007/s10708-013-9516-8
6. Thuzar, M.: Urbanization in Southeast Asia: developing smart cities for the future? In: Urbanization In Southeast Asia: Developing Smart Cities For The Future?, pp. 96–100. ISEAS Publishing, Singapore (2011). https://doi.org/10.1355/9789814311694-022
7. Nguyen, N.P., Mogaji, E.: Information technology for enhancing transportation in developing countries. In: Chemma, N., El Amine Abdelli, M., Awasthi, A., Mogaji, E. (eds.) Management and Information Technology in the Digital Era, vol. 29, pp. 81–94. Emerald Publishing Limited, Bingley (2022). https://doi.org/10.1108/S1877-636120220000029006
8. Cooper, H.M.: Organizing knowledge syntheses: a taxonomy of literature reviews. Knowl. Soc. **1**, 104 (1988). https://doi.org/10.1007/BF03177550
9. Gan, Y., Li, D., Robinson, N., Liu, J.: Practical guidance on bibliometric analysis and mapping knowledge domains methodology – a summary. Europ. J. Integrative Med. **56**, 102203 (2022). https://doi.org/10.1016/j.eujim.2022.102203

# Resource Management in Cloud Applications: Simulation, Streaming Processing and Workflows

# Distributed Simulation with Efficient Fault Tolerance

Javier Vela[1]📷, Unai Arronategui[2]📷, José Ángel Bañares[2(✉)]📷,
and José Manuel Colom[2]📷

[1] Instituto Pirenaico de Ecología, Consejo Superior de Investigaciones Científicas
(IPE-CSIC), Zaragoza, Spain
jvela@ipe.csic.es
[2] Universidad de Zaragoza, Zaragoza, Spain
{unai,banares,jm}@unizar.es

**Abstract.** Fault tolerance is essential for the correct execution of large
distributed simulations of discrete event systems, as the likelihood of
faults increases with the size of the cloud infrastructure used. Achieving
optimal performance and cost in a fault-tolerant distributed simulation
remains a challenge. In this paper, we propose a replication-based approach in a conservative distributed simulation strategy that is specifically designed to minimize latency introduced by fault tolerance mechanisms. Unlike traditional replication methods, our method is tailored for
conservative simulation, leveraging simulation messages and timing to
maintain consistency while decoupling replica execution. As a result, our
approach reduces the need for messaging and synchronization and maintains eventual consistency windows with low latency overhead, achieving
near-nominal simulation performance in the absence of faults. If replicas have similar performance, memory usage can be lower compared to
optimistic approaches, and recovery can be fast following a node failure, despite asynchronous replication. Experimental results show that
without faults, the performance of a distributed simulator with fault
management is similar to one without it. Recovery from a fault reveals
that the main overhead is in replica provisioning, with minimal overhead
for synchronization.

**Keywords:** Distributed Simulation · Petri Nets · Fault Tolerance ·
Cloud

## 1 Introduction

*Discrete Event System* (DES) simulation is a fundamental tool for analysing,
predicting, and designing systems across various domains. For large and complex systems, distributed simulation becomes essential, as it allows for scalable
and efficient analysis. However, as the number of computational resources in
distributed simulations increases, faults become unavoidable, especially in long-
running simulations. Faults can result in the loss of the simulation state, requiring fault-tolerant mechanisms to preserve data integrity and ensure successful
simulation finalization.

© The Author(s), under exclusive license to Springer Nature Switzerland AG 2025
M. Naldi et al. (Eds.): GECON 2024, LNCS 15358, pp. 261–274, 2025.
https://doi.org/10.1007/978-3-031-81226-2_23

The *Cloud* has proven to be an effective platform for distributed simulations [15]. The Cloud offers the ability to scale resources according to model size and dynamically adjust computing as needed during the simulation. Despite these advantages, the adoption of distributed simulation of DESs in industrial and commercial applications remains limited [9,10]. The Cloud's pay-as-you-go model requires efficient solutions that can guarantee the success of the simulation at a limited cost, adding a layer of complexity that hinders industrial adoption.

In distributed simulations of DESs, the success and performance of the simulation depend on each model partition executed on each node. Additionally, the overall processing speed is determined by the slowest simulator in the network. Resilience is crucial for the successful execution of large-scale distributed simulations, as faults become more common with the expansion of cloud infrastructure. Therefore, any fault tolerance mechanism must introduce minimal overhead during normal operations to ensure cost-effectiveness within the Cloud's pay-as-you-go model.

Key factors such as data storage performance, computing processing rates, network latencies, and dynamic model partitioning for load balancing are critical in distributed simulations. As pointed by Ferscha et al. [9], the complexity of these parameters makes it challenging to rely solely on analytical methods to select the optimal simulation strategy, without detailed analysis. The choice of causality consistency protocols is model-dependent and requires extensive parameter evaluation. Performance data mining and statistical analysis are recommended to determine the best approach for specific models and execution environments.

In cloud environments, fault tolerance techniques are a hot topic, focusing on proactive and reactive approaches [14] to predict failures using machine learning and artificial intelligence. A key objective of these techniques is to maintain low overhead during fault-free operations. With this requirement in mind, our work proposes a replica-based approach for large-scale simulations in the Cloud. Our approach is similar to other replica-based fault-tolerance mechanisms proposed for the Cloud [17], but it uniquely employs simulation messages and timing to maintain replica consistency and uses the model and simulation engine to recover consistency efficiently without needing to store large amounts of state data. This innovation reduces overhead and enhances fault recovery, making it a significant advancement over traditional methods.

The remainder of this paper is organized as follows: Sect. 2 summarizes the context of our previous works on distributed simulation, Sect. 3 presents the main assumptions taken into account and the replication model-based approach, Sect. 4 shows that minimum overhead is introduced by the proposed fault-tolerance mechanism in the experimental results, Sect. 5 briefly presents related work, and Sect. 6 provides some final remarks.

## 2    Background: Efficient Distributed Simulation of Petri Nets

The replication fault tolerance method in this study is based on the conservative strategy for distributed simulation. This section presents the fundamental concepts of the conservative approach and explains why it is central to our methodology.

Distributed simulation enhances both the execution speed and scalability when analysing complex models. However, managing causality constraints in the model poses a challenge. Our previous work focused on using *Petri Nets* as the core formalism within a *Model-Driven Engineering* approach to leverage the model at every stage of the DES lifecycle. This framework addresses challenges such as bridging the gap between model specification, code deployment in distributed simulators, and simulation load balancing [3,4].

In distributed simulation, the model is divided into partitions that are simulated on different nodes. Each partition corresponds to a *Logical Process* (LP), which performs tasks related to its assigned portion of the model and interacts with other LPs through message exchange. The model partitioning is defined at compilation time, and LPs cannot be changed dynamically. In our approach, LPs act as simulator engines executing Petri Nets, interpreting the *Linear Enabling Function* (LEF)-coded transitions specific to their partition. The LEF function defines whether transitions in the system can be triggered, based on the state of the Petri Net, reducing the time needed to determine enabled transitions and the size of data structures representing the system's subnetwork. Therefore, dynamic workload balancing between LPs can be done by redistributing their LEF-coded transitions between them [11].

We refer to the micro-kernels (LPs) in our distributed simulation as *simbots*. Each simbot operates independently, with its own clock, and is connected to others via a communication network. They execute partitions of the overall Petri Net model, which contain transitions that either originate from or are directed to other partitions. The set of all simbots in the simulator completes the Petri Net model of the DES.

To maintain causality, distributed simulation employs two primary protocols: conservative and optimistic. *Conservative protocols* use null messages to inform neighbouring model partitions about the simulation time that can advance without causing causality errors, such as receiving an event with an earlier timestamp than the current simulation time. This approach can lead to idle periods in distributed simulators waiting for events from others. *Optimistic protocols* allow the simulation to proceed, with the capability to roll back to a previous state if a causality error occurs. An *Ideal Simulation Protocol* (ISP) [12] was introduced to compare these methods. The idea is to use prior simulations to compute the *lookahead*, a lower bound for the *Local Virtual Time* (LVT) that an LP communicates to its neighbours, enabling safe advancement. While ISP serves as the optimal efficiency reference that can be achieved, it is impractical as it does not consider any overhead communications between LPs.

While our approach cannot eliminate communication overhead, exploiting the Petri Net model allows us to obtain precise lookahead and minimize waiting times. Consequently, we adopted a conservative strategy. Automating Petri Net analysis using software tools for optimal model partitioning and estimating lookahead is crucial for accelerating simulation on distributed platforms [5]. Murata and Wu [13] demonstrated that synchronic distances in a Petri Net, which measure the degree of mutual dependence between occurrences of two transitions, can be used for synchronization in distributed processing systems and can be used to compute when events will be delivered to neighbouring LPs.

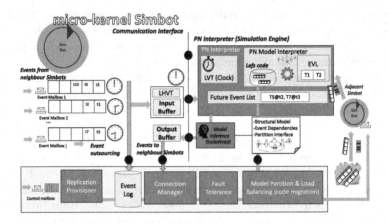

**Fig. 1.** Simbot Architecture

Figure 1 illustrates the architecture of a simbot as an LP using a conservative approach. Initially, the simbot calculates enabled transitions in the *Event List* (EVL). Firing these transitions produces future events stored in the *Future Event List* (FUL). Events can be internal or updates that must be communicated over the network to the affecting adjacent simbots. The simbot processes FUL events only when it is guaranteed that no events with an earlier execution time will arrive from other simbots. Each event has a timestamp indicating its occurrence time, ensuring that the simulation proceeds accurately and in order. In LEF-based transition encoding, each transition in the Petri Net has an associated value and a duration. When an event occurs, an integer updating factor is added to the LEF value. If the resulting LEF value is zero or negative, the transition becomes enabled and is added to the event list. The event's timestamp is determined by the current simulation time plus the transition's duration.

A simbot synchronizes with others via a *Communication interface*, which includes a queue of incoming messages from other simbots, ordered by timestamp. Each input queue has a timestamp field showing the timestamp of the queue's front event or the last received message if empty. The *Local Horizon Time* (LHT) is the minimum of all queue fronts, indicating the latest point to which the local clock can advance without inconsistencies. The simbot interleaves events from its queue (FUL) with incoming message events up to the LHT, processing the earliest events first. Events are processed until the LHT is reached. Continuing the simulation beyond the LHT could result in receiving an event with an earlier timestamp, leading to inconsistencies in the simulation. If an LP's input queue is empty, the LP must wait for new messages. This mechanism can lead to deadlock, so simbots send empty messages, called null messages, with a timestamp indicating the lookahead to neighbours. The lookahead specifies the future time when it guarantees no events will be sent.

On the left, Fig. 1 shows the Communication interface responsible for maintaining message consistency by computing the LHT. On the right, there is the Petri Net interpreter used for processing events. At the bottom, the figure displays basic services, including communication, an event repository, load balancing, and fault tolerance, which will be explained in subsequent sections.

# 3    A Performant Simulation Approach with Fault Tolerance

The approach proposed in this paper is based on the following assumptions: 1) only crash failures are considered, meaning nodes stop working; 2) communication of events and lookahead between simbots is ordered and reliable; 3) each node runs only one simbot, so if a node fails, its corresponding simbot also fails.

A replicated state machine model, implemented within a replica group, processes all events in each simbot. Each replica of a simbot processes events in the same sequence from the same initial state, which justifies our preference for a conservative approach. Although our mechanism currently assumes a leader and a single replica per replica group, it can be easily extended by adding additional replicas to enhance robustness.

In the non-fault-tolerant operation configuration, a simbot receives event messages from its predecessors, which are the simbots simulating the subnetworks with transitions leading to it, and sends event messages to its successors, the simbots simulating the subnetworks with transitions originating from it.

In contrast, in the fault-tolerant configuration, only the leader within each simbot replica group sends event messages to its successor simbots to prevent them from receiving duplicate messages. However, all replicas of a simbot receive messages from predecessor simbots, ensuring that in the event of a crash within a replica group, one of the replicated simbots maintains the complete and correct state of the simulation. These connections between neighbouring simbots are illustrated in Fig. 2. In summary, all replicas of a simbot run asynchronous, complete simulation steps using received and local events to produce new events as nominal simbots, but only leaders are allowed to send events and lookaheads to successor simbots.

If a replica fails, the leader requests a replacement to keep the simulation's integrity. However, if the leader fails, the replica is promoted to leader and continues the simulation with a new provisioned replica. In either case, synchronization is needed to ensure all replicas remain consistent. The subsequent sections describe the mechanisms used to maintain consistency between replicas both before and after a crash, as well as how to detect and recover from crashes.

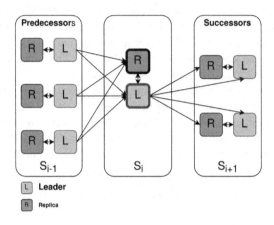

**Fig. 2.** Distributed Relations of Replicated Simbots

## 3.1 Decoupled Replication

Distributed simulations, particularly when executed across many nodes with varying capabilities, can lead to differing simulation speeds among simbots. To address this, implementing a more lenient consistency model by decoupling the execution of the leader from its replicas minimizes the risk of slowing down the entire simulation if one part lags due to delayed execution. This approach necessitates integrating techniques that ensure strict consistency convergence if a failure occurs when the leader and its replica have divergent states.

In non-fault conditions, decoupling the leader from its replicas reduces the need for constant synchronization, enhancing overall simulation efficiency. This configuration allows the leader simbot to handle the sending of external events to successor simbots, while the replica generates but does not send these events. Should the replica fail, the leader can continue the simulation unaffected, regardless of whether the replica was ahead or behind in processing. Conversely, if the leader fails, the replica can be found in one of these states at the time of the crash:

- **State D: Delayed Replica**. The replica is lagging behind the leader in processing events. When the leader crashes, the replica could resend events already dispatched by the leader when promoting as the new leader and resuming the simulation. These events should not be sent to avoid duplicates.
- **State A: Advanced Replica**. The replica has produced events, without sending them to its successors, that the leader has not yet reached. When the leader crashes, the replica could skip sending the already produced events

to its successors when promoting. These events must be stored to maintain consistency and sent when the promotion takes place.

- **State S: Synchronized Replica**. If the leader and replica are processing events at the same pace, the replica can continue seamlessly and resume event dispatch to successors.

## 3.2 Consistency

Tracking the state of each leader and replica is crucial for determining the correct course of action when handling events after a crash, particularly when the leader of a simbot crashes and a replica needs to be promoted. This mechanism enables the system to seamlessly restore and maintain consistency.

In this system, the *events-sent* message serves as a confirmation from the leader that an event has been sent to successor simbots. Each event produced is assigned a unique identifier, which is consistent across both the leader and the replica due to the deterministic nature of the simulation. The unique identifier ensures that every event and its confirmation carry the same serial number, thus confirming the simulation step across all replicas reliably. The reception of an events-sent message allows a replica to validate the progression of the simulation state up to the received serial number, assuming that any event not validated by a leader has not been transmitted to successor simbots.

The replication system operates within an eventual consistency window, which must converge at the point of a failure. The leader sends event confirmations to the replica but does not wait for a response, and the replica does not need to wait for these confirmations to continue the simulation. This process reduces the number of messages and the waiting time required to maintain consistency.

When a leader crashes, the events-sent message allows a replica to establish whether it is in State D (Delayed) or A (Advanced). If the replica is in an Advanced State, it must store generated event messages that the previous leader had not yet validated with an events-sent message. The stored event messages are then sent in order by the new leader before producing new ones. Conversely, if in a Delayed State, the new leader, previously a replica, might avoid sending the messages that the leader had already confirmed, as these would be duplicated to the successors.

An essential aspect of this process is the invalidation mechanism employed by successor simbots, which might receive duplicated messages: first from the crashed leader and then from the newly promoted leader (formerly a replica). The duplication issue can arise if the leader sends a message to its successor but crashes before it can confirm this action to the replica. To address this, successors store unique identifiers of received event messages, enabling them to detect and discard any duplicates. Achieving an optimal balance between the frequency of confirmations from the leader to the replica, and the number of messages that successors need to store for detecting duplicates, is crucial for minimizing overhead and maximizing the system's efficiency.

Algorithm 1 is executed by the replica to manage the differential state between the leader and itself. It tracks the last message confirmed by the leader and the last message produced by the replica, allowing for the identification and invalidation of potential duplicate messages, and avoid sending these to the successors when promoting.

---

**Algorithm 1.** Differential State between Leader and Replica Registration

---

*// Differential state between leader and replica. Init.: empty list*
$Q^R \leftarrow []$
*// Last message produced by replica and not confirmed by leader. Init: ID null message*
$M^R \leftarrow 0$
*// Last message acknowledged by leader. Init.: ID null-message*
$M^L \leftarrow 0$
*// Register reception of acknowledgement message of an event from the leader*
**procedure** REGISTERACKNOWLEDGEMENTRECEIVED($M$ : Acknowledgement)
   $M^L \leftarrow M_{ID}$
   **if** $M^R >= M^L$ **then**
      $Q^R.deleteFirst()$  *// Replica is in advance or at the same point as the leader*
   **else**
      $no-op$  *// ($M^R < M^L$) Replica is behind*
   **end if**
**end procedure**
*// Event produced in replica*
**procedure** REGISTERPRODUCEDEVENT($M$ : Message)
   $M^R \leftarrow M_{ID}$
   **if** $M^R > M^L$ **then**
      $Q^R.insertLast(M)$  *// Replica is in advance*
   **else**
      $no-op$  *// ($M^R <= M^L$) Replica is behind or at the same point as the leader*
   **end if**
**end procedure**

---

### 3.3 Fault Detection

If a simbot crashes, the entire simulation stops as the flow of event messages ceases and simulation time cannot advance. To mitigate this, adjacent neighbouring simbots are monitored, to efficiently detect and respond to potential crashes. Additionally, within each replica group, both the leader and the replicas actively monitor each other to ensure any faults are quickly identified.

Fatal faults occur when every member of a replica group, including the leader, crashes. This scenario results in the triggering of notifications from neighbouring simbots, leading to a complete halt of the distributed simulation. Terminating the simulation is necessary because the state of the partition of the model in the crashed simbot is irretrievably lost, compromising the integrity of the entire simulation.

## 3.4  Fault Recovery

Fault recovery for each simbot is managed by its surviving replicas and coordinated with its adjacent neighbours.

**Replica Fault.** When a simbot replica crashes, the leader promptly notifies the *Replica Provisioner*, an external service that prepares the infrastructure and initiates the simbot to simulate a specific subnetwork of the model. The Replica Provisioner then dynamically provides a new replica node. Subsequently, predecessor simbots synchronize with the new replica, and the leader transfers its state to it, allowing the new replica to start connections and resume the simulation from the same point as the leader. Finally, all neighbours resume simulation with the leader and the new replica.

**Leader Fault and Replica Promotion.** If the leader fails, the replica is promoted to become the new leader, notifies this role change to its predecessor neighbours, and establishes new connections with the successor leaders and replicas. Depending on its state at the time of the leader's failure, the new leader will take different actions to re-establish simulation consistency:

- **State D**: The new leader is behind the old one, so it abstains from sending event messages until it produces an event with the last serial number confirmed by the old leader.
- **State A**: The new leader is more advanced than the old one, so it replays all stored messages from the last confirmation received from the old leader.
- **State S**: The new and old leader are in the same state, so no additional action is needed.

Finally, all steps of replica fault recovery are applied, involving a request for a new replica to the Replica Provisioner to ensure continuous simulation operation.

## 3.5  Simbot Architecture

Figure 3 illustrates the architecture and software components of a fault-tolerant simbot. The architecture is split into two primary threads: the *Simulation thread* and the *Communication thread*. The Simulation thread runs the *Simulation Engine* and the *Fault Tolerance Manager*, while the Communication thread manages the reception of messages from other simbots via the network, utilizing the *Mailbox* and the *Network Message Receiver*. The *Simbot* component is the coordinator of these threads and components. The *Connection Manager* is responsible for maintaining persistent network connections with neighbouring simbots established in Fig. 2, managing both the connections established at the beginning of the simulation and new connections created when new replicas are added after a crash. The Replica Provisioner and *Debug Server* serve as auxiliary external services.

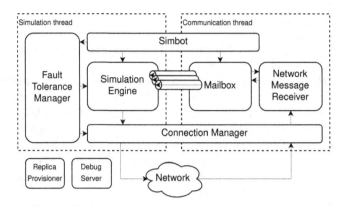

**Fig. 3.** Simbot Architecture for Fault Tolerant Simulation

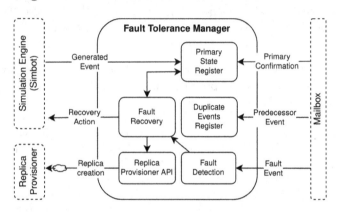

**Fig. 4.** Components of Fault Tolerance Manager of a Simbot

Figure 4 describes the internal elements of the Fault Tolerance Manager, which is a crucial component highlighted in Fig. 3. The Fault Tolerance Manager's functionalities include the detection and management of faults, synchronization, recovery of neighbour faults, coordination with the Replica Provisioner, and consistency management. The *Leader State Register* executes the procedures of algorithm Algorithm 1 on the replica node. The Mailbox component redirects acknowledgements from the leader and facilitates the production of local events by the Simulation Engine. The Leader State Register plays a vital role in fault recovery to ensure consistency across the simulation. The *Duplicate Event Register* manages the reception of duplicate events post-fault and ensures their dismissal. Each message is registered by the Mailbox before processing to detect any duplicates. The Network Message Receiver is tasked with the detection of faults in other simbots, with any detected faults reported to the Fault Tolerance Manager, which then manages these faults as allowed by the ongoing simulation execution. Finally, the *Fault Recovery* component initiates activities that include requesting a new replica from the Replica Provisioner.

# 4    Experimentation

The distributed simulator has been developed in the Rust language. The test environment consists of a cluster of 20 Raspberry Pi 4 model B with 8 GB of RAM and 1Gb Ethernet links through a 1Gb Ethernet switch. The fault-tolerant configuration includes two nodes for each simbot, a leader and one replica.

**Table 1.** Comparison of the Execution Time for Non-fault-tolerant vs. Fault-tolerant Distributed Simulators with Different Simulation Times and Low Simulation Load

| Total Simulation time (*simseconds*) | Wall clock time (*seconds*) | |
|---|---|---|
| | non fault-tolerant | fault-tolerant |
| 20 | 0.0067 | 0.0108 |
| 1000 | 0.162 | 0.253 |
| 10000 | 1.643 | 2.478 |
| 100000 | 17.655 | 22.751 |

Table 1 illustrates the execution time differences between the fault-tolerant simulator and the non-fault-tolerant simulator in a worst-case scenario with minimal simulation load, emphasizing the communication and coordination overhead. This minimal load represents all the operational overhead as pure communication, which is typically where fault tolerance could add significant overhead. The simulation time goes from 20 to 100000 simseconds to measure the wall clock time. However, it is evident from the results that the difference in execution times between the versions, even under these conditions, is minimal.

Figure 5 displays the average execution time for each phase of the simulation (reception, simulation, and sending) for versions without fault management and with fault management. A minimal simulation load is calculated based on a model [16] where the efficiency of distributed simulation outweighs centralized approaches. A simulation load of 0.035 wall clock time seconds is used, when the load is large enough to make the distributed coupling factor $\lambda > 100$. The negligible difference of 0.269% between both simulator versions underscores that, in scenarios without faults, there is almost no overhead introduced by fault management.

Experiments in our test environment indicate that it takes approximately 0.4 s to recover from a fault, with 99% of this time spent provisioning a new node and copying all state to the new replica. For simulations involving large models, the state copy process constitutes the most significant portion of time spent in fault recovery. This insight is beneficial as most of the time added by fault tolerance is concentrated in the fault recovery process (specifically, replica provisioning and state copy) which occurs only when faults arise, not during normal operation.

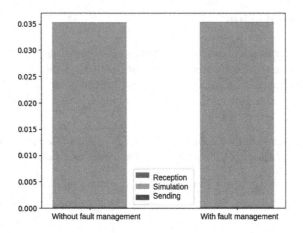

**Fig. 5.** Execution Time of Simulation with Minimal Efficient Load (0.035 s.)

## 5   Related Work

Fault tolerance techniques in distributed simulations are broadly categorized into two main strategies: replication and checkpointing [6]. Replication increases the demand for computational resources and introduces synchronization overhead to ensure consistency between replicas. Checkpointing, on the other hand, involves storing recovery points and requires synchronization among processes to determine the recovery moment. Optimistic protocols maintain causality consistency through a rollback mechanism, which restores the simulation to a previously stored checkpoint when an out-of-order event is received. Consequently, the choice of fault tolerance technique often depends on the protocol used to maintain the consistency of the distributed simulation. Traditional methods generally incur significant computational costs, storage demands, or synchronization overheads.

Recent advancements in fault tolerance for distributed simulations have primarily focused on optimistic protocols, exploiting rollback mechanisms inherent to optimistic simulations to revert to states prior to faults [1]. These techniques have occasionally been adapted for conservative simulation approaches as well [8]. Fault tolerance methods have been developed for specific simulation architectures or frameworks, such as Time Warp [2], GAIA/ARTIS [7], and High-Level Architecture (HLA). These methods typically require extensive computational and network resources, which can increase simulation latency and reduce overall performance. Conversely, techniques designed to preserve performance tend to be complex and less flexible.

In contrast to the aforementioned systems, which prioritize interoperability, our approach focuses on efficiency and scalability. Our fault tolerance strategy enhances performance with minimal impact on latency compared to other methods. By tailoring our approach to conservative simulation, and leveraging simulation messages and timing, our model achieves greater resource efficiency and adaptability, avoiding the significant computational and network overhead often associated with other fault tolerance systems.

## 6   Conclusion

In this paper, we have presented a replication-based approach to fault tolerance within distributed simulations, that highlights performance and resource efficiency during non-fault conditions. Our approach adopts a conservative strategy to optimize resource utilization effectively. Notably, even when fault tolerance mechanisms are active, a fault-free distributed simulation maintains performance levels comparable to those with fault tolerance disabled. Additionally, memory usage remains minimal when replicas perform similarly. Thus, this approach facilitates cost-effective deployment and execution in cloud environments, ensuring fault tolerance for extended simulations without sacrificing performance or resource efficiency.

As future work, other failure models, as network partitions and byzantine faults, could be addressed to enhance the resiliency of distributed simulations.

**Acknowledgments.** This work was co-financed by the Aragonese Government and the European Regional Development Fund "Construyendo Europa desde Aragón" (COSMOS research group); and by the Spanish program "Programa estatal del Generación de Conocimiento y Fortalecimiento Científico y Tecnológico del Sistema de I+D+i ", project PGC2018-099815-B-100.

## References

1. Agrawal, D., Agre, J.: Recovering from multiple process failures in the time warp mechanism. IEEE Trans. Comput. **41**(12), 1504–1514 (1992)
2. Agrawal, D., Agre, J.R.: Replicated objects in time warp simulations. In: Proceedings of the 24th Conference on Winter Simulation, pp. 657–664 (1992)
3. Arronategui, U., Bañares, J.Á., Colom, J.M.: A MDE approach for modelling and distributed simulation of health systems. In: Djemame, K., Altmann, J., Bañares, J.Á., Agmon Ben-Yehuda, O., Stankovski, V., Tuffin, B. (eds.) GECON 2020. LNCS, vol. 12441, pp. 89–103. Springer, Cham (2020). https://doi.org/10.1007/978-3-030-63058-4_9
4. Bañares, J.Á., Colom, J.M.: Model and simulation engines for distributed simulation of discrete event systems. In: GECON 2018 - International Conference on the Economics of Grids, Clouds, Systems, and Services, pp. 77–91. Springer (2018)
5. Colom, J.M.: Harnessing structure theory of petri nets in discrete event system simulation. In: Kristensen, L.M., van der Werf, J.M. (eds.) Application and Theory of Petri Nets and Concurrency, pp. 3–23. Springer, Cham (2024)
6. Damani, O.P., Garg, V.K.: Fault-tolerant distributed simulation. In: Unger, B.W., Ferscha, A. (eds.) Proceedings of the 12th Workshop on Parallel and Distributed Simulation, PADS '98, Banff, Alberta, Canada, May 26-29, 1998, pp. 38–45. IEEE Computer Society (1998)

7. D'Angelo, G., Ferretti, S., Marzolla, M., Armaroli, L.: Fault-tolerant adaptive parallel and distributed simulation. In: 2016 IEEE/ACM 20th International Symposium on Distributed Simulation and Real Time Applications (DS-RT), pp. 37–44. IEEE (2016)
8. D'Angelo, G., Ferretti, S., Marzolla, M.: Fault tolerant adaptive parallel and distributed simulation through functional replication. Simul. Modelling Practice Theory **93**, 192–207 (2019), modeling and Simulation of Cloud Computing and Big Data
9. Ferscha, A., Johnson, J., Turner, S.J.: Distributed simulation performance data mining. Future Generation Comput. Syst. **18**(1), 157–174 (2001), i. High Performance Numerical Methods and Applications. II. Performance Data Mining: Automated Diagnosis, Adaption, and Optimization
10. Fujimoto, R.M.: Research challenges in parallel and distributed simulation. ACM Trans. Model. Comput. Simul. **26**(4), 22:1–22:29 (2016). https://doi.org/10.1145/2866577
11. Hodgetts, P., et al.: Workload evaluation in distributed simulation of dess. In: GECON 2021 - International Conference on the Economics of Grids, Clouds, Systems, and Services, pp. 3–16. Springer (2021)
12. Jha, V., Bagrodia, R.: A performance evaluation methodology for parallel simulation protocols. In: Proceedings of Symposium on Parallel and Distributed Tools, pp. 180–185 (1996). https://doi.org/10.1109/PADS.1996.761576
13. Murata, T., Wu, Z.: Fair relation and modified synchronic distances in a petri net. J. Franklin Inst. **320**(2), 63–82 (1985)
14. Rehman, A.U., Aguiar, R.L., Barraca, J.P.: Fault-tolerance in the scope of cloud computing. IEEE Access **10**, 63422–63441 (2022)
15. Vanmechelen, K., De Munck, S., Broeckhove, J.: Conservative distributed discrete-event simulation on the amazon ec2 cloud: an evaluation of time synchronization protocol performance and cost efficiency. Simul. Model. Pract. Theory **34**, 126–143 (2013)
16. Varga, A., Sekercioglu, Y., Egan, G.: A practical efficiency criterion for the null message algorithm. In: Verbraeck, A., Hlupic, V. (eds.) Simulation in Industry: Proceedings of the 15th European Simulation Symposium (ESS 2003), pp. 81 – 92 (2003)
17. Zhao, W., Melliar-Smith, P., Moser, L.: Fault tolerance middleware for cloud computing. In: 2010 IEEE 3rd International Conference on Cloud Computing, pp. 67–74 (2010)

# Strainer: Windowing-Based Advanced Sampling in Stream Processing Systems

Nikola Koevski, Sérgio Esteves, and Luís Veiga[(⊠)] [ID]

INESC-ID, Instituto Superior Técnico, Universidade de Lisboa, Lisboa, Portugal
luis.veiga@gsd.inesc-id.pt

**Abstract.** Stream Processing is a very effective predominant paradigm for data processing. It provides an efficient approach to extract information from new data, as the data arrives. However, spikes in data throughput, can impact the accuracy and latency guarantees stream processing systems provide. This work proposes data sampling, a type of data reduction, as a solution to this problem. It provides a user-transparent implementation of two sampling methods in the Apache Spark Streaming framework. The results show a reduced amount of input data, leading to decreased processing time, but retaining a good accuracy in the extracted information.

## 1 Introduction

Big Data has brought a revolution to data processing. With commodity hardware becoming cheaper and widely available, constraints on the amount of data to be collected have been lifted. As a result, useful information, patterns and insights have become far easier to extract. A variety of Big Data processing is on-the-fly data processing called stream processing.

For stream processing systems to provide an efficient service, data needs to be processed as fast as it arrives. When a sudden peak in data throughput occurs, greater than the processing capabilities of the system, several problems arise. When possible, the system will utilize additional computing resources. Next, if the available resources are not enough, the system will try to queue new data while it processes available data. This in turn may lead to a delay in the results, lowered accuracy from an overflowing queue, and an eventual crash of the system.

An obvious solution to the problem is to scale out by adding machines to the system. Next, changing the size of the data to be processed may be attempted [5]. Another approach is to use controlled data reduction methods like load shedding [19–21] or sampling [9,12], alternatives to compression [16].

However, additional machines may be unavailable or too costly to provide, and altering the input data size would increase latency. Although effective, load shedding may skew the data distribution lowering the result accuracy. In contrast, sampling decreases data size by producing a subset retaining desired characteristics of the whole data set. This provides lower resource requirements, lower latency, but maintains a good result accuracy.

© The Author(s), under exclusive license to Springer Nature Switzerland AG 2025
M. Naldi et al. (Eds.): GECON 2024, LNCS 15358, pp. 275–285, 2025.
https://doi.org/10.1007/978-3-031-81226-2_24

This paper contributes to the utilization of sampling in stream processing systems. We implemented Strainer, a stream processing sampling framework. Coupled with the Apache Spark Streaming framework, in Strainer we employ two sampling algorithms. We evaluate the advantages and cost this usage of sampling techniques incurs in the accuracy guarantees of systems like Spark. The result is an early-stage data reduction in the workflow producing a smaller processing load, shorter execution times while keeping a limited result error.

The remainder of this paper is structured as follows. Section 2 presents the necessary background to frame the paper. Section 3 details the design and implementation of Strainer, and its evaluation follows in Sect. 4. Then, Sect. 5 reviews and contrasts relevant work within the state-of-the-art, and Sect. 6 concludes the paper and gives insights on future directions.

## 2    Background and Assumptions

Sampling methods and their application in Big Data are initially thoroughly analysed in earlier work [4]. As their work suggests, among the varied methods of data reduction available, sampling provides an intuitive and straightforward way to obtain a smaller subset of the data with the same structure. Thus, they show it a valid choice as a method to reduce data for real-time data processing.

Apache Spark Streaming is a mature data processing framework, speeding up processing times by performing in-memory processing. Furthermore, Spark's modular design allows it to integrate with a multitude of different technologies, from Hadoop's HDFS for distributed storage, YARN or Apache Mesos for resource management, to providing libraries for connecting with data sources like SQL, Apache Kafka, Cassandra, Kinesis, as well as Twitter.

As seen in Fig. 1, in Spark Streaming, the data is admitted into the system through the Receiver module. The Receiver provides the flexibility to connect with various data sources. Moreover, it allows data items to be pre-processed before being admitted into the workflow. Through the Receiver Supervisor, the Receiver gathers the data items into blocks and then stores them into memory. Furthermore, the Supervisor generates block meta-data and then inserts it into a queue at the Receiver Tracker. Next, Spark Streaming utilizes an interval to build a small batch from the enqueued meta-data. The length of this batch interval determines the size of the micro-batches which are then processed by a user-defined streaming application.

While micro-batches are the reason Spark does not provide "true" real-time stream processing, they are useful to us. Spark Streaming abstracts the data stream into micro-batches, so each micro-batch can be processed as a regular Spark batch application, and have a known size to be considered when sampling.

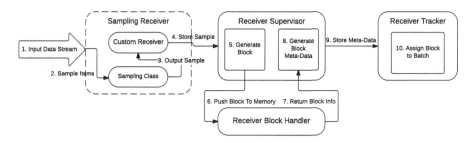

**Fig. 1.** Basic Architecture of Batching module in Spark Streaming

## 3  Framework Integration and Sampling Techniques

### 3.1  Framework Integration

The micro-batch abstraction mentioned in the previous section is what allows a seamless integration of Strainer with Spark Streaming. Figure 1 shows the sampling framework implemented as a wrapper at the Receiver module. Strainer intercepts each data item before it is stored and passes it through a class implementing a sampling algorithm. Next, before the batch interval passes, the framework outputs the sampled items to the Supervisor. It uses the sampled data to generate blocks, continuing a standard batching operation. Thus, with Strainer the pre-existing functionality of the batching module remains unaltered.

### 3.2  Sampling Techniques

Before the implementation, several sampling techniques were considered. The following criteria were used for selecting the sampling methods [4,11]. The algorithms needed to implement the reservoir scheme, providing a one-pass sample over an unbounded data stream. The reservoir sampling scheme provides a fixed size sample with a single pass over an arbitrary sized data stream. However, reservoir scheme algorithms use uniform sampling which can skew the data distribution of the sampled set. Thus, algorithms that use techniques that can counter this data distribution skew were required. Finally, an algorithm needed to provie a bounded error guarantee in order to be selected.

**Congressional Algorithm.** [1] Congressional sampling is an efficient method of performing sampling when data is partitioned in groups. A considerable number of data processing applications group data by key. The MapReduce paradigm is a relevant example of this. Furthermore, Congressional sampling is a hybrid of uniform and biased sampling. This guarantees that both large and small groups will be represented in the sample, preventing data distribution skew. Algorithm 1 shows the algorithm for Congressional sampling.

As can be seen on lines 5, 6 and 8, in the first stage, the algorithm performs three types of sampling. First, it performs a *house* (standard uniform reservoir)

**Algorithm 1.** Congressional algorithm

```
1: initialize(sampleSize, group)
2: sampleCount ← 0
3: houseSample ← ∅
4: senateSample ← ∅
5: groupingSample ← ∅
6: for all item ∈ dataStream do
7:     doHouseSample(item)
8:     doSenateSample(item)
9:     for attribute ∈group do
10:         doGroupingSample(item)
11:     end for
12: end for
13: getFinalCongressionalGroups(groupingSample)
14: calculateSlots(houseSample,senateSample, groupingSample)
15: scaleDownSample()
```

sample. Next, a *senate* sample is performed, which assigns an equal slot of the sample size to each group. Finally, a *grouping* sample is performed for each attribute in the group-by set, where each attribute's "grouping" is assigned a sample slot proportional to the size of the grouping in the data set. Second, in the grouping sample, the slot size for each group is recalculated (line 13).

Equation 1 shows the equation, where $S$ is the sample size, $mT$ is the number of distinct groups, $N_g$ is the number of items for the attribute and $N_h$ represents the number of items in the distinct group. In the next stage (lines 14 and 15), the group sizes of the uniform, senate and grouping samples are evaluated and the final slot size for each group is calculated from the house, senate and grouping samples.

$$GroupSize = (S/mT) * (N_g/N_h) \tag{1}$$

In Eq. 2, $S$ is the sample size, $max_{g \in G} S_g$ is the size of the largest slot for a group from the house, senate and grouping samples and it is divided by the sum of all the slot sizes for that group. Finally, each group is re-sampled with reservoir sampling to generate a sample slot with the new size. The house sample allocates more space for larger groups. On the other hand, the senate sample allows smaller groups to enter the sample. Finally, the grouping sample optimizes the separate attribute representations inside each group.

$$SlotSize = S * (max_{g \in G} S_g / \sum_{sampletype} max_{g \in G} S_g) \tag{2}$$

**Distinct Value Algorithm** [7]. As its name suggests, the Distinct Value sampling method approximates the number of distinct values of an attribute in a given data stream. As with the previous algorithm, determining the distinct values of a certain attribute is frequently used in the optimization of the computation flow. The DV sampling algorithm provides a low, 0–10% relative error, while providing a low space requirement of $O(log_2(D))$, where D is the domain size of the attribute.

**Algorithm 2.** Distinct Value algorithm

```
1: initialize(sampleSize, threshold)
2: level ← 0
3: sampleCount ← 0
4: Sample ← ∅
5: CountMap ← ∅
6: for all item ∈ dataStream do
7:     hashValue ← dieHash(item)
8:     if hashValue ≥level then
9:         if Sample(hashValue) <threshold then
10:            Sample(hashValue).add(item)
11:            CountMap(hashValue) + +
12:            sampleCount + +
13:        else
14:            Sample(hashValue).sample(item)
15:        end if
16:    end if
17:    if sampleCount>sampleSize then
18:        sampleCount− =Sample(level)
19:        Sample(level).remove
20:        level = level + 1
21:    end if
22: end for
```

Algorithm 2 presents the Distinct Value algorithm. It requires two additional parameters besides the sample size. The second parameter is the maximum sample slot size per value, called the threshold. The third parameter is the domain size, representing the number of possible values that can occur.

The algorithm works as follows. As each data item arrives, the domain size is used to generate a hashed value of the data item. Next, if the hashed value is at least as large as the current level, an attempt to put the item in the appropriate hash value slot is performed. If the slot size is smaller than the threshold value, the item is simply placed in the slot. Otherwise a uniform sample is performed which can result in the new item replacing an item currently in the slot. When the items in the sample exceed the sample size, the slot whose value equals the current level number is removed from the sample and the level is incremented.

By randomly mapping the attribute values to hashed values and only allowing hashed values equal or greater than the current level to enter the sample, the algorithm ensures that the sample contains a uniform selection of the scanned portion of the data stream. As an addition, the threshold value keeps the level from frequently incrementing and skewing the data distribution.

# 4  Experimental Evaluation

For the experimental evaluation, we employed an instance of a server representative of elements in typical cloud deployments. The server runs on an 8-core, 2.93 GHz Intel i7 processor with 12 GB of RAM, using 64-bit Ubuntu Server. The system was implemented on Apache Spark, while the data streams were created using the Netcat Linux command-line tool. For measuring the maximum heap memory usage, a light-weight console application was used, called Jvmtop.

*Metrics and Benchmarks.* In order to understand the gains of the implemented system, four metrics were used. Two are performance metrics, evaluating the speed-up in processing time and the variation in memory consumption. The other two are error metrics, estimating the relative error in the generated sample and the relative error in the results of the benchmark applications. Two benchmark applications were used, usually employed in streaming benchmarks. The first is one that provides the most used payment type in New York taxis. The second provides the country with most customers of an online retail website.

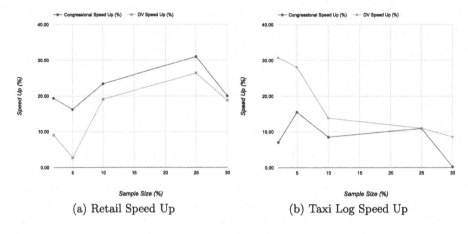

(a) Retail Speed Up    (b) Taxi Log Speed Up

**Fig. 2.** Processing time speed up benchmark applications

*Results.* The speed-up in processing time for both applications is shown in Fig. 2. For the Online Retail application (Fig. 2a), both algorithms show a high speed-up in processing time (20–30%) for sampling sizes of 10, 25 and 30%, but the 2 and 5% sample shows that sampling is rendered ineffective for too small data inputs. However, the Taxi log application (Fig. 2b), which has a much smaller domain size for the target attribute of the sampling, shows a steady decrease of speed-up, providing high values for the smaller sample sizes.

On Fig. 3 the relative error of the application results is presented. As can be seen on Fig. 3a, the algorithms in the Online Retail application maintain steadily decreasing error with a maximum of 20%, while the error in the Taxi log application (Fig. 3b) is kept bellow 1%. Exceptions are the 2% sampling sizes, where, because of the greatly decreased data size, the differences in the results are much more noticeable.

The plots in Fig. 4 detail the maximum heap memory usage of Spark Streaming during the execution of the benchmark applications. As can be seen, the sampling runs actually consume more memory for most of the sample sizes. The reason behind this is that both algorithms obviously require some constant extra amount of memory for the data structures they use for maintaining the metadata of the sampled elements; meanwhile, all events are still injected in Spark

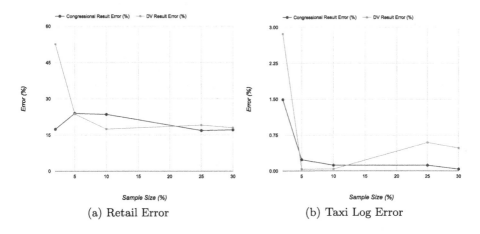

**(a) Retail Error**                    **(b) Taxi Log Error**

**Fig. 3.** Result error plots for benchmark applications

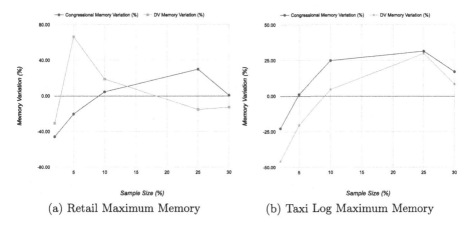

**(a) Retail Maximum Memory**           **(b) Taxi Log Maximum Memory**

**Fig. 4.** Maximum memory usage variation for benchmark applications

even if not fully processed, with the garbage collector sometimes freeing their memory only lazily in the background. An exception is the DV algorithm for the Taxi log application, where because of the smaller domain size, the DV sample actually performs better. This is affected by the threshold value which greatly impacts the slot sizes and increment frequency of the level value, thus increasing or decreasing the memory usage.

From the evaluation metrics, it can be summarized that the system can provide significant gains in processing time for the sample sizes between 5 and 25%, while maintaining a low error rate. However, this is done at the cost of additional memory consumption.

## 5    Related Work

Strainer is an approximate computing system that intersects data reduction with data processing platforms. There are several notable works in these areas.

In the area of sampling, several one-pass sampling algorithms can be adapted to streamed data. Reservoir sampling [22] is a uniform sampling algorithm. It provides a bounded error, but may skew data distribution. Count and Weighted sampling [2,8] use biased sampling methods. However, both have no error bounds. Furthermore, Weighted sampling introduces overhead information about the weights of the data items in advance.

Currently, there is an abundance of data processing platforms. Apache Flink, Storm and Samza offer stream processing libraries. In contrast to Spark, they use a streaming dataflow engine which performs true streaming, thus immediately processing each data element. However, this becomes an obstacle when trying to sample data, since most sampling methods need to first build a sample set.

Approximate computing systems use two approaches in data reduction. Works on Aurora and Borealis [20] tightly integrate load shedding operators that discard tuples throughout their operation paths. Another work on Aurora/Borealis [19] groups tuples into blocks, which then selectively discards. Comparably, the system in [21] divides the input data stream into windows which are probabilistically discarded. Like Strainer, IncApprox [12] uses sampling to reduce the input data. However, it additionally utilizes incremental computing to increase the efficiency of the system. Finally, ApproxHadoop [9] uses multi-stage sampling as the first stage of data reduction, and adds task dropping as a load shedding approach for the second stage.

In the realm of big data analytics, a plethora of research has been outlined [15], delving into the intricacies of resource efficiency within large-scale data processing clusters. A relevant contribution to this field is the utilization of hidden Markov models to predict frequent patterns and approximate computation, a method that has achieved a notable level of accuracy as discussed in [13]. Additionally, the study presented in [18] introduces a model for predicting applications' resource allocation needs by using *a priori* knowledge, which is also beneficial for effective resource mapping. Another significant approach is found in [10], where the focus is on the estimation of actual available resources to prevent scenarios of resource wastage. Furthermore, the innovative application of game theory in managing container allocation for streaming applications, as explored in [17], presents a unique perspective in resource management. Each of these studies offers distinct insights and solutions to the challenges associated with resource management in the context of big data.

Other approaches employ parameter tuning [14] to Map-Reduce and Spark workloads, or employ machine learning in order to determine how to ensure a specific error bound in continuous Map-Reduce workflows [6] while delaying reexecution as much as possible when new input data arrives. This has also been attempted in iterative or continuous graph processing [3].

Overall, none of the previous works employ sampling as a means to ensure application quality-of-service during overcommit/overallocation situations, in a way that does not risk dropping relevant, yet possibly under-represented, types or values of data (as uniform-based sampling approaches typically employed in load-shedding can incur in).

# 6  Conclusion

Strainer implements the approximate computing paradigm by leveraging the advantages of sampling as a data reduction technique. It utilizes the modularity of the Apache Spark Streaming to create a seamless merging of this established data processing framework with the Congressional and Distinct Value sampling methods. Thus, it provides a user-transparent framework for the development of approximate computing applications.

The experimental results indicate that the system can be employed in data stream environments and provide a faster execution time while maintaining a low error bound. Although it is fully functional for stable data streams, the introduction of a variable arrival rate in the data stream may impact the accuracy of the results. This is because the sample size would maintain a fixed value while the amount of data fluctuates. Implementing a self-adjusting sampling size depending on the error measurement and processing time would alleviate this problem. Finally, sampling could be performed in a dedicated component with custom memory management or more frequent GC to promote memory savings.

**Acknowledgments.** This work was supported by national funds through FCT, Fundação para a Ciência e a Tecnologia, under project UIDB/50021/2020 (DOI:10. 54499/UIDB/50021/2020). This work was supported by: "DL 60/2018, de 3-08 - Aquisição necessária para a atividade de I&D do INESC-ID, no âmbito do projeto SmartRetail (C6632206063-00466847)". The authors would like to thank colleague Rodrigo Rodrigues for the initial collaboration in this work.

# References

1. Acharya, S., Gibbons, P.B., Poosala, V.: Congressional samples for approximate answering of group-by queries. In: Proceedings of the 2000 ACM SIGMOD International Conference on Management of Data, SIGMOD '00, pp. 487–498. ACM, New York (2000)
2. Chaudhuri, S., Das, G., Datar, M., Motwani, R., Narasayya, V.: Overcoming limitations of sampling for aggregation queries. In: Proceedings of the 17th International Conference on Data Engineering, pp. 534–542. IEEE (2001)
3. Coimbra, M.E., Esteves, S., Francisco, A.P., Veiga, L.: Veilgraph: incremental graph stream processing. J. Big Data **9**(1), 23 (2022)
4. Cormode, G., Duffield, N.: Sampling for big data: A tutorial. In Proceedings of the 20th ACM SIGKDD International Conference on Knowledge Discovery and Data Mining, KDD 2014, pp. 1975–1975, New York, NY, USA, (2014)
5. Das, T., Zhong, Y., Stoica, I., Shenker, S.: Adaptive stream processing using dynamic batch sizing. In: Proceedings of the ACM Symposium on Cloud Computing, SOCC '14, pp. 16:1–16:13. ACM, New York ( 2014)

6. Esteves, S., Galhardas, H., Veiga, L.: Adaptive execution of continuous and data-intensive workflows with machine learning. In: Proceedings of the 19th International Middleware Conference, Middleware '18, pp. 239–252. Association for Computing Machinery, New York (2018)

7. Gibbons, P.B.: Distinct sampling for highly-accurate answers to distinct values queries and event reports. In: Proceedings of the 27th International Conference on Very Large Data Bases, VLDB '01, pp. 541–550. Morgan Kaufmann Publishers Inc., San Francisco (2001)

8. Gibbons, P.B., Matias, Y.: New sampling-based summary statistics for improving approximate query answers. In: Proceedings of the 1998 ACM SIGMOD International Conference on Management of Data, SIGMOD '98, pp. 331–342. ACM, New York (1998)

9. Goiri, I., Bianchini, R., Nagarakatte, S., Nguyen, T.D.: Approxhadoop: Bringing approximations to mapreduce frameworks. In Proceedings of the Twentieth International Conference on Architectural Support for Programming Languages and Operating Systems, ASPLOS '15, pp. 383–397. ACM, New York (2015)

10. Ha, S.-H., Brown, P., Michiardi, P.: Resource management for parallel processing frameworks with load awareness at worker side. In: 2017 IEEE International Congress on Big Data (BigData Congress), pp. 161–168. IEEE (2017)

11. Hu, W., Zhang, B.: Study of sampling techniques and algorithms in data stream environments. In 2012 9th International Conference on Fuzzy Systems and Knowledge Discovery (FSKD), pp. 1028–1034. IEEE (2012)

12. Krishnan, D.R., Quoc, D.L., Bhatotia, P., Fetzer, C., Rodrigues, R.: Incapprox: a data analytics system for incremental approximate computing. In: Proceedings of the 25th International Conference on World Wide Web, WWW '16, pp. 1133–1144, Republic and Canton of Geneva, Switzerland, 2016. International World Wide Web Conferences Steering Committee

13. Liu, C.-M., Liao, K.-T.: Efficiently predicting frequent patterns over uncertain data streams. Procedia Comput. Sci. 160, 15 – 22 (2019). The 10th International Conference on Emerging Ubiquitous Systems and Pervasive Networks (EUSPN-2019) / The 9th International Conference on Current and Future Trends of Information and Communication Technologies in Healthcare (ICTH-2019) / Affiliated Workshops

14. Lu, J., Chen, Y., Herodotou, H., Babu, S.: Speedup your analytics: Automatic parameter tuning for databases and big data systems. Proc. VLDB Endow. **12**(12), 1970–1973 (2019)

15. Mohamed, A., Najafabadi, M.K., Wah, Y.B., Zaman, E.A.K., Maskat, R.: The state of the art and taxonomy of big data analytics: view from new big data framework. Artif. Intell. Rev. **53**(2), 989–1037 (2020)

16. Morais, B., Coimbra, M.E., Veiga, L.: pk-graph: Partitioned k 2-trees to enable compact and dynamic graphs in spark graphx. In: International Conference on Cooperative Information Systems, pp. 149–167. Springer (2022)

17. Runsewe, O., Samaan, N.: Cram: a container resource allocation mechanism for big data streaming applications. In: 2019 19th IEEE/ACM International Symposium on Cluster. Cloud and Grid Computing (CCGRID), pp. 312–320. IEEE Computer Society, Los Alamitos (2019)

18. Shukla, A., Simmhan, Y.L.: Model-driven scheduling for distributed stream processing systems. CoRR, abs/1702.01785 (2017)

19. Sun, L., Franklin, M.J., Krishnan, S., Xin, R.S.: Fine-grained partitioning for aggressive data skipping. In: Proceedings of the 2014 ACM SIGMOD Interna-

tional Conference on Management of Data, SIGMOD '14, pp. 1115–1126. ACM, New York (2014)

20. Tatbul, N., Çetintemel, U., Zdonik, S.: Staying fit: Efficient load shedding techniques for distributed stream processing. In: Proceedings of the 33rd International Conference on Very Large Data Bases, VLDB '07, pp. 159–170. VLDB Endowment (2007)

21. Tatbul, N., Zdonik, S.: Window-aware load shedding for aggregation queries over data streams. In: Proceedings of the 32Nd International Conference on Very Large Data Bases, VLDB '06, pp. 799–810. VLDB Endowment (2006)

22. Vitter, J.S.: Random sampling with a reservoir. ACM Trans. Math. Softw. **11**(1), 37–57 (1985)

# On Digital Twins for Cloud Continuum Applications

Luiz F. Bittencourt[1]([✉]) [ID], Kelly R. Braghetto[2] [ID], Daniel Cordeiro[2] [ID],
and Rizos Sakellariou[3] [ID]

[1] Instituto de Computação, Universidade Estadual de Campinas, Campinas, Brazil
bit@ic.unicamp.br
[2] Universidade de São Paulo, São Paulo, Brazil
{kellyrb,daniel.cordeiro}@usp.br
[3] The University of Manchester, Manchester, UK
rizos@manchester.ac.uk

**Abstract.** Digital Twins (DTs) are digital representations of physical objects or processes that can be used for their computer-based analysis. This technique has been used in different fields to analyze, simulate, and optimize various scenarios in real time without interfering with the real twin. Using Serverless Computing as a use case, this paper discusses the underlying costs of using DTs when applied to analyze and optimize the management of computational resources for cloud-continuum applications. We argue that, although feasible, using DTs for Digital Systems can be prohibitively expensive. Defining the ideal DT fidelity for a given application is challenging, as this impacts both system management and performance through heavy monitoring as well as the DT running costs.

**Keywords:** Digital Twins · Cloud Continuum · Resource Management

## 1 Introduction

Creating Digital Twins (DTs) of *physical systems* is a complex task that requires in-depth modeling and mapping of real-world variables and processes into digital variables and digital representation of processes. On the other hand, creating DTs of *computer systems* is straightforward: simply duplicate the whole system (infrastructure, management system, and applications) as well as all requests and tasks, and the DT is ready to use. However, the costs of duplicating a complete digital system can be prohibitively high in many cases.

According to Ahlgren et al. [1], recent developments in DTs have focused primarily on cyber-physical systems, where simulations interact with real-world physical systems. However, there is significant untapped potential in cyber-cyber DTs, which offer complete malleability, meaning that any aspect of the simulated software system can be changed automatically in response to the simulation. This creates a different paradigm, as the distinction between the simulator and the simulated system can blur, with either being able to inform and adapt the other.

© The Author(s), under exclusive license to Springer Nature Switzerland AG 2025
M. Naldi et al. (Eds.): GECON 2024, LNCS 15358, pp. 286–293, 2025.
https://doi.org/10.1007/978-3-031-81226-2_25

Useful implementations of DTs for digital systems should bring high fidelity and real-time reproduction of the real system to support what-if scenarios and uncertainty mitigation. Modeling digital systems into twins with fundamental variables and mathematical models representing processes is challenging. Techniques from computer simulation and emulation can be used, as they help understand the general behavior of computer systems, but DTs should be one step ahead in terms of fidelity and real-time mimicking of a real twin using appropriate inputs monitored from the real system. Thus, the set of variables, their relevance, and the formulation of models that are able to generate a DT of the real digital system should be carefully chosen to enable a cost-efficient yet representative twinning process.

The complexity of building digital twins for digital systems does not come from the modeling and understanding of physical phenomena, but from understanding how simplified the original digital system can be represented by a DT such that uncertainties and costs of the DT do not surpass or are supplanted by the potential gains in resource management to fulfill application requirements. In this sense, we discuss in this paper challenges that must be considered when modeling, building, and running DTs for digital systems focusing on a resource management perspective. To illustrate these challenges, we describe a use case of DTs as a resource manager for serverless computing and applications implemented using the Function as a Service (FaaS) paradigm considering a computing continuum environment. We also discuss research challenges to be addressed to make DTs feasible in this context.

## 2 Concepts

### 2.1 Digital Twins

Digital Twins (DTs) were introduced in the early 2000 s by Michael Grieves in a product lifecycle management course. Initially considered complex to implement, DTs gained traction with advancements in cloud computing, IoT, and big data, extending from the aerospace industry to manufacturing around 2012. Industry 4.0 developments, data digitization, and embedded sensors were key to this evolution, making realistic virtual testing feasible [10].

Despite the large amount of scientific literature around the theme, there is no consensual definition of a DT and its components. However, recent standardization efforts, including a new ISO standard (ISO/IEC 30173:2023, "Digital twin—Concepts and terminology"), may help address this issue. For the purposes of this work, DTs can be understood as *digital representations of physical objects or processes used for computer-based analysis of their properties.*

Analyzing digital twins typically requires significant computational capacity, which may include diverse computing resources. In a nutshell, the DT's virtual, computer-based representations are fed with data from multiple sensors, and they demand high processing power and rapid networking data transfers to be able to digitally mimic physical objects and their dynamic processes. Therefore, managing DTs execution in a (potentially distributed) computing system is crucial to achieving acceptable performance that enables timely visualization of the DTs physical objects, processes, and their potential outcomes [2].

The main benefit of having digital twins representing physical systems is to allow simulations, analyses, and optimizations in real time without interfering with the real twin. These simulations help to understand scenarios and support decision-making even before actual events occur in the real system. Analyzing the DT's behavior allows following the real twin more closely to identify and mitigate potential problems and inconsistent states that may derive from the current state and as a consequence of different, sometimes unpredictable, factors.

As virtual representations of physical objects and/or processes, DTs should be able to allow real-time analytics and corrective actions. As such, DTs can be modeled as self-interested agents acting in pursuit of their goals. Multiple types of applications can be represented by DTs to visualize how data input can impact processes and how such impact affects other objects/processes in a chain of digital twins. Therefore, digital twins can be standalone entities, can depend on other digital twins, or can even be part of larger digital twins, organized in a hierarchical structure or interacting in a collaborative model [9].

The level of detail in modeling a physical system for desired outcomes is crucial, as it determines DT's *fidelity*. This fidelity depends on the number, accuracy, and abstraction of parameters exchanged between the real and virtual twins. While high-fidelity models provide detailed and accurate representations, they can be complex, costly, and computationally intensive [6]. Conversely, low-fidelity models are simpler and faster but may fail to capture essential interactions. Balancing fidelity and practicality is essential for a cost-effective DT implementation.

### 2.2  Resource Management in Serverless Cloud Computing

Managing cloud services presents significant challenges in providing availability, load balancing, auto-scaling, security, and monitoring. These complexities have driven the development of serverless cloud computing. This model abstracts infrastructure management, allowing developers to focus on coding applications without worrying about resource allocation and scaling.

Serverless cloud computing provides both Backend as a Service (BaaS) and Function as a Service (FaaS), with the latter being the most prevalent model. BaaS encompasses services such as storage, messaging, and user management. FaaS allows developers to deploy and execute their code on computing platforms, relying on BaaS services [3]. According to [5], three characteristics mainly differentiate serverless from serverful computing: (i) storage and computation scale independently, with storage provided by a separate cloud service and computation being stateless; (ii) automatic resource allocation, where the cloud automatically provisions the necessary resources for execution of the code provided by users; (iii) billing based on actual resource usage, such as execution time, rather than on the size and number of VMs allocated.

Serverless computing enables developers to break down applications into smaller, manageable functions, allowing for individual scaling of components. On the one hand, this approach can lead to improved efficiency and resource utilization. On the other hand, it introduces challenges related to managing and coordinating numerous functions effectively. The interactions between different functions can be seen as workflows; some providers offer tools to simplify the orchestration of these workflows, such as the AWS Step Functions service [7].

To offer serverless computing in the form of Function as a Service, the cloud provider needs to choose the most suitable computing resource (machine) to run the function code. Also, when functions call each other, forming a workflow, data transfers take place in the computing infrastructure, and delays are introduced between function calls. Moreover, a function in FaaS is often run as a container-ized software, which allows a sandboxed environment that can be instantiated on demand and replicated when demand for that function. All these details should be taken into account during the decision-making on where each function should be run in the provider infrastructure, which makes resource management challenging in this context. Digital twins can be used as decision-makers on scaling resources to keep the performance of functions' execution at acceptable quality of service levels.

## 3 The Case for Digital Twins for Digital Systems

### 3.1 FaaS Characterization and Modeling

Let $\mathcal{A} = \{f_1, f_2, ..., f_n\}$ be the set of $n$ serverless functions that compose an application $\mathcal{A}$ designed and implemented considering the FaaS paradigm with an associated Service Level Agreement (SLA). Each function $f_i \in \mathcal{A}$ has an associated invocation pattern $p_{f_i}$, representing the frequency of calls to $f_i$ in the application and a set of resources utilized per invocation, such as CPU instructions, memory size, and input/output parameters. The SLA of the application contains information about what the user expects, for example, the maximum response time of a submitted request for $\mathcal{A}$.

The service provider should be able to allocate and run each $f_i \in \mathcal{A}$ in the computing continuum infrastructure in such a way that the composed response time of all functions does not violate the application's SLA. Suppose the continuum provider will run all functions of $\mathcal{A}$ in a set $\mathcal{M} = \{m_1, m_2, ..., m_k\}$ of $k$ machines connected by network links $\mathcal{L} = \{l_{m_i, m_j} \mid \forall m_i, m_j \in \mathcal{M}, m_i \neq m_j\}$. Each machine $m_i \in \mathcal{M}$ has an associated computing capacity, modeled as a set of computing characteristics such as CPU, memory, and storage; and each network link $l_{m_i, m_j} \in \mathcal{L}$ connecting machines $m_i$ and $m_j$ has a set of associated network characteristics, such as the available bandwidth and latency. The modeling of each machine and each link can be as detailed as needed to represent the desired *computing model resolution* $\mathcal{R}$. The computing model resolution will impact the digital twin precision and running costs.

Matching the function's requirements with the machine's capacity allows estimating the number of concurrent invocations to a function a given machine supports without getting overloaded. This kind of estimation is widely used when modeling applications and systems in parallel and distributed computing scheduling algorithms. However, precisely estimating application requirements and machine capacity when running different kinds of workloads in a highly heterogeneous environment as the computing continuum cannot always be achieved. Thus, estimating the actual performance when executing functions is prone to uncertainties, potentially leading to overloaded resources and unpredictable turnaround times if static modeling is used. Using digital twins to understand and manage uncertainties through what-if scenarios can help guarantee functions' performance in the computing continuum.

## 3.2   Digital Twins for Serverless Computing

A digital twin for managing serverless scenarios will support decision-making on resource allocation to handle requests and keep the quality of service at acceptable levels. Figure 1 overviews the resource management process in a cloud-edge infrastructure that offers Function as a Service through the deployment of containerized services. First, the cloud-edge clients access an application interface to submit requests to be processed in the cloud (step 1). These requests will be fulfilled by running (a set of) containerized functions $\mathcal{A}$, as defined in Sect. 3.1, which will be invoked by a service composition engine (step 2). Once the functions are invoked, a scheduler should decide which instance of a (potentially) replicated function should actually run the function(s) needed to fulfill the request (step 3). These instances can be deployed in any machine $m_i \in \mathcal{M}$, which can satisfy the functions' resource requirements.

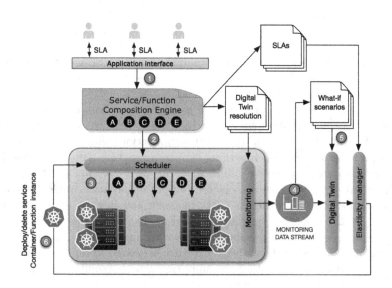

**Fig. 1.** Digital twins for resource management in FaaS.

One of the main characteristics that differentiate digital twins from standard simulation and emulation is the need for real-time feedback through the adoption of what-if scenarios based on instantaneous information from the monitored system. We define the *digital twin resolution* as the main driver of the digital twin fidelity when running the what-if scenarios of a digital system. The digital twin resolution $\mathcal{R}$ should define the granularity of the monitoring and how frequently the twin evaluation process is performed using the collected data from the real system. In our of FaaS use case, we illustrate this resolution as a configuration derived from the function invocation patterns $p_{f_i}$ and their Service Level Agreements (SLAs), which are used as input in the infrastructure monitoring services that will feed what-if scenarios and the digital twin with a data stream representing the current status of the whole system (step 4). A function invocation pattern $p_{f_i}$ can determine how frequently monitoring is needed at different points in time, and how frequently the twin should be used to assess performance and what-if scenarios to handle potential performance uncertainties. Note that the monitored data (CPU, I/O, memory utilization, application profiling, etc.) and monitoring frequency are a direct result of the defined DT model resolution $\mathcal{R}$, impacting the data stream flow and, consequently, the digital twin precision, computing costs, and delays. Moreover, the monitored system state allows what-if scenarios to be generated and inputted into the digital twin (step 5). Based on the observed DT behavior, an elasticity component will be able to make decisions on increasing/decreasing the amount of computing resources (e.g., replicas) dedicated to a set of functions based on their SLAs (step 6).

### 3.3   Challenges

In general, modeling and running digital twins has several challenges [10]. In this paper, we focus on challenges related to twinning digital systems for resource management with a holistic approach, taking an illustrative use case of serverless computing implementing FaaS. We are motivated by recent research that presents encouraging results for using DTs in some form of resource management for specific applications [4,8,11,12]. In this section, we highlight the challenges of using DTs for resource management for computing continuum systems.

The Digital Twin resolution defines how precisely the digital twin model represents the twinned digital system and is dependent on the characteristics of the modeled system. The resolution of a DT can be a direct consequence of how the DT of a digital system is modeled (i.e., the model resolution $\mathcal{R}$), e.g., as a set of mathematical representations of the real system or by a full replica of the system running every request as a duplicate. In the first case, the resolution can be determined by the complexity of the modeling utilized to represent the system's processes and also by the amount of monitoring performed in the system and the frequency of the inputs provided to the digital twin. Defining the ideal resolution for a given application is challenging, as this impacts both the system management and performance through heavier monitoring and the digital twin running costs. In addition, dynamically controlling the DT resolution can be effective in handling unexpected scenarios where more frequent analyses are needed, but this adaptive behavior also brings challenges in terms of modeling and system adaptation to varying DT resolutions.

Automating the definition of what-if scenarios to serve as input for the digital twin is also challenging. A set of pre-defined what-if scenarios can be loaded into the system with the most frequently expected events, such as a workload increase or decrease. In our illustrative FaaS use case, adding and removing service/function replicas can be explored as what-if scenarios. This way, the DT can recommend system configuration changes based on how it would behave, improving applications' QoS. For example, what is the impact on an application if the system reduces the number of replicas of a given function/application component? From a resource management perspective, this answer is important to reduce costs, improve system utilization, and also guarantee QoS, but if this is done in a trial and error approach in production, the system can get overloaded, and the application can be severely impacted until the misbehavior can be detected and corrected.

Even though DTs can help in resource management, managing the DT execution itself can be challenging. Keeping DT response times acceptable to provide timely responses when running (potentially multiple) what-if scenarios concurrently should be attached to the DT's resolution: is it more effective, for a given application/infrastructure, to run multiple what-if scenarios in low DT resolutions, or is it better to focus on a few frequently expected scenarios with higher DT resolutions?

Finally, incorporating the DT costs into business models in a way that improves resource management and the system customers observe concrete advantages can also be challenging. Offering DTs as an improved resource management service can be attractive but challenging to design, implement, and price.

## 4   Conclusion

DTs can simulate different scenarios and workloads, helping to optimize resource allocation in cloud environments. By monitoring and analyzing how resources such as CPU, memory, or network are being used, DTs can suggest optimal configurations and scaling strategies to improve performance and efficiency. DTs can also facilitate dynamic reconfiguration of computer systems, automatically adapting to varying loads and resource availability, ensuring SLAs are met.

The challenge of employing DTs to manage cloud-continuum resources for executing serverless applications has analogies with DT-assisted dynamic production scheduling in manufacturing, a topic extensively studied [8]. Dynamic production scheduling optimizes resource allocation and task sequencing over time to achieve various goals, such as minimizing makespan, cost, or the number of tardy jobs. It enhances the responsiveness of manufacturing systems by allowing schedule rearrangements to mitigate disruptions.

However, scheduling serverless applications in cloud platforms presents specific challenges. These include large-scale (in terms of both the number of resources and workload), highly heterogeneous resources, varying pricing and business models, and real-time requirements. These factors complicate modeling and simulation, increasing both complexity and costs, which can render high-resolution modeling impractical. Yet, the potential for using Digital Twins to optimize resource management in computer systems is vast. However, more research is needed to develop modeling strategies and DT architectures that effectively balance the costs and benefits of DT implementation.

**Acknowledgments.** Grants #2019/26702-8, #2023/00702-7 (in collaboration with the University of Manchester), and #2024/01115-0, São Paulo Research Foundation (FAPESP), CAPES (grant 88887.954253/2024-00) and CNPq (grants 405940/2022-0 and 421787/2022-8) partially fund this work.

**Disclosure of Interests.** The authors have no competing interests to declare.

# References

1. Ahlgren, J., et al.: Facebook's cyber–cyber and cyber–physical digital twins. In: Proceedings of the 25th International Conference on Evaluation and Assessment in Software Engineering, pp. 1–9 (2021)
2. Bellavista, P., Bicocchi, N., Fogli, M., Giannelli, C., Mamei, M., Picone, M.: Exploiting microservices and serverless for digital twins in the cloud-to-edge continuum. Futur. Gener. Comput. Syst. **157**, 275–287 (2024)
3. Hassan, H.B., Barakat, S.A., Sarhan, Q.I.: Survey on serverless computing. J. Cloud Comput. **10**(1), 1–29 (2021). https://doi.org/10.1186/s13677-021-00253-7
4. Jeremiah, S.R., Yang, L.T., Park, J.H.: Digital twin-assisted resource allocation framework based on edge collaboration for vehicular edge computing. Futur. Gener. Comput. Syst. **150**, 243–254 (2024)
5. Jonas, E., et al.: Cloud programming simplified: A Berkeley view on serverless computing. arXiv preprint arXiv:1902.03383 (2019)
6. Kshetri, N.: The economics of digital twins. Computer **54**(4), 86–90 (2021)
7. McGrath, G., Brenner, P.R.: Serverless computing: Design, implementation, and performance. In: 2017 IEEE 37th International Conference on Distributed Computing Systems Workshops (ICDCSW), pp. 405–410. IEEE (2017)
8. Ouahabi, N., Chebak, A., Kamach, O., Laayati, O., Zegrari, M.: Leveraging digital twin into dynamic production scheduling: a review. Robot. Comput.-Integr. Manufact. **89**, 102778 (2024)
9. Segovia, M., Garcia-Alfaro, J.: Design, modeling and implementation of digital twins. Sensors **22**(14), 5396 (2022)
10. Sharma, A., Kosasih, E., Zhang, J., Brintrup, A., Calinescu, A.: Digital twins: State of the art theory and practice, challenges, and open research questions. J. Ind. Inf. Integr. **30**, 100383 (2022)
11. Yu, H., Han, S., Yang, D., Wang, Z., Feng, W.: Job shop scheduling based on digital twin technology: A survey and an intelligent platform. Complexity **2021**(1), 8823273 (2021)
12. Zhao, J., Xiong, X., Chen, Y.: Design and implementation of a cloud-network resource management system based on digital twin. In: 2023 IEEE 3rd International Conference on Digital Twins and Parallel Intelligence (DTPI), pp. 1–5 (2023)

# Specification of Complex Analytics Workflows: A Formal Language Model of Decision Options

Pouriya Miri[1], Petar Kochovski[1], Marcela Tuler de Oliveira[2], and Vlado Stankovski[1(✉)]

[1] Faculty of Computer and Information Science, University of Ljubljana, Ljubljana, Slovenia
{pouriya.miri,petar.kochovski,vlado.stankovski}@fri.uni-lj.si
[2] Department of Engineering Systems, Delft University of Technology, Delft, Netherlands

**Abstract.** The specification of experiments expressed as Complex Analytics Workflows is a complex task that involves many decision-making steps with various degrees of complexity. The use of the context, the expert knowledge, and the potential for its sharing and reuse in the context of experiment specification have not been addressed sufficiently until now. Moreover, to make such knowledge instrumental, it should be coupled with specific probabilistic measures, such as particular assurances, ranking, and verification of various options. The paper aims to present a novel semantic model for probabilistic reasoning in any experimentation context coupled with a functional system for knowledge generation, reuse, and sharing. The result of our work can be used within existing experimentation engines.

**Keywords:** Semantic model · Complex Analytic Workflow · Markov Decision Process

## 1 Introduction

Complex Analytics Workflows (CAWs) provide an advanced framework for managing data-driven analytics, leveraging technologies such as Artificial Intelligence (AI) and Machine Learning (ML). These workflows are crucial for handling multifaceted tasks that require precision, flexibility, and integration of heterogeneous data sources. Unlike traditional workflows, CAWs are designed to adapt and optimize scientific experiments, simulations, and real-world scenario analyses, incorporating feedback and learning mechanisms throughout the process.

The importance of CAWs is highlighted in projects like ExtremeXP[1], demonstrating their ability to fit AI/ML models to specific tasks, involving humans in

---

[1] https://extremexp.eu/.

© The Author(s), under exclusive license to Springer Nature Switzerland AG 2025
M. Naldi et al. (Eds.): GECON 2024, LNCS 15358, pp. 294–299, 2025.
https://doi.org/10.1007/978-3-031-81226-2_26

the control loop to achieve the highest possible accuracy and precision. However, specifying CAWs requires expert knowledge, particularly when selecting data and defining experiment configurations.

This paper proposes a semantic model for CAWs that incorporates probabilistic reasoning through a Markov Decision Process (MDP), facilitating knowledge generation, sharing, and reuse. The model is designed to be integrated into existing workflow tools, like Taverna[2], or Ascalon[3], enhancing their capability to manage complex decision-making processes with formal assurances, ranking, and verification. In Sect. 2, we provide background on CAWs. Section 3 analyzes a public administration use case that could be fit on the high-level CAW. Section 4 elaborates on the semantic language model that represents the concepts that are involved in the EMF model for the CAW. Finally, Sect. 5 discusses the current development in the context of the aims of the ExtremeXP project.

## 2 Background

The evolution of workflows, particularly in handling complex, multi-step analytic tasks, has been a focal point of research since Casati et al. (1970) [1] introduced the conceptual modeling of workflows. Gil et al. (2013) [2] advanced this field by exploring the dynamic configuration of workflows to manage large datasets, which has become increasingly relevant in today's data-driven environments. Deelman et al. (2016) [3] contributed to this evolution by introducing performance modeling and diagnostic approaches for extreme-scale workflows, emphasizing the importance of assessing workflow efficiency.

In modern technological advancements, the Horizon Europe ExtremeXP project redefines workflows within the framework of IoT, Blockchain, AI, Cloud-to-Edge computing, and Digital Twins. These technologies are pivotal in developing and executing CAWs, essential for achieving high precision in scientific experiments and decision-making processes. Krishnan et al. (2021) [4] and Forkan et al. (2023) [5] have also contributed by developing workflows tailored to specific applications, such as germline variant calling and spatial analytics, respectively, highlighting the diverse applicability of CAWs. Oliveira et al. (2022) [7] proposed a transparent access control mechanism using Attribute-Based Access Control (ABAC) integrated with blockchain technology. This model offers a sophisticated approach to security, providing fine-grained access control, accountability, and transparency in CAWs. Their work is instrumental in ensuring that workflows can be securely shared, reused, and monetized, making it a cornerstone of decentralized knowledge systems.

Integrating a semantic model of CAWs with an MDP, as pursued in the ExtremeXP project, builds upon these advancements. By capturing, sharing, and reusing expert knowledge in experiment specification, this integration ensures that workflows are precise, adaptable, and capable of providing formal assurances, ranking, and verifiable results.

---

[2] http://www.taverna.org.uk/.
[3] https://ascalon.fr/.

## 3  High-Level CAW Knowledge System Design

This section analyses complex interactions among expert users and a workflow system. An example of a CAW is a workflow in which the user intends to realize a Sustainable Development Goal (SDG)[4]. Workflows of this kind can be implemented in many domains, such as science, engineering, and public administration. In a CAW, complex decision-making involves evaluating various options, considering uncertainties and probabilities, making optimal choices in the short term, and aligning with long-term sustainability goals. In this context, sustainable use cases involve decision options that contribute to the UN's SDGs, minimize negative environmental impacts, promote social responsibility, and support long-term economic viability.

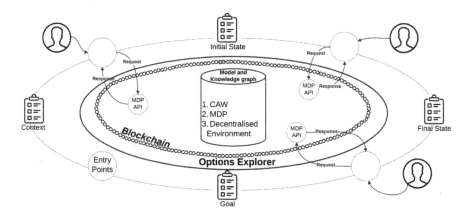

**Fig. 1.** A decentralized ecosystem for expert users of Complex Analytic Workflows

As illustrated in Fig. 1, a semantic model of (1) CAWs, (2) MDP, and (3) Smart Contracts allows expert users to generate, share, reuse, and otherwise exchange knowledge about workflows in a decentralized manner. Our decentralized system assists expert users in navigating through various states in different use cases by accessing the knowledge stored in a knowledge graph. The CAW employs MDP method to suggest ranked sequences based on users' entry points and desired outcomes. With this workflow, users can obtain answers to their needs with diverse levels of knowledge and varying degrees of specificity within the system. Users who begin with specific initial states are guided through sequences of actions that lead to potential outcomes. The system analyzes the current state, identifies available transitions, and suggests sequences that maximize the likelihood of achieving optimal outcomes. The machine identifies potential starting points and suggests sequences of actions that lead to the known final state. Users who know their goals but lack knowledge about specific starting or ending points are guided through sequences that bridge the gap between

---

[4] https://sdgs.un.org/goals.

their current knowledge and desired objectives. The decision-maker assesses the user's goal, identifies relevant starting points and potential outcomes, and suggests actions aligning with the user's objectives. In the following, we present a use case of smart public administration that motivated our research.

Each government aims to address specific citizen issues. Currently, integrating multiple public services into effective workflows is inefficient. Successful processes should be recorded, stored in a knowledge base, and used to resolve new cases based on similarity. By doing this, public administration decision-makers can create efficient workflows that leverage various services to address citizen situations. They can record successful processes, store them in a knowledge base, and access them to resolve new cases. This enhances efficiency by making effective methods readily available and adaptable to each citizen's unique needs. The model helps decision-makers assess applicant eligibility and compliance, prioritize evaluations, and expedite processes. Applicants can select workflows, prepare requirements, and verify completeness. Verification protocols ensure data integrity and security, building trust. Officials can analyze historical data to identify effective processes, speed up query resolution, and optimize resources.

## 4   Semantic Model for Probabilistic Reasoning

The Eclipse Modeling Framework (EMF) offers a robust infrastructure for developing structured data models, defining model structures, maintaining instances, and generating code. Our model leverages EMF as a foundational tool to orchestrate complex analytical processes, addressing the challenges organizations face with growing data sources and increasingly intricate tasks.

The CAW EMF model provides a comprehensive framework for designing and executing complex analytical workflows. It incorporates six fundamental concepts that form the basis for constructing detailed analytical models, guiding users systematically from data intake through to insight generation.

**Table 1.** The concept of complex analytics workflow and the concept of MDP state.

| Complex Analytics Workflow | | | MDPState | | |
|---|---|---|---|---|---|
| Properties | Range | Card | Properties | Range | Card |
| :hasMDPState | :MDPState | 1...* | :hasContextFeature | :ContextFeature | 1...* |
| :hasContextFeature | :ContextFeature | 1...* | :hasInitialState | xsd:boolean | 1 |
| :hasTransition | :Transition | 1...* | :hasFinalState | xsd:boolean | 1 |
| :isSequential | xsd:boolean | 1 | :hasGoal | xsd:boolean | 1 |
| :isConsensual | xsd:boolean | 1 | :hasReward | xsd:boolean | 1 |
| :hasExpertName | xsd:string | 1 | :hasIndicators | xsd:string | 1 |

The CAW concept, detailed in Table 1, encompasses all possible MDP states, features, and transitions within a workflow. CAWs may be performed by one or

more experts, adhering to a sequence of transitions where the property isSequential is set to true. In cases without a specific sequence, isSequential is set to
false. When user choices are involved, the property isConsensual is set to true.
The MDPState concept, also outlined in Table 1, represents the current state
within an MDP model. Each MDP state can exhibit characteristics like being
an initial state, final state, goal, or offering a reward, with relevant properties
set to true. MDP states may hold multiple actual properties simultaneously.
As shown in Table 2, indicators quantify aspects such as accuracy, precision, and
user scores, providing insight into state dynamics. These indicators, expressed as
integer values, reflect varying performance and engagement levels. MDP states
are defined by features that describe the state's attributes and dynamics. The
transition concept defines the movement from one state to another within a
CAW. These transitions, integral to the CAW framework, align with predefined
workflow sequences and are crucial in guiding system dynamics and decision-
making processes. Transitions also incorporate MDP actions, which are tailored
to respond to specific trends, whether increasing or decreasing, ensuring that the
workflow adapts to changing conditions.

**Table 2.** The concepts of indicators, MDP action, and transition.

| Concept: Indicators | | Concept:Transition | | Concept:MDPAction | |
|---|---|---|---|---|---|
| Properties | Range | Properties | Range | Properties | Range |
| :hasAccuracy | xsd:int | :hasStartState | xsd:string | :hasAccuracyTrend | xsd:string |
| :hasPrecision | xsd:int | :hasEndState | xsd:string | :hasPrecisionTrend | xsd:string |
| :hasUserScore | xsd:int | :hasMDPAction | xsd:string | :hasScoreTrend | xsd:string |

The operational workflow of the CAW system highlights the interactions
among various components involved in decision-making and knowledge management. Domain experts with digital credentials (1) contribute by adding states to
the knowledge graph, enriching the system with their expertise. AI algorithms
(2) continuously monitor the system's performance, recommending updates to
optimize efficiency. Entity Embeddings (3) store all available states, providing
necessary information when requested by the MDP machine (4), which acts as
the system's decision-making core. The MDP machine simulates and evaluates
actions, interacting with the reward simulator (5) to validate outcomes. Users (6)
engage with the system by sending requests to the server (7), facilitating interaction and monitoring CAW performance. The MDP machine generates and ranks
user action recommendations, ensuring informed decision-making.

## 5  Discussion and Conclusions

This paper introduces a new Options Explorer that is designed to aid expert
users in exploring various solutions to a given problem. Experts' decisions are

influenced by their goals, intentions, context, and method limitations, often made under complex, non-deterministic conditions. The paper emphasizes the importance of the Options Explorer, highlighting possible decision options and providing probabilistic assurances, ranking, and verification based on previous executions. The model comprises three sub-models: (1) a CAW, (2) an MDP model, and (3) Blockchain-based Smart Contracts environment. These components enable decentralized knowledge generation, sharing, and reuse among expert users stored in a knowledge graph. The model offers assurances, ranking, and verification of options and supports trustworthiness, transparency, traceability, and access control. This ongoing work under the ExtremeXP research project aims to develop a prototype for integrating existing workflow systems.

**Acknowledgment.** The research and development reported in this paper have received funding from the European Union's Horizon Program under grant agreement no. 101093164 (ExtremeXP: EXPerimentation driven and user eXPerience oriented analytics for eXtremely Precise outcomes and decisions).

# References

1. Casati, F., Ceri, S., Pernici, B., Pozzi, G.: Conceptual modeling of workflows. In: Papazoglou, M.P. (ed.) ER 1995. LNCS, vol. 1021, pp. 341–354. Springer, Heidelberg (1995). https://doi.org/10.1007/BFb0020545
2. Gil, Y., et al.: Time-bound analytic tasks on large datasets through dynamic configuration of workflows. In: Proceedings of the 8th Workshop on Workflows in Support of Large-Scale Science (WORKS '13). Association for Computing Machinery, New York, NY, USA, pp. 88–97. https://doi.org/10.1145/2534248.2534257
3. Deelman, E., et al.: PANORAMA: An approach to performance modeling and diagnosis of extreme-scale workflows. Int. J. High Perform. Computi. Appl. **31**(1), 4–18 (2017). https://doi.org/10.1177/1094342015594515
4. Krishnan, V., Utiramerur, S., Ng, Z., et al.: Benchmarking workflows to assess performance and suitability of germline variant calling pipelines in clinical diagnostic assays. BMC Bioinform. **22**, 85 (2021). https://doi.org/10.1186/s12859-020-03934-3
5. Forkan, A., Both, A., Bellman, C., Duckham, M., Anderson, H., Radosevic, N.: K-span: Open and reproducible spatial analytics using scientific workflows. Front. Earth Sci. (2023). https://doi.org/10.3389/feart.2023.1130262
6. Merkle, N., Mikut, R.: Context-Aware Composition of Agent Policies by Markov Decision Process Entity Embeddings and Agent Ensembles. arXiv eprint=2308.14521 (2023). https://doi.org/10.48550/arXiv.2308.14521
7. Tuler De Oliveira, M., Reis, L.H.A., Verginadis, Y., Mattos, D.M.F., Olabarriaga, S.D.: SmartAccess: attribute-based access control system for medical records based on smart contracts. IEEE Access **10**, 117836–117854 (2022). https://doi.org/10.1109/ACCESS.2022.3217201

# Author Index

© The Editor(s) (if applicable) and The Author(s), under exclusive license
to Springer Nature Switzerland AG 2025
M. Naldi et al. (Eds.): GECON 2024, LNCS 15358, pp. 301–302, 2025.
https://doi.org/10.1007/978-3-031-81226-2